Theories
of
International Cooperation
and the
Primacy of Anarchy

SUNY series
in
Global Politics

James N. Rosenau, Editor

Theories
of
International Cooperation
and the
Primacy of Anarchy

Explaining U.S. International
Policy-Making After Bretton Woods

Jennifer Sterling-Folker

State University of New York Press

Published by
State University of New York Press, Albany

For information, contact the State University of New York Press, Albany, NY
www.sunypress.edu

Production by Michael Haggett
Marketing by Michael Campochiaro

Library of Congress Cataloging-in-Publication Data

Sterling-Folker, Jennifer Anne, 1960–
    Theories of international cooperation and the primacy of anarchy : explaining
U.S. international policy-making after Bretton Woods / Jennifer Sterling-Folker.
        p. cm. — (SUNY series in global polics)
    Based on the author's dissertation (University of Chicago, 1993).
    Includes bibliographical references and index.
    ISBN 0-7914-5207-7 (alk. paper) — ISBN 0-7914-5208-5 (pbk. : alk. paper)
    1. Monetary policy—United States.   2. United States—Foreign economic
relations.   3. Economic policy—International cooperation.   4. International
cooperation.   5. International agencies.   6. United Nations Monetary and
Financial Conference (1944 : Bretton Woods, N.H.)   I. Title.   II. Series.

HG540.S735 2002
337.73—dc21   2001049285

10 9 8 7 6 5 4 3 2 1

Contents

Preface and Acknowledgments

Methodological and historical disciplinary differences aside, why is the study of political science divided into the subfields of international relations (IR), comparative politics, and American politics when clearly political outcomes result from an interaction of factors that cut across each of these subfields? My professional inquiries are driven by this central conceptual question, and it has informed this present study. It is a "second-image reversed" question because it presumes that it is impossible to treat the systemic environment in which nation-states exist, the internal composition and politics of nation-states, and the institutions and politics of the United States in particular, as if they were in causal isolation from one another. It presumes instead that processes and outcomes in each of these areas are caused by variable interaction across them.

Much of the IR scholarly community remains convinced that because the liberal IR theoretical paradigm explicitly recognizes the causal role of subsystemic variables, it adequately allows for the integration of subfield analysis. I am firmly convinced otherwise, however, and one of the goals of this work is to reveal why that particular paradigm is insufficient to the task at hand. Alternatively I seek to develop a more holistic explanatory approach which can deductively combine the three standard levels-of-analysis under the same causal framework, but which is also concerned with the totality of historical and global political phenomenon. I believe realism offers such an approach, if the explanatory implications which might be derived from its ontology are fully considered.

Hereto, however, I recognize that this view is not widely shared by other scholars who seek a holistic perspective, which is why this work involves the careful analysis of theoretical approaches as comparative alternatives to one another. Such comparisons reveal that there is enormous potential in realist theorizing *if* it is carefully developed and *if* theoretical boundaries are recognized and acknowledged. This means, to put it bluntly, that realism cannot do everything. Indeed a core argument of this book is that realism needs an approach like constructivism in order to complete its narratives of social reality. However realism still does provide the basis from which we may begin to think about human social activity writ large and to understand why it is a fundamental truism of human existence that the more things change, the more they stay the same.

In developing the ideas and arguments in the book I owe an enormous debt of gratitude to numerous individuals. The most important of these is my husband, friend, and colleague, Brian Folker, who has always supported my personal and professional efforts and who is responsible for pushing my intellectual development beyond the confines of what is considered standard realist theorizing in the discipline. His intellectual input into the process was tremendous, and exposure to ideas from his discipline of literary theory and criticism led me to reconsider the relationship between realism and constructivism specifically. His commitment to me and our family remains a source of professional inspiration and personal joy. My daughter, Katherine Folker, also deserves special mention, not because she personally assisted the intellectual development of this book. Far from it, her birth in the middle of its writing held up the process considerably. But her presence has confirmed for me a central aspect of my argument, which is that to be a "nurturing realist" is not an oxymoron.

A number of scholars reviewed the manuscript. Their recommendations not only helped the book find a congenial home at State University of New York Press, but their suggestions also shaped the structure of the present manuscript and the substantive revisions to my theoretical arguments. These scholars include Yale Ferguson, Patrick Thaddeus Jackson, Jeff Taliaferro, Joe Grieco, and Donald Puchala. Each one of these scholars provided me with insights, suggestions, and personal encouragement. Significantly many of them are not realists or do not practice the "neoclassical" variant to which I subscribe, yet all were willing to give this variant a fair hearing, which I believe amply testifies to the extensive intellectual and personal capacities that each of these individuals brings to the profession. All of them have also been professionally supportive well beyond the confines of the manuscript itself and in ways that I only hope I may repay in the years to come.

The book was presented at the "Northeast Circle: New Scholarship Roundtable" during the International Studies Association—North East's Annual Meeting in Albany in November 2000. There I received more valuable advice from the roundtable participants just as the book was being finalized. Yale and Patrick agreed to participate and read a draft of the manuscript yet one more time, and suggestions from Eric Leonard, Craig Murphy, Dan Nexon, and audience participants were incorporated as much as possible into the final draft. Portions of the present chapters 3 and 7 should demonstrate that I was indeed listening and taking your advice quite seriously. Thank you all for being willing to participate and helping me revise the work accordingly. I would also like to thank the ISA-NE Governing Council, State University of New York Press, and Michael Rinella for their support at the conference.

Various other scholars have read portions of the manuscript while it was in progress and provided detailed suggestions. These include Jon Mercer, Ernie Haas, Jack Snyder, Chuck Gochman, and Annette Freyberg-Inan. Each of these scholars let me use them as sounding boards for my ideas and provided me with honest reactions that I very much appreciated. Once again many of these scholars are not realists, which leads me to value all the more their willingness to seriously consider the ideas involved.

Two individuals whom I would like to single out for particular thanks are Mark Boyer and Randy Schweller. Both of them have provided me with intellectual and personal encouragement not only regarding the manuscript but regarding my work in general. At certain points during the process each of them kept me from despairing about the book and the profession at large (without even realizing it I'm sure), and at other points in time their intervention and involvement tipped the professional scales in my favor. I will be eternally grateful to each of them for their encouragement and support.

Although pieces I presented in several other forums during the writing of the manuscript were not part of the final copy, those pieces proved foundational for the development of the neoclassical realist-constructivist perspective I provide in chapter 3. The participants in the October 1999 ISP Friday seminar series, Belfer Center for Science and International Affairs, at Harvard University, deserve thanks for providing their reactions and comments. The support I received from Colin Elman and Miriam Fendius-Elman in that venue and in other situations has been steadfast, considerable, and instrumental to the development of this book. Their feedback and comments on other pieces I have written has also been insightful and of tremendous value.

Another forum which allowed me to develop ideas related to the book was the "Conference on Evolutionary Approaches to International Relations," organized by Bill Thompson at Indiana University in December 1998. Bill has consistently encouraged my work and provided me with publication opportunities that were absolutely essential to my ability to continue working as an academic. Hereto I only hope that I may repay his support in kind someday. Participant feedback at the conference was useful in formulating the arguments which became chapter 3. Comments and support from fellow participants Vincent Falger and John Vasquez were particularly pertinent and continued well after the conference had ended. In an entirely different venue, at the 1999 ISA Annual Meeting Marty Finnemore also provided comments on a paper that informed some aspects of the realist-constructivist perspective I develop in the book.

The graduate students in my International Organization seminar during the 1998 spring semester deserve special mention for allowing me to organize the class around the themes of my book and using them as sounding boards for my own critiques of the interdependence and regimes literature. Their skepticism regarding those critiques forced me to hone the arguments further and, I hope, make them even more convincing. One of those students, Javier Morales-Ortiz, later served as my research assistant and I appreciate all of the preparations he undertook in order to get the book ready for publication.

I would like to acknowledge the International Studies Association and Blackwell Publishers for their copyright permission. Portions of chapters 1 and 6 first appeared as "Competing Paradigms or Birds of a Feather? Constructivism and Neoliberal Institutionalism Compared," *International Studies Quarterly* 44 (March 2000): 97–119, © by the International Studies Association, adapted by permission of Blackwell Publishers. Portions of chapters 3 and 6 first appeared as "Realist Environment, Liberal Process, and Domestic-Level Variables," *International Studies Quarterly* 41 (March 1997): 1–26, © by the International Studies Association, adapted by permission of Blackwell Publishers.

There are also various organizations I would like to thank for their financial support in developing this project. During the writing of the dissertation upon which the book was based, I received a Dissertation Fellowship from the Mellon Foundation-University of Chicago, a MacArthur Scholarship from the Council for Advanced Studies on Peace and International Cooperation at the University of Chicago, and a Margaret Yardley Fellowship from the New Jersey State Federation of Women's Clubs. I also received a Junior Faculty Summer Fellowship and a Small Faculty Research Grant both from the University of Connecticut Research Foundation.

Finally, I would like to thank the members of my 1993 dissertation committee at the University of Chicago. That committee included Duncan Snidal, Lloyd Rudolph, Bernard Silberman, and (as an unofficial reader) Stephen Walt. These scholars gave me the freedom to pursue a topic which attempted to blend IR, comparative politics, and American politics and which produced a decidedly untidy dissertation. For their willingness to encourage me in this endeavor I thank them. I hope this book will prove that their support at that point was not in vain and well worth the wait.

Glossary of Abbreviations

BIS	Bank for International Settlements
BOJ	Bank of Japan
C20	Committee of Twenty
CEA	Council of Economic Advisers
EEC	European Economic Community
EMS	European Monetary System
EMU	European Monetary Union
ESF	Exchange Stabilization Fund
EU	European Union
FOMC	Federal Open Market Committee
GAB	General Arrangements to Borrow
GATT	General Agreements on Tariffs and Trade
GNP	Gross National Product
G5	Group of Five
G7	Group of Seven
G10	Group of Ten
IBRD	International Bank for Reconstruction and Development (The World Bank)
IMF	International Monetary Fund
IO	International Organization
IPE	International Political Economy
IR	International Relations
MOF	Ministry of Finance
NATO	North Atlantic Treaty Organization
OECD	Organization for Economic Cooperation and Development
OPEC	Organization of Petroleum Exporting Countries
SCR	Strategic Capital Reserve
SDR	Special Drawing Right
USTR	United States Trade Representative

blank xii

Chapter 1

Explaining International Cooperation

How do we as international relations (IR) scholars explain international co-operation? Given that cooperation and peace are commonly associated with one another, and that the search for explanations of peace and war have largely driven the discipline's development, it would seem reasonable to assume that we had developed a relatively good understanding of this important phenomenon. The central contention of this book, however, is that we still do not adequately understand or explain international cooperation. In fact, the theories of cooperation which dominate its study obscure more than they reveal about the subject.

The problem is rooted in a common reliance on interdependence as *the* permissive condition for international cooperation. This reliance is ubiquitous within the cooperation literature and yet, amazingly, its causal connection to cooperative outcomes has never been sufficiently tested. If the causal chain which supposedly links the condition of interdependence to international cooperation is mapped out and then tested against empirical events, three very interesting conclusions emerge. First, while most explanations for international cooperation adopt a systemic orientation, the pivotal causal link in the interdependence-cooperation chain involves national decisionmakers learning to perceive their policymaking situations in new ways. Yet despite the fundamental role this causal link plays in explanations for cooperation, the importance of decisionmaker cognition and learning, as well as the assumptions regarding what it is that decisionmakers are suppose to learn, are insufficiently acknowledged and considered.

What makes this lack of acknowledgment or consideration particularly disturbing is that embedded in almost every existing theory of cooperation is the assumption that national decisionmakers will want to pursue the functionally efficient course of action within their assigned policy spheres more than they will want to fulfill any number of role-related, domestic institutional, and daily practical demands which conflict with functionally efficient outcomes. According to the cooperation literature, the phenomenon results because as policymakers interact transnationally they come to recognize that all of these other demands are in the way of a more efficient and hence desirable means of obtaining goals derived from their assigned issue area. Ultimately this efficiency can only be achieved through multilateralism.

While there are considerable dangers with deriving explanations from such a presumption, not the least of which is that it produces expectations for which there is no empirical evidence, what makes this conclusion particularly interesting theoretically is that explanations for cooperation have generally developed within the liberal IR paradigm. The practitioners of this paradigm have consistently claimed that its explanatory parameters allow systemic, domestic, and individual level variables to be simultaneously combined in a deductively coherent manner. In fact, however, domestic institutional variables, and the cognitive roles associated with them, do not play any independent causal role in explanations for cooperation derived from an interdependent basis. This point has been missed by proponents and critics alike, largely because most scholars have tended to take at its word the liberal claim to alternative level-of-analysis inclusiveness.

The second conclusion which emerges from a more careful consideration of the interdependence-cooperation connection is that explanations of cooperation have too often taken the existing correlation between post-World War II increases of interdependence and cooperation among the major industrials as confirmatory evidence that the first phenomenon caused the second. The connection is treated as though it were a self-evident reality in the cooperation literature, rather than a potential subject of empirical inquiry in its own right. Yet it is important to remember that correlation is not causality. In this context it is worth underscoring the fact that this study does not deny relations among the major industrials since 1945 may be characterized as interdependent, however problematic attempts have been to define, measure, or identify that condition. Nor does it deny that these relations, and capitalist economic relations in particular, have involved a great many cooperative efforts with the United States being a regular, sometime enthusiastic participant in those efforts. It does not even deny that the phenomenon of interdependence and cooperation are linked in some way.

What it does seek to challenge is the particular causal chain by which the cooperation literature presumptively connects these two empirical phenomena. As with Gilpin, "I thus accept economic interdependence as a 'fact' or 'condition,' but do not accept many of its alleged economic and political consequences" (1987: 18; see also 1996b). Once the presumed causal chain linking interdependence and cooperation is sufficiently revealed and the empirical record examined, what becomes obvious is that there is little empirical evidence to support the posited causal chain, largely because policymakers do not behave according to liberal theoretical expectations. They either do not learn the lessons anticipated by standard theories of cooperation, or they do not have sufficient political capacity and will to make the lessons stick institutionally. When one takes a closer look at why and how decisionmakers choose to cooperate with their counterparts transnationally, it is clear that while interdependence may have many effects, a capacity to engender cooperation on the basis of elite learning about functional institutional efficiency is not one of them.

In fact, a closer look reveals the third startling conclusion. There may indeed be a link between interdependence and cooperation, but it is not a link in which the first encourages the second and in so doing the two phenomena mutually reinforce one another. The link is instead that cooperation can be pursued as a means to *deflect* the interdependent demands for functionally more efficient strategies and institutions. Its track record for achieving this goal within the American international monetary policymaking context has been particularly remarkable. Even as the condition of interdependence frequently imposes the necessity for action upon American monetary policymakers, international cooperation has been one of the instruments they have utilized to *avoid* making the types of structural adjustments anticipated by the cooperation literature.

Multilateralism has done so by taking on the form of adjustment necessary to assuage critics and markets alike, while simultaneously containing none of the institutional substance. Since 1971 American policymakers have become particularly adept at nodding in the cooperative direction during a monetary crisis, but making none of the structural or behavioral adjustments actually required in order to obtain more efficient monetary outcomes in economic interdependent conditions. The result is that cooperation with their transnational counterparts has allowed American policymakers to ensure that the business of monetary policymaking continues as usual. This means that decisionmaking remains autonomous relative to the institutions of other nation-states and responsive to domestic political and social demands that continue to contradict the more efficient course for international monetary policymaking. The ability to make unilateral decisions within the issue area relative to the decisionmaking units of other nation-states has continued unabated as a result. Far from being the mutually exclusive antithesis of unilateral decisionmaking, as it is represented in the cooperation literature, multilateralism can instead reinforce unilateralism.

What is wrong, then, with the causal chain posited by the cooperation literature is not simply that within the parameters of interdependence a much wider latitude for policymaking choice exists. It is instead that because the standard theories of cooperation misread what the phenomenon is all about to begin with, they have no capacity to recognize why and how policymakers actually make the decisions they do. The result is that each act of cooperation is misread by IR theorists as confirmatory evidence that decisionmakers have learned to value multilateralism over unilateralism in an interdependent world, when in fact they typically have learned nothing of the kind. What they appear to have learned instead is that unilateralism is just fine if one occasionally "toasts," as Volcker has put it, "the god of international cooperation" (Volcker and Gyohten 1992: 144). Theories which continue to ignore what decisionmakers and national populations want or do socially and politically, and choose instead to derive explanations from the abstract condition of interdependence itself and the institutional imperative that condition implies, will remain incapable of explaining why cooperation occurs and what it means for global world order.

These arguments and the nuances their development require will be explored in the pages which follow, as will the delineation of connections these arguments have to existing theories of international relations. Much of the existing literature on cooperation has been developed within the liberal IR paradigm, where the assumption that a condition of interdependence will demand a functionally efficient institutional response has a considerable pedigree. It may be found in the original formulation of functionalism by Mitrany, itself inspired by the evolutionary functionalism of "in-use" inheritance proposed by Lamarck.[1] It may be traced through all subsequent liberal cooperation theories and approaches including neofunctionalism, transnational relations, complex interdependence, and neoliberal institutional regimes. The pervasiveness of this assumption has effected explanations for cooperation from other approaches as well, so that even many constructivist accounts have relied upon it.

There is nothing about constructivism which demands it tow the liberal cooperative line however. Indeed in the context of the arguments presented here "Wendtian" constructivism serves as a link between the phenomenon of cooperation, domestic political institutions and social practices, and the realist paradigm. Realism has remained the odd-man-out in the cooperation literature, due in part to the choices its own practitioners have made about the subjects they wish to study, and in part because immediate post-Cold War events have not conformed to some of realism's better-known expectations. Yet the realist-constructivist combination has a great deal to offer the study of international cooperation. Not only does it have no investment in the interdependent functionalism of prior cooperation theories, but it can also provide a framework for understanding why the policymaking commitment to unilateralism would remain institutionally and cognitively dominant even as systemic conditions appeared to warrant new commitments.

In developing an alternative theoretical perspective on cooperation, realism brings to the table its long-standing insights into inter- and intragroup behavior in anarchic conditions, while constructivism brings an understanding of how social practices create and reinforce identities and preferences. Such a combination produces a direct challenge to the pivotal causal assumption in liberal cooperation theories that national decisionmakers learn from interdependent conditions to value multilateralism over unilateralism and change their behaviors and institutions accordingly. It explains why interdependence has no capacity to engender cooperation on such a basis and why American monetary policymakers then continue to care more about the next presidential election than how transnational cooperation could maximize national economics. It also explains how the choice of cooperation may be derived from and reinforce the preference for unilateral decisionmaking, and why the American commitment to multilateral efforts is characterized by such a high degree of recidivism. In other words, a realist-constructivist combination explains everything that the field's dominant theories of cooperation cannot.

This chapter begins to lay the groundwork for these assertions by first establishing just how pervasive the assumption of interdependent functional efficiency has been in our explanations for international cooperation and to our approach to the subject in general. It demonstrates how little attention has been paid to the implicit causal chain linking interdependence to cooperation in these explanations, and it takes a second look at this chain in order to reveal the centrality of subsystemic variables to it. In so doing it highlights the striking paucity of studies which empirically examine or test cooperation theories along lines that their own assumptive frameworks would suggest. Thus the chapter seeks to underscore why this book, as both an examination of liberal cooperation theory's explanatory powers and the proposition of an alternative perspective on the cooperative phenomenon, is necessary.

THE "NEW" INTERNATIONAL ORGANIZATION

Since the end of the Cold War, the literature on "governance without government" has burgeoned in both scope and proportion. It has become routine for scholars and policymakers of IR to declare the dawning of a new age in global politics. Held claims, for example, that "the development of international and transnational organizations has led to important changes in the decisionmaking structure of world politics" (1996: 411).[2] Fliers for professional conferences baldly assert that "dramatic transformations in the global order pose serious challenges for educators, as power shifts from nation-states and superpowers to subnational, international, and nongovernmental entities."[3] And much of this literature is in accord with Zacher that "there are grounds now for thinking that there are significant changes occurring in the growth of international cooperation or regimes—consequently in the strength of governance in the international system" (1992: 59).

If, as Kratochwil has argued, "the study of international organization . . . can be conceived of as the investigation of the various organizational forms that populate the international arena" (1994: ix), then much of the IR theoretical community appears to share a common assumption about post-Cold War organizational forms. The system's organization differs in fundamental ways from other, prior, and even coexisting International Organization (IO) forms and principles, because cooperative interaction is in ascendance. While cooperation had been a subject of extensive study throughout the Cold War, the end of bipolarity has given impetus to the assertion that cooperation is now *the* dominant organizational principle in many geographic and issue-specific sectors of the present international system. This means that it now dominates at the expense of prior IO forms.

The most obvious prior alternative is the realist model of IO, with its anarchic environment, aggressive behaviors, and balances-of-power. Even its critics usually acknowledged that the realist model of IO provided a relatively accurate description of nation-state interaction before the latter half of the twentieth century. But according to the new model of IO, realism's anarchic demands have been, or are in the process of being, transcended in portions of the globe and/or in particular issue areas. Lebow asserts, for example, that

> The allegedly inescapable consequences of anarchy have been largely overcome by a complex web of institutions that govern interstate relations and provide mechanisms for resolving disputes. These institutions reflect and help sustain a consensus in favor of consultation and compromise that mute the consequences of power imbalances among states (1994: 269).

In a similar vein, Goldgeier and McFaul argue that "balance-of-power politics will not be the defining feature of interactions among great powers in the coming decades, since the nature of states and the nature of the international system differ fundamentally from those described by structural realists." Instead, "the collapse of communism will continue to move the world closer to an international order governed politically by collective action among the great powers," and such an order may be characterized as "a great power society" (1992: 486, 477).

One of the reasons why a cooperative model of IO has been achieved among the major industrialized societies is because these societies share a common set of Western values, norms, preferences, and institutions which are assumed to have peace-inducing qualities. So, for example, Jervis describes the major industrials as "stable, democratic governments that have learned to cooperate and have developed a stake in each other's well being" (1991/92: 56). Biersteker argues that "a limited degree of transnational convergence of foreign and domestic economic policies is likely to facilitate governance (or a change in the nature of governance) in the international political economy" (1992: 104). Zacher asserts that it is because the world "is becoming sufficiently homogeneous (especially at elite levels among many countries) that higher levels of coordination are becoming more feasible" (1992: 98). And Goldgeier and McFaul claim that because the major industrialized societies have similar economic and political processes, they will choose to "settle conflicts and enhance their security through negotiation and compromise rather than through the use or threat of force" (1992: 468). In fact, Rasler and Thompson point out that it is a common feature of "endism" arguments to presume that homogeneity of political, economic, and social institutions leads to peace (1994: 186).

Homogeneity means not only that the major industrials find violent behavioral patterns among themselves unattractive, but they have also developed a preference for transnational policy coordination, particularly in the sphere of economics where their societies share the common capitalist-market motivation for profit. This preference for coordination was produced by a process begun during the Cold War in which, as their economies became increasingly intertwined via trade and monetary transactions, degrees of autonomous decisionmaking had to be relinquished in order to obtain economic and social benefits. As Jessop puts this, changes involved "a movement from the central role of official state apparatus in securing state-sponsored economic and social projects and political hegemony towards an emphasis on partnerships between governmental, para-governmental and nongovernmental organizations in which the state apparatus is often only first among equals" (1997: 574–575). While this form of IO is clearly not global, there is a presumption within the IO literature that it will become generalizable as more states adopt capitalist and democratic reforms.

Much of what is asserted and predicted in the "governance" literature should sound familiar to IO scholars acquainted with the liberal IR theoretical tradition. In fact there is an overwhelming sense of *déjà vu* in the presumptions and descriptions of the brave "new" IO with which we are now supposedly faced. What is being asserted is, in essence, that with the end of the Cold War earlier models of IO based on liberal theorizing about transnational relations in conditions of interdependence have finally achieved empirical and theoretical salience. The theoretical insights, arguments, hypotheses, and predictions of David Mitrany, Ernst Haas, Leon Lindberg, Karl Deutsch, Joseph Nye, Robert Keohane, James Rosenau, and Wolfram

Hanrieder (to name only a few of the most obvious) are being resurrected in order to characterize, explain, and make predictions about the present and future international system. This resurrection is occurring despite the fact that many of the prior liberal theoretical perspectives were abandoned by their own proponents for having been, as Haas put it earlier, theoretically "obsolescent." Much of this earlier theorizing about cooperation was associated with the study of the European Union (EU), and in her review of these alternative perspectives Webb arranged them chronologically precisely because "each is an attempt to correct the omissions of earlier theories"(1983: 10).[4]

What the contemporary IO literature appears to assume, on the other hand, is that far from being obsolete or rife with omissions, much of this liberal theoretical tradition was actually ahead of its time. Present international conditions apparently warrant a reclamation of what could now be considered liberal "pre-" theorizing.[5] Such claims remind one of the doctor in Hitchcock's film *The Lady Vanishes* who asserts, when confronted with falsifying evidence, "My theory was a perfectly good one. The facts were misleading." This assertion may actually be quite consistent with the fundamental tenets of liberal IR theory itself. Liberalism purposely adopts an evolutionary perspective which means, according to Keohane, that it "believes in at least the possibility of cumulative progress" (1990: 174) or, as Zacher and Matthew have put it, that "the possibility of progress is constant but its realization . . . vary over time and space" (1995: 121). It may be legitimate to argue then, as Keohane and Nye did in their preface to the second edition of *Power and Interdependence,* that while events subsequent to the 1970s had not entirely supported their model of IO, "the real questions are not about obsolescence, but about analytical cogency" (1989: xi). A brief review of what is old about the "new" IO is pertinent not only to the issue of analytical cogency but also to the counterarguments made in this book.

PRIOR PERIODS OF LIBERAL COGENCY

Even a cursory comparison of present and prior liberal descriptions of the international system reveal striking similarities. In a precursor to *Power and Interdependence,* Keohane and Nye argued for a "world politics paradigm" which would "transcend the 'level-of-analysis problem' both by broadening the conception of actors to include transnational actors and by conceptually breaking down the 'hard shell' of the nation state" (1971: 380). They argued that as interdependence increased, the developed countries were experiencing a "loss of political and economic autonomy" and that this "loss of control is probably most acute . . . in regard to welfare objectives" (393–394). The policy option which would yield "optimal results" was argued to be the adoption of "cooperative policies involving joint coordination of policy through international institutions."

Yet even as Keohane and Nye were proposing "transnational relations" as a new perspective, the ideas upon which it were based could be traced back to functionalism and neofunctionalism. In his vision of post-World War II Europe, Mitrany had argued for the "functional selection and organization of international relations" which meant "the binding together [of] those interests which are common" (1943: 32). While it remains unclear in much of the early functionalist literature whether interdependence was a new phenomenon or had always existed and human beings were only just becoming cognizant of it, functionalist proponents argued that interdependence was an environmental condition that demanded institutional innovation if commonly-shared interests were to be fulfilled. Reinsch provides a typical example in claiming that "recognizing interdependence with other civilized nations of the world," meant recognizing that "there is a broader life; there are broader interests and more far-reaching activities surrounding national life in which it must participate in order to develop to the full its own nature and satisfy completely its many needs" (1911: 8, 4).[6]

Functionalism's proponents were also firmly convinced that the nation-state was *the* problem that prevented common interests from being obtained. Mitrany argued, for example, that "fidelity to outgrown administrative divisions and instruments" was "hamstringing the new goals" and that, although this "clamors for their being linked together in the most suitable practical way" and that "we are favored by the need and habit of material cooperation," the problem was that "we are hampered by the general clinging to political segregation" (1945: 10; 1948: 351). The only answer to this problem was the transcendence of national institutional structures themselves. Institutional form would instead follow function because "the organizational component of each functional unit is intimately related to the need which it is to satisfy" (1943: 35), and the new institutions would be "functionally efficient" because they matched a set of pregiven collective interests to demands for how to best obtain them in an interdependent environmental context. As Sewell later noted, the functional approach was hopeful rather than "debilitating" in this regard, because "the separation of functional needs into specific tasks and their reassignment to new structures will itself presumably ease the strain wrought by the present disparity" between "functional assignments and 'outgrown administrative divisions and instruments'" (1966: 33).

This perspective quickly ran into empirical trouble, however, in that it had all along assumed a relative ease in the ability "to breed a new conscience" in "nonpolitical" tasks once the functional way revealed that it "would promise something for the purse of necessity" (Mitrany 1943: 40, 29). By the early 1960s, functionalism had spawned a neofunctionalist variant which recognized the difficulties in defining an interest as "nonpolitical," as well as the necessity for persuading "political actors in several distinct national settings . . . to shift their loyalties, expectations, and political activities toward a new and larger center" (E. B. Haas 1961: 366–367). Yet even with its greater sensitivity to these issues, neofunctionalism continued to assume that once the cooperative regional effort began to reap greater benefits, loyalty to the regional institutions would gradually develop. E. B. Haas argued, for example, that integration was to be "conceived not as a condition but as a process" which "relies on the perception of interests . . . by the actors participating in the process" so that "interest will be redefined in terms of regional rather than a purely national orientation."[7] Loyalty-shifting and interest-redefinition would occur first among national elites who would find themselves "sucked in" to cooperative efforts and "would transfer their support and loyalties away from national authorities towards the Community institutions in return for the satisfaction of vital interests" (Webb 1983: 17–18).

The continued reliance on functional assumptions about interests, institutions, and identity led neofunctionalists to overestimate the degree to which elite identities and loyalties could be changed by strategic interaction. Webb observed that neofunctionalism continued to assume that "the staking of claims and demands in return for exchanges of political loyalties reinforced the authority of the system as a whole," and it "regarded this pattern of political activity as directly transferable to an international setting" (1983: 17). In other words, it never strayed far from Mitrany's original assumption that "each of us . . . is in effect a collectivity of functional loyalties; so that to build up a world community . . . is merely to extend and consolidate it also as between national sections and groups" (1959: 647). By the mid-1960s, neofunctionalism was having an increasingly difficult time explaining empirical events in the region for which its explanatory scope and focus had been developed, and Haas tactfully suggested that the pursuit of other theoretical approaches might be more fruitful.[8]

The first stab at a new theoretical approach was Keohane and Nye's study of "transnational relations" which was again premised on the notion that interdependent conditions demanded cooperative institutions for conducting intrastate business and obtaining common interests (1971: 375, 395). This approach was quickly superseded by their 1977 *Power and Interdependence*, which proposed an IO model of the "world political structure" that finally placed the condition of interdependence front and center in its theoretical framework. In doing so Keohane and Nye expressed their belief that "many of the insights from integration theory could be transferred to the growing and broader dimensions of international economic interdependence" (1989:

247–248). In this endeavor they were encouraged by E. B. Haas himself, who suggested that neofunctionalism be "both included in and subordinated to the study of changing patterns of interdependence" (1975: 86).

Not surprisingly then, the IO model which would be relevant under conditions of "complex" interdependence contained most of the theoretical assumptions that could be found in functionalism and neofunctionalism before it. In order to cope with growing interdependence, nation-states would have to accept responsibility for both collective leadership and policy coordination. This responsibility would involve "mutual surveillance of domestic and foreign economic policies, criticism of these policies by other governments, and coordinated interventions in certain international markets" (Keohane and Nye 1989: 232). The model's salience was contingent on higher levels of complex interdependence which, Keohane and Nye argued, had increasingly come to characterize "trends in the conditions of world politics over the past half century" (161). And they predicted that the IO world political structure "will frequently be needed for understanding reality and framing appropriate polices" while "traditional theories of world politics . . . are becoming *less useful*" (161, their emphasis; see also 223–229).

In the same decade, authors such as Rosenau, Hanrieder, and Morse were making similar arguments about the impact of interdependence on the international politics of the major industrials.[9] Rosenau argued that "by their very nature interdependence issues tend to require multilateral cooperation among governments for their amelioration," and predicted that, "as interdependence impinges ever more tightly, so may the adaptive capacities of states allow them to evolve a greater readiness for multilateral cooperation" (1976: 48–49). One could speak then of a "domestication" of international politics, in which interdependence as a "permissive context" encouraged "global political processes" to "approximate domestic political processes" (Hanrieder 1978: 1278–1279). While none of these authors dated the end-point at which Keohane and Nye's IO model would become the dominant world political structure, all of them assumed that levels of interdependence among the major industrial were increasing so that a model along the lines specified by Keohane and Nye had the potential to be more relevant in the future.

The subsequent literature on international regimes in the 1980s took the condition of complex interdependence as a given in order to argue that "international coordination of policy seems highly beneficial in an interdependent world economy" (Keohane 1984: 49; see also Krasner 1983a). Yet it acknowledged that cooperation could be difficult to achieve initially and posited that existing regimes would be of assistance in the post-hegemonic transition to collective leadership and policy coordination. The regime literature, dubbed by Grieco in 1990 as "neoliberal institutionalism," also adopted a presumption of future salience based on increasing levels of interdependence. Keohane argued that "there is likely to be increasing demand for international regimes as interdependence grows" (1984: 79–80), and Krasner noted that "if, as many have argued, there is a general movement toward a world of complex interdependence, then the number of areas in which regimes can matter is growing" (1983a: 7–8). In discussing how to falsify his regimes theory, Keohane pointed out that its explanatory applicability would occur in the future and that "scholars may *later* be able to conduct a full evaluation of the theories of cooperation and international regimes put forward in this book" (1984: 219; my emphasis). Thus the theme of future analytic cogency, itself contingent on sufficiently high levels of interdependence among the major industrials, has been an ongoing presumption in liberal theorizing.

The post-Cold War "governance" literature continues this tradition in its universal reliance upon complex interdependence as a necessary or permissive cause (and regimes as one of the sufficient causes) for cooperative behaviors and outcomes among the major industrials.[10] But what makes this literature so distinctive is the certain conviction expressed within it that the levels of interdependence necessary for Keohane and Nye's IO model to gain analytic cogency have now been achieved. Adler, Crawford, and Donnelly claim, for example, that "complex interdependence is a model that is widely acknowledged to provide a fairly accurate account of large portions of contemporary [IR]," and that progress (defined as "changes in the policies and relations of states that reduce conflict or increase cooperation . . . that further human interests") is relatively likely (1991: 23, 9). Held argues that "while a complex pattern of global interconnections has been evident for a long time, there is little doubt that there has recently been a further 'multinationalisation' of domestic activities and an intensification of decisionmaking in multinational frameworks" (1996: 414).

In a similar vein, Zacher claims that "it is clear to anyone who studies the development of the modern interstate system that states have sought to evade international constraints on their behavior," but that "it was around 1990 that a good number of observers of the international system began to recognize that a network of formal and informal international regimes was developing to a point where states' enmeshment in them marked the advent of quite a different type of international order" (1992: 62, 67). And Jessop notes that while "it is hard to discern a marked discontinuity in the organization of the capitalist economy during the 1970s to 1990s," a number of factors including the Soviet communist collapse have produced "a trend which partly returns the world economy . . . to the levels of interdependence prevailing in 1913 but which nonetheless has a qualitatively quite different significance" (1997: 572, 571). One of these significant qualitative differences is "a shift from govern*ment* to govern*ance* on various territorial scales and across various functional domains" (574; his emphasis).

Thus the end of the Cold War represents a disjuncture for the capitalist world economy which can be associated with a certain level of "maturity" from mere interdependence to a condition of complex interdependence. It is never made clear in this literature why it is such a disjuncture, but according to the new "governance" literature what *is* clear is that a world political structure approximating the IO model proposed in the 1970s by Keohane and Nye is no longer just a potential. It is now *the* dominant world political structure.

CONSTRUCTIVISM IN AN ERA OF LIBERAL COGENCY

There is perhaps no better proof of the firm grip which the assumptions of interdependence and functional efficiency have on our theories of cooperation than attempts within the constructivist literature to explain the phenomenon. The accumulated study of norms, ideas, learning, and identity-formation has produced what Checkel has called "the constructivist turn in IR theory" in which theorists open up "the black box of interest and identity formation," in order to argue that "state interests emerge from and are endogenous to inter-action with structures" (1998: 326).[11] This is important because, as Kratochwil and Ruggie put it, "social institutions, before they do anything else—for example, act as injunctions—express rule-like practices . . . that make routine social interaction possible by making it mutually comprehensible" (Ruggie 1998: 91). Thus constructivism is, according to practitioners such as Ruggie, Finnemore, and Wendt, about recognizing "the fact that the specific identities of specific states shape their perceived interests and, thereby, patterns of in-ternational outcomes," that "interests are not just 'out there' waiting to be discovered; they are constructed through social interaction," and "that through interaction, states might form collective identities and interests."[12]

Because functionalism could not be more antithetical to the constructivist approach, most constructivists explicitly seek to distance their accounts of cooperation from it. It is because constructivist explanations rely on a "logic of appropriateness," rather than on a "logic of consequences" that they sup-posedly avoid the demand-driven trap that neofunctionalism and neoliberal institutionalism (as well as realism) fall into.[13] In addition, neoliberal institu-tionalism has consistently been one of the targets of constructivist ire because it, along with neorealism, attempts to hold identity constant and treat inter-ests as exogenously-given. States are assumed to be self-interested actors seeking to maximize utility functions which are theoretically designated prior to the strategic interaction and behavior under inquiry. In other words, actor pref-erences and values "become inputs into the analysis rather than the subject of analysis."[14]

However within the interdependence literature which grounds the concept of regimes itself, there is some confusion on this score. Keohane and Nye, for example, frequently referred to changes or transformations in "how states define their interests," in "perceptions of self-interest," and to the possibility that "interactions facilitate learning" (1989: xi, 35, 241). Conceptual clarity on this point was provided in their later-published afterword, where they acknowledged that although they had assumed "interests as formed largely exogenously, in a way unexplained by our theory," in fact "changes in definitions of self-interest . . . kept appearing in our case studies . . . without adequate explanation"(256).[15] Ultimately it is the constancy of exogenously-premised interests which allows for predictable outcomes in complex interdependent issue areas. Because one can assume, as Hanrieder does, that "one of the central functions of state activity" has become "the improvement through state intervention of the material (and perhaps even psychological) well-being of its citizens," it is also possible to posit the existence of "powerful incentives to cooperate with one another" (1978: 1278–1279).

Given this earlier confusion, most regime theorists were particularly careful to specify their assumptions regarding exogenous interests. According to Stein, for example, it is necessary to emphasize strategic interaction among states because while "structure and sectors play a role in determining the constellation of actor preferences . . . it is the combination of actor preferences and interactions that result from them that determine outcome" (1983: 140). Thus the analysis of regimes begins with the "different patterns of interest that underlie the regimes themselves," which Stein argues must be distinguished from the structural bases for regime formation "as constituting the determinants of those different patterns of interests" (135). Keohane also specified his assumptions that "rationality and conceptions of self-interest are constants rather than variables," and that among the "advanced market-economy countries" one can assume the "existence of mutual interests as givens" (1984: 27, 6).[16] Again, it is this constancy which allows neoliberal institutionalism to predict the post-hegemonic continuation of regimes while avoiding the criticism that it is suggesting a "beyond the nation-state" thesis.

One of the more important implications of the assumption of exogenous interests is that it excludes from the analysis of cooperation any concern with identity formation issues. This was, in fact, the theoretical attribute which distinguished the complex interdependence and the regimes literature from prior strands of liberal cooperation theory. Although all of these strands share the assumption of interdependent functional efficiency, functionalism and its neo- variant had assumed that changes in elite loyalty and identity would have to be an important part of the cooperative institution-building process. Complex interdependence and neoliberal institutionalism, on the other hand, attempted to avoid this assumption (and the various problems it had caused for their theoretical predecessors) by positing that interests, and as a logical corollary identities as well, could be treated as given.

Thus the interdependence and regimes literature argued that while the nation-state was still the primary barrier to effectively obtaining collective interests in interdependent conditions, it now remained so only because its decisionmaking elites had failed to recognize the ineffectiveness of the strategies they continued to employ. Their strategic judgment was clouded by an unquestioned reliance on unilateralism held over from the days when the nation-state could obtain its interests autonomously. The offending perceptions were treated as byproducts of behavior, rather than of identity or interest, so that Keohane and Nye could argue that this "illusion" of "total control" reproduced "well-entrenched patterns of governmental behavior" which would "have to be discarded" (1989: 232, also 161).[17] As with functionalism, neoliberal institutionalism derived a hopeful prescription from its analysis of these dysfunctions based on the nature of interdependence itself, which it argued would promote a process of interaction and simple learning among state elites about the greater efficacy of multilateralism.

Since many constructivists have criticized neoliberal institutionalism for its failure to understand how interaction might change not just behavior but identity as well, the notion that they are fundamentally different approaches has generally been accepted within the field. In fact, however, a closer examination of many (although by no means all) constructivist accounts for cooperation reveal a reliance on both the assumption of interdependence and the functional efficiency of cooperation in its context.[18] For example, in order for cooperation to develop in a world of survival-seekers, Wendt asserts that "a necessary condition for such cooperation is that outcomes be positively interdependent in the sense that potential gains exist which cannot be realized by unilateral action" (1992: 416). This assertion grounds his "pretheory" of collective identity formation, which identifies two systemic processes as the necessary incentives to adopt collective identities—interdependence and the transnational convergence of domestic values. Neither is sufficient to produce collective identities without reinforcing strategic practices, yet the reason why both remain incentives is because national institutions no longer efficiently obtain a list of pregiven "corporate needs." The result is that

> As *the ability to meet corporate needs* unilaterally declines, so does *the incentive* to hang onto the egoistic identities that generate such politics, and as the degree of common fate increases, so does the incentive to identify with others. As interdependence rise, in other words, so will the potential for endogenous transformations of identity (1994: 389; my emphasis).

This means that identity is a function of whichever institution and set of social practices best obtains a set of exogenous interests in interdependent systemic conditions. In making this argument Wendt clearly adopts the same assumptions about institutions and identities which prior functional theorizing about cooperation had relied upon as well.

Fellow constructivist Ruggie also takes the condition of interdependence as *the* general model of IO and hence the starting point for his explanations of international cooperation. Ruggie argues that nation-states face a tradeoff between the efficacy of organizing multilaterally in economic interdependence and "the general desire to keep that dependence to the minimum level necessary" (1998: 48). That tradeoff does not favor the continuation of autonomous national policymaking, however, because the "generic forms of international 'collective action problems'" which confront the nation-state are in reality "the 'social defects' that inhere in the modern construction of territoriality" (266, 195). That is, because the collective action problems confronting nation-states derive from their own construction as territorially-based entities, nation-states are incapable of addressing the "nonterritorial functional space" (191). This space demands institutional forms consistent with it, which is why the "negation of the exclusive territorial form has been the locale in which international society throughout the modern era has been anchored" and why a "multiperspectival polity" such as the EU has emerged (195). While the constructivist terminology utilized to describe multilateral efforts may sound different, Ruggie's approach manages to replicate the explanatory content and form of functionalist accounts which proceed it.

Finnemore provides another example of replication in arguing that "states are embedded in an international social fabric that extends from the local to the transnational," thereby creating an international society that looks like "the world of complex interdependence or turbulence described by liberals" (1996: 145). Because this society remains inexplicable if interests are held constant, a constructivist approach is required in order to explain "why groups or individuals want what they want" as well as "changes in collectively shared social values or definitions of what is good and appropriate" (147). Ultimately, however, nation-states want what they want according to Finnemore because enough other nation-states want it too. It is because "the driving force behind adoption of . . . innovation" is "a new understanding of necessary and appropriate state behavior," that the pregiven desire to simply *be* appropriate to international society produces norms and behaviors which conform to that society (65). While Finnemore insists that this "logic of appropriateness" avoids the "logic of consequences" upon which functionalism relies, in reality the two logics have simply been merged so that the functional consequence of causal import is whatever has become appropriate socially. As the definition of what constitutes "being appropriate" changes systemically, social practices which are more efficient at obtaining this exogenous collective interest (and hence are more appropriate to the new systemic circumstances) will be supplied.

Although it would be inaccurate to generalize from these examples to all constructivist accounts of cooperation, the examples cited represent a strand of mainstream American constructivism which has been consistently touted as a new theoretical approach to the study of IR. Closer examination reveals this claim to be erroneous. In addition, the extent to which neoliberal institutionalism should be differentiated from constructivism on the basis of its exogenous interests assumption is also highly questionable. While this is an argument that is developed in chapter 6, it is pertinent here because it again underscores the firm grasp which functionalism retains on our theoretical explanations for international cooperation. In order to explain regime creation the regimes literature does indeed initially bracket interests and identities, but in order to account for subsequent regime maintenance an implicit elite identity transformation is inserted into the argument's causal chain. Thus contrary to the accepted wisdom, neoliberal institutionalism does not exclude the possibility of collective identity transformation and must actually rely on such an eventuality in order to complete its stories of the cooperative phenomenon.

One of the reasons why neoliberal institutionalism and constructivism have more in common than not is because they share a process-based ontology which anticipates the transformation of identity through interaction with others. Certainly the two approaches may differ with regards to their explanatory ambitions and the interactive processes they identify as most pertinent to identity transformation, but constructivist accounts of cooperation simply make explicit an assumed but unexplored step in situationally-strategic neoliberal arguments. When their assumptive structures and contents are closely examined, it becomes difficult to differentiate functional-constructivist accounts of cooperation from prior theorizing on the subject. Far from being a step in a new explanatory direction, many constructivist accounts have been about retracing steps along a well-trodden path while proclaiming that the terrain covered is all new. Constructivism threatens to become just another strand of liberal cooperation theory in the process, and the stranglehold which the mechanisms of interdependence and functional institutional efficiency have on our explanatory imaginations is reinforced.

The relationship between liberalism and constructivism may be even cozier when one considers the fortifying effects which each approach may have on the other's assumptive framework. The liberal assumption that many states in the post-Cold War system have common interests and are engaged in collective problem-solving paves the way for an acceptance of constructivist subjects as legitimate areas of inquiry in a way that realist assumptions of unending anarchy producing zero-sum interests and competition would not. As Haggard notes, constructivist approaches require the existence of common norms (1991), and Wendt echoes this in asserting that in order to explain cooperative outcomes with constructivism, joint gains must be assumed (1992: 416-418). This latter assertion is not entirely correct if one is careful *not* to equate the concept of common norms with the concept of joint gains when developing constructivist explanations for cooperative outcomes.

Yet the theoretical space necessary for the exploration of constructivist subjects such as norms, ideas, learning, and identity-formation may have been made possible only because vast portions of the American IR theoretical community already share the certain conviction that something approximating Keohane and Nye's IO model of complex interdependence is now an accurate description of global affairs. The ready acceptance of constructivism within that community could owe much to the dominance of the liberal perspective in the study of IO, even as many of constructivism's practitioners would hope to distance themselves from the theoretical straitjackets of either liberalism or realism.

A SECOND LOOK AT INTERDEPENDENCE AND REGIMES AS EXPLANATIONS FOR COOPERATION

Yet does complex interdependence and its associated regimes produce cooperation in the manner specified by liberal theories? This is a fundamental question because as we have seen almost all liberal arguments rely upon interdependence as a permissive condition for the occurrence of cooperation among the major industrials. Economic relationships are consistently singled out as the issue area in which complex interdependence is most obvious and in which transnational coordination has been realized. The growth of economic interdependence is assumed to both reflect and reinforce the steady displacement of military-security interests by economic ones which can only be maximized via coordination. Existing economic regimes are routinely thrown into the explanatory mix so that the two concepts are assumed to work together in encouraging cooperative outcomes in economic issue areas. Given the causal centrality of interdependence and regimes to liberal explanations for major industrial cooperation from the 1970s on, it is startling how little work has actually been done on testing the causal chain for interdependence and regimes.

There is certainly a body of literature (much of which could be termed *realist*) which questions the assertion that interdependence produces cooperation and argues instead that it is just as likely to produce conflict.[19] The interdependence argument has also been challenged on the grounds that its relationship with cooperation is spurious, since military-security alliances could potentially account for both phenomena.[20] And the regimes concept itself has come under considerable scrutiny from a variety of quarters.[21] What is striking about these critiques and counterarguments, however, is that most of them do not seek to test the interdependence and regimes argument on its own terms. The preferred mode of attack is at the systemic level-of-analysis rather than at the domestic or the individual levels. In other words, the relationship between interdependence, regimes, and cooperation has been challenged by alternative explanations that "account for state behavior on the basis of attributes of the system as a whole" and regard "internal attributes as constants rather than variables" (Keohane 1984: 25).

This systemic orientation initially appears to be consistent with the parameters specified by liberal theorists themselves. Keohane and Nye state in the first-edition preface to *Power and Interdependence* that they are attempting to develop a systemic-level explanation because it is "essential to know how much one can explain purely on the basis of information about the international system" (1989: vi). Keohane's *After Hegemony* regimes argument adopts a systemic level-of-analysis and so does much of the subsequent regime literature.[22] It would appear inappropriate, then, to argue that interdependence and regime arguments should be tested and critiqued at the domestic and individual levels-of-analysis instead. Yet any attempt to map out the cooperative causal chain for the interdependence and regimes argument quickly reveals that it is precisely at these alternative levels-of-analysis that measurement and testing should occur. What is this causal chain which claims to be systemic in focus but actually relies upon domestic and individual level variables to do the causal work for cooperation?

A central tenet of liberal cooperation theory is that the condition of complex interdependence has implications for the way in which national foreign policy is conducted. Keohane and Nye argue, for example, that when complex interdependence exists, "certain well-entrenched patterns of governmental behavior will have to change," and that "the illusion that major macroeconomic policies can be purely domestic will have to be discarded, along with the search for total control over one's own economic system" (1989: 232). National decisionmakers will, instead, have to "accept much more international participation in their decisionmaking processes," and all economic policymaking (including fiscal, monetary, foreign trade, capital, and exchange rate) will "have to come under surveillance by the international community." In a similar vein, Rosenau argues that "the declining capacity of governments to mobilize domestic support, and the technical, decentralized, fragmented, and accommodative structure of interdependence issues" means that there are "substantial changes in the capabilities that states bring to world politics" (1976: 43–44).

The implications of interdependence extend to the study of comparative foreign policy as well so that it is possible to argue, as Smith has, that "the rise of interdependence and transnationalism poses a fundamental challenge to the basic assumptions of the discipline" (1984: 66). The reason for this challenge lies in the common distinction within the field between the domestic and international spheres, which is now supposedly rendered meaningless by a phenomenon that makes it impossible for the state to act as "a self-contained and a sealed unit" (68). A revamping of other fields of study is also required according to Keohane and Milner, since interdependence is a context in which "crossnational comparisons are meaningless without placing the counties being compared in the context of a common world political economy within which they operate" (1996: 257). Hence complex interdependence "should sound the death-knell of the anachronistic divisions, institutionalized in universities, between 'comparative politics' and 'international relations.'" Presumably American politics, public policy, and law as separate fields of study would have to undergo a similar melding. The study of complex interdependence may eventually be the only game in town.

The radical implications for domestic politics and the study of IR suggested by the condition of interdependence are consistent with a "second-image reversed" perspective. Such a perspective begins with the premise that a given external condition has a particular type of impact on the domestic politics and decisionmaking structures of states. Domestic politics and structures are then assumed to have a particular type of effect on the state's international behavior and hence the external condition in which it finds itself. Precisely what the relationship is between the first loop of causality (external's impact on domestic) and the second loop (domestic's impact on externals) is left unclear by Gourevitch, who argued that while "the environment may exert strong pulls . . . some leeway in the response to that environment remains" (1978: 900; also Almond 1989). In liberal cooperation theory, the leeway in response is largely circumscribed by the first loop of causality, though the second loop is where the actual cause for cooperation is ultimately placed.

What liberal cooperation theories assume is that interdependence encourages decisionmakers to make certain types of choices. In particular, it encourages elites to choose cooperation over other policy options and to induce a reworking of domestic decisionmaking structures and processes in order to facilitate this choice. As Rosenau puts this,

> The fact that interdependence issues cannot be handled unilaterally, that foreign policy officials must engage in a modicum of cooperation with counterparts abroad in order to ameliorate the situations on which such issues thrive, means that the rhetoric, as well as the substance, of control techniques must shift toward highlighting the common values that are at stake. . . . That is, appeals to national

interest and loyalties seem likely to become less compelling as means of mobilizing domestic support, so that positions on interdependence issues will have to be sold internally in terms of their consistency with the aspirations of external parties to situations (1976: 44).

National decisionmakers and their constituents are willing to sacrifice decisionmaking autonomy and to engage in this transnational coordination because doing so allows them to maximize their nation-state's economic interests. It is only when governments "regard themselves as having small stakes and no margin for maneuver, [that] parochial and self-protective responses are likely to result" (Keohane and Nye 1989: 233). The economic benefits which are reaped from transnational coordination will reinforce the willingness of domestic actors to continue revamping decisionmaking processes in accordance with transnational imperatives.

Central to the second loop of interdependent causality, then, is the decisionmaker's interests, behaviors, and choices which will produce outcomes that subsequently reinforce the impact of the first loop. Issues of learning and cognition are clearly pertinent to this second loop since national leaders and elites (along with their constituents) must correctly *perceive* that they have a stake in interdependence and that they can only obtain their self-interests through cooperation. "Effective strategies," Keohane and Nye argue, "will have to appeal to elites' perceptions of their self-interests. . . . Government leaders are often capable of learning how to achieve their goals in a more cooperative way; over time, their perceptions of self-interest may change. Such a learning process will be of critical importance internationally in future years" (1989: 235).[23] As a result, and despite the declared intention in these arguments to maintain a clear-cut separation between the levels-of-analysis for the purposes of explanation, cooperation would not occur in the absence of particular types of changes to individual and domestic level variables. It is simply impossible to explain interdependent cooperation without examining, as Keohane and Nye later put it in their afterword to the second edition of *Power and Interdependence*, "the reciprocal connections between domestic politics and international structure—and the transmission belts between them" (261).

Such a transmission belt also occurs in the regimes argument which attempts to explain why, despite the given condition of complex interdependence in economic issues among the major industrials, national decisionmakers do not easily sacrifice decisionmaking autonomy or engage in transnational coordination. Complementary interests in joint gain exist, but issues of uncertainty, such as the potential for cheating or hidden transaction costs, inhibit cooperation. In order to cooperate states must learn why it is not in their interest to cheat one another, as well as whom among potential cooperative partners can be trusted, and they do so through regime communication and information exchange. Yet as with interdependence it is the national decision-maker who must actually do the learning by realizing that "maintaining un-restrained flexibility can be costly" because "attainment of their objectives may depend on their commitment to the institutions that make cooperation pos-sible" (Keohane 1984: 259). In the absence of a cognitive learning process at the individual level-of-analysis, which connects tangible domestic level benefits obtained with the act of cooperation itself, the decisionmaker would not choose to support regime. Regimes would be unable, in turn, to provide the benefits reinforcing the decisionmaker's choice to support international regimes.

As it turns out, then, liberal cooperation theories does not actually "black box" variables at the domestic and individual levels-of-analysis in order to provide a systemic explanation for cooperation. Such "black boxing" is rou-tinely cited as a critical flaw of systemic level theories on the grounds that alternative causal variables are being missed, and certainly Waltz's theory of realism has been vociferously attacked on this very point. What liberal coop-eration theories does instead with such variables is to smuggle them into explanations for cooperation without explicit acknowledgment that they are centrally important to the cooperative causal chain. Amazingly no one has challenged liberal cooperation theories on this score, despite that fact that some scholars have already recognized that in order to test propositions drawn from liberal cooperation theories one must take a closer look at evidence from the other levels-of-analysis.

It is no small matter in this regard that Keohane and Nye admit in their afterword to the second edition of *Power and Interdependence* that when com-plex interdependence is subjected to a closer examination, "the sharp bound-ary between what is 'domestic' and what is 'systemic' breaks down" (1989: 257). They then suggest that in order "to ascertain the impact of the regime, we must trace internal decisionmaking processes to discover what strategies would have been followed in the absence of regime rules," and that "only by examining internal debates on such issues could the analyst go beyond the self-justificatory rhetoric of governments" (259).[24] These observations are con-sistent with those of Haggard and Simmons who had noted in their review of regimes theory that "even if one adopts a structural explanation of com-pliance and defection, validating such claims demands careful reconstruction of decisionmaking at the national level," and that "surprisingly little work of this kind has been done" (1987: 513). Despite the passage of time, this observation retains a great deal of validity. After a small but enthusiastic burst of late-1970s research into the impact of interdependence on foreign policy-making by Hopkins and Dickerman, the subject simply vanished from the research agendas of IR theorists.[25]

The most frequently utilized type of evidence to support propositions drawn from liberal cooperation theory remains systemic in origin. The pro-

vision of data on growing trade flows, transnational lending, foreign investments abroad, and a concomitant increase in IOs and treaty numbers are
employed to support the assertion that "one impact of these trends is that
states are losing their degree of autonomy in managing their domestic and
international economic policies" and that "there has been a movement toward
coordination of those policies" (Zacher 1992: 81, 88).[26] Since cooperation
depends on nonsystemic variables, this type of data actually proves nothing
about the causal connection between interdependence and cooperation. Worse
still, and as Jones illustrates in his detailed examination of interdependence
measurement indicators, economic statistical data proves nothing about the
phenomenon of interdependence itself when pulled out of its appropriate
political-economic context (1984).[27] Thus it is the case, as Jones and Willetts
put it, that "many popular statements about interdependence, by whatever
definition, rest upon insecure empirical foundations," and that "other claims
are either contradicted by such empirical evidence as is available or, perhaps
more frequently, rest upon data which are open to differing, if not clearly
contrary, interpretations" (1984: 8).

A good example of contradictory interpretation may be found in Keohane
and Milner's *Internationalization and Domestic Politics* which, despite its stated
intentions "to build on the interdependence literature," contains no evidence
that interdependence has caused an increased tendency among states to cooperate (1996: 7). One could argue that the primary focus of the volume is
on the pressures interdependence exerts for policy but not necessarily cooperative convergence.[28] Yet within the parameters of the interdependence argument itself it is analytically impossible to separate the two, since the primary
policy convergence which interdependence is supposed to cause *is* cooperation. Significantly, cooperation is mentioned only once and as a "possible"
policy choice that is difficult to achieve (1996: 257). The volume's case studies
also reveal that while interdependence has narrowed policy choices, the "declining policy autonomy of states" has occurred as states "cede control to
markets," and not because control has been ceded to the multiple leadership
and policy coordination envisioned by the interdependence argument (249).[29]
Hence even with detailed case studies specifically designed to test the impact
of interdependence on domestic politics, there is no evidence to support the
typical post-Cold War assertion that "it is no longer accurate to conceptualize
states as having their traditional degree of autonomy because of the network
of formal and informal regimes in which they are becoming increasingly
involved" (Zacher 1992: 60).

Other scholars have also observed that a great deal of nonsystemic empirical evidence contradicts the expectations of the interdependence-regimes
argument. Works influenced by the "historical-structural branch of new institutionalism," such as that of Garrett and Lange, take issue with the functional

orientation of liberal cooperation theory and argue that "institutions invariably outlive the constellations of interests that created them and hence they provide barriers to market-driven policy change" (1996: 49).[30] The conditions under which domestic decisionmakers will restructure domestic institutions and policies in accordance with interdependent pressures is highly restrictive as a result. Numerous regime theory case studies have also concluded that domestic political forces frequently prefer what could only be considered suboptimal outcomes from a functionalist perspective that emphasizes market failure and the need for transnational coordination.[31] Yet despite these observations there has been no systematic attempt to examine or explain how and why nonsystemic empirical evidence contradicts the expectations of liberal cooperation theory, nor to defend and substantiate its expectations on these same grounds.

That this subject has received no systematic treatment in the IR theoretical literature has enormous implications. It means that the asserted causal connection between interdependence, regimes, and cooperation amounts to little more than an imagined possibility which has never actually been subjected to rigorous examination, measurement, or testing. This means, in turn, that liberal characterizations of, and predictions about, cooperation in the post-Cold War international system rest upon a theoretical and empirical foundation that is precarious at best and erroneous at worst. In their desire to rush to a liberal judgment, proponents of the "new" governance perspective are rushing past both a responsibility to test theoretical propositions and the contradictory evidence that might be produced by such inquiries. They are also rushing past alternative explanations for that evidence and the cooperative phenomenon in general.

A REALIST-CONSTRUCTIVIST ALTERNATIVE

In order to move beyond liberal dominance in theorizing about international cooperation, a major reconceptualization of the subject will be required. Liberal cooperation theories have consistently relied upon issue area functionalism and interdependence in order to explain cooperation. As Crawford has succinctly put that proposition, "the existence of interdependency dynamics in a widening range of functional issue areas does not merely constrain the policy efficacy of states, but *forces them to pursue collective responses* to these collective problems" (1996: 50; my emphasis). Alternatively the approach I am proposing here refuses to think in terms of the efficacy of international cooperation within the context of functional interdependent issue areas. It instead considers other contexts which might be more pertinent to the cooperative choice, and it seeks to derive that choice from alternative mechanisms, even as that choice occurs within a context of economic interdependence.

The starting point for the development of this new approach is realism. Yet why realism? My insistence that it is the appropriate venue through which to develop an alternative might be viewed as unnecessarily irksome to some IR scholars. After all, why is it necessary to invoke the orthodox opponent of liberalism to make the case for an alternative perspective on international cooperation? Why not simply describe this as a "new" theory? There are, however, several theoretically-determined reasons why the realist umbrella provides a conducive if not necessary paradigm within which to develop an alternative explanation for the cooperative phenomenon. Realists have traditionally been skeptical of the cooperation-inducing abilities attributed to the condition of economic interdependence. One of the reasons for this skepticism points to a possible alternative site or context from which the choice to engage in international cooperation may be derived—the state.

According to Gilpin, the relationship between the state and the market is "the crucial problem in the study of political economy" (1987: 11). This is because "for the market, the elimination of all political and other obstacles to the operation of the price mechanism is imperative," and "the logic of the market is to locate economic activities where they are most productive and profitable" (10). For the state, on the other hand, "territorial boundaries are a necessary basis of national autonomy and political unity," and "the logic of the state is to capture and control the process of economic growth and capital accumulation." What is produced as these contradictory logics interact has been the subject of ongoing philosophical debate, and it is a debate which clearly informs the interdependence literature. When markets become entwined, as they had among the major industrials by the late twentieth century, the logic of the market is to coordinate economic policy. Yet this is in fundamental contradiction to the (historical) logic of states for which "concepts of territoriality, loyalty, and exclusivity" have been central components. Thus the logic of states must be overcome to some degree because it is what prevents mutually advantageous cooperative efforts from taking place.

Realist International Political Economy (IPE) scholars have remained skeptical that the market can be assigned causal precedence over the state, because from a realist perspective the maximization of capitalist profit for its own sake has never been the state's *raison d'être*. But the implications this has for the cooperative choice (that is why and how states might still choose to cooperate with one another) remains underdeveloped in the realist IPE literature. Of course the subject of cooperation in general has always been relegated to the outskirts of realist scholarly concerns, with only a few notable exceptions.[32] But this underdevelopment also arises because realist IPE tends to replicate the same dichotomy found in liberal cooperation theories. States are assumed to prefer autonomy and hence pursue autonomous policymaking, while markets are equated with a policymaking preference for cooperation with other nation-states. The preferences are treated as mutually exclusive so that either the state is determining and elites choose to make policy autonomously or markets are determining and elites choose to make policy cooperatively.

This dichotomy inhibits any consideration of how the two types of preferences and policymaking might actually mix together. State elites could initiate the cooperative choice not because they are relinquishing state autonomy in favor of the market, for example, but because some forms of cooperation can actually protect the state's ability to autonomously make policy. Realists in particular should be attuned to such a possibility since they have long argued that security alliances in the face of a common, immediate threat represents one form of cooperation which seeks to achieve this precise outcome. Yet by taking the state-autonomy and market-cooperation dichotomy at face value, important interactive possibilities between these alternative entities and the policies pursued are missed. The failure to recognize such possibilities is also encouraged by a preference for systemic level-of-analysis, which misses how these possibilities may inhere to the process of policymaking and to the domestic political issues and institutions which inform and comprise that process.

While much of the realist literature continues to subscribe to systemic level-of-analysis theorizing, at least one variant places domestic and individual level variables front and center in its analyses of international behavior and outcomes. A small but growing contingent of realist scholars practice what Rose has called "neoclassical realism," which maintains that the impact of the international system "must first be translated through intervening variables at the unit level such as leaders' perceptions and domestic state structure" (1998: 4).[33] While the anarchic system and polarity remain primarily causal for neoclassical realists, they also argue that international behaviors and choices remain inexplicable based on systemic input alone. This is because domestic institutions and cognitive variables act as filters through which systemic conditions must pass in order to be realized in policymaking form. It is a type of realism that appears to have been influenced by March and Olsen's "new institutionalism" (1998; 1989; 1984), at least in its greater sensitivity to the role which existing internal institutions and their parameters play in deflecting systemically efficient outcomes.

This aspect of neoclassical realism is one of its more important for the purposes of this particular study. Because domestic and individual level practices and institutions act as filters for systemic conditions, neoclassical realism explicitly rejects the assumption that systemic conditions can generate a functionally efficient institutional response within the nation-state. While it is other realists who do presume such a match that are usually the targets of neoclassical realists, the latter's perspective on this issue applies equally well to the way in which liberal cooperation theories explain the cooperative phenomenon. Whether the systemic context is anarchy or economic interdependence, the baseline for neoclassical realism involves challenging the notion that the form which a behavioral output takes is determined by whatever constitutes the functionally efficient institutional course of action within the systemic context. Specific domestic and cognitive factors intervene instead to produce outcome parameters that could not be anticipated on the basis of systemic conditions and attributes alone.

From a neoclassical realist perspective the filtering that occurs involves the concrete institutions and practices which dominate daily politics within the nation-state. It is not the lofty heights of systemic IR that occupies center stage here but the internal, frequently messy, and seemingly inefficient processes of electoral, bureaucratic, and interest group politics which comprise the politics specific to any capitalist, democratic nation-state. Systemic input must work through these processes which have alternative logics of their own. In the case of international monetary policymaking in the United States, for example, every aspect of policymaking is affected by the context of presidential electoral politics (itself a process comprised of various interacting institutions and practices). Decisions are made by a small group of bureaucrats all of whom are appointed by particular and usually incoming presidents. Some of them are the president's close personal friends who place loyalty to the president above all other goals while in office. Those who seek to strike out on their own bureaucratically and without the consent of the president do so at considerable risk, since they can and frequently are removed from office by the president who appointed them.

While in these positions of authority, monetary elites must interact with a variety of other bureaucratic actors and government subdivisions, as well as answer to the congressional committees who hold their department's purse strings or the particular interest groups and clientele their bureaucracies service. Yet ultimately their role-related fortunes rise and fall with those of the president, who is in turn continually attentive to the electoral cycle upon which his own future and that of his party's depends. Not only does that electoral cycle produce recognizable patterns to policymaking (Quandt 1988), but winning the internal game of electoral politics remains the primary filter through which any concern with maximizing capitalist profits in interdependent economic conditions must pass. This is an essential point from a neoclassical realist perspective because if internal processes such as democratic elections and bureaucratic politics are acting as filters for choice, they could also deflect pressures emanating from economic interdependent systemic conditions to cooperate with transnational counterparts.

Some IPE scholars have attempted to avoid this obvious conclusion by equating a desire to effectively maximize capitalist profits with winning elections in a capitalist democracy. Milner provides a typical example in asserting that "in order to maximize their chances of reelection, executives have to worry about two factors: the overall economy and the preferences of interest groups that support them" (1997: 34–55). Because all of the interest groups in question want to improve their own economic lot, the "political leaders' electoral prospects depend on the state of the economy," and because that economy is increasingly interdependent with other capitalist economies, executives "may not be able to achieve their economic goals without other states' help" (62, 44). Ergo state elites will choose to cooperate internationally in order to both improve their overall national economies and to get reelected to office. What provides the basis for such a conclusion are the underlying assumptions that responsiveness to societal demands is the democratic nation-state's *raison d'être* and that the primary demand of both society and the international system is economic well-being. Much of the democratic peace literature also rests on a similar, easy equation of democratic processes with capitalist profit-maximization.

Yet this equation can only be achieved by ignoring or willfully misreading the historical institutional record. The political institutions internal to the state developed as social practices in their own right and, as I will argue more extensively in chapter 3, these social practices cannot be equated with market practices simply because their societies are today reaping the benefits of participation in a capitalist interdependent system. The state and the market have each evolved a set of social practices which generate identities and interests that are not just dissimilar but in direct conflict with one another. Maximizing national economic welfare is about participation in the market, while electoral and bureaucratic politics is about who within the nation-state controls the decisionmaking apparatus of the state. The two involve different logics and social practices and that is the case even when the latter must make decisions about market participation. In fact, the problem the market faces is that maximizing capitalist profits can only be realized by and through the practices and institutions of the state, which has an alternative logic of its own and, if Gilpin's dichotomous characterization is correct, it is also a logic that is antithetical to the marketplace.

What neoclassical realism suggests, then, is that the logic of the market would have to be filtered through domestic institutions, thus implying that the logic of the state would dominate even in decisions that involved marketplace participation. More specifically it would anticipate that a preference for decisionmaking autonomy would continue to take precedence over multilateral decisionmaking even when doing so meant sacrificing efficient profit maximization. This conclusion is similar to that reached in other realist IPE approaches, particularly Grieco's neorealist argument regarding the state's concern with relative over absolute gains and the willingness to sacrifice the latter in a context of anarchy. The difference is that neoclassical realism traces the preference for autonomy not to the anarchic environment but to the domestic institutions and social practices which comprise the state and which then act as the institutional, cognitive filters through which systemic capitalist forces must operate. The origins of these state institutions and practices may be traceable to external anarchic pressures, but they are now also independent variables in their own right which may remain sources for autonomy preference even when systemic economic conditions appear to demand alternative institutions and practices.

Neoclassical realism points us toward this conclusion and provides us with an initial basis from which to explore it empirically. Yet as with other approaches in realist IPE, it is an implication which has remained underdeveloped in the neoclassical realist literature. In keeping with realism's traditional focus on war, neoclassical realists have usually been concerned with cooperation only when it manifests itself as security alliances. And there has been little effort within the neoclassical realist literature to specify the deductive logic whereby nonsystemic variables may be included in realist theorizing while still granting the anarchic environment primary causality. The result is that in its present form the approach cannot provide the theoretical underpinnings to explain why, in spite of changing systemic conditions, domestic institutions remain sources for autonomy preference or how and what we might generalize from this observation.

One of the ways in which neoclassical realism's analytical framework might be developed is to tie it to insights regarding social practices, identities, and interests drawn from Wendtian constructivism.[34] Despite the connections some constructivists have rushed to establish with liberal functional explanations for cooperation and systemic level-of-analysis theorizing, constructivism need not remain wedded to either. In fact, Wendt's formulation of constructivism provides a theoretical foundation from which to understand how and why state institutions would continue to reify autonomous policymaking even in systemic conditions favoring institutional alternatives. From a Wendtian perspective the institutions and practices of the state are both abstractions and material structures simultaneously. They provide meaning to participant behavior by establishing identity and interest parameters which determine what it means to be a state elite in the first place. These parameters are reinforced through ongoing participation in those institutions. State institutions also provide material benefits such as paychecks and promotions which reward behavior that conforms to institutional expectations and parameters, thereby also contributing to the reification of identities and interests specific to the state.

What is significant about this for the choice of international cooperation is that the state is comprised of a series of entwined institutions which, relative to other nation-states, developed as internal autonomous decisionmaking structures particular to each nation-state. Thus the practice of autonomy is not simply a behavioral predisposition which may be changed through strategic interaction; it is instead embodied in, and propagated by, the very existence of each nation-state's separate, internal political institutions and social practices. Autonomy is present and reinforced in every daily act participated in and taken by those individuals who occupy the roles of national bureaucrat, politician, or lobbyist. This means that not only is the systemic condition of economic interdependence confronted by state institutions which are informed by an alternative logic, but that interdependent effects must be felt by, and work through, agents who have no capacity to experience the logic of the marketplace absent that of the state's.

To put this another way, from a constructivist perspective how the practice of autonomy would prevail goes far beyond particular policymaking situations or specific concrete institutions. It involves what Reus-Smit calls the "*mentalities* of institutional architects" which are derived from the moral purpose of the state and limit as well as make possible historically-situated institutions and choices (1999: 39; his emphasis). It is their very identities as state elites which make national decisionmakers incapable of recognizing what the more efficient response should be or acting upon it even if they did recognize it. State institutions would provide no ideational avenues or material incentives for thinking and behaving otherwise. The practice of autonomy would instead define "the horizons of their institutional imagination and expectation," and represent one of the "significant cognitive and discursive limits to the forms of institutional cooperation that are possible" (149, 169).

As a result, the social practices and institutions of the state cannot be treated as causally ineffectual when confronted with external conditions which demand different institutions. In fact, those conditions can only be experienced through existing political and social institutions particular to each nation-state. From such a perspective it is not the practice of multilateralism derived from systemic functional demands which would prevail, but the practice of autonomy reproduced by existing domestic institutions and social practices. Nor does the mentality of autonomy preclude cooperation with other nation-states (as Reus-Smit's sweeping historical study of alternative systemic institutional arrangements amply demonstrates). It does mean, however, that the practice of autonomy is the institutional and cognitive template through which the choice and act of cooperation will be interpreted and conceived by state agents. The cooperative choice cannot be mutually exclusive to the practice of autonomy in this regard, because it can only be derived *from* the institutions and social practices of autonomy.

In reconceptualizing the subject of international cooperation in this way, we begin to move beyond the field's own licensing mentalities which have consistently conceived of autonomy and cooperation as mutually exclusive phenomena, with the latter derived from its greater functional efficacy in a systemic context of capitalist interdependence. As it turns out, international cooperation can only be realized through institutional contexts that embody the practice of autonomy. As a phenomenon international cooperation must be reconceptualized within this context. The combination of neoclassical realism and a constructivism which purposely distances itself from liberal systemic theorizing is capable of providing such a re-conceptualization. The combination suggests that the institutions and practices which comprise the state would have no capacity or incentive to adopt international cooperation in response to the functional pressures of systemic interdependent conditions. Alternatively the combination recognizes that economic international cooperation might be attractive to state elites for reasons that are largely domestic and unrelated to economic efficiencies. That is, how decisionmakers view the option to cooperate with their transnational counterparts and why they might find such an option attractive would be informed by, and internal to, the institutional context of the state itself rather than the marketplace.

The empirical case study undertaken in this book reveals, for example, that when American economic elites have chosen to cooperate in post-Bretton international monetary affairs, they have done so *as the result of* insular domestic processes which are unrelated to the goal of achieving functional institutional efficiency in the interdependent issue area over which they have responsibility. The choice has been driven instead by a desire to shield the president from domestic criticism and opponents, to improve his electoral fortunes, and to protect their own bureaucratic jurisdictions. From the national decisionmakers' perspective international cooperation is just one more policymaking tool or instrument that can be as useful as various domestic tools and instruments for expanding and protecting bureaucratic jurisdictions, promoting or defending executive policies and prerogatives from legislative encroachment, and deflecting both legislative and media scrutiny. International cooperation can be a domestic strategic choice resulting not from a desire to maximize national economic welfare, but from cooperation's efficacy in the context of domestic electoral and bureaucratic politics. That cooperation may also be more efficacious in the marketplace is causally spurious.

This perspective on cooperation explains why U.S. behavior in international monetary policymaking not only *cannot* be characterized as functionally efficient but frequently undermines transnational coordinating mechanisms which American decisionmakers themselves have proposed and established. It also explains why American international monetary policymaking since 1971 has been recidivistic, so that during an economic crisis American policymakers have consistently touted the virtues of international cooperation but made none of the substantive, behavioral commitments necessary to see these virtues implemented in practice. The public and rhetorical support for cooperation serves an important causal function, but it does not derive from the discovery that cooperation is efficacious in interdependent economic conditions. Nor should rhetorical support be confused with behavioral and institutional adjustments implied and which never actually materialize. Cooperation derives instead from domestic pressures and threats confronting decisionmakers, who discover that gesturing at cooperation can be an effective means of deflecting internal threats in the midst of a domestic political crisis. Such gestures have proven so effective that real adjustment is never necessary and, not surprisingly, rhetorical support for international cooperation never lasts for long within American policymaking circles.

As this brief overview indicates, there are many virtues to a realist-constructivist alternative to the subject of cooperation. Such an alternative avoids the licensing mentalities which dominate our approach to the subject, and it sheds new light on what it is that American monetary policymakers are actually up to when they choose to cooperate with their counterparts. The alternative is also capable of accounting for patterns in the U.S. international monetary policymaking record that standard liberal theories of cooperation cannot. It contradicts liberal expectations regarding the capacity of interdependence and regimes to affect changes in the way in which Americans think about and make economic policy. Obviously one must be cautious not to generalize from the American situation to other nation-states and interdependent issue areas. Yet the deductive framework for the realist-constructivist alternative provided in chapter 3 does have broader application in that it suggests that interdependence would confront similar cognitive, institutional barriers elsewhere. If we are to sufficiently understand why and when cooperation is chosen, these domestic political institutions and social practices must become central to our analyses. Not only will we produce more accurate accounts of cooperation than we do at present, but alternative expectations and policy suggestions will also be generated.

OVERVIEW OF THE BOOK

The chapters that follow will explore the relationship between interdependence and regimes, the practices of autonomy and cooperation, and the various theoretical approaches which are relevant to the subject. Chapter 2 examines the liberal literature on interdependence and regimes in order to delineate the causal chain which purportedly generates international cooperation. Such an exploration underscores the centrality of subsystemic variables to the liberal functional causal chain and demonstrates that the chain assumes that the state's economic decisionmaking processes and individuals will place national economic well-being over all other interests. Those readers who are already convinced that such presumptions inform liberal cooperation theories may wish to skip to chapter 3, but an in-depth examination of the liberal causal chain connecting interdependence and regimes to international cooperation remains desirable for the sake of skeptics. Such an examination also provides the basis for delineating the appropriate empirical propositions and indicators which are suggested by the literature and which may then serve as the means to later test liberal explanations for cooperation in the American monetary policymaking context.

The deductive foundations for a realist-constructivist alternative to international cooperation are provided in chapter 3. The chapter specifies the logic that allows systemic realists to incorporate the causality of domestic and individual level variables into their explanations and that therefore grounds neoclassical realism as an approach. It also derives from realist theory a theoretical relationship between the anarchic environment, individuals, and the institutions and social practices they create which anticipates the formation of groups as a central attribute of the anarchic environment. One of the patterns produced by a group context that is relevant to the practices of autonomy and cooperation is the tendency toward in-group favoritism and out-group discrimination. Cooperative practices would be fundamental to the process of group formation, yet that process would also involve the establishment of internal decisionmaking practices particular to groups and that effectively excluded nongroup members from decisionmaking participation. This suggests that the practice of autonomy would be the cognitive template from which group members viewed their interaction with other groups.

While realism's anarchy provides the basis for approaching the subject of cooperation as a phenomenon bounded by a context of groups, rather than as a freely-floating functional concept, anarchy alone cannot explain or predict how particular groups will constitute their internal decisionmaking practices, why and how these practices remain unreceptive to pressures emanating from the international environment for alternative institutions, or how transgroup cooperation may be generated by, and simultaneously sustain, internal decisionmaking practices. It is here that realism must turn to constructivism to complete its picture of social reality. Constructivism directs our attention to the internal political institutions and practices of the modern nation-state which reinforce exclusion from intragroup decisionmaking by their very existence and design. Such exclusion is not simply strategic behavior or misperception which can be altered through the greater exchange of information or interaction with members from other groups. It is instead the mentality which generates the cooperative choice on behalf of itself, so that cooperation is about protecting intragroup social practices and institutions that exclude nongroup members by design.

The empirical propositions and behavioral expectations that may be derived from liberal cooperation theory and from a realist-constructivist alternative are outlined in chapter 4. The chapter seeks to explain and justify the empirical indicators which are suggested by these competing explanations for international cooperation and in so doing justify why particular research design strategies are more appropriate than others to the task at hand. Because an effective delineation of empirical expectations can only occur within the context of the issue area itself, the chapter begins with a review of the decision-making institutions and actors relevant to American international monetary policymaking. It also reviews the international cooperative forums which evolved in the issue area after 1945 and in which American monetary elites have been regular participants.

Chapter 5 examines the chronological record for U.S. participation in international monetary cooperative episodes and the international and domestic contexts for those episodes. In so doing it compares and contrasts patterns in post-Bretton Woods U.S. international monetary policymaking to the empirical expectations of liberal cooperation theory and a realist-constructivist alternative. The chapter utilizes a method of "process tracing" cited by Haggard and Simmons as the most appropriate means for testing the regimes argument (1987: 514).[35] Such a method is also consistent with Keohane and Nye's recommendation that internal decisionmaking processes be traced in order to establish the impact of regimes (1989: 259). The goal of chapter 5 is to establish whether the behaviors and choices of American decisionmakers conformed to liberal or realist-constructivist expectations about patterns of cooperation.

Chapter 6 begins with the conclusion that post-Bretton Woods U.S. international monetary policymaking does not support liberal expectations. Despite the ongoing liberal presumption that "with increasing economic interdependence, the ministers and central bank governors cannot effectively fulfill their domestic responsibilities without cooperating extensively with one another" (Bergsten and Henning 1996: 19), post-Bretton Woods monetary cooperation has been sporadic at best and marked by a high degree of recidivism at worst. Obviously liberal cooperation theories should not be dismissed on the basis of a single issue area case study from one nation-state. But in its attempt to understand why liberal theories of cooperation fail to account for this particular empirical record, chapter 6 traces the failure to deductive flaws embedded in the causal chain that supposedly links interdependence and regimes to international cooperation. Liberal arguments fail empirically precisely at those points where their deductive logic fails as well, so that the need for transnational coordination does not create its own supply. When the case study findings are combined with a new understanding of these deductive flaws, a compelling case can be made for questioning the cooperative causality of interdependence and regimes and hence liberal explanations in general.

In the final chapter of the book the empirical record of post-Bretton Woods U.S. international monetary policymaking is reexamined in the context of the realist-constructivist alternative. Despite the condition of economic interdependence and supporting regimes, there is no discernible pattern of either an increase or a maintenance of cooperative policymaking efforts in the issue area after the end of Bretton Woods. In fact, the one pattern of behavior that *is* discernible in the post-Bretton Woods period is the continued preference for, and adherence to, unilateral policymaking. The relevant domestic institutional contexts in the issue area have remained unaffected by interdependence or by the participation of American decisionmakers in established economic regimes as a result.

Chapter 7 outlines how a realist-constructivist alternative would account for this outcome and for the cooperative efforts in which Americans have participated. It demonstrates that episodes of U.S. monetary cooperation can be explained without reference to functional institutional efficiency in the issue area and by focusing instead on domestic electoral and bureaucratic practices and the role-specific interests they engender. The chapter concludes with a more general discussion of a realist-constructivist perspective on international cooperation, the possibility of fundamental systemic transformation, and the research agenda implied by such a perspective. While the goals of this book are ambitious, I hope for some scholars and students it will at minimum represent what Ruggie has eloquently referred to as yet another "welcome antidote to the prevailing superficiality of the proliferating literature on international transformation, in which the sheer momentum of processes sweeps the international polity along toward its next encounters with destiny" (1983a: 285).

blank 36

Chapter 2

Liberal Cooperation Theory

This chapter will map out the causal chain in the liberal IR literature which purportedly connects interdependence, regimes, and international cooperation. This will serve as the basis for comparing theoretical expectations to the empirical evidence and for examining potential flaws in the deductive logic. Throughout the discussion the term *liberal cooperation theory* will be utilized as a short-hand means of referring to theories which rely on economic interdependence and regimes to explain cooperation. Although this reliance is common to so much of the liberal IR literature, differences remain among authors over how to define, measure, or apply these concepts. There is also variety in the extent to which causal chains are made explicit and in whether the concepts of interdependence and regimes are the focus of study or merely employed as permissive conditions. While these differences must be acknowledged, this examination of the interdependence and regimes literature will also confirm that there are threads of consensus in this literature that have been consistently tied together in order to create a coherent liberal theoretical package.

It is also important to acknowledge from the outset that even as it attempts to review and recognize differences, this discussion ultimately singles out particular texts as more representative of liberal cooperation theory than others. Some justification of this practice is obviously in order. In part the selection of particular texts is a function of the exercise at hand. Studies which rely upon interdependence and regimes merely as permissive conditions for cooperation will generally fail to shed much light on the precise causal relationship between these concepts. Hence the focus here is on those studies which attempt to delineate this relationship in some fashion, though even within these parameters scope and emphasis make a difference to pertinence. The close attention to particular texts is also a function of their popularity and influence because, regardless of reason or merit, it is clear that some texts have left a decisive mark on the study of international cooperation. Keohane and Nye's *Power and Interdependence,* for example, introduced the concept of "complex interdependence" which, as noted earlier, is still routinely employed in the IO literature to describe segments of international relations and post-Cold War major industrial relations in particular.

In a similar fashion, Hasenclever, Mayer, and Rittberger point out that although there are many regime theorists, Keohane "is the author of the most elaborate and also most widely discussed theory of international regimes to date," that "the influence of this formulation has been so strong that observers repeatedly were led to equate Keohane's approach with 'regime theory' as such," and that it "has indeed left its stamp on the research program centering on the concept of regime" (1997: 27–28).[1] Thus the discussion of regimes presented here tends to rely upon Keohane's formulation as if it were a definitive statement on the subject. Perhaps the discernible common threads in causal arguments related to interdependence and regimes are the direct result of the ongoing popularity of particular texts. Whatever the case may be, this study acknowledges as much of the relevant interdependence and regimes literature as possible, while at the same time treating particular texts as first-among-equals for the purposes of theoretical delineation and critique.

DEFINING INTERDEPENDENCE

Interdependence is both a process and a condition. Examining empirical cooperative efforts in order to assess the accuracy of purported causal chains requires treating interdependence as a process. Yet in order to do so it is first necessary to delineate what the condition of interdependence entails and how, according to the scholars who have written extensively about it, we know interdependence when we see it. Keohane and Nye offer one of the more widely utilized definitions. Interdependence is "mutual dependence" which can be differentiated from mere interconnectedness on the basis of "reciprocal (although not necessarily symmetrical) costly effects of transactions (1989: 8–9)."[2] The degree of costs is dependent upon "sensitivity" and "vulnerability," which means the extent to which a country will be affected by the actions of another or can insulate itself from the costly effects of events occurring elsewhere. According to Keohane and Nye, the condition of interdependence involves both reciprocal costs as well as reciprocal effects, so that even relationships which do not provide mutual benefits, such as Soviet-American Cold War strategic relations, can be defined as interdependent.

Several aspects are striking about this definition. First, interdependent relationships do not necessarily obtain actor interests and can include intentional, unintentional, and even noncooperative relationships. This suggests a relatively broad application for the concept, since even situations of mutual threat (in which utilities are independent and relational effects unintended) could produce an interdependent relationship. Jervis has made this argument about the two superpowers during the Cold War, who became increasingly dependent on the self-restraint of the other in order to avoid their own nuclear destruction (1984). Second, interdependence is not the same thing as cooperation. As Adler, Crawford, and Donnelly note, "there is no reason to believe that simply because states are more connected or because societies increasingly affect one another, that violence, poverty and human rights violations will be minimized" (1991: 20).

Third, there are "costs" related to the relationship which are an ongoing and inherent feature of the relationship irrespective of whether it obtains the actor's value or whether the relationship ends. Costs that would be incurred from ending a relationship of mutual benefit are not precluded; rather the definition indicates that they are an ever-present feature of *any* interdependent relationship. In other words, actors within the relationship are continually confronted with costs associated with maintaining the relationship. Yet if potential costs are not necessarily measured in units of the value one is deriving from the relationship, what constitutes costs in Keohane and Nye's definition of interdependence?

The answer to this becomes a fourth noteworthy aspect of the definition. According to Keohane and Nye, "interdependent relationships will always involve costs, since interdependence restricts autonomy" (1989: 9–10). Cost applies to relationships of mutual gain as well as to mutual threat, since in the latter type of interdependency "costly effects may be imposed directly and intentionally by another actor." So for example, Adler, Crawford, and Donnelly argue that "unilateral decisions are thus constrained because payoffs for acting in the 'common interest' of avoiding nuclear war are increased" (1991: 20). In a similar fashion, Keohane and Nye assert that interdependencies of mutual gain incur costs which are indirect and unintentional, because "collective action may be necessary to prevent disaster for an alliance the members of which are interdependent, for an international economic system (which may face chaos because of the absence of coordination, rather than through the malevolence of any actor), or for an ecological system threatened by a gradual increase of industrial effluents" (1989: 9). In all types of interdependencies, the cost of the relationship is the constraint on unilateral behavior and may be measured in units of lost autonomy.

The notion that a loss of autonomy is the price of an interdependent relationship is endemic to almost all the literature on cooperation, whether it can be labeled *liberal, realist,* or *constructivist.* Baldwin, for example, defines interdependence as both "international relationships that would be costly to break" and relationships in which "the opportunity costs of autonomy are prohibitively high" (1980: 485, 489). According to Adler, Crawford, and Donnelly, interdependence is a situation in which "common constraints impose an 'authority' over states that set limits on unilateral action" (1991: 19). In a similar vein, Rosecrance concludes that "in an interdependent world the state is no longer in command and its ability to control economic events is declining" (1986: 175, also 167). The theme of lost autonomy is also central to both Rosenau's (1976) and Zacher's (1992) treatment of interdependence, and it is the impact of interdependence on "central control" which leads Waltz to conclude that it "hastens the occasion for war" (1979: 138). Finally it is a perspective echoed by Ruggie who cites Buchanan and Tullock in arguing that the cost of interdependence is "circumscribed options or general loss of autonomy" so that "in calculating whether to organize activities internationally, a state will include not only the direct gains and the direct costs of producing a good with others, but also the overall interdependence costs of international organization" (1998: 48).

While one of the reasons to maintain an interdependent relationship is apparently the potential costs incurred from ending it, there is also an overwhelming consensus in the literature that a reduction in autonomous choice and behavior is an ongoing cost of *maintaining* an interdependent relationship.[3] This effectively introduces into the theoretical discussion a specific correlation between the condition of interdependence and a particular type of behavior. Because an interdependent relationship constrains autonomous choice and behavior, there is a mutually exclusive tradeoff between maximizing one's utility function and behaving autonomously. Actor utility functions in interdependence are necessarily in conflict with unilateralism specifically. This conflict between interests and behavior apparently exists regardless of the content of actor utility functions, and it does not automatically lead to cooperation as an intentional process of policy coordination.

Yet it is difficult to make sense of lost autonomy or its relevance to interdependence when taken out of its theoretical and historical context. What exactly does lost autonomy mean and how is it being measured? Why is autonomy of any relevance to the actors involved? How and why is it defined as a cost in cases when the interdependent relationship is allowing actors to maximize their utility functions? Why is autonomy only a behavior and not a potential utility function in its own right? And why, if cooperation is not inherent to an interdependent relationship, is there a common association between the two concepts? Clearly a host of assumptive building blocks underlie the concept of lost autonomy in liberal cooperation theory, and these begin to move us beyond basic definitions to the theoretical framework that

connects interdependence to state decisionmaking and to international cooperation as an outcome.

AUTONOMY AND SOVEREIGNTY IN INTERDEPENDENCE

The reason why liberal cooperation theory assumes that autonomy is an issue
for actors in a condition of interdependence is because the dominant unit-of-
analysis in recent world politics has been the nation-state, and autonomy has
been an historical, behavioral characteristic of nation-states. Liberal cooperation theory accepts as appropriate to prior historical periods the realist proposition that nation-states are unitary actors capable of controlling decisions
and events within their territorial jurisdictions.[4] Interdependence scholars do
not entirely reject a state-centric perspective then; rather they believe, as
Thomson notes, that such a perspective "was appropriate in theorizing about
world politics in the past but is of decreasing utility in the twentieth century"
(1995: 216). It is only within this presumptive historical context of nation-
state centralization and control that the IO changes wrought by interdependence become both meaningful and radical.

In *Transnational Relations and World Politics,* for example, Keohane and
Nye assert that the state-centric model "was approximated in the eighteenth
century when foreign policy decisions were taken by small groups of persons
acting within an environment that was less obtrusive and complex than the
present one" (1971: 371, also 375). What makes the post-1945 growth of
transnational relations significant, they argue, is that it "creates a 'control gap'
between the aspirations for control over an expanded range of matters and the
capability to achieve it" (393). They continue this theme in *Power and Interdependence* by juxtaposing realism and complex interdependence as ideal types
of international systems. The latter has become increasingly more relevant
over the past half-century, and by it very definition involves characteristics
and political processes which make it increasingly difficult for governments to
obtain their interests autonomously (1989: 161).

Rosecrance provides another example of autonomy in an historical perspective, organizing his argument around a dichotomy between a military-
political orientation, which dominated world politics between 1500 and 1945,
and a trading orientation, which became prominent among the major industrials after World War II (1986: 22, 67). In defining the two orientations, he
specifies that the military-political involved "a continual recourse to war,"
because each nation-state was afraid that others would "undermine its domestic autonomy and perhaps its very existence" (23). The trading orientation, on
the other hand, involves "accepted interdependence" in which nation-states
now "recognize that the attempt to provide every service and fulfill every

function of statehood on an independent and autonomous basis is extremely inefficient, and they prefer a situation which provides for specialization and division of labor among nations" (24). Similarly Zacher describes the traditional Westphalian system as one in which "war for the purpose of territorial revision was accepted and frequent" and "states had a very high degree of autonomy in their international relations in that they accepted very few international obligations" (1992: 59, 60). Today, however, "the world is in the process of a fundamental transformation from a system of highly autonomous states to one where states are increasingly enmeshed in a network of interdependencies and regimes"(98).[5]

While there are a number of acknowledged reasons for this interdependent transformation, the most widely cited—scientific advancement and technology—is also what makes it possible to speak of interdependence across issue areas and regardless of their contents. Modern technology has produced nuclear weapons and the telephone, neither of which can be cited as a sufficient condition for international cooperation. "Just as technological changes can be a boon to welfare and global connectedness," Adler, Crawford, and Donnelly accept that "they can make war far more destructive, lead to environmental degradation, and make torture and repression more efficient" (1991: 18). What nuclear weapons and the telephone do have in common is that they both impose a relational dimension on choice and activity which is beyond the control of the actors involved. As Rosecrance puts it, "modern technology, transportation, communication, and international sources of energy bring nations into greater contact. They cannot avoid interaction and are required to deal with one another" (1986: 31).

Rosenau strikes a similar theme: "an ever more dynamic technology and ever growing demands on the world's resources have shrunk the geographic, social, economic, and political distances that separate states and vastly multiplied the points at which their needs, interests, ideas, products, organizations and publics overlap" (1976: 38). The belief that interdependence and technology go hand-in-hand to constrain autonomous policymaking has changed little over the years. In a later consideration of how the information revolution may have affected power and interdependence, Keohane and Nye once again conclude that "cheap flows of information" mean that "states are more easily penetrated and less like black boxes" so that "political leaders will find it more difficult to maintain a coherent ordering of foreign policy issues" (1998: 94). Modern technology shrinks the world so that action is impossible without interaction, thereby producing a systemic context in which the ability of states to obtain objectives independently of one another is seriously compromised.[6]

Autonomy is relevant to interdependence, then, because it was a prominent behavioral characteristic exhibited (or enjoyed) by the dominant units-of-analysis within the international system during the premodern period, when interdependence was *not* a prominent characteristic of the system. As the condition of interdependence began to increase during the nineteenth and twentieth centuries, the pursuit of interests became increasingly relational and began to impinge upon the ability of nation-states to behave as they were accustomed. This makes it an historical attribute of nation-states which is now in fundamental contradiction to the new conditions in which nation-states find themselves. According to Rosenau, "quite aside from the activities of governments, what happens within states would appear to have wider and wider ramifications across their boundaries and these proliferating ramifications have created, in turn, an ever-widening set of external control (i.e., foreign policy) problems for governments" (1976: 38). This means in turn that although "states ultimately relied on the use of force" in order "to achieve wealth and power and to ensure security" prior to the twentieth century, "assuming that states are unitary actors is counterproductive for developing theories about the behavior of great powers today" (Goldgeier and McFaul 1992: 475).

While interdependence has increasingly constrained the nation-state's ability to behave autonomously, it is not immediately obvious that this also implies a loss of state sovereignty. In her review of the sovereignty literature Thomson argues that liberals and realists define sovereignty differently: "For liberal interdependence theorists sovereignty is defined in terms of the state's ability to control actors and activities within and across its borders. For realists, the essence of sovereignty is the state's ability to make authoritative decisions—in the final instance, the decision to make war" (1995: 213). Yet interdependence scholars are quick to deny that lost autonomy amounts to a demise of the nation-state or to its replacement as a central unit-of-analysis. According to Keohane and Nye the loss of autonomy "does not mean that governments will give up control over their economies to international organizations with sovereign power" (1989: 232), or for Zacher that "the present international transformation is undermining the centrality of states" (1992: 64), or for Held that "sovereignty is wholly undermined in contemporary circumstances" (1996: 415). As Caporaso succinctly summarizes the liberal argument, "interdependence and limitations on autonomy, 'yes,' but the erosion of state sovereignty, 'no' " (1997: 580).

These disavowals are undoubtedly driven by the associations which the "demise" thesis has with earlier functionalist theorizing about the EU. But they are also the result of an assumed distinction between sovereignty and autonomy which remains consistent with realist definitions of sovereignty as Thomson has described them. Held argues, for example, that sovereignty must be distinguished from autonomy in that sovereignty is power and control over one's future or the ability to take final decisions, while autonomy is "the capacity of nation states, not to set goals, but to achieve goals and policies once they have been set" (1996: 407; see also Zacher 1992: 61). Sovereignty, or the ability to make authoritative political decisions, may remain in tact even as autonomy, or the ability to independently achieve goals and policies, begins to erode. Interdependence affects the ability to unilaterally control outcomes and to obtain interests in the manner to which nation-states were accustomed, but it does not necessarily affect the state's authority to make final decisions for the societies that they represent. This is the idea behind Rosecrance's "mediative state," which he defines as "an instrument that balances the pressures of international life on the one hand with domestic life on the other" (1986: 221–222). He argues that "despite the inability to control its fate, the modern state remains the primary unit of international politics" because other entities "cannot be held fully accountable for their actions" and "the state remains as flawed but still the only reliable instrument of popular will."[7]

Underlying this distinction between sovereignty and autonomy is a theory of state-society relations which will be explored later in this chapter. But the relationship being hinted at by interdependence scholars is relevant here because it underscores why lost autonomy, but not necessarily lost sovereignty, is so central to their arguments. Thomson notes that both realist and liberal scholars tend to adopt a holistic view of the nation-state in that the state is assumed to represent society and to act upon its wishes or needs (1995: 217). Thus, Keohane and Nye assert that "governments will be highly responsive to domestic political demands for a rising standard of living" (1989: 40, also 227), and Hanrieder claims that "the satisfaction of rising claims by citizens has become a major source of the state's legitimation and of a government's continuance in office" (1978: 1278). Even under interdependent conditions, society will recognize and grant legitimacy to the state's authority to make decisions on its behalf so long as the state continues to pursue societal interests. According to liberal scholars what changes in a condition of interdependence is not the state's authority to make decisions, but the manner in which the state acts upon its decisions. Because unilateralism, as a particular type of interest-obtaining behavior, is no longer as efficient as it once was, the state has an incentive to abandon it as a behavior, although this incentive varies according to types of interests as we will see in the next section.

It is this perspective on autonomy, sovereignty, and state-society relations which makes it possible for interdependence scholars to argue that "formal sovereignty remains but actual control diminishes or even disappears" (Thomson and Krasner 1992: 311). Of course this raises the interesting question, as both Thomson and Held note, of how much control the state could lose before society no longer recognized it as being legitimately capable of making authoritative decisions on its behalf. As theoretical precursors to interdependence, neofunctional theories tended to assume that only a minimal level of lost control would be necessary before society began to transfer loyalty and legitimacy to other administrative structures. Interdependence arguments assume that society's level of toleration for lost control is much higher, but ultimately the long-term relationship between autonomy and sovereignty is not clear. For the immediate future, however, liberal scholars envision the condition of interdependence as "a halfway house between disintegration and integration of political and economic processes" and the international system as remaining "an interstate system in many of its essential features" (Hanrieder 1978: 1286, 1277).

INTERDEPENDENCE AND COOPERATION
ACCORDING TO ISSUE AREAS

While the relational dimension of interdependence is what poses a significant imposition on the behavior of nation-states, it still tells us nothing about the nature of outcomes in interdependent conditions. This is because whether or not interdependence leads to conflict or cooperation still depends on which interests one assumes nation-states have in particular situations. Interdependence and the loss of autonomy it entails may have a blanket effect on the system and interests within it, but if one assumes (as realists do) that security is a nation-state's ongoing primary interest (with violence the primary means to obtain that interest), then armed conflict would necessarily predominate in a world of increasingly forced interaction. Liberal cooperation theory agrees with realism to a point. When security and economics are in competition, security and its associated behaviors take precedence.[8] The concern with lost autonomy is also derived to some extent from agreement with realism that "the priority of security fosters centralization" so that the condition of "interdependence may create tension, friction, or conflict and thus actually impede progress or even lead to regressive forms of interaction" (Adler, Crawford, and Donnelly 1991: 22, 20).

However unlike realist theory, liberal cooperation theories do not accept the proposition that anarchy necessitates a constant, overriding concern with security. As Grieco has pointed out, at issue are two fundamentally different perspectives on anarchy (1990: 37–40). For realists, anarchy is an environment which is intrinsically threatening because the absence of a central authority means that the potential for war and domination are ever-present. In such an environment, the nation-state's primary interest will remain survival. For liberals, on the other hand, the absence of central authority does not necessarily induce an ongoing security dilemma because various forces in the twentieth century have alleviated that dilemma, at least among the major industrials.[9]

"Simply ameliorating the security dilemma will," according to Adler, Crawford, and Donnelly, "allow states to pursue a broader range of objectives" (1991: 22), so that liberals move beyond realist expectations that higher levels of interaction will lead to conflict even as they accept some realist propositions as historically accurate.

As a corollary to alleviated security concerns, liberal theorists also tend to assume that interests other than security are interests of absolute or mutual gain. The relevance of this to interdependence is that how states deal with the loss of autonomy will vary according to the interest being pursued. While interdependence may constrain autonomous behavior in general, for some types of interests this constraint may be less problematic than for others and will therefore produce outcomes that vary according to issue areas. For example, while higher levels of interaction in security affairs may constrain unilateral decisions by forcing a relational dimension upon them, it does not necessarily make unilateral decisionmaking impracticable. Given that it is an issue area dominated by relative gains concerns, states may still obtain a modicum of security by behaving unilaterally (and violently). Higher levels of interaction in economic or ecological affairs, on the other hand, make unilateral decisionmaking impracticable because the degree to which these interests are obtainable with such behavior is so minimal as to be unacceptable to nation-states. Because these types of issue areas are dominated by mutual gains concerns, the incentive to abandon unilateralism in them is much higher.

Games theory is frequently employed in order to analyze and differentiate types of interests, issue areas, and the outcomes they produce. In his appendix Rosecrance examines a number of games which are meant to illustrate how the incentives for unilateralism varies according to his military-political and trading dichotomy. He argues that "the relationship of the players in international relations is of two possible sorts: it is either constant-sum (with zero-sum as a variant) or variable-sum in character. Zero or constant-sum games are those of the military-political world" (1986: 232). The games of the trading world, on the other hand, are "increasing-sum games of either a collective or individual nature in which the parties do not defect or seek to take one-sided advantage." While there is some disagreement in the literature over whether interests can be so neatly categorized according to game-type, there is still agreement with Rosecrance's general point that, as Axelrod and Keohane have put it, "the context within which [an issue] takes place may have a decisive impact on its politics and its outcomes" (1986: 227).[10]

Three context dimensions appear to be particularly important—that actors have interests in common, that their relationship involves the expectation of future interaction, and that a small number of actors are involved. These dimensions are pertinent because increasing-sum games become possible when mixed-motive games, in which cooperation is a pareto-optimal but not preferred outcome, become iterated among a small group. According to Rosecrance, "when play is repetitive; when there is a small number of players; when players may meet and interact in other situations, agreements often can be kept," and "after a sequence of cooperative responses, two parties can build trust between themselves to the point where it can be assumed that their agreements will be carried out" (1986: 235, 237). He goes onto assert that the development of trust then shifts the game from mixed-motive to increasing-sum in which "agreement is essential to obtaining favorable outcomes."

All of this is relevant to the condition of interdependence because interdependence signifies an increase in the level of interaction among the players. This may not change interests associated with zero-sum games, but it can encourage a shift in the relationship between players from mixed-motive games to increasing-sum games in which cooperation is more likely. In other words, the relational dimension forced upon nonsecurity issues in interdependence is the element of iteration necessary for a mixed-motive situation to become an increasing-sum situation among the players.[11] Higher levels of interaction force repeated plays of mix-motive games which then allows for the employment of strategies such as "tit-for-tat" and issue-linkage, as well as for the trust necessary to shift games to increasing-sum. As Rosecrance puts it, "when interdependence exists between parties on a range of issues, there is an overwhelming incentive to avoid Prisoner's Dilemma outcomes on one particular issue. In iterative play the strategies which players use also matter. Tit-for-tat strategies reward cooperation, punish defection, and help to buttress cooperative relationships, once achieved" (1986: 235).

Once increasing-sum games have been established, none of the players can obtain their interests in the absence of agreement from others. This necessarily connects cooperation as an outcome to interests characterized by increasing-sum games in interdependence. Keohane provides a widely-adopted definition of cooperation as a process of policy coordination in which "actors adjust their behavior to the actual or anticipated preferences of others" so that "the policies actually followed by one government are regarded by its partners as facilitating realization of their own objectives" (1984: 51). Cooperation is, in short, "*conscious* policy coordination" (Oye 1986: 6; my emphasis), and when all the players have mutual-gain objectives it becomes the pareto-optimal choice in every play of the game. Actors may still prefer to make independent decisions, and difficulties may still occur when attempting to agree upon the precise point along the pareto-optimal line where cooperation should occur. Yet because opting for unilateralism in increasing-sum games does not obtain the interests of *any* of the actors involved, according to Stein "jointly accessible outcomes are preferable to those that are or might be reached independently"(1983: 127, also 120).[12]

Based on the types of interests involved, it is possible to predict when and where the incentive to cooperate in interdependence will occur. The condition of interdependence imposes a relational dimension on all interests, but the ability to still obtain those interests via unilateralism varies according to the nature of the interests themselves. Unilateralism could still adequately obtain zero-sum interests in conditions of high interaction capacity, so the incentive to abandon it in favor of multilateralism would remain relatively low. Under the same conditions unilateralism would no longer adequately obtain increasing-sum interests, however, and so the incentive to abandon it in favor of multilateralism would be much higher. According to liberal cooperation theory, then, the condition of interdependence induces behavioral incentives which vary according to the type of interest the nation-state is seeking to obtain.

Interests of similar type may also be grouped together into issue areas because governments actively link interests of functional-type together. Keohane and Nye argue that an issue area is created "when governments active on a set of issues see them as closely interdependent, and deal with them collectively" (1989: 65).[13] In summary, the intervening variable between the general condition of interdependence and the outcome of cooperation in liberal cooperation theory is the nature of interests themselves, which are typically categorized according to issue areas. Still left to be explained is which interests and issue areas may be categorized as "mutual gain" (and why), as well as how the condition of interdependence affects these issue areas specifically. It is at this juncture that the concept of "complex" interdependence becomes relevant.

COMPLEX INTERDEPENDENCE: ISSUE AREAS OF MUTUAL GAIN IN CONDITIONS OF INTERDEPENDENCE

Economics is the issue area which is universally cited by the liberal cooperation literature as providing the best example of the interdependence-driven shift from mixed-motive to increasing-sum games. More specifically, this literature is interested in those issues most pertinent to capitalist-market economies, such as trade balances and barriers, reserve assets, exchange rates, and fiscal policies, which may be bounded together into a common "economic" issue area because they are pertinent to capitalist-market operations. Such operations are contingent on the presence of mutual-gain interests within a society, since as Gilpin points out "a basic long-term harmony of interests underlies the market competition of producers and consumer" (1987: 31).

Although problems of collective action, market failure, and differing relative gains occur, it is still assumed that "everyone will, or at least can, be better off in 'absolute' terms" under market operations. When the market expands beyond nation borders, the potential to extend an interest of mutual gain across societies occurs as well. Indeed, Gilpin notes that as "the normative commitment to the market has spread from its birthplace in Western civilization to embrace an increasingly large portion of the globe," this has also created "bonds of mutual interests and a commitment to the status quo."

Such a perspective on the cooperation-inducing capacities of capitalist-markets clearly informs Rosecrance's trading world. Similarly Keohane assumes that "utility functions (such as profit maximization)" are "independent of one another: they do not gain or lose utility simply because of the gains or losses of others" (1984: 27). This makes profit maximization an interest of mutual rather than zero-sum gain, although Keohane recognizes that it cannot serve as a common interest of mutual gain across societies until interaction among advanced capitalist-markets increases. When this occurs "international coordination of policy seems highly beneficial in an interdependent world economy," Keohane asserts, because "in the absence of cooperation, governments will interfere in markets unilaterally in pursuit of what they regard as their own interests," thus producing "suboptimal outcomes of transactions" (1984: 49–50, see also 10–11). Keohane and Nye also consider the common pursuit of capitalist wealth a mutual gain interest, denying at first that economics may be characterized as such, then later differentiating wealth from power on the basis that "most economic and ecological interdependence involves the possibility of joint gains, or joint losses" (1989: 32).[14] Indeed, their entire argument regarding regime maintenance only makes sense if it is premised on an "economic process model" which assumes that capitalist governments have a common interest in maximizing their economic welfare and that economic interdependence necessitates coordination among them in order to obtain this interest. Such a model may not be a sufficient explanation for why cooperation occurs, but it is clearly a necessary one as they themselves admit (129–130).

Economics is not the only issue area in which an interest in mutual gain necessitates cooperation in conditions of interdependence. Ecological issues such as pollution, agriculture, population, and health care might qualify as well, and as the level of interaction capacity increases among nation-states these types of issue areas begin to take on particular characteristics which cannot be understood by referencing the general phenomenon of interdependence alone.[15] An entirely new explanatory model is required, which is what prompted Keohane and Nye to introduce "complex interdependence" as a means to characterize the specific effects which increasing interdependence has on mutual gain issue areas (1989: 23–24, 249). Such issue areas will come to exhibit three primary characteristics: multiple channels connect societies, there is an absence of hierarchy among issues, and military force is irrelevant to resolving disagreements. Multiple channels involve interstate, transgovernmental, and transnational ties which blur the distinction between domestic and foreign affairs. Although this characteristic is distinguished from the absence of issue hierarchy, the two are related. Different channels of interaction encourage multiple issues to be placed on the interstate agenda so that military security no longer consistently dominates, and issues once considered low and domestic become the stuff of high international politics. These new issue areas involve overlaps which make the pursuit of interests and the resolution of problems more complicated.[16]

The primary effect of these complications is that traditional mechanisms of problem-solving become inappropriate, and "a host of new types of abilities have become increasingly relevant if states are to maintain any control over their environments" (Rosenau 1976: 37). Military force, as one of those traditional mechanisms, becomes increasingly irrelevant in interdependent issue areas of mutual gain. So too does centralized decisionmaking which, as another traditional problem-solving mechanism, is negatively effected by the development of multiple, overlapping, complex issues. These create what Keohane and Nye refer to as "a nightmare of governmental organization" (1989: 27), because multiple bureaucratic agencies are involved, representing various and often conflicting internal and transnational coalitions. Thus according to Rosenau "the problems of formulating a coherent and consistent foreign policy increase" (1976: 42).

The final traditional problem-solving mechanism which proves inappropriate in issue areas characterized by complex interdependence also leads us back to the role of autonomy in these arguments. Unilateralism cannot even begin to address the problems generated by these issue areas, nor can it obtain the interests associated with them. As Rosenau argues, because many of these issues create conflicts "which do not conform to political boundaries and which most governments can thus neither dismiss nor handle on their own," these issues "do not lend themselves so readily to unilateral action" and "require cooperation among states if obstacles to goals are to be diminished or eliminated" (1976: 43, 36).[17] Similarly Keohane and Nye assume that "in the organization of collective action to cope with economic and ecological interdependence, leadership is often crucial to ensure that behavior focuses on joint gains rather than the zero-sum aspects of interdependence" (1989: 229). Yet in order to obtain effective nonhegemonic leadership, nation-states will have to accept some form of joint decisionmaking and be "reluctant to seek short-term victories (either though majoritarian resolutions or unilateral action) if such victories could jeopardize the negotiating process over the long term" (235).

DOMESTIC STRUCTURAL AND
COGNITIVE BARRIERS TO COOPERATION

If the condition of interdependence produces tension between what a nation-state wants and how it is accustomed to obtaining it, then the concept of "complex interdependence" theoretically refines this point by indicating that the tension will be strongest when the interests being pursued are of the mutual-gain variety. As Keohane and Nye note in the afterword to the second edition of *Power and Interdependence*,

> Interdependence generates classic problems of political strategy, since it implies that the actions of states, and significant nonstate actors, will impose costs on other members of the system. . . . From the foreign policy standpoint, the problem facing individual governments is how to benefit from international exchange while maintaining as much autonomy as possible (1989: 249).

Whether or not states actually do cooperate "is partly determined by whether states are prepared to extend their involvement in the network of interdependencies, giving up some of their autonomy in return for concrete benefits" (Rosecrance 1986: 235). Thus the presence of "complex interdependence" identifies where within the international system one might expect the greatest incentive for cooperation under conditions of interdependence to occur.

Liberal cooperation theorists are quick to point out, however, that an incentive to cooperate does not necessarily translate into the act of cooperation itself. Keohane uses the example of Romeo and Juliet to observe that "actors may fail to cooperate even when their interests are entirely identical" (1984: 65). In the case of complex interdependent issue areas, the foundation of common interests necessary for post-hegemonic or multilateral cooperation exists, but the abandonment of autonomy and adoption of cooperation is not a foregone conclusion. Scholars have identified a number of factors that can prevent incentive from automatically translating into action, including iteration, number of actors involved, and "market failure" in which, according to Keohane, "the difficulties are attributed not to inadequacies of the actors themselves (who are presumed to be rational utility-maximizers), but rather to the structure of the system and the institutions, or lack thereof, that characterize it" (82–83, see also 1983: 150–151).[18] What these problems of cooperation have in common, as Keohane notes, is that they "draw our attention to ways in which barriers to information and communication in world politics can impede cooperation" thereby promoting uncertainty (1984: 69). They are also all ameliorated to some degree by the provision of information and by the development of trust in one another's preferences (1983: 162–163; see also Jonsson 1993).

While the identification of these problems has led to some important insights about the nature of cooperation in general, in the context of *international* cooperation specifically these factors do not move us beyond the basic tension between autonomy and cooperation already central to the interdependence argument. This is because when these problems are applied to interstate relations, they all become products of nation-state autonomy again.[19] The barriers to information and communication that exist in world politics are due to the fact that nation-states developed as centralized, autonomous units with differing political, economic, and social structures. Historically each nation-state purposely protected these structures from intrusion by others. As a result the primary units of world politics do not have access to one another's preferences or decisionmaking processes and cannot reliably know on their own terms what other units are about. This makes the problem of uncertainty in IR largely a function of the way in which nation-states developed autonomously from one another. Even though some nation-states may now share interests of mutual gain and would benefit from policy coordination, existing differences associated with the historical pursuit of national autonomy continue to prevent them from recognizing or pursuing cooperation as an option.

Given that the public goods and collective action literature cannot shed much light on the specific barriers which still exist to international cooperation in complex interdependent issue areas, we are left with two fundamental questions. Why does the interdependence literature assume that autonomy will continue to be a barrier to cooperation even when mutual gain interests exist? And how does this literature believe the tension is resolved in practice so that cooperation is the outcome? The first question is particularly interesting because the model of state-societal relations upon which liberal cooperation theorists rely would suggest that the tension should be resolved in favor of cooperation. As noted earlier, both realism and liberalism assume "the state and sovereignty are institutions that developed to serve societal needs like economic growth and protection from military attack" (Thomson 1995: 216).[20] Rosecrance attributes this to the development of liberal societies after the American and French revolutions, which reflected a belief that "the nation was to be run to help society not the other way around" (1986: 94–95). The result is, according to Cerny, that the "legitimate, holistic political authority characteristic of the traditional state reflects either an institutionalized commitment to provide public goods efficiently, or the presence of extensive specific assets, or both" (1995: 601).

Added to this presumed state-societal relationship is the assumption that societal wishes have increasingly involved the maximization of economic welfare in the twentieth century. This point is actually crucial to the connection between complex interdependence and cooperation, because if a nation-state's economic interest were the maintenance of a subsistence standard-of-living then it would still be possible to obtain this with unilateralism (as Burma and North Korea in the early post-Cold War period could attest). Rosecrance explicitly acknowledges this point:

> Individuals in a state of nature can be quite independent if they are willing to live at a low standard of living and gather herbs, nuts, and fruits. They are not forced to depend on others but decide to do so to increase their total amount of food and security. Countries in an international state of nature (anarchy) can equally decide to depend only on themselves. They can limit what they consume to what they can produce at home, but they will thereby *live less well* than they might with specialization and extensive trade and interchange with other nations (1986: 144–145; my emphasis, see also 40, 94).

Alternatively it is the demand for higher standards of living being generated from a capitalist-market society which undergirds the state's incentive to abandon unilateralism as a behavioral practice. According to Hanrieder, "domestic demands can be satisfied only by intense participation in international or transnational activities—providing governments with powerful incentives to cooperate with one another" (1978: 1279). The condition of complex interdependence increases this incentive because it "has meant that individual states do not have the jurisdiction to control economic forces which might determine their level of socioeconomic living" (Rosecrance 1986: 167).

The state's function as a provider of societal interests is reflected in the implicit political model relied upon as well. Domestic policy preferences are translated into state behavior according to an "economic pluralism" model. According to Garrett and Lange such a model assumes that "policy outcomes are a function of political conflict shaped by the preferences of different actors, weighted by their market power and their propensity for collective action" and that "domestic economic preferences will be quickly and faithfully reflected in changes in policies and institutional arrangements within countries" (1996: 49). Based on this perspective on state-societal relations and the incentives supposedly provided by complex interdependent conditions, one might expect economic cooperation among the major industrials to be a foregone conclusion. That is, if the state's function is to satisfy societal demands, if society is demanding that a mutual-gain interest be satisfied, if interdependence has encouraged mutual-gain interests to extend across societies, and if transnational cooperation would obtain these interests, then it would seem logical to presume that cooperation would be automatic. Indeed most liberal cooperation theorists continue to project, as Zacher does, "a willingness of states to sacrifice autonomy over time" (1992: 64–65), yet simultaneously concur with Rosenau that "the capability for multilateral co-operation will not come readily to governments" (1976: 49).

One clue to explaining this type of anomalous statement is the consistent analytic focus on governments rather than societies as the source of the difficulty. Keohane and Nye provide a good example:

> Governments will argue over the distribution of gains and complain about the loss of autonomy entailed in rising economic interdependence, . . . but they will generally find that, when there are domestic political demands for greater economic welfare, the welfare costs of disrupting international economic relations, or allowing them to become chaotic, are greater than the autonomy benefits. Reluctantly, they will permit economic interdependence to grow, and even more reluctantly, but inexorably, they will be drawn into cooperating (1989: 40).

Such a description implies that it is the state, not society, which is unwilling to relinquish the practice of autonomy. While societal barriers are sometimes acknowledged in the interdependence and regimes literature,[21] ultimately the overwhelming attention of liberal scholars is on the barriers to international cooperation at the state level and among its decisionmakers.

Such attention is suggested by the model of state-societal relations relied upon by liberal cooperation theory itself. Society at large would expect the state to satisfy its interests regardless (to some extent) of the methods involved. In a period of rising standard-of-living expectations one might expect society to accept whatever methods were deemed appropriate by the state as long as its economic interests were obtained by them. Rosecrance suggests this is the case: "information that can be evaluated by people themselves can lead in the same direction as policies enforced by government. A nation which founds its fortunes on exports can explain the problems posed by international competition, and electorates can judge accordingly" (1986: 224). Such a perspective places the burden of active adjustment on the shoulders of the state and its members since they are, in the final analysis, responsible for making the policies which obtain interests, while society's response is one of more passive acquiescence just so long as economic benefits are being obtained.

However from a traditional political economy perspective, this expectation of active state adjustment poses a fundamental dilemma. As noted earlier the state and the market have diametrically opposed logics because while the market seeks to eliminate obstacles to economic interaction, the state seeks to establish obstacles and control interaction. For liberal cooperation scholars the logic of the state appears to distill into a fundamental obsession with its

own autonomy, which then manifests itself as a barrier to economic cooperation in two interrelated ways. First, this obsession has informed the organizational development of the state itself and this then makes intergovernmental
cooperation pragmatically difficult. The problems posed by these structures
involve divergent administrative practices, as Hanrieder points out:

> Aside from conflicting interests, the obstacles to policy coordination
> stem from differences among national styles of problem solving and
> decision making. . . . In each country there are entrenched adminis-
> trative practices that are unique and that resist international or
> transnational coordination. While the bureaucratic instinct may be
> universal and timeless, it cannot be stripped totally of its local his-
> torical and institutional context (1978: 1285).

If "rivalry is probably more securely embedded in bureaucratic structures than
coordination," as Rosenau also argues, then state decisionmaking structures
would have to change if international economic cooperation were to be realized in complex interdependent issue areas (1976: 47; 1988).

The changes envisioned are relatively dramatic since they involve the
reorganization and reorientation of national administrative structures. In order to facilitate decisionmaking penetration, for example, Keohane and Nye
assert that "governments must be organized to cope with the flow of business," and "the function of central foreign policy organs such as the State
Department should be to encourage constructive transgovernmental contacts, . . . and to orient the agencies involved toward broader views of world
order, rather than toward their narrowly defined problems" (1989: 242). States
must also accept greater international participation in their decisionmaking
processes, because "governments that successfully maintain 'closure,' protecting the autonomy of their decisionmaking processes from outside penetration, . . . will be viewed with more skepticism by potential partners, who will
anticipate more serious problems of bounded rationality in relations with
these closed governments" (Keohane 1983: 163). In addition, states must
better train and utilize scientific expertise, "sensitize officials to the implications of their choices for other governmental units," and find techniques "for
transforming destructive rivalries into creative tensions" (Rosenau 1976: 48).
In other words the state must revamp its own administrative structures and
procedures so that it may more effectively achieve the objectives imposed
upon it by its own society and complex interdependent conditions.

Autonomy manifests itself as a barrier to cooperation in a second way in
the liberal cooperation literature in that its practice has provided state
decisionmakers with a cognitive map of the world which is antithetical to the
recognition of common interests and to the necessity for cooperative efforts

in order to achieve them. Hence the very way in which decisionmakers conceive of their nation-state's own interests, problems, and solutions must change if cooperation is to be realized. As Keohane and Nye note, "the growth of economic and ecological interdependence does not provide clear, deterministic guidelines for foreign policy," and so "there is still a 'necessity for choice'" (1989: 242). Whether state elites accept or fight interdependence depends on the degree to which they accurately recognize its existence and assess its implications, which means according to Rosecrance that "interdependence only constrains national policy if leaders accept and agree to work within its limits" (1986: 141). Thus it is the decisionmaker's perceptions and ability to recognize new contexts that are the keys to unlocking the practice of autonomy and allowing cooperation to be substituted in its stead.[22]

Rosecrance asserts, for example, that "how leaders act is partly determined by the theories and past experience that they bring with them" (1986: 41). The Westphalian system has endured because "it has continued to capture the imagination of statesmen and peoples" (190), and it reflects a "widespread inculcation and acceptance of nationalist and military values" (213). Along similar lines, Rosenau argues that although interdependent issues require cooperation,

> The ability to contribute to the evolution of such institutions and patterns can vary considerably, depending on the readiness of societies, their publics, and their governments to acknowledge that their futures are interdependently linked and to adapt to the changing circumstances which may thereby arise. . . . Adaptation and maladaptation involve *nothing less than the images* which citizens and officials hold of themselves in relation to their external environments; and if these images are unrealistic and fail to account for the need to sustain cooperative foreign policies, then burdens rather than benefits are bound to mount with interdependence (1976: 48; my emphasis).

Cognition serves as a barrier to cooperation in Keohane and Nye's treatment of complex interdependence as well. It is because "state choices reflect elites' *perception* of interests," that "a critical question for research is how different sets of elites *perceive* and redefine the constraints and opportunities of the international system and the appropriate goals and means of states" (1989: 264–265; my emphasis). All states *"must believe"* and share "the widespread *perception* that it is indeed in the interests of all major parties" to cooperate in the absence of hegemon (231; my emphasis). And in order for such cooperation to appear legitimate to the poorest and weakest states, "they must *perceive* that they are receiving a significant share of joint gains" (235; my emphasis).

In fact of the two barriers to cooperation identified in the interdependence argument, cognition is actually the more important of the two. This is because the definition of complex interdependence itself implies that many of the state's structural barriers have already broken down. Its presence indicates that multiple linkages exist to connect governments and societies within mutual-gain issue areas and which "act as transmission belts, making government policies in various countries more sensitive to one another," so that "the domestic policies of different countries impinge on one another more and more" (Keohane and Nye 1989: 25–26, also 34–35). If state decisionmaking structures have already been penetrated to such a degree, then their conscious redesign is not actually necessary in order to remove them as impediments to cooperation. That is, because "the direct-dial telephone, the videocassette, the short-wave radio, and the personal computer all will facilitate a rising degree of crosspenetration of every political system" (Maynes 1989: 53), the sheer weight of technology and transnational communications has already and will continue to force interpenetration upon states.

But since interdependence scholars already disaggregate the nation-state on the basis of issue areas that are affected differently in conditions of interdependence, only particular segments of the state are actually confronted by the condition of complex (as opposed to ordinary) interdependence. This means that the potential for overcoming autonomy's cognitive historical imprint only exists (at least for the moment) in particular segments of the state. Those elements of the state which are responsible for making and executing foreign policy in mutual-gain issue areas become the central focus of liberal analysis as a result. Empirically, for example, the conduct of economic foreign policymaking has been conducted by the executive branch, specific bureaucratic units within it, and a number of independent agencies. Hence it is within these elements of government that structural penetration should be most advanced and the necessity for cooperation in order to achieve common issue area interests most pressing.[23]

In a sense, the condition of complex interdependence presents particular state elites with a situational and structural decisionmaking *fait accompli*. What has apparently not kept pace with the structural reality in these issue areas, however, are elite perceptions because they are accustomed to thinking and acting autonomously. This is a real problem for policymaking because, according to Keohane and Nye's blunt assessment, "outdated or oversimplified models of the world lead to inappropriate policies" (1989: 242). What must be shed is the cognitive imprint of autonomy which involves not only a change in the state elite's perception of their environment but also of their self-interests and how precisely to obtain them. Interdependence and regimes scholars do not mean that interests in these issue areas have changed, although as noted earlier their own language often generates considerable confusion on this score. What changes instead are "perceptions of self-interest" that "depend on actors' expectations of the likely consequences that will follow from particular actions and on their fundamental values" (Keohane 1984: 63). Thus "under conditions of complex interdependence, state elites must recognize that, at a minimum, national interests cannot be achieved at the expense of others, and at a maximum, their own interests depend on the realization of others' interests" (Adler, Crawford, and Donnelly 1991: 27).

Autonomy remains the fundamental *problematique* of international cooperation then, because it is the historical lesson nation-states must now unlearn. Yet not all components of the nation-state are equally pertinent to or complicitous in autonomy's perpetuation. Although structural and societal constraints are acknowledged, it is primarily because the practice of autonomy continues to shape decisionmaker perceptions that international cooperation is not a foregone conclusion in complex interdependent issue areas. It is the cognitive mind-set of the decisionmakers who control foreign economic policymaking, rather than the decisionmaking structures within which they act, which has proven to be the more intractable barrier. And the economic gains necessary for society's acquiescence to both penetration and multilateralism will never be realized if state elites remained incapable of recognizing that mutual interests exist, that these can now only be obtained via cooperation, and that behavior must be adjusted accordingly. Cooperation in conditions of complex interdependence ultimately depends on "intelligent and farsighted leaders" who must develop "sophisticated attitudes toward international cooperation, and increased sensitivity to the international aspects of problems" (Keohane 1984: 259).[24]

CHANGING COGNITIVE MAPS: LEARNING, INFORMATION, LINKAGES, AND REGIMES

What remains to be examined is how state elites have the opportunity to overcome the cognitive barriers of autonomy so that interdependent cooperation may occur. This is the second fundamental question raised by the tension between autonomy and cooperation in the interdependence literature and it involves a process of learning. Keohane and Nye underscore this point in their afterword's discussion of perception and learning. Utilizing what they call a "spare definition" of learning, that is, "alteration of beliefs through new information," they argue that "one form of such learning is increasing awareness of strategic interdependence" (1989: 265). In considering the impact of international political processes such as interdependence, they note that some learning is incremental, continuous, and "occurs when bureaucracies or elites come to believe that certain approaches work better than others for their purposes" (266). Rosecrance relies on a similar conception called "social learning," which is "the ability of one generation to innovate to remedy the failures of its predecessors," and it "will partly determine the acceptance of the trading or the military-political world in the years to come" (1986: 172, 41–42). The concept of learning is central to Adler, Crawford, and Donnelly's treatment of cooperation in complex interdependence as well in that when interdependence rises "to the level of political collective consciousness," it can "break old ideas and beliefs about the autonomy of political actors in the international arena" (1991: 29).

This means that lying at the heart of the causal chain between interdependence and cooperation posited by liberal cooperation theorists are the perceptions of individual decisionmakers and their ability to learn and unlearn what liberal cooperation theorists believe should be the correct lessons of complex interdependence. In order for elites to learn that the new international reality in which they exist requires cooperation to obtain interests, they need to understand the degree to which their societies and the pursuit of their own mutual-gain interests have become interconnected. In other words, they must learn that "governmental jurisdiction no longer coincides . . . with control over the essential elements of a national livelihood," that "policy is no longer governed by fiat; it is a matter of negotiations," and that "it is the reciprocal exchange of benefits within each other's territories that facilitates the adjustment process" (Rosecrance 1986: 220–221). They must also develop confidence in one another's preferences and intentions in order to overcome fears of cheating as an inhibiting factor. That is, they "need to know whether other participants will follow the spirit as well as the letter of agreements," as well as "whether they will share the burden of adjustment to unexpected adverse change" (Keohane 1984: 94). And, based on their new understanding of their common situations and problems, they must have the opportunities to actually pursue and implement cooperative efforts with one another in their respective issue areas.

All of the lessons necessary to overcome autonomy's imprint on elite cognition depend in some way on elites acquiring information about one another, which is not only the same general solution suggested by the study of cooperation in the contexts of public goods, games theory, and market failure, but also a solution subscribed to by almost *all* strands of liberal IR theorizing. Informational exchanges and communicational forums are believed to encourage the learning and development of trust necessary for cooperation to occur because, according to Keohane and Nye, "the ability to communicate and cooperate can provide opportunities for the redefinition of interests and for the pursuit of strategies that would not be feasible if the only information available to states were about other states' preferences and available power resources" (1989: 262).[25] Such information encourages the recognition that elites have ongoing interests and problems in common and that the policy choices they make do not stop at the water's edge. It also helps build confidence about one another's intentions.

The manner in which elites acquire the necessary information is through recurrent interaction and ongoing communications with one another. Keohane and Nye caution the IR analyst not to neglect "the important role of communications in slowly changing perceptions of self-interest," because transgovernmental contact and "recurrent interactions" encourage a convergence of perspectives so that "national interests will be defined differently on different issues, at different times, and by different governmental units" (1989: 34–35). In addition, "contacts between governmental bureaucracies charged with similar tasks may not only alter their perspectives but lead to transgovernmental coalitions on particular policy questions" (34). Such coalitions are essential to the successful management of complex interdependence and are "particularly beneficial when officials from technical agencies of different governments work together to solve joint problems, or when interactions facilitate learning" (241).[26]

It is therefore essential to have ongoing opportunities to communicate and exchange information if autonomy's hold on elite perceptions is to be undermined. Only if elites know one another better can they develop the policies more appropriate to obtaining their state's interests in conditions of complex interdependence. Liberal cooperation theory singles out three specific facilitators for elite contact and communications: the multiple linkages which already exist due to technological ability and the growth of ordinary interdependence, formal IOs, and regimes. Multiple linkages are important because they indicate that every level of the state's administrative structure is in contact with its counterpart, from summitry all the way down to the "informal networks of working relationships at a lower level of the bureaucracy," and that "the convergence of views and perspectives that these multiple contacts can create will be crucial in effectively coordinating policy" (Keohane and Nye 1989: 233). IOs also play a significant function in promoting communications because they provide ongoing forums where elites may physically meet and exchange ideas and information. Thus they "provide the arena for subunits of governments to turn potential or tacit coalitions into explicit coalitions characterized by direct communications" (234, also 35–36, 240).

Associated with these formal organizations are informal institutions that include the intergovernmental and transgovernmental networks which have developed among elites, as well the practices and expectations they share about the mutual-gain issue area in which they interact. It is here that regimes finally enter the cooperative picture. The concept of regimes has been embraced by liberal theorists as a means to analyze the extensive yet informal relationships among the major industrials which developed to manage mutual-gain issue areas in interdependence. Krasner defined regimes as "sets of implicit or explicit principles, norms, rules, and decisionmaking procedures around which actors' expectations converge in a given area of international relations" (1983a: 2). This definition is also employed by Keohane in *After Hegemony*, and remains one of the most frequently cited, probably because it was "a collective definition, worked out at a conference on the subject" and so it already bears a stamp of approval from established theorists in the field (1984: 57).[27] Keohane and Nye had employed a similar definition of regimes based on the work of Ruggie, as "networks or rules, norms, and procedures that regularize behavior and control effects" that could be analyzed as "sets of governing arrangements which affected relationships of interdependence" (1989: 19).

The primary function of regimes in liberal cooperation theory is to provide opportunities for, and the reinforcement of, the elite learning necessary to cooperate in post-hegemonic, complex interdependent conditions. Keohane pointedly denies that learning is a necessary component to his rational choice, functionalist theory of regimes or that he is attempting to "go beyond the acknowledgment that self-interests can be redefined" (1984: 132). Yet while most IO theorists have accepted this denial as valid, and the neoliberal institutional approach is usually criticized for not including a theory of learning and interest-formation, learning is actually central to the entire argument. The difference here is that Keohane is consistent with the "spare definition" of learning utilized in the interdependence literature, rather than with the "complex" definition of learning which critics argue is warranted. Nye has argued that "simple" learning may be distinguished from "complex" learning because

> Simple learning uses new information merely to adapt the means, without altering any deeper goals in the ends-means chain. The actor simply uses a different instrument to attain the same goal. Complex learning, by contrast, involves recognition of conflicts among means and goals in causally complicated situations, and leads to new priorities and tradeoffs (1987: 380).[28]

The interdependence literature and Keohane's influential theory of regimes both rely on simple learning to explain cooperation in complex interdependent conditions. The "perception" of self-interest is redefined only to the extent that new means are adopted to obtain them, while the content of interests remain fundamentally unchanged and may be taken as givens for the purposes of theorizing about behavior in that issue area.

While actors engage in simple learning about their "proper political context," in the neoliberal institutional literature that context is not only one of complex interdependence but also of post-hegemony. The relevancy of regimes to cooperation is explicitly premised on an existing condition of interdependence and on the types of mutual-gain issue areas relevant to complex interdependence. But the decline of the hegemon triggers the need for additional learning, because while "cooperation can take place in the absence of hegemony," its erosion "makes it necessary to do so in new ways" (1984: 16). That is, because according to Keohane, "hegemony rests on the subjective awareness by elites in secondary states that they are benefiting," in a situation of post-hegemony these elites would have to develop a new subjective awareness that these benefits would continue if they supported cooperative practices on their own (45, also 137). The common interest in mutual-gain remains the same, but elites now have to learn new methods in order to obtain them.

Clearly Keohane's emphasis is on specifying the functions served by *existing* regimes, but post-hegemonic cooperation will only occur if elites learn how to behave appropriately within the context of these regimes. The lessons they must learn include the importance of sharing information, the development of a "farsighted" perspective about their own interests that recognizes how issues are linked, the consequences of establishing and maintaining a good reputation (while avoiding "collective bads"), the usefulness of substituting multilateral for unilateral rules of thumb in domestic decisionmaking processes, and the potentials for binding successors to present policy decisions (1984: 97–120). The systemic context in which these lessons are appropriate is one in which complex interdependence, but not a hegemon, continues to exist and increase. Thus these lessons are part of the package of cognitive changes required if the practice of autonomy is to be overcome in such a context.

According to Keohane's regimes argument, most of these lessons are learned by informational exchange which only occurs through recurrent interactions and communications between state elites. Monitoring one another's behavior in order to encourage self-induced compliance and linking issues together to discourage deceptive practices depend on a high degree of similar *self-awareness* among elites. This point is worth underscoring because it has received almost no attention in the regimes literature.[29] Much like the condition of interdependence itself, regimes only have causal weight if elites recognize why it is in their interest to limit their own actions. And if governments are willing to commit themselves to agreements, it is only because state elites have come to know one another through ongoing contact. So, for example, Keohane argues that the "close ties among officials involved in managing international regimes increase the ability of governments to make mutually beneficial agreements" (1984: 97), because ongoing interaction

> may lead to "transgovernmental" networks of acquaintance and friendship, supposedly confidential documents of one government may be seen by officials of another; informal coalitions of like-minded officials develop to achieve common purposes; and critical discussions of professionals probe the assumptions and assertions of state policies (101, see also 1983: 165).

All of these potentialities are premised, in turn, on the assumption that changes in the way elites conceptualize the pursuit of nation-state interests is essential to the choice of cooperation and that contact among elites facilitates the simple learning necessary to overcome the cognitive barriers posed by the practice of autonomy. Regime maintenance relies on recurrent contact, particularly at lower levels of state bureaucracy, and is part of the process by which the cognitive barriers to nation-state autonomy are overcome in the major industrials, rather than the condition which necessitates that state practices be adapted in the first place.[30]

INTERDEPENDENCE AS PROCESS AND BY WAY OF CONCLUSION

Earlier in this chapter it was asserted that interdependence was both a condition and a process. The focus of this chapter has principally been on interdependence as a condition and on delineating its connection to international cooperation in the liberal cooperation literature. In order to specify more clearly how interdependence is also a process, it is useful to work backward for a moment in summarizing the arguments of the chapter. Interdependence is a process in which state decisionmakers learn to cognitively and behaviorally adapt to new systemic conditions. This adaptation involves learning how to abandon unilateralism for multilateralism, and it occurs when elites have the opportunity to engage in recurrent interactions and informational exchanges. Technologically-driven interpenetration, IOs, and regimes all provide the necessary opportunities for cognitive adaptation to occur.

The incentives to adapt derive from the development of interdependence as a systemic condition and the impact this has on interests and issue areas that have the potential to become mutual-gain. The interdependent condition forces higher levels of interaction on nation-states which, because they were unaccustomed to such levels, had relied primarily on the practice of autonomy to obtain their interests. Although this reliance continues to pose structural and cognitive barriers to adaptation, these barriers can be overcome because higher levels of interaction also force the iteration necessary for the common pursuit of increasing-sum interests. Additional inducement to adapt derives from the mutually-felt societal pressures to maximize standards-of-living. Thus there are powerful pressures on state elites within the major industrials to adapt their cognitive perspectives and policymaking strategies to the new systemic conditions.

These incentives are reinforced by the actual attainment of greater benefits which are realized when cooperative methods and strategies are adopted, and so there is a reinforcing "feedback" loop with each successive act of cooperation (Krasner 1983b: 361–362; Jervis 1991/92: 51). Elites come to recognize not only that "independent self-interested behavior can result in undesirable or suboptimal outcomes," but also that joint decisionmaking does produce "the optimal nonequilibrium outcome" (Stein 1983: 120, 139). Behavior is adjusted to suit regime parameters because elites perceive that regimes "can correct institutional defects in world politics" and "may become efficient devices for the achievement of state purposes" (Keohane 1983: 154). Once decisionmakers accurately correlate cooperation with efficient interest maximization, the incentive to continue cooperating is reinforced and iterated cooperative acts produce a progressively expanding commitment to cooperation itself. That is, regimes can "make a difference to actors' beliefs by helping to 'lock in' and to further develop the learning that had prompted their creation" (Hasenclever, Mayer, and Rittberger 1997: 147–148).[31] The flip side of this growing commitment to cooperation is the willingness of elites to sacrifice ever greater amounts of state autonomy over time. Because elites would increasingly recognize that it produces suboptimal outcomes, the practice of autonomy should gradually fall by the wayside.

While protests abound in the liberal cooperation literature to the assertion that international cooperation's progression in conditions of complex interdependence will be seamless and smooth,[32] the logic employed makes it difficult to deny the progressive quality to interdependent adaptation nonetheless. It is because "each act of cooperation or discord affects the beliefs, rules, and practices that form the context for future actions," that cooperation "must therefore be interpreted as embedded within a chain of such acts and their successive cognitive and institutional residues" (Keohane 1984: 56). If these residues have causal weight, then cooperation in issue areas of complex interdependence must inevitably evolve into Keohane and Nye's IO model of the world political structure, which represents a world of "governance without government." For many IO scholars that world has already arrived.

As this chapter has sought to make clear, however, the development of such a world political structure is premised on a particular set of assumptions about autonomy, the state, the individuals who comprise the state, and the state's relationship to its respective society. It combines these with particular perspectives on anarchy, technology, learning, and evolution in order to explain international cooperation and to predict cooperative trends in the international system. Ultimately the realization of systemic "governance without government" depends on subsystemic variables changing and being changed in particular ways. State penetration and recurrent elite contact are assumed to promote a process of elite learning. This learning process depends, in turn, on the ability of state elites to accurately assess the opportunities and constraints of the new international environment in which they operate. It depends on their willingness to abandon cognitive and structural manifestations of autonomy in return for greater economic benefits. It depends on their faith in one another's intentions and in the stability of their relationships. It depends on their capacity to accurately attribute maximization of interests to the act of cooperation and on their ingenuity at responding behaviorally to this attribution. It depends on society's acquiescence to elite choices in return for the maximization of economic welfare. And it depends not simply on the continuation of all of these conditions, but on their progressive evolution as well. These are obviously a set of highly stringent assumptions, but before turning to the question of whether this stringency can withstand empirical scrutiny, the realist-constructivist alternative to the subject of cooperation will be explored.

blank 66

Chapter 3

A Realist-Constructivist Alternative

This chapter specifies the logic which allows subsystemic variables to be incorporated into systemic realist theorizing and which therefore grounds neoclassical realism as an approach. By reexamining the concept of anarchy in realist theorizing, it demonstrates that it is deductively possible to treat domestic social practices, institutions, cognition, and even emotion as intervening variables between the systemic impact of anarchy and the choices and behaviors of nation-states. Revealing this logic provides the deductive foundations for linking neoclassical realism to a Wendtian constructivist concern with social practices and identity formation, and for outlining a realist-constructivist approach to international cooperation. While multiple implications may also be drawn from a neoclassical realist approach to process, one of the purposes of the chapter is to lay the groundwork necessary to examine post-Bretton Woods U.S. monetary policymaking for patterns which conform to realist-constructivist expectations.

THE "CONVENTIONAL WISDOM"

In turning to the development of a realist-constructivist alternative explanations for international cooperation, one is immediately confronted with the "conventional wisdom" that subsystemic variables can play no part in realist theory. Realism's critics have charged that the expanded uses to which realism is being put, and the ad hoc addition of variables to account for outcomes anomalous to realist expectations, are the hallmark of a "degenerating paradigm" (Vasquez 1997; see also Legro and Moravcsik 1999). Certainly the standard realist approach to cooperation has done little to acknowledge the fundamental role played by domestic social practices, and even among realists there is disagreement over precisely what their own theory is capable of explaining (see, e.g., Waltz 1996; Elman 1996; Spirtas 1996; and Jervis 1999, 1998).

According to most realist accounts, limited acts of alliance cooperation in the face of shared threat are consistent with anarchy because they are self-help behaviors meant to obtain immediate survival. In order to explain a situation such as the EU, in which cooperation has been ongoing and expansive, realists have typically expanded the time-horizon of alliance cooperation. According to Waltz, "politics among European states became different in quality after World War II because the international system changed from a multipolar to a bipolar one" (1979: 71). Under the unique conditions of bipolarity, European nation-states shared a common threat from the Soviet Union and a common benefactor in the United States. As Mearsheimer puts it, both "mitigated the effects of anarchy on the Western democracies and facilitated cooperation among them" by, in the first instance, reducing their fears of one another and, in the second instance, acting as the alliance's ultimate arbiter and protector (1990: 47). These were unusual international circumstances which allowed European societies to pursue cooperative and economic enterprises that would normally have been impossible in other polarities.

While the development of cooperative institutions is taken as an outgrowth of systemic permissive conditions, such institutions are generally not treated as causal variables in the realist argument. Instead most realists have proscribed to Mearsheimer's perspective that "institutions are merely an intervening variable in the process" and "largely mirror the distribution of power in the system" (1995: 340).[1] According to realists, then, cooperative interaction does not have the capacity to transform intersubjective meanings in ways that deny self-help. Post-1945 cooperation among the major industrials is simply an outcome dependent upon particular international circumstances. This lends an element of pessimism to all realist accounts of such cooperation and of Europe's future in particular because, as Snyder puts it, "to the extent that these benign domestic conditions may in part be consequences of the bipolar stalemate, a shift in international structure may undermine them" (1990: 12).

One of the more obvious problems with the type of explanation realism provides for post-World War II cooperation is that it only highlights the permissive condition for this cooperation. It does little to specify the sufficient conditions which determined whether it would in fact develop, how precisely it would do so, and what form such cooperation would take. Grieco highlights this problem in his examination of polarity's role in realist arguments (1999). Bipolar permissive conditions existed in both Europe and Asia, yet as

Grieco points out no institutions comparable to the EU developed in Asia. Bipolarity is necessarily underdetermining if it cannot account for these qualitative differences in institutional arrangements. In order to fully explain the qualitative differences in the cooperative efforts of each region, realists typically end up relying on unit level attributes to complete their analyses. This means that realists are in effect allowing social practices and domestic institutions to do much of the causal work without sufficiently specifying how it is still logically possible to assign causal primacy to anarchy and systemic variables such as polarity.

In part the problem derives from the original goal of systemic realism, which was to avoid reductionism and a reliance on human nature assumptions while providing an explanation for common behavioral patterns within the international system. Subsequent realist scholarship neither explored nor sufficiently clarified the causal role of collective practice, social institutions, or domestic political processes in systemic realism. As Kratochwil observes, "the unchanging or cyclical nature of international politics substituted for the investigation of actual processes and decisions" (1993: 64). Domestic social practices and institutions have not been realism's major investigatory concern as a result, and those realists who have examined process in the context of anarchy have tended to concentrate on institutions which produce conflict.[2] It is still possible to count on one hand the number of systemic realists who study cooperation beginning with the work of Grieco in the late 1980s. And concepts such as intersubjective meaning, agency intent, social practices, and identity transformation have generally not been a part of the realist lexicon.

It has seemed to most of its critics, then, that realism is incapable of explaining a great deal of international activity and, because many of its practitioners rely on domestic social practices and cognitive processes to complete their analyses, it should be subsumed under the rubric of liberal IR theory.[3] Yet in justifying the use of realism in ways for which it may initially seem unsuitable, this chapter's central premise is that the explanatory power of systemic realism has been vastly underutilized by realists and nonrealists alike. That realists have not been speaking the language of social construction is due to the latter's sudden and unexpected popularity in IR theoretical circles and not the result of realism's theoretical framework or any faults which may be found therein.[4] In fact, realism can offer a logically tenable account of both change and the relevance of social practices in anarchy, and its account is fundamentally different from that offered by all other theoretical approaches in the field.

What makes a realist account so different is that realism has an environment-based ontology, while other IR and American social scientific theoretical approaches rely on a process-based ontology instead. Realism separates the context of an anarchic environment from what agents do within it and considers the social practices and institutions human beings create to be both affected by, and the active means to, any given end within the anarchic environment. This separation allows realism to incorporate the causality of social practices and institutions, but also suggests that the historical development and evolution of human processes occurs within boundaries that are not determined or controlled by human beings themselves. Such an ontological claim has proven to be an anathema in the American "Enlightenment" context and may help explain why realism has remained the object of such vitriolic and at times near-hysterical attack by its American critics.[5] Because the realist approach to process is different, it also reaches very different conclusions about what causes international cooperation and what its implications are for international relations. No revision of systemic realism is necessary in order to make this argument. What is required instead is to highlight the implications for process, cooperation, and international change which can be drawn from realism's ontology. Contrary to Wendtian expectations, realism can accomplish these goals without conceding that anarchy is simply what states have made of it.

REVISITING THE CONCEPT OF ANARCHY

At the heart of systemic realism lies the concept of anarchy which, in encouraging a primary concern with survival, generates a process of imitative socialization and competitive interaction. Through this process units discover relative to one another which behaviors are more or less supportive of their own survival and thus they come to look and behave alike. These behavioral patterns are encouraged and reinforced by an unintended and spontaneous structure created among states by their positional maneuvering relative to one another. Yet while *structure* is the term Waltz uses for what is created as units interact, its meaning in realist theory goes beyond denoting the configuration of states in relation to one another. Its usage is also different from the term's meaning in a constructivist context, where it is used to denote collective intersubjective meanings.

The impact of structure on state behavior in realist theory is akin to an environment that surrounds states and that acts as an extrinsic physical condition affecting and influencing the growth and development of states. As Dessler puts it, in realist theory "structure is an *environment* in which action takes place. Structure means the 'setting' or 'context' in which action unfolds" (1989: 466, his emphasis). Hence realists operationalize the concept of anarchy as an environmental context, arguing that states exist "*in* anarchy," or are "living *under* anarchy."[6] Dessler then draws a useful analogy between realist environment and an office building, because both provide a "fixed, enduring set of conditions that constrains and disposes, shapes and shoves behavior." Each of these environments generates broad behavioral patterns for the units that seek to survive within them, but central to the realist environment is the intrinsically threatening character of anarchy. It is as if the office building has hidden trapdoors which could end life suddenly and without cause. Such a potentially threatening environment ensures not only that a state's primary interest will be in survival, but that this concern will be ever-present and ongoing. Hence, "the aims of states may be endlessly varied," Waltz argues, but "survival is a prerequisite to achieving any goals that states may have, other than the goal of promoting their own disappearance as political entities" (1979: 91–92).

One of the more significant implications of this perspective on anarchy is that it contains a causal element which is underivable from, and outside of, human interaction. This element is predictable yet paradoxically uncontrollable and chaotic according to the standards of human intervention. In keeping with Dessler's analogy, office workers are aware that hidden trapdoors exist, but they have no knowledge or control over the placement of these traps. What they do know, however, is that the consequences of falling into one of these traps is death. In fact, the fear of death plays a fundamental role in almost all realist accounts of global politics. While this may seem to be an obvious point, since all realist explanations place survival front and center in their motivation for behavior, its ontological implications have not been obvious to most IR theorists and hence they have remained unexplored.

What anarchy appears to be implicitly equated with in most realist arguments is the *fact* of death which, because it serves as the unavoidable and unknowable end-point for living, is assumed to remain a constant fear shared species-wide across time and human invention. According to Waltz, for example, one of the primary affects which the anarchic environment has on human beings is worry, so that "in any self-help system, units worry about survival and the worry conditions their behavior" (1979: 105). Brooks has also observed that "the internal coherence of the neorealist framework itself depends fundamentally on the psychological assumption that actors are characteristically highly fearful," and that without this feature the theory would make little sense (1997: 449). Because death represents an unknown finality which continually confronts all human beings, according to most realist accounts its unknown nature powerfully frightens and hence motivates behavior in its avoidance. Underlying most realist theorizing, then, is a presumption that the fear of death has a universal, predictable affect on how human beings behave and the social practices in which they engage.

Yet the extent to which a "consciousness" of death automatically generates "fear" as a particular human emotion is an obvious point of contention for nonrealists. Drawing upon Heidegger's notion of "the possibility of an impossibility," for example, Jackson disputes the notion that definitive behavioral implications may be drawn from what he calls "a guess about the meaning of a mystery" (1997). Even if death is an "objective" limit "in that it comes outside of ourselves and cannot, as far as we know, be avoided . . . it is not unique, nor does it have determinate consequences." Indeed, "death's opposite—life, existence, consciousness—has the same 'objective' character in that life is somehow 'given to' human beings and . . . what we have in practice are various attempts to figure out what 'death' or 'life' means." A Hobbesian perspective that the fear of death is a primary human motivation is but one interpretation or response to these "objective" facts, and different philosophical traditions offer alternative responses and perspectives. Ultimately as Wilmer puts it, "the problem with realism is that it validates only one interpretation of reality, or, said differently, it validates only one way of experiencing reality, denying the validity of others" (1996: 348).

Certainly it is the fact of a guess or response which leads realists back to an insistence that death's avoidance must be a prime motivation for human behavior. While there are differences in the philosophical and religious treatments of death, worry about it is what prompts the creation of any treatments of it in the first place. That human beings everywhere have felt the need to give meaning to death and to make it familiar appears to substantiate the claim that its unknown nature is universally motivating. Yet because the emotions of fear and worry are social constructs in themselves and only gain meaning in social contexts, nonrealists have a legitimate point.[7] How is it possible to generalize the fear of death into an ahistorical and universal behavior, when the causes of death have varied across history and according to social situations that have varied dramatically as well? Perhaps it is the case that human beings instinctively fear snakes and so automatically avoid them, but would a Roman citizen suddenly transported to the twenty-first century instinctively know to fear a loaded firearm were it pointed at her?

One solution to this dilemma is to focus instead on the role that death itself can play as a selection mechanism on species-wide characteristics and behavior. While realists have tended to concentrate on the emotion of fear as a generalizable motivation, their own ontology points to a more significant and less problematic theoretical answer. As a theoretical category realism has always been premised on the ontological given that something exists outside both human interaction and human institutions which then affects human behavior directly and shapes the character and composition of the institutions human beings create. Frankel argues, for example, that "there are significant things out there which exist independently of our thoughts and experience" (1996, xiii), and similarly Mearsheimer asserts that the anarchic environment is "an objective and knowable world, which is separate from the observing individual"(1994/95: 41).[8]

Ultimately the environmental attribute that remains objectively pertinent to human beings irrespective of their historical period or the practices in which they engage is not the "fear" of death but death itself. It is nonvariable, ahistorical, and underivable from human-constructed arrangements. And while it is certainly true that human beings directly contribute to one another's death all the time, death is still a "natural" or "biological" rather than "humanist" phenomenon in that it will occur to everyone and every living thing regardless of human intervention or intention. It is something beyond the capacities of human beings and their social practices to change, avoid, or control. Thus from a perspective that considers realist ontology more fully, it is not simply that the anarchic environment leaves actors in it unregulated and unsupervised so that "war may at any time break out" (Waltz 1979: 102). It is instead that the anarchic environment allows death to occur in the first place while providing no guidance for how to avoid it in the short-term and ultimately no means of doing so in the long-term.

It is this lack of guidance which makes anarchy automatically and immutably self-help in quality. Because the environment into which human beings are born does nothing to ensure their survival in the immediate sense, and actually guarantees death in the future, human beings must help themselves if they as a species are to survive at all. Thus the argument that self-help may eventually be overcome as a constitutive principle differentiating units within this environment makes little sense to realist scholars. Realism's environmentally-based ontology implies that the environment in which human beings exist has *always* required that they take responsibility for their own survival. Nature holds plenty of daily, violent lessons on what occurs when an actor is incapable of behaving as its own protector. Without the intervention of other human beings newborns die, and when famine and disease are present it is those who are least capable of acting on their own behalf, such as the weak, the sick, the young, and the old, who die first. "If might does not make right, whether among people or states," Waltz notes," then some institution or agency has intervened to lift them out of nature's realm" (1979: 112).

Whether human beings have obtained their own survival in the normatively best means possible or according to some standard of efficiency is an entirely different matter. What is more significant from a realist perspective is that the displacement of self-help as a constitutive principle could only mean that something nonhuman was ensuring human survival instead or that death's inevitability had somehow been overcome. It is because self-help is a characteristic of the environment and not human intention that the social practices in which human beings engage would have no capacity to overcome it. In fact, the causal role which human process plays in such an environment would, regardless of its qualitative content, serve only to represent and hence reify self-help as an immutable feature of the environment. Many of the self-help behaviors that realism posits are the result of anarchy, such as war-making, balance-of-power, and a mistrust of cooperative efforts, are well-known. Yet the logic which proscribes and predicts these outcomes also points us toward new and unexplored aspects of systemic realism and from which we may begin to theorize about the historically-situated social practices and institutions that human beings create as well.

As a species we produce infants who are helpless at birth and who require the intervention of other human beings if they are to survive and reproduce. If human survival and reproduction are contingent on direct human intervention, then identification with other human beings may be an adaptive mechanism of the species. Based on Freud's work on identification, for example, Bloom points out that it could be a mechanism of defensive adaptation because "for the immensely vulnerable infant, the parents are the only means of survival . . . [and] when a parent threatens the infant with not gratifying primary needs, the threat to the infant organism is ultimately one of death." Thus identification with "the being who supplies food and warmth" is "a *real* source of survival in the infant's threatening environment" (1990: 29; his emphasis). He also points out that while personality was a social construct and the result of social interaction for both Freud and Mead, its dynamic source remained biologically–driven in their arguments as well:

> With the evolution of the human creature who is *per se* a social creature, and the concomitant lengthy and vulnerable infancy and childhood, a personality acceptable to the immediate social group is a simple necessity for social survival—social survival being synony-mous with physical survival (33).

Thus the development of successful identification with others is the means to gratify the primary needs basic to survival and, as Bloom asserts, "this is not simply an academic proposal, but is a blatantly observable part of the general human experience" (1990: 34).

Because identification is a social act, groups and group formations could be a species-wide adaptive mechanism resulting from the anarchic selection pressures on human reproduction as well. According to Bloom, "identification is, from its inception, a group process even if the group or social system is only parent and child," and "once the infant moves beyond one-to-one identifications, the identifications become generalized" to include the ideo-logical and cultural elements of the larger social group (1990: 39; see also Elias 1991). Because identification could promote species reproduction, it could also promote the formation of groups. Druckman notes that the bases for group identification are considered universal in that groups provide individuals with a sense of security, feeling of belonging, and prestige. Groups are attractive because they serve "the individual's need for self-protection and self-transcendence" and hence provide human beings "and their progeny with security and safety as well as status and prestige in return for their loyalty and commitment" (1994: 44–45). Mercer's review of the social identity theory literature also suggests that intergroup biases might have a biological basis and that with the formation of groups inevitably comes competition among them. Such studies reveal that "no matter how trivial or ad hoc the groupings, and in the apparent absence of any competing values, the mere perception of another group leads to in-group favoritism and out-group discrimination" (1995: 238).[9]

While these observations are drawn from the literature of psychology, they are in keeping with long-standing realist propositions about the behavior of human beings in anarchy. Groups are treated as unitary actors in realist theory because, according to Gilpin, "human beings confront one another ultimately as members of groups, and not as isolated individuals" (1984: 290).[10] Systemic realism has tended to concentrate on the nation-state as the primary unit of group identification, but it has always assumed that realist propositions could be applied to other types of groups which should be treated as unitary actors as well. "Whenever human beings band together to act collectively," James argues, "the collective which is created must, if it is to fulfill its purpose, be deemed to have the capacity to act as a unit" (1989: 220). And the reason why human beings enter into collective arrangements and create institutions to assist those arrangements is, according to realism, to obtain species survival in the anarchic environment. Groups and the social practices in which they engage serve a purpose which is necessitated by an environmental context external to the practices themselves. Regardless of the particular form which groups take, be they "tribes, petty principalities, empires, nations, or street gangs," their very formation reflects the imperatives of species survival in anarchy (Waltz 1979: 67).

From a realist perspective, then, death is what has driven human beings to identify with one another, to form groups, and to create social practices and processes that bind individuals together into groups. These are behavioral characteristics which, as our species evolved, may have become part of the biological tool-kit that human beings now carry within them. If group formation and identification allowed early human beings to survive in better health and to reproduce then, due to environmental selection pressures on species reproduction and survival, these attributes could have become part of our adaptive biological evolutionary package. They would have been one of the means by which we as a species survived and reproduced in an environment that not only provides no direct guidance or assistance to achieving these goals, but actually appears to actively promote death from the moment human beings are born. This means that individual identification, group formation, and group social practices are not ends in themselves in the realist argument, but means to the end of species reproduction and survival in an anarchic environment. As such their very existence reflects the constitutive principle of that environment and could provide no means with which to deny it.

HUMAN SOCIAL PRACTICE
IN AN ANARCHIC ENVIRONMENT

By positing a particular relationship between the anarchic environment, individuals, and the institutions and social practices they create, realism contends that the formation of groups is a central attribute of anarchy and anticipates a number of broad patterns to transgroup interaction. These include in-group favoritism and out-group discrimination, a tendency to imitate the social practices of the powerful, and the layering of imitated social practices onto existing group institutions. While the first would seem most relevant to this particular study, understanding the centrality of imitation and the institutional layering effect it produces within groups is actually essential to neoclassical realism's deductive foundations and to how the practices of autonomy and cooperation in the present international system would be analyzed under a neoclassical rubric. This is because neoclassical realism is interested in how, as filtering mechanisms for transgroup interaction, the institutions within the group would promote and preserve the in-group/out-group distinction. Its subsystemic focus is what distinguishes neoclassical realism from neorealism, and because it is interested in how anarchy accounts for patterns in intragroup social practices, neoclassical realism approaches out-group discrimination and its impact on international cooperation from the bottom up. Delineating its approach to social practice in general also underscores why neoclassical realism is not inconsistent with the proposition that anarchy has causal priority.

Because there is an imperative in an anarchic environment for individuals to identify with one another if they are to reproduce and survive, "humans actively seek to glue their cultures and social systems together—and do not have to be constrained or coerced into so doing" (Bloom 1990: 44–45). The development of shared meanings is itself a response to anarchic selection pressures, so that every social practice in which collectives engage, regardless of specific content, contributes either directly or indirectly to the goal of survival and reproduction. In other words, from a realist perspective the social practices and intersubjective meanings which individuals develop with one another in order to interact and operate as a collective are a means by which human survival as a species is obtained. It is not merely the processes of competition and war-making that represent self-help behavior, but all of the social practices in which one group of human beings engage and which ultimately differentiate them from other groups. Contrary to Peterson's claim, then, it is quite possible to tell a story of human survival involving social relations and cooperation which remains profoundly realist in quality (1996: 267).

It is no path-dependent accident of history, for example, that practices which induce loyalty and cooperation within the group, and competition and biases without, would become stable patterns of behavior in an anarchic environment. Loyalty and cooperation within the group would make it more cohesive and capable of acting as a unit in providing for the primary needs of its members, while the promotion of intergroup biases would reinforce internal cohesion. Again these propositions have their corollaries in psychological studies of group loyalty and the evolution of intergroup biases. In his review of this literature, Druckman notes that prosocial behavior has adaptive advantages:

> It has been argued from the perspective of evolutionary psychology that cooperation behavior promotes individual survival, and that groups composed of members who are cooperative are more effective than those with members who are less cooperative. Such behavior also contributes to a person's sense of identity by distinguishing them from those who are like them and those who are not, between friends and foes. This cooperative behavior displayed between members of one's own group, strengthened by pressures of conformity to group norms, is rarely seen in relations between members of different groups (1994: 45).

Cooperative behavior within groups in order to obtain survival would also produce greater intolerance and discrimination toward other groups. While the degree of intolerance can vary according to whether a group is culturally individualistic or collective, and while "antagonism is not fixed or immutable," it is also the case that "some measure of collective antagonism is inevitable in human relations" (Ignatieff 1996: 230). This antagonism generates a concern with relative gains regardless of cultural categorization, and universally it is the case, according to Hogg and Abrams, that "beating the outgroup is more important than sheer profit" (1988, 49).

Shared group social practices are a means to reproduction and survival not only in an immediate physical sense but in a psychological sense as well. Participation in them allows the individual who is ultimately bound by time to experience the timeless. As D. Smith describes this, "a more abstract set of connections builds to a larger community of people with common ways of living, common ways of approaching the basic problems of life and death, and shared assumptions about ethics and social organization" (1996: 204). These commonalties can offer "a sense of continuity and stability," a sense of "geographical and historical location," and "a sense of their place not only in this world but the next." This is one reason, but not the only reason, why social practices are so difficult to overcome once established. Challenging such practices is the equivalent of challenging the glue which binds groups, and so it challenges one of the individual's primary means to survival. The social practices in which groups engage become self-perpetuating not only because identity is derived from them and they materially reward patterns of behaviors, but also because they are the means to an end which remains universally and ahistorically pertinent to the species as a whole. The dynamic which perpetuates the existence of such practices is not purely internal to the processes themselves and may be traced to an external, immutable environment as well.

One of the implications of a realist perspective on human social practices and institutions is that particular patterns of group behavior which liberal cooperation theory and constructivism interpret as historically accidental are instead predictable and ahistorical. The social construction of power politics among groups is but one example. While Wendt argues that "security dilemmas are not given by anarchy or nature," and "if states find themselves in a self-help system, this is because their practices made it that way" (1992: 407), realism's environmentally-based ontology indicates that security dilemmas are ahistorical patterns of behavior which derive from the unchanging anarchic environment in which human beings exist. As Mercer puts it, "self-help is not one of a multitude of plausible institutions in anarchy; instead, it is a consequence of intergroup relations in anarchy" (1995: 251).

Security dilemmas are not processes to which human beings have accidentally committed as a result, but are traceable to an environment that confronts all human beings with death as the ultimate selection mechanism for the species. If the formation of groups was an adaptive characteristic in response to this environmental selection pressure, then intergroup suspicion and wariness would become an ahistorical pattern of human interaction. In other words, security dilemmas would be "discovered" regardless of their particular historical, cultural, geographic, or systemic context because anarchy is an ahistorical teacher with the same lessons to teach each new generation. This is what Waltz means when he asserts that "the enduring anarchic character of international politics accounts for the striking sameness in the quality of international life through the millennia" (1979: 66).

Of course one upshot of realism's insistence that anarchy is immutable is that it is continually criticized for its inability to account for change in historical global politics and in the present international system. Waltz himself was insistent that his was a theory of continuity and not change (1979: 65–69). Yet overlooked by critics and practitioners alike is that it is anarchy's immutability which actually provides the constant source for group innovation and hence for changes to group social practices and intersubjective meanings. This is because if death is an immutable selection mechanism of the anarchic environment, then human survival is never resolved. It remains as pertinent to the species today as it did in our formative evolutionary past, which means that the search for modes of human survival and reproduction remain an ongoing project of the human species. One of the ways in which the human mind appears to have adapted to the constancy of this selection mechanism is an acceptance and active promotion of change in, and innovation to, the social practices they create (Dennett 1995, chapter 13). In fact, without this feature of the environment it would be difficult to understand why human beings strive for or accept change in their social practices at all.

This means that the dynamic for change in realist theory is not purely internal to social practices themselves. Instead its source lies outside of the collective agreements in which humans create and engage. This point may appear to be a contradiction in that anarchy is the source for both the change and stability of social practices in realist theory. Yet from a realist perspective process change is largely the result of imitation, which is a predictable pattern to the evolution of social practices and is derivable from the anarchic environment. Anarchy provides the incentive to change, but how groups of human beings do so is typically by imitating one another's social practices. Thus imitative change is fundamental to all human behavior and to the social practices in which they engage, but the reason why human beings imitate lies beyond or outside of the social practices they create.

Why is imitation central to realism's approach to change? The answer is, in returning to an earlier point, because the environment provides no guide as to how human beings are to obtain their own immediate survival. Anarchy is not a tangible or physical actor but a context that is fundamentally self-help in quality. Thus "it can tell us what pressures are exerted and what possibilities are posed by systems of different structure, but it cannot tell us just how, and how effectively, the units of a system will respond to those pressures and possibilities" (Waltz 1979: 71). Ultimately human beings must make the assessments and choices necessary for their own survival and reproduction. Because the environment provides no guidance in this regard, it is only the behavior of other human beings that provides any clue as to how one survives at all in such an environment. Successful identification clearly involves a high degree of imitation, which makes both identification and imitation pertinent to species survival and reproduction.

From this we may conclude that comparing and assessing how effectively the processes of other groups have obtained their survival, and then imitating those practices that seem relatively successful, would be a predictable, ongoing behavioral attribute of anarchy. Waltz notes, for example, that "states spend a lot of time estimating one another's capabilities, especially their abilities to do harm" (1979: 131). They do so not merely because they fear attack from one another, but also because the practices in which groups engage are the only indicators available to them for assessing how group survival may be obtained in anarchy.

For some realists the anarchic inducement to imitation has pointed toward the importance of "interaction capacity" as an independent variable. Buzan, Jones, and Little argue, for example, that "neorealism is less structurally deterministic than is often supposed," because the logic of anarchy implies imitative change, and the degree to which groups have "the ability and the willingness" to interact makes a difference to imitation incentives (1993: 83, 69, also 23). In this way one can account for process-based differences in historical subsystems, such as the Greek city-state, the empires of South America, or the world order of dynastic China, because groups would imitate one another within these subsystems to the extent that they were able and willing. As the level of interaction among these subsystems increased, there would be a tendency to imitate across subsystems which would then produce a socialization of units on a global scale. Of course whether they are able or willing to interact fails to address whether they *have to* interact. As long as the region in which groups exist contains infinite resources, groups can afford to ignore one another or be tolerantly benign in their interactions because they would not be competing for the same resources in order to survive.[11]

It is an entirely different matter, however, when close geographic proximity is involved because this would make a difference to resource availability. A level of interaction capacity that shrinks the geographic space between groups will begin to affect resources and directly affect their survival. Higher levels of interaction would therefore produce greater inducements for competition and violence and would also geographically expand the number of groups engaging in imitative change and socialization.[12] Under conditions of increasing interaction, groups which engaged in social practices that did not encourage intergroup comparison or were nonadaptive would select themselves as well as their practices out of the system overtime. Such practices would have failed to place ends before means, thus disabling the groups which relied upon them from recognizing the tradeoff inherent to the environment. Such groups would "live at the mercy of their militarily more vigorous neighbors," and be subject to conquest, defeat, and annihilation (Waltz 1979: 102). And, having failed to secure survival in the first place, the processes in which those groups were engaged would not reoccur because other groups wishing to survive would not imitate them. As a result, "the units that survive come to look like one another," and will "share certain characteristics. Those who go bankrupt lack them" (77, see also 127–128).

One of the most basic characteristics that increased interaction among groups would produce, then, is a common tendency to process-comparison and a shared penchant for institutional imitation. Social practices which were nonadaptive and nontransformative could threaten the group's survival, and because groups in anarchy prefer the end of survival over the means of process, they are generally willing to change the means if it appears to no longer suit the end. Thus the anarchic environment, as a "set of constraining conditions" for process (Waltz 1979: 73), would provide a continual incentive for groups to compare, assess, adapt, and reshape the social practices in which they engaged. In this context it is no accident that groups would tend to imitate the practices and institutions of those groups which were most powerful within the system. The concept of power (and polarity) is the shorthand means by which groups identify who among them has greater military, economic, political, and social resources at their disposal. The social practices and institutions in which such groups engage are the means by which they amass such resources; hence those practices are prime candidates for imitation by other groups.

This is why Waltz argues that systemic realism "is written in terms of the great powers of an era," and that "the units of greatest capacity set the scene of action for others as well as for themselves" (1979: 72). Polarity induces predictable variations in balancing and management patterns (Schweller and Priess 1997), and it also produces predictable patterns of imitation that are a source of dynamism within the system. The desire to avoid direct victimization by the powerful may be an immediate motivation to imitate for some groups, while for others the incentive may be less pressing depending on proximity to the powerful and to their interests. But the anarchic incentive for imitation as a means to survival, coupled with material resource differences between groups, would serve as a dynamic source for the propagation of the social practices relied upon by the materially-advantaged groups within the global system.

It is for this reason that the practices of the very powerful during any given time period become the hegemonic discourses of the system. The "inherited language, concepts, and texts that have constituted privileged discourses in international relations," and which remain the focus of post-modern theorists (Der Derian 1989: 4), are privileged for a reason, according to the logic of realism, which lies outside of those discourses and is unaffected by them.[13] Some ideas become privileged over others as a function of imitative change induced by the anarchic environment. It is not the content of these ideas which determines that they will be preferred, but rather that the group which prefers them is materially advantaged and so will be imitated by others in their own quest for survival. Thus realism provides a very different answer than do liberal theories to the question posed by Haggard, "what allows some knowledge to be selected while other knowledge withers politically?" (1991: 431). Liberal cooperation theories and functional-constructivism provide what Woods calls a "logic of discovery" answer, in which systemic "ideas change when new, better ideas are discovered" (1995: 168). This not only fails to explain "why a particular set of ideas gets taken up at a particular point in time" as Woods points out, but also relies on value-judgments about what constitutes "good" or "better" that are motivationally underivable from the social practices in which groups are actually engaged.

Realism's explanation for the selection of ideas relies instead on a "power political answer" in which "ideas enter the political arena because they are favored by powerful states" (Woods 1995: 169). This is typically interpreted to mean that the powerful directly, intentionally impose their ideas upon others through various mechanisms, such as memberships in IOs or in their determination of what will constitute the rules of the international game. But there is a more subtle side to this as well, in that anarchy-induced imitation means groups would have an incentive to adopt the ideas and practices of the powerful regardless of direct imposition. The social practices of the very powerful are attractive objects of imitation by other groups because those practices appear to be responsible for having produced the material advantages enjoyed by the powerful. Because groups equate power and social practices with attaining the only interest that consistently and universally matters in anarchy (i.e., species reproduction through group survival), they will also have a consistent incentive to adopt the ideas of the powerful.

Nor is that incentive limited to the imitation of military-security practices, because economic, political, and cultural practices also appear to contribute to material advantage and hence to group survival. Even norms which may not appear to have immediate material benefits may be part of the package of practices imitated by other groups.[14] What motivates such behavior is not something inherently attractive or compelling about those ideas, but that groups want to survive and will imitate what they think works most effectively to that end. In other words, what makes the comparison and adoption of ideas compelling is the environment in which groups exist, not a logic inherent to the ideas themselves and when compared in some sort of contextual vacuum. Anarchy is the motivation for a pattern of imitative group behavior which then produces the predictable outcome that discourses of the powerful will become hegemonic regardless of intent or imposition.

By positing that change is the result of anarchy-driven imitation, realism can explain the sorts of process-based outcomes which its critics frequently charge it cannot. An example might underscore this point. The nation-state is by no means the teleological end-point of group identification, but its development as the primary constitutive unit of the present global system is explicable as a result of anarchy's imitative dynamics. Although he fails to adequately explain what it is about anarchy that prompts comparison and competition, Spruyt is correct when he states that comparison is the key to understanding why the sovereign state displaced other institutional competitors such as urban-leagues, city-states, and independent communes (1994). As much of the state-building literature has argued, at the time the sovereign state proved to be more effective relative to other organizational forms for managing internal resources and for responding to external pressures from other groups.[15] This prompted a process of comparison and imitation that led to the imitation of the sovereign state and the selection out of the system of competing institutional forms overtime.

Eventually those groups which tied together the sovereign state, as the dominant political unit in a defined territory, and the nation, as a collective with shared cultural features, again appeared overtime to be relatively more successful at obtaining their own survival in comparison to other institutional forms. Indeed, they became the prime exploiters of groups which did not have these attributes, as they sought to colonize much of the rest of the globe. Hence the incentive to imitate the institutional forms and social practices of the nation-state became widespread, although its imitation was not always successful. Some groups lacked the internal resources and cultural unity necessary for the nation-state's replication, or they imitated some of its practices but not others.

Certainly it was this type of comparative assessment that led other Europeans to conclude that the Prussian administrative state of the 1800s was a relatively more efficient institution at mobilizing armies in its defense, and the perception of success led to attempts of emulation. As Hintze described it, "the success of Prussian and German arms made the introduction of universal service a political necessity for the Great Powers everywhere on the Continent" (1975: 213). Its success also made it the administrative structure of choice when Japanese leaders traveled to Europe to study its forms of government in order to emulate them in the late 1800s (Norman 1975: 437). Emulation even led the genro to adopt democratic institutions, such as a national representative assembly, despite the fact that the Meiji Restoration was clearly an oligarchy (Ishida and Krauss 1989: 5–7).

This brief historical example hardly does justice to what are complex and multifaceted historical, global developments, but its intent is to illustrate that systemic realism is far from being a theory of stasis with no ability to account for change. Why a dynamic of competitive institutional selection and imitation would exist at all is the stuff of systemic realism, which makes the charge by its critics that it cannot account for such changes all the more curious.[16] Realism can explain group transformation and change because its central component—anarchy—is what provides a constant and predictable incentive for groups to modify the social practices in which they are engaged. That groups engage in process-comparisons and are willing to adopt and imitate new practices can be traced to ongoing anarchic selections pressures on human beings as a species. The primary response of the species to those pressures has been the formation of groups, the development of intragroup social practices, and the promotion or acceptance of innovation to those practices.

Whether there is a biological bases for these ongoing behavioral characteristics is not addressed here, though such a presumption would certainly be consistent with a neoclassical realist approach which, as the name suggests, harks back to earlier forms of realism that explicitly relied on human nature assumptions in a way that neorealism purposely did not.[17] But of greater pertinence to this discussion is that imitative choice is not derived from qualities inherent to the social practices themselves in realist theory, but rather derived from their relation to materially-advantaged groups. What has yet to be addressed is what the logic of anarchy implies about how imitation will affect the processes in which groups are already engaged, and how it is that groups may entirely opt out of such imitations despite ongoing pressures from the anarchic environment. It is here that we turn to neoclassical realism's approach to the practices of autonomy and cooperation specifically.

THE FOUNDATION FOR A NEOCLASSICAL REALIST APPROACH TO AUTONOMY AND COOPERATION

In its explanations for group social practices and their transformation, systemic realism emphasizes similarity over difference. The incentive to imitate one another's social practices provides an element of dynamism in the system, but why differences in group process would continue to exist when imitation is a pattern basic to anarchy or how those differences might affect choices and outcomes must still be explained. Doing so will also underscore why the anarchic environment of realism is not teleological. At first glance it would appear that anarchy must be so because "behaviors are selected for their consequences" (Waltz 1979: 76), thereby implying that groups would eventually discover, through experimentation, comparison, and competition, the best means to survival and, through imitation and socialization, should come to look and act not merely similar but almost identical. Yet while anarchy produces similarity among groups, Waltz was cautious to stress that this did not mean they were identical because differences within groups would still be logically and historically expected (88, 122–123).

The development of cooperative, altruistic processes within groups would assist group survival vis-à-vis other groups, but differences within could be initially accounted for by ongoing subgroup tensions between individual re-production and group survival. While cooperative practices would be fundamental to the process of group formation and maintenance, they would also involve the establishment of internal decisionmaking practices particular to groups. The development of these decisionmaking institutions would be an internally contentious process, since what they involve are fundamental questions of resource allocation within and by the group that would affect individual survival. Thomson notes the historical grounds for distinguishing between the state and society (and for theorizing accordingly), because the latter "was largely an adversary" in the process of state-building "as it resisted state rulers' efforts to extract resources and monopolize political and judicial authority" (1995: 216). This tension between individual and group survival is one of the reasons why groups always look different; the different types of extractive bargains struck during the process of governance-building would produce internal process differences between groups.

The internal institutions and practices produced by these historical extractive bargains would remain as important to group members as external pressures from other groups. This is because these institutions involve the power to determine resource allocation within the group, and so they affect individual members quite directly. It would matter very much to group members, then, who was in charge of group decisionmaking institutions and how much jurisdictional power over resource allocation these institutions had relative to each other. Given their function within groups, the importance of intragroup decisionmaking institutions would remain even if political and judicial authority were no longer the subject of violent confrontation among subgroups or between state and society.

These internal decisionmaking institutions would also effectively exclude nongroup members from participation, which suggests two conclusions pertinent to the topic of transgroup cooperation. First, because internal cooperative processes serve the function of reinforcing group parameters, they also reinforce differences between groups. Contrary to many functional-constructivist claims, even when internal processes are similar across groups the act of transgroup cooperation does not in and of itself provide any means by which to overcome an "us versus them" cognitive or material distinction. Second, internal group practices and structures act as barriers to transgroup cooperation because they reinforce institutional differences between groups and these differences are felt at the most basic levels of identity and cognition. That is, group members would develop identity commitments to the intragroup decisionmaking practices in which they were engaged, and this would effect how members of groups responded to external stimuli. This is the foundation for the neoclassical realist perspective in general, as well as its insistence that the practice of autonomy would be the cognitive template from which group members viewed their interaction with other groups. Clearly it needs further elaboration.

Although realism appears to treat process as if it were merely a dependent variable that is affected by anarchy and cannot affect it in turn, the fact that process serves a survival function in anarchy also means that process itself is immediately causal in the realist argument. The differences between social practices obviously matter to outcomes because they encourage or prevent groups from recognizing and addressing external threat in an effective manner or in imitating one another's practices more effectively. While the anarchic environment encourages the goal of survival and the comparative assessments of process, it is the social practices in which groups engage that is immediately responsible for their ability to survive and to emulate the practices of others. Thus it is process that acts as a final arbiter for group survival within anarchy.

As with the pursuit of power, process in such an environment is a means to a particular end and not an end in itself. Groups who lose sight of this, as with those who pursue power for its own sake, risk their own extinction (Waltz 1979: 126–127). Yet groups are free to undertake such risk and frequently do so because "in pursuit of its security no state will act with perfect knowledge and wisdom—if indeed we could know what those terms might mean" (92). Groups are free to pursue any goals they desire and to allow their interests and behaviors to be determined by the processes in which they are engaged. They are also free to die, but it is the choices they make vis-à-vis themselves and others that determine whether such an outcome will actually come to pass.

Because it is only through the mechanism of process that groups can obtain their immediate survival, effective imitations of seemingly successful processes are not and cannot automatically be induced by the anarchic environment. Anarchy exerts an immutable and constant pressure, but it is not a tangible actor which can insist that groups and the individuals who comprise them behave in a particular manner. As Dessler puts it, in returning to his office-building analogy, "structure constrains and disposes behavior but does not determine it. The actual paths taken by workers will be determined by the nature of the job, the requirements of interoffice communications, and so on—considerations properly the focus of 'unit level' theory" (1989: 466). Although security alliances may sometimes provide an external source of power, ultimately groups have only their own resources, whether material or ideational, upon which to rely in order to obtain their own immediate survival. Even the choice to enter into security alliances can only be derived from the practices in which the group is already engaged. This means that group social practices act as perceptual filters through which the assessment of more successful or efficient means to survive are made.

In other words, even if there were an objectively best means to obtain survival in anarchy, groups and the individuals who comprise them would have no way to access it. Groups would have no capacity to experience this objective standard absent their social practices, and those practices would also prevent identical emulation of one another. Systemic realism is quite specific, in fact, that groups may simply blunder into successful processes or fail to imitate them altogether. According to Waltz, "competitive systems are regulated, so to speak, by the 'rationality' of the more successful competitors. What does rationality mean? It means only that some do better than others—whether through intelligence, skill, hard work, or dumb luck" (1979: 76–77, see also 92 and 118–119). As a result, "nations rarely learn any one lesson from specific events in the past, what each nation learns is never the same as the other, and each applies these lessons in a different manner" (Zakaria 1992: 195). None of the European powers or Japan applied the lessons of the Prussian bureaucracy in quite the same manner. What stood in the way of identical emulation was existing group social practices which acted as perceptual filters that changed the meaning and application of alternative social practices in each case.

Once again it is the anarchic environment itself that suggests a consistent dynamic by which perceptual differences across groups would remain and would produce differences in the way in which each group imitated the same social practices. Given the function that process serves within the environment, one could expect that groups would tend to rely on and commit to those processes which they believed had successfully obtained group survival in the past. As Gilpin has noted, "past success itself can become an obstacle to further innovation and adaptation," because it becomes "very difficult to convince a society that what has worked so well in the past may not work in an unknown future" (1996a: 413). Such a commitment also provides the opportunity for subgroups to develop vested interests in these social practices which need not be derived from the group's original motivation for adopting those social practices.

The modern nation-state bureaucracy was created as a means to mobilize and allocate resources in order to ensure group survival, for example, and so it served a function made necessary by a context external to the institution itself (Hintze 1975). Yet the modern bureaucrat would undoubtedly not describe the purpose of the institution of which they were a member in terms of the allocation of group resources for security purposes. She might instead be more concerned with protecting her department's own jurisdictions and prerogatives because her own immediate self-interests in employment and advancement lay in the maintenance of interbureaucratic power. Rather than being a means to obtain survival for the entire group, the maintenance of particular processes may become ends in themselves for the individuals who are engaged in them.

Their identities, interests, and behaviors would become tied to those processes, which would then act as opaque filters through which assessments, choices, and judgments were being made with regards to intergroup relations.

What is interesting about this conclusion is that it is reachable not from a process-based ontology, but from an environment-based ontology. It is precisely because process plays such an important causal role in the specified environment that realism anticipates strong group attachments to the practices which members believe have been successful at obtaining group survival in the past. It is this attachment which opens up the possibility that, for the individuals engaged in those practices, their identities and interests would be largely determined by the specific social practices in which they were engaged. This would inhibit them from ever objectively judging choices, behaviors, and outcomes, and should even serve as a barrier to efficient choice and hence to their own group's survival during times of immediate external threat. The vested subgroup interests that would develop in existing institutional arrangements would not disappear or suddenly become less causal simply because the group was faced with external threat or because the social practices of another group appeared to be more efficient at obtaining security or wealth.

What decisionmakers would be confronted with instead in such situations was contradictory pressure on the multiple identifications they had formed as a means to obtain their own individual survival. The external environment would exert pressure on these individuals to respond, adapt, and emulate in order to protect the group as a larger unit, yet identification with specific subgroups and institutions would also encourage them to protect subgroup institutional interests against emulation and change. Thus there would be pressure from within to protect existing institutional arrangements, and this would act as a counterweight to the environmental pressure from without to adapt institutional arrangements. Such a dynamic can explain why conflicts of interest between subgroups sometimes take precedence over external threat considerations. The behavior of other subgroups may pose a more immediate threat to the domestic institutions from which individual decisionmakers derive their identity and interests than does the behavior of external groups (David 1991).

The proposition that individual decisionmakers operate under a dual pressure from both the anarchic environment and the subgroup practices in which they are engaged goes a long way in explaining why foreign policy choices often appear to be objectively inefficient.[18] Behavior such as the U.S. Navy's failure to place Russian interpreters on board blockading ships during the Cuban Missile Crisis, Roosevelt's inability to obtain swifter congressional approval for U.S. involvement in World War II Europe, and Patton's decision to use military resources to personally beat Montgomery to Messina appear to be inefficient if external threat is primarily causal. Such outcomes are often cited as evidence for realism's lack of explanatory power and are sometimes even presented as alternative models to realism (Allison 1971; Rosecrance and Stein 1993).

Yet is it only with the theoretical framework specified by realism, which places process within the context of an anarchic environment, that these outcomes make any sense. The individuals involved were simultaneously attempting to balance group interests engendered by the environment with the subgroup processes to which they owed their immediate identities. Both were threatened by other actors and institutions that were simultaneously external and internal to the group. The Navy was protecting both the nation-state and itself from jurisdictional encroachment by other military services, Congress was balancing national security needs with reelection by isolationist voters, and Patton was satisfying both his own personal ambitions and his immediate duties in battle.

This contradictory pressure also explains why and how the study of decisionmaker perception and misperception is central to the realist research program. As Rose notes, "there is indeed something like an objective reality of relative power, which will, for example, have dramatic effects on the outcomes of state interactions," but "states [do not] necessarily apprehend that reality accurately on a day-to-day basis" (1998: 153; see also Schweller and Priess 1997). Not only does perception play a role in chain-ganging and buck-passing, as Christensen and Snyder have pointed out (1990), but so too do domestic political benefits and costs. In the face of external threat, nation-states rely on some combination of arms and alliances to obtain their security, "but the comparison of internal costs and external benefits drives the choice at the margin" (Morrow 1993: 232).[19]

The choices made are meant to simultaneously address external threats to the group and internal threats to the particular subgroup practices in which individual decisionmakers are engaged. The choices appear to be contextually efficient to the individuals involved. This does not mean that the individual decisionmaker stops identifying with the larger group of which she is a member, nor does it negate intergroup competition as a basic feature of anarchy. It is, after all, the group's reliance on, and commitment to, particular social practices which provides individuals with the opportunity to develop immediate vested interests in those processes in the first place. But individual decisionmakers do have simultaneous and sometimes competing identities within the context of their group, and it is the individual's attempt to balance these conflicts that serves as an ongoing source for perceptual and institutional differences across groups.

In other words, it is the tension between the imperatives of group formation in anarchy and the vested interests that subgroups then develop in particular group practices which accounts for the continuation of process differences in anarchy. This tension produces social practices and institutions which are unique to each group and this uniqueness determines the specifics of any particular foreign policy choice that a group makes. Whether the choices made are efficient or successful according to an objective standard is irrelevant according to this formulation, because choice is always being exercised within a given context. That is, choices are not selected because they are objectively more rational, but because they make sense to individuals given their contexts. The particular practices in which the individual is engaged within the group serve as such contexts, but they do not exist in a vacuum. They are, instead, contexts within the group context, which itself exists within, and as a function of, the larger environmental context of anarchy.

Thus the social practices of the group act as causal variables within a given environment that encompasses all social practices and exerts a constant, immutable pressure on them. At the same time, group social practices and institutions are causal variables and, because those practices will engender their own interests and behaviors over time, their attributes will affect the choices individuals within the group make as they attempt to deal with the pressures of anarchy. By relating the environment to process in this way, the systemic and the domestic can act as simultaneous independent variables in realist theory. The anarchic environment remains primarily but indirectly causal, while process remains secondarily but directly causal. Death remains an immutable selection mechanism of the environment, yet human interaction is the only means by which the individual and the species can avoid its immediacy. It is because environment and process work in tandem to produce behaviors and outcomes that realism can explain why there is a species-wide incentive for process malleability at the same time that such malleability is ultimately constrained.

The simultaneous impact of environment and process also affects if and how groups will imitate alternative social practices. In addition, it prevents imitation from ever producing an identical outcome between groups, and it promotes institutional variation that serves as the resource pool from which future rounds of emulation will be drawn. Internal process differences will affect how amenable a group is to change and emulation, as well as what in particular it chooses to imitate. The environment explains the tendency toward similarity, since it is an unchanging context that exerts the same pressure on all groups, but existing internal group processes explain why the choices in response to this environment are not identical, so that no group addresses the pressures of anarchy in quite the same way or emulates the processes of others in quite the same manner. The interpretation of success itself is filtered through perceptual lenses colored by existing social practices and their differences. And because groups never start with a clean institutional slate, imitation is layered onto existing group practices which then produce a unique amalgamation of intended similarity and unintended difference.

These amalgamations can be infinitely varied and may serve as sources for imitative change in the future. The unique institutional product produced in each case will have varying affects on the group's ability to amass resources. Those institutional amalgamations which appear to be more or less successful at accomplishing this goal could become the source for avoidance or imitation by other groups in the future. Thus social practices and institutions change and evolve over time in response to the immutable anarchic environment, but that evolution can never be teleological because it is based on process comparison and imitation that must work through existing social practices with causal properties of their own. Consistent with Bowler's observation that "evolution can only work by modifying the structures available to it" (1984: 182), anarchic imitation works by layering similarity on top of and thereby modifying existing differences. What is produced are unpredictable institutional variations that might become the stuff of systemic institutional imitation at a later point in time.

While I recognize that the discussion to this point has been sweeping and abstract in content, its goal has been to develop the deductive foundations for the neoclassical realist approach itself. Such a foundation has remained underdeveloped by neoclassical realist practitioners, and in delineating it here my hope is that I have managed to accentuate the enormous potential it holds as an approach to historical global politics and to the present international system. Neoclassical realism allows institutions to be important causal variables in their own right, yet they are not the only context that matters to choice. Those institutions must be embedded within the larger group context which is itself a function of the environmental context. This is a point entirely lost in the liberal literature on interdependence because its proponents have, as Waltz put it, "discovered the complexity of processes and have lost sight of how processes are affected by structure" (1979: 145). It is this ontological approach to social practice as a means within a given environment that allows realism to incorporate the causality of domestic institutions and then approach the subject of cooperation from an alternative direction. That direction recognizes that existing social practices and institutions play an immediate causal role in producing the choice to engage in international cooperation.

According to neoclassical realism, and unlike liberal cooperation theories or functional-constructivism, elites make choices which are derived from internal existing group institutions and which serve as guides to what they believe would be rational behavior. Elites deal with external pressure through the prism of their own group processes. They do not disengage themselves from the group practices which create their immediate interests and behaviors in order to objectively evaluate their own situations and that of their group.

The determination of efficiency remains grounded in the processes from which state elite identities, interests, and behaviors are derived, so that even in their attempt to obtain survival for their larger group, individual decisionmakers make choices which have meaning to them only within ongoing process contexts. The practice of autonomy could be such a context and should be treated as one of the perceptual prisms through which choices regarding international conflict and cooperation are made. Neoclassical realists would concur with Mann, then, that "the potential universalism of the [capitalist economy] is undercut by the particularisms of nation-states—and indeed also by the particularisms of human social practices at large" (1997: 489).

Thus a deductive basis exists for neoclassical realism to examine subsystemic variables as intervening causal variables, even as it also accepts the systemic realist proposition that anarchy is causally primary. Anarchy provides the basis for approaching the subject of cooperation as a phenomenon bound by a context of groups, rather than as a freely-floating functional concept, and neoclassical realism specifically points us toward the possibility that, within this context of groups and the internal decisionmaking practices they would develop, autonomy might be a social practice in its own right. Yet this tells us nothing about what group decisionmaking practices and institutions would actually look like, or how they would operate to reproduce identity and choice in practice. The presumption of groups in anarchy cannot explain or predict how particular groups will constitute their internal decisionmaking practices, why and how these practices remain unreceptive to pressures emanating from the international environment for alternative institutions, or how transgroup cooperation may be generated by and simultaneously sustain internal decisionmaking practices. It is here that neoclassical realism must turn to constructivism to complete its picture of social reality.

AUTONOMY AS A SOCIAL PRACTICE

According to liberal theories of international cooperation, the perceptions and preferences of nation-state elites and their ability to learn lessons appropriate to their issue area and interdependent context are central to the cooperative choice. In assessing such centrality, Wendtian constructivism directs our attention to the practices and institutions of the modern nation-state which provide state elites with the basis for action and which give meaning to their activities in the first place. We need to think of "the structures which organize our actions" as "collective meanings," because it is by participating in such meanings that we "acquire identities—relatively stable, role-specific understandings and expectations about self" (1992: 397). In fact, interests and behaviors would have no meaning outside the particular process-context, which is Wendt's point when he asserts that identities and interests "are produced in and through 'situated activity' " and "are constituted by collective meanings that are always in process" (1992: 407).

In considering how nation-states developed their internal decisionmaking practices and institutions, it is hard to escape the conclusion that notions of autonomy are fundamental to the very definition of what constitutes a nation-state. Based on a cumulative review of the literature, Barrington argues that nations are "collectives united by shared cultural features and the belief in the right of territorial self-determination," while a state "is the principal political unit in the international political system corresponding to a territory, a relatively permanent population, and a set of ruling institutions" (1997: 713). According to this definition, autonomy is a fundamental component of nation-states since, even if cultural or territorial boundaries may be social constructs themselves, every element of the definition implies that collectives are attempting to demarcate themselves in the pursuit of self-determination.

· Certainly what was external to the group had to be influential to the group's notions of autonomy and to the internal decisionmaking institutions it would create in order to pursue self-determination. The state formation literature, for example, has generally supported the thesis that external competitive pressures, and in particular waging war, had a centralizing effect on state structures.[20] And as post-modern theorists have pointed out, independence can only have meaning if an "other" exists from whom "self" can be independent.[21] Connor argues, for example, that nations and states must be separately defined, and that "a group of people must know ethnically what they *are not* before they know what they *are*," so that "while an ethnic group *may*, therefore be other-defined, the nation *must* be self-defined" (1994: 45–46; his emphasis).

Yet if self-determination is the goal of self-definition, then the postulated absence of "other" from the ability to actually achieve self-determined intragroup goals meant the practices that developed in order to obtain interests for "self" were necessarily insular and parochial. Actors and subgroups within nation-states focused on one another as potential competitors and cooperative partners in the process of their development, so that internal decisionmaking institutions were designed to deal with one another while excluding participation by actors from other nation-states. It was, after all, the ability to independently achieve goals for the nation within its boundaries that gave the state its *raison d'être* or, as Reus-Smit has argued, defined "the terms of legitimate statehood and the broad parameters of rightful state action" (1999: 6). The nation-state's domestic practices and formal institutions reflected the constitutive norm of autonomy from the start. It was, in Ruggie's words, one of the "principles on the basis of which the constituent units are separated from one another" (1983a: 274).

Unlike sovereignty, then, which is a systemic social practice in that it is an intersubjective meaning shared and reified by the interactive behaviors and practices of nation-states, autonomy is a social practice which acquires much of its intersubjective meaning from the collective that *is* the nation-state. In other words, if sovereignty is, as Thomson puts it, "what some collectivity of state leaders say it is" (1995: 218), then autonomy is what some collectivity of actors *within* the nation-state have made it. It is an intersubjective meaning shared and reified by the practices of state and societal actors, and so it has consequences for state identity, interests, and behavior even as the systemic conditions change or as interactive capacity increases. This suggests that the predisposition to insularity and parochialism brought to the bargaining table by the nation-state's representatives would not be a behavioral misperception, but a component of identity itself.

Note that one need not agree with neoclassical realists or Mercer that self-help is the spontaneous outcome of group interaction in order to concur with this point. It is enough that the state became the repository for national loyalties and that each nation-state was a group which differentiated itself from other nation-states. Goals were believed to be achievable through interaction with actors who were already designated as "self," and "self" did not need to interact with "other" in order to achieve them. These beliefs were translated into intragroup decisionmaking structures that were designed (either willingly or through imposition) to settle resource allocation issues within the group. Such decisionmaking institutions and social practices were specific to each group and involved who held the power to make resource allocation decisions. They also involved whether and how this power might be balanced between competing subgroups, and their parameters effectively excluded the participation of other groups in resource allocation decisions.

The implications of this from a Wendtian constructivist perspective is that the practice of autonomy would be felt and propagated by the most fundamental level of identity formation itself. Self-determination was one of the norms that informed how nation-states determined who constituted a member of its group and how members of another nation-state were different. As such it would be internalized by individual members as group identity was developing within and becoming tied to the specific confines of the nation-state as an organizational form. It would therefore act as a mechanism of reinforcement for established group differences and hence for myopic perspectives and biases that would be derived from identity as a group member.

As a result the logic of the state may be felt in places one least expects, and this is because each new generation of human beings develop social identities in the context of domestic social practices and governing structures that remain specific to each nation-state. These structures and practices involve not just political decisionmaking bodies, but also the practices and structures of education, communication, commerce, health, and transportation that are all internal and specific to each nation-state. There is no evidence that systemic interdependence has managed to subvert or displace these internal structures. As Thomson notes, these institutions are part of the historical extractive bargains struck between states and societies which are not just "unique to each national state; they also shape personal identities," so that "human beings are separated not just by geographical boundaries, but by a set of unique relationships with their respective states" (1995: 227). Insular group identities are reinforced by these insular structures and institutions, which developed and continue to operate separately from other nation-state groupings (which, in turn operate their own structures and institutions in these areas).

This has important implications for the classic IPE tension between the market and the state, because it indicates that capitalists, as an individual or a class, cannot exist in a cognitive space that is devoid of a logic antithetical to the market. Individual identity is still formed within the context of a nation-state collective that has reified the practice of autonomy in the pursuit of its goals. Institutions are powerful mechanisms of consolidation, as Gramsci insightfully argued, but if capitalism and the state are competitive and not reinforcing institutions then the individual pursuit of capitalist profit would already be informed by the logic of the state. This may explain why, even in a world of global capitalism, multinational firms continue to place ownership, assets, and research and development within their "home" states, fix their shares to particular national stock markets, and abide by national corporate laws and accountancy practices.[22] It also raises questions about the extent to which an international capitalist business class really exists to propagate liberal economic ideas and so assist in the dismantling of the Westphalian system.

The tendency to differentiate according to the norm of autonomy would also be reinforced by the parochial political decisionmaking structures of which state elites would be members. This is the second way in which autonomy would continue to leave its mark even if systemic conditions were not conducive to its practice. The formal decisionmaking structures that developed within each nation-state have remained different and disconnected from the political structures developed in other nation-states. The state's executive-legislative-judicial branches are exclusive to it, as are the practices that connect state to society, such as political parties, elections, media, and education. The decisionmaking structures that developed were also extremely complex since they reflected a host of material and ideational legacies which were specific to each nation-state.

In the American case, for example, its constitution had to specify vertical decisionmaking procedures and relationships between the local and state levels of governance which already existed and a federal government which did not. It also specified the horizontal practices that would link the components of the federal together, the electoral practices that would link the state and society, and it even attempted to delineate the relationship between the state and the individual. Yet even though the constitution remains a working blueprint for American governance, various particular practices still filled in the cracks it had left between state and society. The reliance on party politics, caucuses, and conventions to delineate the field of electable candidates was one such practice. The issues which political parties represented as well as their goal to obtain elected office only had meaning within social practices specific to the American context. And as Quandt observes, "the electoral arrangements for the presidency and Congress have rarely been justified by the contribution they make to sound foreign policy. The rationale is almost entirely domestic" (1988: 88). In other words, even if one could argue with the notion that "politics stops at the water's edge," it was a concept that informed the very development of intersubjective meanings and formal governing structures within nation-states and continues to be relevant today.

The practice of autonomy informs the choices of the appointed civil servant who must balance the conflicting yet institutionally-specific demands of bureaucratic department, executive leader, and legislative branch. It informs the choices of the executive head who is more preoccupied with upcoming elections than external events because, as Garrett and Lange note, "the proximate objective of all governments is to retain office" because "politicians cannot afford to ask what is good for society as a whole in the long run, lest they lose power in the interim" (1996: 50). And it informs the choices of the legislator who must answer to a narrow constituency dominated by domestic manufacturing firms or who care more about American abortion-rights than international affairs. The social practices in which these actors are engaged developed in the context of a particular state and society and provide no means to even reference the concerns, needs, or demands of other nation-states. No votes are reserved for other nation-states in national and subnational elections, and there are no electoral practices that allow another nation-state to keep a legislator in office in spite of local constituency wishes.

Nor do national administrative structures include bureaucratic agencies which are on an equal footing (in both resources and prerogatives) with nationally-oriented agencies and whose sole function is to represent the interests or needs of other nation-states. In fact, in the American context the State Department is frequently criticized simply for raising the obvious point that other nation-states have different interests and concerns, and congressional legislators who are too interested in foreign affairs are often punished electorally.[23] This is hardly a phenomenon specific to the American nation-state. In the case of the EU, supranational governing processes have failed to replace national practices and instead coexist uneasily with them. The resilience of national governing practices and the parochialism which they engender is a result, reflection, and reinforcement of the social practice of autonomy.[24]

In addition, regardless of how personally enthusiastic a civil servant might be about the benefits of multilateralism, the social practices from which her role is derived exert both material and ideational pressure in the opposite direction, that is, to remain parochial and insular in her perspectives. It may seem tempting to argue that state monetary elites can be conceptualized as temporary appointees who are, prior to and after appointment, individual capitalists in the private sphere and thus bring this motivation to bear on their role as elites. However, the moment such individuals become elites they become embedded in the practices of the state.[25] The paychecks and promotions of life-time civil servants also depend on their conformity to expectations derived from within the department and from its relationship to the state's other bureaucratic departments, branches of government, and society.[26]

None of these expectations or relationships are derived from or include the social practices and formal institutions of other nation-states. Lines of promotion and pay do not translate from one national bureaucratic apparatus to the next, and there are no direct mechanisms whereby other nation-states and IOs can reward or punish the national civil servant for behavior within their own national governing structures. Instead the civil servant has an incentive to remain focused on the national rather than the international, and this conservatism is the direct result of the embedded practices of autonomy. If civil servants are instinctively protective of their national governing structures, it is because those structures reward them in both a material and ideational sense for behaving in such a manner.

The result is that almost every social practice related to governance within the nation-states reflects the practice of autonomy. The formal institutions of each nation-state are interconnected within the nation-state, but have no formal or ideational connection with the governance structures in other nation-states. *These institutions don't just pursue autonomy as a policy; they embody it.* They are the structural manifestations of the practice of autonomy and their very existence propagates it within each nation-state. Autonomy is the foundational concept upon which the nation-state's governing practices developed and, because it informs the content of those practices, the practice of autonomy is continually reinforced by them. This means that the individuals who act in the capacity of "state elites" have group identities and loyalties which already predispose them to the practice of autonomy. This predisposition is continually reinforced by the structures in which they participate as state elites. While they may be charged with responsibility for international economic affairs, those responsibilities are embedded in social practices that have been informed by the narrow logic of the state, not by the expansive logic of the market. Even if the decisionmaker is well acquainted with liberal economic arguments regarding open trade and the efficiencies of multi-lateralism, countervailing pressure to think and act according to the parochial and insular would be exerted from their own governing structures.

What the parochial and insular involve are the daily domestic political battles over the allocation of intragroup resources. The decisionmaking institutions in which state elites participate are not only a source of identification, but also the only legitimate basis from which intragroup allocation battles may be waged. This makes these institutions targets of competition in their own right, as subgroups and state elites vie for control over them and seek to either expand or contract particular institutional jurisdictions in resource allocation decisionmaking for the group. From this perspective it is clear that domestic decisionmaking structures should not be an afterthought in the study of IO and international cooperation. They serve as the prisms through which state decisionmakers interpret activity that is both internal and external to the group, and so they shape choice in a very direct manner. And it is precisely because these institutions reify the identity of state decisionmakers that the institutions themselves can become objects of intragroup competition and protection in their own right.

The point of these observations is not to insist that the formal and informal institutions in which the practice of autonomy are embedded and reified can never change. It is instead to confirm that the practice of autonomy cannot be treated, as it is by the interdependence and regimes literature, as if it were merely strategic misperception on the part of unenlightened state elites. It is odd, given constructivism's theoretical parameters, that so many of its practitioners have overlooked autonomy's potential causality in favor of a systemic functional explanation. Wendt acknowledges that by bracketing some domestic variables he may have excluded rival hypotheses to his claim that collective identities may be promoted by systemic processes (1994: 391; 1992: 423).[27] His justification for this practice is that standard domestic approaches still "treat interaction as affecting only the price of behavior and thus assume that a rationalist research agenda exhausts the scope of systemic theory" (1994: 391). However, there is no a priori reason why the same process-based approach which Wendt has reserved for systemic practices may not also be applied to domestic practices.

When autonomy is examined as a social practice in its own right, rather than merely a behavioral or strategic perception, it becomes a much more formidable obstacle to functionally efficient interdependent cooperation than either standard liberal theories of cooperation or functional-constructivism have acknowledged. As this section has sought to demonstrate, there is good reason to argue that autonomy is fundamental to what constitutes nation-states as entities. The concept of autonomy informed the establishment of what Ruggie describes as the "territorially fixed state formations" of the modern world, in which "territorial domains were disjoint and mutually exclusive" (1998: 189). It is one of the constitutive principles differentiating nation-states from one another, and it has produced observable, material, ideational, and reinforcing governing structures and institutions within each nation-state. Every governing practice in which state elites participate embodies the concept of autonomy, and it has been manifest and reified in numerous ways within the nation-state.

Because the practice of autonomy exerts a powerful countervailing pressure on the incentive to cooperate, it is not enough that a particular set of elites learn a specific set of strategic lessons in order to overcome it. Nothing short of a complete identity transformation would be required in order to remove it as an obstacle to functionally efficient interdependent cooperation. Yet such an identity transformation could only transpire if the domestic sphere were fundamentally reordered. Without changes to the governing structures in which state elites operate, parochial perspectives and choices antithetical to cooperation would continue to be reinforced by them. To expect national economic elites to accomplish the task of structural revision obviously places far too great an expectation on their shoulders.

It also ignores the way in which internal decisionmaking structures define what Reus-Smit calls "the cognitive horizons" of their participants. Such structures "shape the institutional imaginations of those political actors engaged in producing and reproducing fundamental institutions, making some practices appear mandatory and others unthinkable" (1999: 34). This means that while astute observers may recognize what constitutes "objective" efficiency in an issue area, they cannot and will not act upon this recognition as participants in the most basic subgroup governance structures that are reifying their group as a group distinct from other groups. The institutions and practices in which policymakers would participate are not objectively derived from the issue area; therefore the interests and policies which they pursue cannot be objectively derived from the issue area either.

As daily participants in the social practices of governance, elites would propagate the insularity of those practices and could only abandon this insularity if they refused to participate in the very social practices that define them as elites. They would have to refuse to participate in bureaucratic standard operating and promotional procedures, to attend to international events rather than participate in campaign activities and fund-raising, and to argue for international openness on principle alone. In doing so it is doubtful that they will remain elites for long, since they would be refusing to participate in the social structures which give meaning to modern state governance in the first place. Refusal to participate in the "situated activity" that gives the identity of "state elite" its meaning is essentially a refusal to be an elite at all, a choice that is certainly open to individuals but not individuals as elites.

It should come as no surprise, then, that state decisionmakers would be incapable of rising above the logic of their own group processes in order to assess the inefficiencies of those processes and to modify them accordingly. Internal group practices and institutions would continually reify the practice of autonomy vis-à-vis other groups and would remain causally dominant regardless of particular interests, definitions of functional institutional efficiency, and interdependent conditions. And because systemic conditions in particular issue areas have no independent or objective capacity to induce particular interests or behaviors, issue area interests can only be derived from the context of the group and its social practices. In other words, since the pursuit of wealth has no meaning absent the social practices of the group, the choice of transgroup cooperation must ultimately be derived from internal group practices that have causal precedence.

THE REALIST-CONSTRUCTIVIST APPROACH TO INTERNATIONAL COOPERATION

What, then, does the neoclassical realist-constructivist combination have to offer by way of an alternative explanation for international cooperation? And given a realist perspective on anarchy and a constructivist perspective on the practice of autonomy, what patterns would one anticipate for international cooperation? Based on realism one would anticipate that cooperation within groups and competition between them would be the historical, global norm. This does not mean that transgroup relations must necessarily be violent or that transgroup cooperation is precluded. There are a host of factors which can affect the strength of out-group biases and hence the extent to which intergroup competition is marked by aggression. Ignatieff observes, for example, that while "hostility and antagonism are built into the human negotiation of difference . . . these differences can become less murderous with time" (1996: 231).[28] And realists have consistently argued that, depending on variations in external threat, transgroup cooperation can be treated as a recurrent pattern of behavior. Such transgroup cooperation is not easily obtained, due to the ongoing pressures of anarchy and subgroup investiture in differing social practices, yet it is a relatively common form of cooperation consistent with realist theorizing.

Polarity and hegemonic stability are also factors that realists have argued give the theory a legitimate and logical purchase on the subject of international cooperation. Schweller and Priess argue, for example, that from polarity variance one can derive a number of implications for the development and nature of international institutional arrangements:

> unipolar distributions of power tend toward imposed orders; bipolar structures generate spontaneous, informal orders between the two poles and more formal institutional arrangements within the attendant blocs; and multipolar systems engender both imposed and spontaneous orders (1997: 8; see also Buzan 1984).

Thus the extensive institutionalization of international cooperation begun in the latter half of the twentieth century may be explained with reference to bipolarity. Realist variants of hegemonic stability propose similar types of explanations for the same historical pattern. The United States encouraged the institutionalization of cooperation among its trading partners in order to support a liberal free trade order in which its own economic interests would be heavily invested.

From a realist-constructivist perspective, however, none of this cooperation or its institutionalization translates into a fundamental change in the international system or in the nature of international, global politics. Transgroup cooperation, even if extensive and highly institutionalized, does not have the capacity to counteract the competitive effects of anarchy. This is not simply because cooperation is contingent upon power, either in its polarity or hegemonic stability forms, although power is an important part of the problem since change in polarity or the hegemon's capacities would affect the development and nature of cooperative institutionalization. But power is not the entire answer realism has to offer to support its insistence that "the range of expected outcomes falls within certain limits, . . . patterns of behavior recur," and "events repeat themselves, including events that none or few of the actors may like" (Waltz 1979: 69). Also relevant are the inter- and intragroup dynamics induced by the selective pressures of an immutably self-help anarchic environment. When transgroup cooperation occurs, its capacities to transform the essentially competitive nature of transgroup relations is so restrictive as to be, for all practical purposes, nonexistent.[29]

This is because transgroup cooperation *results from* group social practices and institutions, and so it has no capacity to displace the practice of autonomy which domestic decisionmaking institutions embody. Transgroup cooperation can even reinforce the practice of autonomy, particularly in conditions of complex interdependence. This proposition may be derived from neoclassical realist's assumptions about group formation and group dynamics in an anarchic environment. Intergroup practices and institutions bind subgroups within and are mechanisms of differentiation without. Further differentiation occurs because subgroups develop vested identities and interests in particular institutions, structures, and processes within the group. These subgroups compete with one another for resources and power within the context of that group; hence parochial biases and perspectives are continually reinforced by the domestic social interactions, practices, and institutions in which subgroups and individuals are engaged. Such practices give meaning to action not just within the group but vis-à-vis nonmembers as well, which means they are not simply structural or strategic barriers that have to be overcome in order for a particular type of action to occur. They are instead the very cognitive filters through which actions toward other groups have any meaning to the participants involved.

The choice to engage in transgroup cooperation cannot therefore be derived from a process whereby policymakers recognize that the external environment has changed, that it requires new behaviors in order to obtain the same old interests, and so behaviors and institutions are adapted accordingly. If domestic processes act as the filters through which the external environment is perceived, then the very definition of what constitutes the external environment and a transgroup cooperative act is determined by those processes and the boundaries they proscribe for what constitutes another group. It is the social practices and institutions that give meaning to behavior *within* the group which must explain why transgroup cooperation occurs and why policymakers would be willing to engage in it. In other words, choice cannot be derived from a process in which actors step outside of the practices in which they are engaged in order that they might objectively and hence accurately assess their environmental situation and the efficacy of cooperation within its context. They must want cooperation within the context of the domestic practices and institutions in which they are engaged; otherwise the act of cooperation itself would have no meaning to them.

Logically this suggests that the choice of international cooperation *must* be derived from the practice of autonomy itself and from the specific institutions and social practices which reify it on a daily basis within the group. As the latest incarnation of groups, the nation-state's decisionmaking institutions and the individuals who participate in these institutions have been primed to defend their institutional piece of the intragroup decisionmaking pie. They are primed to do so both by the material rewards and incentives inherent to domestic decisionmaking structures and by the role-specific identities derived from participation in those structures. These effectively prevent interdependence from "sneaking up" on nation-state autonomy and continually reify the successful exclusion of other nation-states from participation in internal resource allocation decisions.

The domestic decisionmaking structures in which they participate also make state elites particularly sensitive to jurisdictional encroachment by subgroup institutions and actors. Consistent with long-standing behavioral patterns associated with traditional security alliances, domestic institutional actors often seek intergroup alliance partners in their domestic political battles with one another. In Japanese politics it is known as *gai-atsu,* or "foreign pressure," but it is a common tactic in American national bureaucratic circles as well. These moments of transnational bureaucratic cooperation depend on the fortuitous convergence of state decisionmakers whose institutions are simultaneously being threatened by other internal actors and who also have the opportunity to hijack foreign policymaking for their own internal institutional purposes. And, as with traditional security alliances, these cooperative moments are of short duration because their impetus passes as internal threat is deflected.

The kind of transgroup cooperation this produces has no capacity to displace the institutions and social practices of the state. Its purpose is to ensure that the particular state actors and institutions involved will retain their jurisdictions and control in a domestic decisionmaking arena which continues to exclude the participation of other nation-state. Hence the cooperation is not about opening up and including transgroup actors in the state's decisionmaking process and it cannot serve as an avenue for doing so behind the backs of the participants involved. Rather it is about protecting and reifying the institutional differences that already exist between nation-states and maintaining resource allocation jurisdictions within them. In the process it manages to reify the practice of autonomy rather than displace it, and if systemic interdependence has provided greater opportunities for contact between state elites then it is making a significant contribution to this reification as well.

What I am arguing here in no way contradicts the basic proposition of systemic realism that, as Elman puts it, "system level dependent variables describe international outcomes which may be arrived at regardless of the idiosyncratic behavior of individual units" (1996: 12–13). After all, it is the anarchic environment which determines that groups remain primary to begin with, while some combination of threat or power determines the extent to which transgroup cooperation may be desirable or possible for existing groups. The result is, as Copeland has observed, that "domestic level constructivism reinforces the value of a systemic realist view of world politics, at least as a baseline starting point for theory-building" (2000: 204). The starting point for the theory-building exercise provided in this chapter is that in the realist argument anarchy is not a variable and its effects, as well as that of systemic factors which do vary, must work through domestic processes and institutions that act as filters for the nation-state's foreign policy choices. This is true for all types of choice, but it may be particularly true for the choice of transgroup cooperation which appears to work against the predisposition to in-group favoritism and out-group discrimination.

Because group social practices and institutions are a means to survival for individual members, such practices and institutions are reinforcing the group's boundaries and its autonomy from other groups. The behavioral patterns this would induce, such as intragroup cooperation and transgroup competition, would ensure that autonomy and not multilateralism would remain the transgroup norm. These patterns of behavior can be attributed directly to the anarchic environment regardless of variance in threat or power in the system. Transgroup cooperation such as security alliances, on the other hand, are a product of particular systemic conditions such as threat or power within the anarchic environment (which are particularly relevant to groups concerned with survival in anarchic conditions).

This means that transgroup cooperation is not a prime or first-order behavioral pattern of anarchy. The immediate source for transgroup cooperation, as a pattern of behavior, must be the social practices and institutions of the group as a group. This is because transgroup cooperation is something that works against the competitive predispositions of groups in anarchy, and if it cannot be derived directly from the anarchic environment then it must be induced by group domestic practices themselves. Hence it is affected, perhaps more than any other international phenomenon, by the practices and institutions in which groups are already internally engaged. Any particular instances of transgroup cooperation results from domestic rather than from international influences *precisely because* anarchy remains primarily causal.

Chapter 4

Empirical Propositions
and the Bretton Woods Monetary Regime

In this chapter we move from theoretical delineation to the alternative empirical expectations and propositions which can be derived from the theories of international cooperation which have thus far been reviewed. A careful consideration of how liberal cooperation theories and the realist-constructivist alternative may be operationalized is required in order to accurately access what within the empirical record would constitute evidence to support or refute either approach. The first step in doing so is to examine the issue area and its appropriateness as a subject of comparison for alternative empirical expectations. The second step involves specifying the American actors and institutions responsible for, and involved with, the issue at the domestic level, as well as providing a historical overview of cooperative efforts and U.S. involvement in the issue area prior to the end of Bretton Woods. The third and final step requires that empirical expectations derived from these alternative theoretical perspectives be outlined within the context of the issue area. Because such expectations are rarely or explicitly identified within the interdependence and regimes literature,[1] and because the realist-constructive alternative being proposed is new, a relatively precise discussion and justification is necessary for the empirical expectations and indicators utilized.

The first step in operationalizing empirical expectations may be dealt with relatively quickly. One of the issue areas most frequently cited by liberal scholars themselves as evidence for the growth of economic interdependence among the major industrials has been international finance.[2] Within this issue area, international monetary policymaking has received particular attention, and Keohane and Nye define it as the cluster of issues seen as relevant by policymakers to decisions about what kinds of international arrangements should exist on exchange rates, reserve assets, and control of international capital movements, *along with* issues seen as relevant to adjustment, liquidity, and confidence within a given regimes or nonregime (1989: 66, their emphasis).

Monetary relations are also frequently cited as a prime example of cooperation induced by conditions of complex interdependence. Zacher asserts, for example, that "perhaps the most dramatic increases in international economic interdependence have occurred in the financial sector," which has produced "a movement toward coordination of those policies that have traditionally been regarded as most central to state autonomy—namely fiscal and monetary, and this has occurred significantly because of the integration of national capital markets" (1992: 81, 88).

In addition, Rosenau lists "monetary stability" as one of the "diverse issues of interdependence" and cites it repeatedly in his discussion of the behavioral characteristics induced by such issues (1976: 40–43). Keohane argues that persistent post-hegemonic monetary cooperation among the major industrials supports his thesis regarding the functional institutional efficiency of existing monetary regimes (1984: 187, 215). And although Keohane and Nye later acknowledged finding less evidence for complex interdependent processes in international finance than they had expected, they still conclude that politics within the issue area "lie closer to complex interdependence than to realism" and that elite interaction was significant enough to policy coordination that "those who ignore the effects of elite networks created under a previous regime risk misinterpreting reality" (1989: 112, 152).

The empirical examination offered in this study picks up chronologically where Keohane and Nye's scrutiny of, and assertions about, complex interdependence and monetary policymaking left off in *Power and Interdependence*. The focus is on post-Bretton Woods monetary cooperation in the late 1970s through the early 1990s. This also covers the period identified by Keohane in *After Hegemony* as appropriate for an analysis which seeks to test his regimes theory (1984: 218). By conforming to these parameters, this study examines empirical evidence in an issue area and time period that should be the most conducive to liberal theorizing and explanations. It is also an issue area about which most scholars believe realism has little to say.

The selection of the United States as the focus for this detailed case study is also consistent with prior liberal theorizing on interdependence and regimes. This may not initially appear to be the case since it could be argued that, because of its size, power, and particular type of government-bureaucratic structures, the United States may be unique. Keohane notes, for example, that as the declining hegemon who helped shape the post-World War II international system, the United States might be able to retain a "greater leeway for autonomous action than other countries" (1984: 26; see also Rosecrance 1986: chapter 10). However the United States has also been routinely utilized in liberal cooperative case studies precisely because size and traditional conceptions of power are assumed to become less relevant to policymaking as the condition of complex interdependence increases. The undifferentiated impact that interdependence and regimes are suppose to have means that U.S. size and power should not be able to entirely counteract their effects. In fact, as the declining hegemon grappling with the constraints and opportunities of interdependence, one would expect the impact on U.S. decisionmaking to be all the more obvious. Keohane even singles out the United States as a prime example of a government with an open decisionmaking structure which facilitates transnational cooperation (1984: 93–95, 258). Based on parameters specified by the liberal cooperation literature itself, then, the United States is a suitable selection upon which to base a case study of this kind.

In the next section the domestic actors and players within the United States who are responsible for decisionmaking in international monetary policymaking are examined. The transnational elite networks which developed prior to 1971 and which have continued to operate in various forms to this day are also examined, with particular attention to the participation in them of American economic elites. An overview of the historical record reveals that the United States has been intimately involved with, and at times a major promoter of, these transnational networks. In fact, the development of international monetary elite networks during the Bretton Woods period and any discussion of relevant American monetary decisionmakers and their bureaucratic jurisdictions are intimately bound together.

MONETARY ELITE NETWORKS AND OPPORTUNITIES IN THE AMERICAN CONTEXT

At first glance it would appear to be only natural that the Treasury Department would have the dominant role in international monetary policymaking. Yet Treasury involvement in international monetary affairs is relatively recent, beginning only with the creation of the Bretton Woods system. Strange notes that "though negotiations had often been conducted by central banks" prior to that time, "any formal commitment on trade or money matters had usually been handled by Foreign Ministries" (1976: 114). It was during the negotiations for Bretton Woods that the U.S. Treasury became involved with, and took a lead role in, international economic affairs for the first time. The Americans and British began to draft, negotiate, and implement their vision of a postwar economic order for the world before World War II had even ended (Ikenberry 1992). The first discussions between U.S. and British officials on post-war economic questions took place during the summer of 1941 between the U.S. State Department and the British Treasury. However at the State Department's insistence these discussions concentrated on trade arrangements and quickly became deadlocked over the British system of imperial preferences.

In early 1942, the U.S. Treasury began to draft a plan for the post-war economic order which shifted the focus of negotiations from trade to monetary arrangements. What followed was a particularly intense bureaucratic struggle between the State and Treasury departments in 1942 and in 1943 for control over the formulation of U.S. international monetary policy. According to Gowa, the Treasury won this struggle primarily because of the philosophical and personal compatibility between President Roosevelt and Secretary of the Treasury Henry Morgenthau (1983: 108–109). Ikenberry adds that unlike trade policy and the State Department, a consensus on monetary policy existed among British and American treasury officials which proved essential in breaking the deadlocked negotiations (1992: 319). Negotiations between the United States and Great Britain over the post-war economic question were conducted between their respective treasuries thereafter. These negotiations led to the July 1944 UN Monetary and Financial Conference held at Bretton Woods, New Hampshire, which established the International Monetary Fund (IMF) and the International Bank for Reconstruction and Development (IBRD or World Bank). The IMF began its operations in Washington in 1947 and was charged with oversight of a system of parity values for currencies with gold, whose value was set at $35 per fine ounce, as the common denominator. Member states retained the right to propose exchange rate adjustments for their currencies, and the IMF provided short-term finance in order to cover temporary balance of payment deficits.

From its inception the IMF bore the stamp of U.S. Treasury preferences and perspectives. This is nowhere more apparent than in the formal designation that the Bretton Woods agreements gave to finance ministries as the chief representatives of their government in international monetary affairs. Each nation-state was to be represented in the IMF by the top political leadership of the finance ministries and were to be accompanied by the governors of their central banks but not by foreign ministry officials. The American and British treasuries had, in effect, institutionally carved out an international economic policymaking domain from which foreign ministries were excluded in spite of their prior oversight of that domain.[3] The designation also had a blanket effect on international monetary relations thereafter in that it set a precedent with regards to representation that had significant implications for internal bureaucratic jurisdictions in other nation-states as well.[4]

While the Treasury has since become a major participant in all aspects of international economic policy, it is most dominant in the formulation of international monetary and exchange rate policy. In his review of different decisionmaking models of international economic policy, S. Cohen cites the Treasury and its control of U.S. international monetary policy as the best example of decisionmaking by a single, dominant agency (1988). In other elements of economic policymaking, such as trade or interest rates, the Treasury shares responsibility with other agencies, departments, or offices in the White House. And as Bergsten and Henning point out, because the American executive branch shares responsibility for budgets and taxes with Congress, the Treasury cannot speak with authority on fiscal policy (1996: 88–89). But the Treasury does have responsibility for policy on balance of payments, exchange rate adjustments, use of monetary reserves, voting in the IMF, the monetary role of gold, and it has direct legal responsibility for international monetary policy. In 1934 Congress appropriated funds for an Exchange Stabilization Fund (ESF) so that with presidential approval the Treasury Secretary could trade in gold and foreign currencies in order to influence the dollar's exchange rate.[5] Technically this meant that the Treasury owns most of the U.S. international reserve assets.

Prior to the end of the gold standard in 1971, the Treasury could exercise little control over the dollar's exchange rate since the dollar could only be revalued by an act of Congress. But even then Parks noted that

> there is room for a great deal of discretion in the operation of the Stabilization Fund, the control of foreign assets, the management of government cash balances, and the decisions as to types, interests rates, marketing politics, and maturities for the public debt. Congress had provided very little general guidance for the exercise of these powers. On the preponderantly international side there is generally a large degree of Treasury discretion (1968: 176).

The Treasury gained direct control over the exchange rate after the introduction of floating exchange rates in the early 1970s. Decisions about exchange rate policy are now made and executed by a narrow group of officials led by the Secretary of the Treasury and typically including the Deputy Secretary of the Under Secretary for Monetary International Affairs, the Assistant Secretary for International Affairs, and the Chair of the Federal Reserve.

While the Federal Reserve has little formal authority over the international aspects of U.S. economic policy, it is involved with international monetary policy due to its role in domestic monetary policy and foreign currency operations. The Treasury has responsibility for formulating exchange rate policy, while the Federal Reserve has independent legal authority to operate in foreign currency markets, and it acts as the executing agent for the Treasury in these markets. It does so, however, only under authorization of the Treasury which by law has responsibility for such matters. Destler and Henning have observed about their organizational relationship that

> the law grants both organizations the right to intervene in the markets, but the Treasury argues that it is first among equals and has the right both to prevent the Fed from intervening and to instruct the Fed to intervene on the Treasury's account. The Fed has challenged neither assertion by action (1989: 88).

The Federal Reserve's role in international monetary policymaking is clearly subordinate to that of the Treasury. According to Bergsten and Henning, it is because the Treasury prefers it that way that attempts to give central bankers equal status in international economic negotiations are frequently blocked by the Treasury and by the other finance ministries of the major industrials (1996: 88, 109–112).[6]

In practice, however, the Treasury and the Federal Reserve work closely with one another, and the Federal Reserve's Chair and his staff are included in all interagency coordinating and decisionmaking groups related to external monetary affairs. The Treasury and the Federal Reserve consult frequently and coordinate policy at weekly meetings held at the Secretary-Chair level as well as through daily senior staff consultations on conditions in the foreign exchange markets. The working relationship between the two agencies reflects none of the public jurisdictional wrangling that is frequently observed between the Japanese Ministry of Finance (MOF) and its central bank (Horne 1985; Rosenbluth 1989). In fact there is a marked deference to Treasury Secretary leadership in U.S. delegations to the international monetary forums that developed after Bretton Woods. While delegations typically consist of the Secretary, a deputy, and the Federal Reserve Chair, "the [Treasury] Secretary . . . is the acknowledged leader in committing the United States to any international accord" (Destler and Henning 1989: 90). In addition, the deputies who do all the preparatory work for these international meetings come from the Treasury Department, not from the Federal Reserve or the State Department.

The development of international monetary networks and forums outside the formal boundaries of the IMF occurred in the early 1960s, when the United States moved into heavy and persistent balance of payment deficits and foreign dollar holdings grew out of proportion to U.S. gold reserves. Confidence in the U.S. commitment to convert gold was shaken, and the dollar became an increasingly less attractive asset to hold as well as a focal point for massive speculation. The burden of initiating parity adjustments in these crises fell largely on the shoulders of other countries, because it was assumed that the United States was not free to alter its par value. Contrary to what had been intended at Bretton Woods, however, the devaluation of a country's currency came to be perceived as a sign of government policy failure, and so governments sought to evade devaluations for as long as possible.[7] In addition, persistent asymmetries began to appear between countries with chronic surplus or deficit balance of payments accounts. The result was a patchwork of undervalued and overvalued currencies that owners of short-term mobile capital exploited, thus putting increasing strains on the fixed value of currencies and relations between the major industrials.

The IMF's Board of Governors proved to be too large and unwieldy to effectively negotiate these issues, and only a small group of states within that body could directly affect solutions to the problems in any case. The first international monetary forum to attempt a defense of the Bretton Woods system was actually the Bank for International Settlements (BIS) which was conceived in the late 1920s as a means to depoliticize financial matters regarding German reparations, and continues to hold monthly meetings among central bank officials in Basel, Switzerland. The United States was initially suspicious of the organization when it was created in 1931, and the Treasury even recommended at Bretton Woods that it should be liquidated (Camps and Gwin 1981: 222).[8] Federal Reserve officials did not begin regularly attending its meetings until December 1960, and the United States has never officially joined the organization. But it was at the BIS's March 1961 meeting that the first attempt to stabilize the financial system outside of IMF institutions occurred. In response to considerable turmoil in the gold and foreign exchange markets following a revaluation of the deutsche mark and Dutch guilder, the central bankers issued their first press statement subsequently called the "Basle Agreement." BIS central bankers announced they would hold each others' currencies to a greater extent than they had previously, instead of converting them immediately into gold or dollars, and would make available to one another short-term lending or currency swaps of needed currencies.[9]

The Basle Agreement is significant not only in that it was produced by an informal, ongoing elite network which already existed in the issue area, but also because it was quickly followed by (and may have prompted) the creation of another informal monetary network outside the institutional boundaries of the IMF. During the 1961 IMF annual meeting in August, the U.S. Treasury Secretary called together representatives from the nine leading industrial countries (Japan was not initially included) to discuss the possibility of developing a supplementary borrowing fund among themselves which the United States could tap in order to resolve its balance of payments deficit. What grew out of the negotiations over the General Arrangements to Borrow (GAB) was the Group of Ten (G10) which was an informal negotiating network composed of finance ministers, finance deputies, and later the central bankers from Belgium, Canada, France, the Federal Republic of Germany, Italy, Japan, the Netherlands, Sweden, Great Britain, and the United States.[10] Strange notes that "included in the commitments to the GAB was the important provision that members would consult together and would keep each other informed of developments in their respective balances of payments positions 'to insure the stability of the international monetary system' " (1976: 116).

The G10 would go onto become *the* forum in which attempted solutions to international monetary problems would be negotiated in the 1960s. As G10 meetings continued throughout the decade much of the more significant intergovernmental discussions and negotiations during this period, on issues such as the balance of payments, the liquidity problem, and the creation of the Special Drawing Right (SDR), took place at G10 meetings, although final stages of negotiation were often moved to the IMF.[11] Between October 1963 and June 1964, for example, the G10 deputies conducted a study of monetary reform during which the group held monthly meetings at the French Finance Ministry.[12] The G10 was also the forum through which an initial effort to resort some currency stability was made following the end of Bretton Woods. By the late 1960s the U.S. balance of payments deficit had worsened and its commitment to the gold standard was shaky. In March 1968 the G10 negotiated the Washington Agreement which established a two-tier gold market, separating the free market from the official market, and adopted other restrictions on the conversion of dollars into gold. This essentially ended the free convertibility of gold into dollars, although the exchange rate system did not officially collapse until August 1971 when the Nixon administration announced it would no longer support it.

The Smithsonian Agreement in December 1971 partially restored the fixed exchange rate system by providing the first multilateral realignment of exchange rates among the major industrials. As had been the case throughout the 1960s, the Smithsonian Agreement was the result of G10 negotiations. The U.S. Treasury was quite public and specific in its preference for the G10 over the IMF secretariat as a forum for monetary reform consultation and negotiations. The IMF's Managing Director at the time, Pierre-Paul Schweitzer, was not even informed of U.S. plans to end the gold standard until thirty minutes before Nixon's August television broadcast. According to Frank Southard, who was then the IMF's Deputy Managing Director, Treasury Under Secretary Paul Volcker told Schweitzer that the United States preferred "G10 or a special committee of IMF Governors as the vehicle for negotiations and made it clear that the Executive Board of the Fund would not in his view be the focus" (1979: 39). The IMF's Managing Director and his staff were still permitted to attend G10 meetings and present their positions, but they had no direct participation in the group's decisionmaking.

In many ways, however, the Smithsonian Agreement was to be the G10's last hurrah as the primary international forum through which international monetary consultations and negotiations were conducted. Due to unprecedented world inflation and increasingly large accounts imbalances between countries, all major world currencies were floating by 1973 and the fixed exchange rate system had come to a definitive end. The 1970s proved to be the heyday of economic summitry, in which selective executive leaders would meet to discuss global monetary issues accompanied by their finance ministers and central bankers (Putnam and Bayne 1987). The G10 was also displaced by a smaller Group of Five (G5) which was essentially the G10 whittled down to its five most economically powerful members—France, West Germany, Japan, Great Britain, and the United States. Certainly the G10 had established the precedent for ongoing elite communication networks and interaction among the members of the G5, but those networks proved incapable of preventing the G5 from excluding other G10 members from their negotiations on monetary policy thereafter.[13] Regular G10 deputy meetings continued, and G5 treasury ministers and central bankers continued to attend quarterly meetings of the Organization for Economic Cooperation and Development's (OECD) Working Party 3, the annual IMF and World Bank meetings (in September), and the semiannual meetings of the IMF Interim Committee and the World Bank Development Committee (in April). But the networks that proved most pertinent to international monetary affairs after Bretton Woods were those between monetary elites in the G5 countries, which in 1986 officially became the Group of Seven (G7) with the addition of Italy and Canada. Attendance at these other forums has been used by the G7 ministers, deputies, and central bankers as the opportunity to meet separately, although they may even meet at other times, such as in conjuncture with economic summits (Dobson 1991: 43–45).

The G5 was the brainchild of George P. Shultz, Helmut Schmidt, and Valery Giscard D'Estaing, who in 1973 were the finance ministers of the United States, West Germany, and France, respectively. In April of that year they were meeting privately in the White House library to discuss the international monetary crisis surrounding the breakup of Bretton Woods. The idea of creating an international monetary negotiating forum with a more limited membership than the G10 was raised and their discussion became the foundation, with the addition of Great Britain and Japan for the G5. The meeting also established a precedent for G5 representation. Funabashi explains that "at the outset, finance ministers were present, along with a single official on the basis of the so-called 'principal plus one' rule, and sometimes, the central bank governors" (1989: 138). Those G5 meetings which were held separately from economic summits during the 1970s and early 1980s were also extremely informal. One U.S. administrator later described to Funabashi his encounter with the G5 in the spring of 1985:

> Our first experience with the Group of Five was via the telephone—Regan's legacy—and it looked like a chaotic mess, with everybody having misunderstandings, no records, no nothing . . . these guys would sit around and sort of read their public economic forecasts to each other for a good portion of the meeting (1989: 138).

These early meetings may have been less productive because one of the central functions of G5 monetary official meetings in the 1970s was to support the executive leader summits. There was considerably more organized activity at the meetings associated with the summits as a result.

The relationship between the G5 (as an informal and ongoing communication network between the group's monetary decisionmaking elites) and the summits between their executive heads is also interesting in that it underscores how the monetary elite networks actually determined the form and content of the summits. It is a common belief in the IPE literature that beginning with the first summit at Rambouillet in November 1975, the G5 networks were displaced as the pertinent vehicles for international monetary negotiations at least until the 1980s.[14] It was not until the Versailles Summit of 1982 that executive leaders formally recognized G5 meetings as the primary forums for monetary negotiations among their nation-states. Yet this was merely public recognition of what had already been the case for some time, because the summits had always relied heavily on the existing networks between G5 monetary officials. It was membership in the G5, initially established by the treasury ministers in 1973, that would later determine which executive heads would attend the summits. The only country invited to the first summit that was not a member of the G5 was Italy, while Canada was invited to attend subsequent summits. However regular G5 meetings continued to exclude representatives from these two nation-states until the late 1980s, and Dobson points out that G7 ministerial meetings were still sometimes preceded by a separate meeting of the G5 to discuss foreign exchange market issues (1991: 43, 140; see also Funabashi 1989: 137–142).

In addition, it was the finance ministries of the original G5 countries who set the summit agendas throughout the 1970s and early 1980s. Heads of government went to the summits accompanied by both their foreign and finance ministers, but the agenda was almost entirely economic and focused on the performance of the global economy. Because actual monetary policy negotiations were still conducted by the treasury ministers and central bankers, and because most heads of state tended to defer international monetary decisions to their finance ministries, the G5 treasuries and central banks were invariably at the center of summit discussions and negotiations. It is quite common for heads of state to leave international economic policymaking to their Treasury departments since, as Gowa points out, involvement in international monetary policy offers few rewards to the elected official and has the appearance of an esoteric, inaccessible subject area (1983: 130–131).[15] It may be more accurate, then, to view the summits not as an attempt by executive leaders to exert more control over monetary policymaking, but rather an attempt by Treasury ministers to insert greater political weight into their negotiations with one another and with other bureaucratic departments back home.[16]

Since the early 1980s, it has certainly been the case that the centrality of economic summits to the process of G5 monetary negotiations has waned. Summits continue to be important negotiating venues at which G5 monetary consultations and negotiations simultaneously occur, but Dobson observes that since the late 1970s "political oversight of the adjustment process by the summit leaders has not been pursued in any direct way. Instead, leaders have broadly delegated economic matters to the ministers" (1991: 42). The 1982 Versailles Summit is frequently pointed to as the transition point from summitry to G5 preeminence as the forum for international monetary negotiations, since the G5 Treasury ministers were charged with the task of multilateral surveillance of one another's domestic economic policies. G5 minister meetings became ongoing and independent of the actual summits thereafter. The trend in executive head deference to the monetary decisions of their finance ministries continued at the 1983 Williamsburg summit, and the delegation of these responsibilities provides most finance ministries, the U.S. Treasury Department included, with a great deal of independence in determining the institutional form that international monetary policymaking will take.

The fact that elite communication networks existed prior to the end of Bretton Woods and continued in modified form thereafter is important not only as a background for understanding post-Bretton Woods events but also for operationalizing both liberal and realist-constructivist theoretical expectations. In order for the liberal causal chain connecting interdependence and regimes to cooperation to work, state decisionmakers must have the opportunity to both learn from transnational networks and translate that learning into actual policy outcomes. In the case of American monetary affairs, it appears that both opportunities were present. American monetary elites were centrally involved with transnational networks and in the various negotiating forums which were supported by those networks. Those same elites had, within the context of American bureaucratic structures, control over policymaking in the issue area and hence the ability to determine whether American monetary policy would be conducted in unilateral or multilateral fashion. This latter attribute is important to the realist-constructivist causal chain as well, since state decisionmakers must have access to, and control over, their interaction with issue area counterparts if they are to coopt the foreign policymaking process for their own domestic, institutional ends.

That decisionmakers have this type of access, control, and hence opportunity is certainly the case in U.S. international monetary affairs. The Treasury's jurisdictional prerogatives within its own national administrative structures, coupled with the established tendency of presidents to defer to its decisions in the issue area and to its representation and dominance in international monetary forums, allows the Treasury to largely determine the course of America's international monetary policy. While it does so in consultation with the Federal Reserve, the Treasury dominates the elite communication networks in the issue area and also has the policymaking powers necessary to pursue multilateral efforts in monetary affairs. The historical record also supports the proposition that in bringing elites together, formal IOs and informal regime networks provide a useful platform whereby elites may coordinate policy if they so choose.

American monetary elites have indeed taken advantage of those platforms to engage in several periods of particularly intensive monetary cooperation since the end of Bretton Woods. The form such cooperation has typically taken is exchange rate interventions in which American monetary elites coordinate with the central banks of other major industrials to buy and sell currency in order to affect their value on the open market. Whether post-Bretton Woods U.S. monetary decisionmakers have engaged in these cooperative efforts for the reasons anticipated by either liberal cooperation theory or by the realist-constructivist alternative has yet to be determined. How we might begin to establish elite motivation based on the empirical record and so derive support for the liberal theoretical perspective in particular is the subject of the following sections.

OPERATIONALIZING LIBERAL EXPECTATIONS: A FIRST CUT

What would constitute evidence that in post-Bretton Woods international monetary affairs American monetary elites choose to cooperate because they had learned via elite networks about the limitations of unilateralism and the greater efficacy of multilateralism in interdependent conditions? Establishing why decisionmakers do what they do is always a difficult methodological task,[17] and the common approach in the field is to delineate the behavioral expectations one would anticipate from a theory's proposition, then compare and contrast those expectations to the actual behavior of decisionmakers.

Such an approach is consistent with liberal cooperation theory's causal chain as well, which assumes that lessons learned will be translated into behavior which exhibits a cooperative pattern thereafter. In other words, the theory expects that there will be a qualitative change in the behavior of decisionmakers after they have learned or discovered the realities of interdependence. This means it is the *pattern* of cooperative behavior exhibited by elites during the post-Bretton Woods period that would serve as evidence for elite learning.

It should be possible, then, to compare elite policymaking behavior in the issue area before and after a period of learning in order to determine if a pattern of elite cooperative behavior emerges which is consistent with the theory's behavioral expectations. This would require the delineation of the particular policymaking choices that would be functionally efficient in an issue area marked by increasing interdependence, and then show how elites actually behaved in the issue area. The time period with which this study is concerned lends itself readily to such a task since it involves a change in the management of exchange rates from fixed to floating rates. Hence the study is examining a period in which elites would have to learn what was functionally efficient under new issue area conditions while, at the same time, systemic interdependence remained the same or even increased.

It "should" be a relatively easy task to establish the liberal criteria for making such behavioral comparisons, but as it turns out it is not at all straightforward. The reason for this is because there is disagreement within the liberal cooperation literature itself over whether the end of Bretton Woods required a period of elite learning that would have led to measurable behavioral changes in monetary policymaking. This disagreement arises, in turn, from the two-stage process of regime creation and regime maintenance in ongoing interdependent conditions. Regime creation requires that elites abandon unilateralism for a multilateralism informed by a standard of greater functional efficiency within the issue area. At this stage, elites pursue multilateral efforts in order to overcome the deficiencies created by unilateral policymaking. Hence the form those efforts take is shaped by their immediate assessment of what would be functionally efficient in the issue area.

Regime maintenance, on the other hand, requires a pattern informed only by the type, form, or level of cooperation to which elites are already accustomed. At this stage elites pursue multilateral efforts because they believe that *any* form of cooperation in the issue area is better than reverting to unilateral policymaking. Hence the form those efforts take is shaped by their belief that existing efforts represent sunken costs and that more efficacious forms of cooperation will be too expensive to pursue, rather than an immediate desire to functionally overcome the deficiencies of unilateralism. Bryant nicely captures the difference between creation and maintenance in this regard, in his use of the terms *policy optimizing* versus *satisficing stabilization* (1995: 419).

Regime creation and regime maintenance suggest two very different and ultimately contradictory cooperative behavioral patterns. Whether post-Bretton Woods is a period of creation or maintenance makes a great deal of difference, then, to what liberal theory anticipates about patterns of cooperative behavior in the issue area after Bretton Woods and to how the theory's propositions should be scrutinized empirically. In fact, it makes a great deal of difference to whether the theory is for all practical purposes empirically falsifiable. Much of the liberal cooperation literature argues that the post-Bretton Woods period has been a period of regime maintenance, yet this claim makes it virtually impossible to delineate a pattern of behavior that would contradict the theory's behavioral expectations. Almost any policymaking behavior (even unilateralism!) can be made compatible with the theory's propositions about cooperation from this perspective.

While the problems with treating the post-Bretton Woods period as one of merely regime maintenance are examined in greater detail later, here it is important to underscore the fact that the research design adopted in this study does not dismiss out of hand the possibility that the period may be characterized as either creation or maintenance. Instead it attempts to examine the empirical record for evidence that would support the behavioral patterns and propositions derived from *both* perspectives. Because this is the case, it is necessary to delineate the alternative behavioral expectations and patterns that would be anticipated depending on whether the period under scrutiny is one of regime creation or regime maintenance.

POST-BRETTON WOODS AS REGIME CREATION AND POLICY OPTIMIZING

The literature on interdependence and regimes has been relatively specific that it was in the 1970s that the cooperative causality of complex interdependent conditions and monetary regimes first began to be felt. That decade witnessed a number of international events which realist scholars tended to view as preludes to coming disaster in the international system. Yet as Krasner put it succinctly, "while strains increased, the 1930s were not replayed" (1983a: viii). This was particularly obvious in capitalist-market relations, where trade continued and international liquidity even increased among these nation-states as the decade continued. Thus the end of the Bretton Woods monetary system in 1971 did not signal the demise of the liberal economic order. While the commitment to fixed exchange rates had ended, a commitment to liberal economic principles, or what Ruggie has called "embedded liberalism," had not (1983b). It was, according to Keohane, "the continuation of shared interests in the efficiency and welfare benefits of international economic exchange" that at least partially explained why the liberal economic order persisted (1984: 209).

Within this context, Keohane and Nye initially argued that the period immediately following the end of Bretton Woods was one of regime creation in international monetary affairs. Between 1946–1971 there was first a "recovery" and then an "international" regime in monetary policy, while 1971–1975 was a period of "nonregime" followed in 1976 by another "international" regime (1989: 74). However Keohane and Nye noted that dating the new post-Bretton Woods monetary regime was "somewhat arbitrary," so that the creation period may also have been longer (85). As Cooper points out, "one of the confusions of 1973 was that the old [monetary] regime was clearly breaking up but no new regime was yet agreed" (1975: 91). According to this formulation, then, the behavioral parameters of regime creation would apply to monetary policymaking in the post-Bretton Woods period. What would this imply for the lessons decisionmakers would have to learn, the ways in which choices and actions would become qualitatively different thereafter, and the behaviors that would serve as indicators of an increased commitment to multilateralism over unilateralism?

As we know, liberal cooperation theory is arguing that what prevents cooperation from automatically occurring in complex interdependent issue areas is the practice of autonomy. Strategic misperception on the part of economic elites leads to the continued reliance on unilateral, mercantilist policies which will ultimately produce suboptimal outcomes in interdependent conditions. Ongoing interaction and informational exchange provide the opportunity for elites to transcend this strategic misperception, and as economic elites come to realize that it was their continued reliance on unilateral policymaking which produced the suboptimal outcome, they become increasingly predisposed to multilateral efforts. They adjust their behavior accordingly so that it is supportive of multilateralism and no longer informed by unilateral tendencies. Clearly these adjustments involve a period of elite learning, and the specifics of Bretton Woods would tend to support the proposition that its end would have prompted a period of monetary elite learning, cognitive adjustment, and hence regime creation.

First, while all of the major industrials retained a mutual interest in profit maximization after 1971, the monetary arrangement that had served this goal since the end of World War II had ended. In other words, the fixed exchange rate system supported by a hegemonic power and which had required policy adjustments among the participants in pegging their currencies was no longer available. Whether one defines this as a crisis or not, it is still clear that the issue area after 1971 presented economic elites in these nation-states with new conditions to which they would have to adjust cognitively and behaviorally. The period initially following the end of Bretton Woods witnessed a number of attempts by American trading partners to resuscitate a pegged system in modified form, but with little support from the United States. Keohane and Nye refer to the early 1970s as a "learning period" in which "treasury officials and bankers began to feel more comfortable about, and even to favor, flexible rates" (1989: 83).

That a learning period would have been necessary is underscored by Solomon, who participated in the negotiations for international monetary reform:

> Initially the move to floating was widely viewed as a means of coping with speculation rather than as a basic change in the exchange rate regime . . . the reform discussions continued to envisage a par value system as the norm. . . . It would take some time for the thinking of treasury and central bank officials, businessmen, and bankers to adjust to the new regime (1982: 234).

Elites had to develop new expectation about monetary stability as a result, including a recognition that floating exchange rates did provide some opportunities that a fixed system did not. Bergsten and Henning point out that currency adjustments in a fixed exchange rate system depended on government self-regulation, yet many states during the Bretton Woods period proved unwilling to make the policy choices necessary to the system's stability (1996: 40). One of the opportunities presented by floating exchange rates was that elites "no longer faced the impossible task of defending artificial rates against speculation; the bankers saw their foreign exchange profits soar" (Keohane and Nye 1989: 83). On the other hand, floating exchange rate systems had their own adjustment problems. The private flow of capital could induce market errors pushing "currencies far from the long-run equilibrium levels needed to maintain sustainable national current account positions" (Bergsten and Henning 1996: 40–41).

Because economic elites were accustomed to the problems and virtues of a fixed exchange rate system, it is reasonable to conclude that they would need to discover the problems and virtues inherent in its opposite. Indeed, Dominguez and Frankel note that the exchange rate system which followed Bretton Woods did not involve the pure float of economist theories, in which states refrained from all operations in foreign exchange markets (1993: 6). What evolved instead was managed floating in which state authorities regularly intervened to try to influence the value of their currencies. According to liberal cooperation theory, in order to exploit the opportunities of floating exchange rates, as well as to moderate their effects, some form or level of coordination would still be necessary (Keohane 1984: 209). Authorities would need to learn not simply that some sort of intervention was still necessary to avoid suboptimal monetary outcomes, but also that intervention had to be coordinated with other nation-states.

Although the form that such cooperation would take is not immediately obvious, one form which it could obviously *not* take would be direct and extensive hegemonic management. This is the second way in which the end of Bretton Woods would require a learning period in which economic elites would discover how to more effectively obtain capitalist-market interests in different external monetary conditions. The old monetary system of fixed exchange rates had been managed by a hegemon that had established the rules and decisionmaking procedures by which participating nation-states would cooperate, and it had then used its economic clout to support those rules and procedures. The new monetary system of floating exchange rates meant the absence of such management along with the preestablished rules and decisionmaking procedures.

While there would still be an economic incentive among the major industrials to engage in some form of coordination, the end of Bretton Woods meant that monetary elites had to learn how to reach those agreements without the guidance and oversight of a hegemon. Post-1971 complex interdependent conditions meant that unilateral policymaking would still be economically inefficient and that elites who persisted in this behavior would produce suboptimal economic outcomes for their nation-states. But since elements of the environmental context for monetary policymaking had changed, elites responsible for monetary policymaking would have to discover what cooperative behaviors would be appropriate to post-hegemonic conditions. This was true for elites in secondary states, who had relied upon the hegemon to provide consistency and enforcement throughout the economic system, as well as for elites in the former hegemonic power, who now found themselves to be only one among equals at the bargaining table (Keohane 1984: 138).[18]

In fact, based on this formulation, one would anticipate that the need for perceptual and behavioral adjustment would be greatest among the elites of the former hegemon. If one concurs with liberal cooperation theory that the end of Bretton Woods also marked the end of American economic hegemony, the behavior of its elites after 1971 should serve not merely as an appropriate test case for the theory but as a critical test. That is, if complex interdependence is a systemic condition that universally forces economic elites to cooperate in order to avoid suboptimal economic outcomes, then cognitive and behavioral change should be most obvious among those economic elites who have had the greatest predisposition to unilateralism. Keohane and Nye assert as much:

> Organizing for international collective action poses a particular problem for the Untied States. Americans are so used to being dominant

in the world that, when a problem arises about which important groups in domestic politics feel strongly, there is immediate emphasis on unilateral action (1989: 236).

Of all the nation-states confronted with the necessity to learn how to cooperate in fundamentally different ways after Bretton Woods, it would be the elites of the hegemon who would need to take the biggest learning strides.

In other words, American monetary elites would have retained an interest in profit maximization that would predispose them to prefer multilateralism as a strategy for effectively achieving this goal, but their cognitive predisposition to unilateralism would prevent them from automatically and immediately recognizing that multilateralism was the preferred strategy under these new monetary conditions. In fact Rosenau, as well as Keohane and Nye, single out Secretary Treasury Connally's tendencies toward unilateralism in the early 1970s as a good example of strategic misperception (1976: 43; 1989: 118). According to the theory's parameters, however, such strategic misperception would change overtime as American unilateralism produced suboptimal monetary outcomes. American monetary elites would learn that unilateralism was counterproductive through ongoing intergovernmental contact and the exchange of information. And through these same contacts they would discover the value of multilateralism as well as have the opportunity to pursue it. As Keohane puts this, transgovernmental relations would "increase opportunities for cooperation in world politics by providing policymakers with high-quality information about what their counterparts are likely to do" (1983: 165).

Such a formulation indicates that when confronted with the suboptimal outcomes produced by unilateral policymaking, American decisionmakers would have to assess their own previous behavior, determine what particular behaviors produced the suboptimal outcome, and ascertain what new behaviors would avoid such outcomes in the future. Decisionmakers would then have to actively carry through on these beliefs in their subsequent choices and behavior. This means that one of the qualitative changes we would anticipate in the pattern of subsequent decisionmaking would be the absence of the behavior which had produced the suboptimal outcome in the first place. In addition, we should not see recidivism because, according to the theory, unilateral behaviors are abandoned when decisionmakers recognize that they produced the suboptimal outcome (and are therefore strategically inappropriate). This means that the decisionmaker's cognitive map has been altered by the experience in such a way that returning to the old behaviors that produced the suboptimal outcome would remain inexplicable within the parameters of liberal cooperation theory.

The content of behaviors must also be cognitively tied to ideas about one's own practice of unilateralism and multilateralism specifically. The decisionmaker must perceive that the suboptimal outcome was produced by the practice of autonomy, that such outcomes can only be resolved or avoided through the practice of multilateralism, and that one's own behavior is implicated in either case. In other words, decisionmakers come to recognize that they have been ignoring external conditions and consequences which ultimately do matter in their ability to obtain their own economic objectives. From this recognition they conclude that those external consequences must be taken into account when making their own monetary policies.

At minimum this greater sensitivity could simply mean that decisionmakers attempted to predict the monetary policymaking of other nation-states and to calculate the external consequences of their own unilateral decisions thereafter. But this minimal level is clearly not what liberal cooperation theorists have in mind, since the theory's central proposition is that once decisionmakers recognize those external consequences they will attempt to actively and directly affect them by coordinating their own monetary policies with others. Such a proposition can only be derived from some standard of functional institutional efficiency in the issue area itself, which is why establishing such a standard is highly pertinent to any delineation of the empirical expectations and behavioral patterns associated with regime creation. That is, in trading one type of policymaking for another, the choices made by economic elites are necessarily informed by some standard of efficiency within the issue area for which they are responsible.

Because the form this efficiency would take is part of the lesson package liberal cooperation theory assumes decisionmakers would learn in a period of regime creation in interdependent conditions, it is a guideline to the multilateral behaviors and outcomes that we should expect decisionmakers to engage in thereafter. There are, however, a variety of institutional forms which policy coordination could take and which vary according to the extent that national economic interests would be maximized. Currency integration would maximize economic interests, for example, but so could various levels of exchange rate intervention. What, then, is the standard of functional institutional efficiency implied by the liberal cooperation literature? What forms of policy coordination does the theory anticipate monetary policymakers will aspire to in conditions of economic interdependence and floating exchange rates?

DEFINING FUNCTIONAL INSTITUTIONAL EFFICIENCY IN INTERNATIONAL MONETARY AFFAIRS

The basic logic in support of some form of monetary coordination in conditions of increasing interdependence is well-known. B. Cohen summarizes it by noting that in such conditions, "any one government's actions will generate a variety of 'spillover' effects—foreign repercussions and feedbacks—that can significantly influence it own ability, as well as the ability of others, to achieve preferred macroeconomic or exchange rate objectives" (1993: 135). Bergsten and Henning point out that this creates an unintended causal loop in which, "through flows of trade and investment, monetary and fiscal policy changes in one country affect growth, employment, and inflation in others and feedback into the economy of the first country" (1996: 144). This means that a nation-state which engages in unilateral monetary policymaking will affect the nation-states with whom it is interdependent in such a manner that it causes suboptimal macroeconomic and exchange rate outcomes for itself. Such outcomes provide what B. Cohen calls "the basic rationale for monetary cooperation," because "it can internalize these externalities by giving each government partial control over the actions of others" (1993: 135).

A considerable body of literature exists in support of this basic logic, and there is an equally sizable literature (what B. Cohen describes as "a virtual avalanche") which challenges this logic in some respect. Frequently, however, it is not the logic that is under attack but its applicability to the actual practice of international economics. Much of the argument against monetary coordination is premised on the idea that practical obstacles prevent nation-states from ever sustaining the cooperative effort or from gaining the necessary measure of control over one another's actions. As the editors of one volume on international monetary coordination put it, "the center of debate" does not necessarily involve the "nature of the theoretical case for policy coordination," but instead "the *practice* of policy coordination" itself (Branson, Frenkel, and Goldstein 1990: 2; their emphasis). While the acknowledgment of such obstacles does not sink the logic of coordination, it has generated considerable disagreement in the economic literature over what types of institutional monetary arrangements would be most efficient in a world of floating exchange rates.[19] Unfortunately the interdependence and regimes literature provides little specific guidance in this regard, since it tends to speak in general terms of the desire for functional efficiency and hence the need for cooperation in international monetary affairs. There are, however, a number of institutional arrangements that can obviously be dismissed as inappropriate to liberal cooperation theory expectations.

Some analysts argue, for example, that the growth of private capital flows in conditions of floating exchange rates make any intervention, control, and hence coordination of monetary policy among national authorities a practical impossibility. The result, as Bergsten and Henning note, is a fairly widespread view in the economic literature that "the only two viable exchange rate regimes are freely floating rates and a currency union à la European Monetary Union (EMU)—the two polar extremes" (1996: 89–90). Neither of these extremes appear to be consistent with the expectations of the interdependence and regimes literature. Lack of control over transnational activity is certainly posited as an attribute of complex interdependence, but it is supposed to cause a desire to coordinate policy, not a complete policymaking acquiescence to currency market speculation. What makes multilateralism an attractive strategic choice in such a condition is that it allows nation-states to *re*exert some control or influence over international monetary affairs, albeit by influencing the policies of one another. Since "clean" or freely floating exchange rates would mean that policymakers disdained from *any* policy intervention or operations in foreign exchange markets, this is clearly not the standard of functional institutional efficiency which liberal cooperation theorists have in mind.[20]

As discussed earlier, the interdependence and regimes literature also distinguishes between a loss of autonomy, which interdependence has encouraged, and a loss of sovereignty, which is supposed to remain relatively intact. Because currency integration would have dramatic implications for national sovereignty, it would not be consistent with liberal cooperation theory expectations in this context. Hanrieder clearly differentiates coordination from integration, for example, arguing that despite pressures for the latter, governments resist it for a variety of reasons so that "policy coordination has become a substitute for integration" (1978: 1284). As a result, it is possible to reject as appropriate to liberal cooperation theory the two extremes of institutional efficiency by which many economists have argued monetary policymaking should be organized. Yet along the spectrum between these two extremes there is still room for variation in the level of optimality and hence cooperative institutional form that one could argue is desirable in international monetary affairs. Williamson and Miller point out that there are at least three alternative international monetary systems which involve some level of coordination short of currency union (1987: 39).[21]

The first monetary arrangement would be the resurrection of a fixed exchange rate system in which currencies are pegged and only occasional parity changes are expected in the face of fundamental disequilibrium (see McKinnon 1971, 1984). The second arrangement would be a system of managed exchange rates such as the post-1979 European Monetary System (EMS) in which expectations regarding pegging and parity changes are considerably more flexible. And the third would be acceptance of floating exchange rates but with intervention adjustments according to jointly-agreed nominal national targets. That the first two institutional systems would involve a high degree of policy coordination among their participants is clear from the Bretton Woods system and from the "blueprint" for a managed exchange rate system which Williamson and Miller go onto propose (1987).

Coordination in the latter would involve not only exchange rate interventions, but also automatic adjustments in both short-term interest rates and fiscal policies according to preaccepted growth and exchange rate targets. While the precise policy formula could vary in a managed system (as a comparison between Williamson and Miller's blueprint and the EMS would attest), the degree to which macroeconomic coordination must occur in support of the system is still relatively significant.

In this regard the intensive policy coordination required of the first two institutional arrangements does not appear to be consistent with liberal cooperation theory expectations. Keohane and Nye's description of the behavioral patterns necessary to support post-hegemonic cooperation is relatively modest in comparison, involving a willingness "to accept mutual surveillance of domestic and foreign economic policies, criticism of these policies by other governments, and coordinated interventions into certain international markets" (1989: 232). Central to their vision of interdependent cooperation is the cognitive recognition of international constraints so that "there will need to be a general acceptance of 'collective economic security' as a principle for the conduct of international economic policy," as well as "more international participation in their decisionmaking processes." The need to recognize international constraints when making policy is reemphasized by Keohane in his discussion of "myopic self-interests" which are pursued "without regard to the effects of one's actions on other issues or other values" and must be converted into "farsighted" self-interests "taking into account the impact of violating international rules and norms on other state objectives" (1984: 99, 124). Thus the emphasis is on decisionmakers becoming more accepting of some minimal level of policymaking coordination in general.

Keohane's discussion of post-Bretton Woods monetary cooperation in *After Hegemony* also implies considerably less coordination than what would be required of a managed exchange rate system. Although "shared interests in efficiency and welfare benefits" provided continuity for international economic exchange after Bretton Woods, "obtaining these benefits, however, requires a continual series of agreements—for instance, to monitor exchange rate interventions, expand resources at the disposal of the IMF, or lend money to countries in difficulty in conjunction with austerity programs" (1984: 209). Such a description implies a relatively low level of coordination in comparison to a managed or fixed exchange rate system. In addition, at no point does Keohane discuss the necessity for intensive policy coordination in short-term interest rates, fiscal policies, and so on. While other liberal cooperation theorists are even less specific with regards to their institutional expectations in the issue area, almost all would accept minimal levels of coordination in the issue area to be consistent with the theory's empirical expectations. Zacher is representative in this regard, as the institutional forms he cites as evidence for the theory's propositions about economic collaboration are quite varied (1992: 87–88).

It seems reasonable to conclude, then, that what liberal cooperation theorists have in mind is the evolution of Williamson and Miller's third type of monetary management in the post-Bretton Woods period. That is, the theory anticipates that the major industrials would accept the general principle of floating exchange rates and would not seek to reestablish a fixed exchange rate system. However because a freely floating exchange rate system means that monetary policymaking is conducted in an uncoordinated and autonomous fashion, suboptimal monetary outcomes such as currency misalignments would result. Elites would then learn from such outcomes (and from the international monetary crises that might be generated by them) that unilateral policymaking was undesirable while some degree of policy coordination in foreign exchange markets was necessary. This would lead them to establish a system of national exchange rate targets and to participate in coordinated interventions in order to support those targets.

Such a system sets the definitional threshold of international monetary efficiency and anticipated behaviors on its behalf at a relatively low level. Hereto, however, one cannot escape differences of opinion over the precise details of such a system. Williamson has provided what is perhaps the most detailed and frequently cited proposals regarding a target-driven post-Bretton Woods floating exchange rate system whose minimal goal would be the limitation of severe and protracted currency misalignments (1985; Marston 1988: 121–125). He differentiates target zones from pegs with formal margins, arguing that the former "have 'soft margins' which the authorities are not committed to defending," and that this makes a target zone system more flexible with regards to coordination requirements (Williamson 1985: 64). Williamson also argues that the target zone widths should be set relatively high, perhaps as high as 20 percent, before a joint exchange rate intervention was required (in comparison the Bretton Woods system had a 1 percent band on either side of its par value), that the target zones be publicly announced, and that the zones be continually adjusted to reflect differential inflation and changes in real exchange rates (64–72).

Some critics disagree with Williamson over whether publicity is a necessary or even beneficial component of such a system, arguing that it encourages speculators to mount frequent attacks on the set margins thus forcing national monetary authorities to continuously defend them.[22] Goldstein is not adverse to a target zone system, for example, but argues that because "a move to 'loud' target zones" might be "counterproductive" in this regard, targets should be set quietly with private consultation among the G7 being the first step should a problem arise (1994: 303). Yet much of Goldstein's disagreement with Williamson's proposal hinges on a more fundamental difference over how much emphasis the exchange rate, as opposed to other indicators and objectives such as domestic price stability, should receive in establishing target zones and in triggering a coordinated response.[23]

One of Williamson's justifications for choosing the exchange rate is that it forces attention to external affairs:

> [It] is an attempt to introduce an element of concern for external factors into domestic policymaking without any risk of making the external element dominant, motivated by the political judgment that this is the most internationalist solution that several of the major powers might be prepared to contemplate in the foreseeable future (1985: 88).

He is echoed in these sentiments by Bergsten and Henning, who argue that in Williamson's target zone system, "monetary policy would be called upon to address the exchange rate only when the rate had moved to a considerable extent," but that constant monitoring would provide a "sensible injection of external considerations" into policymaking and hence make it more consistent with external conditions (1996: 102, 105).[24] Thus, "an international monetary regime that would enhance the role of external factors, particularly the exchange rate, in the determinations of national monetary and eventually fiscal policies could help tilt domestic outcomes in desirable directions and play such a role" (109).

In addition, most scholars appear to concur with Williamson that publicity is an essential mechanism of credibility in that it "encourages honesty and improves the information available to the market," which then acts as pressure on policymakers to take external conditions into account and ensure that policy will be "sensibly conducted" (1985: 68).[25] Bergsten and Henning argue that the public announcement of the target zones is an instrument of compellance for decisionmakers to continually monitor the exchange rates, adjust the bands accordingly, and intervene to prevent dramatic and protracted misalignments from occurring. The concern about speculators is misplaced, they argue, because it is applying behavior induced by a fixed exchange rate system to an entirely different type of system in which, "if the zones are based on underlying economic fundamentals and the authorities establish their credibility in defending them, speculators would have little incentive to push rates to the edges of the zones" (1996: 115).

Cohen concurs that regardless of the form monetary coordination takes, it must be visibly sustained because while a modicum of cheating might be acceptable, "the commitment of the collectivity" to monetary cooperation "must be seen to be enduring" or else "incentives will indeed be distorted for state and nonstate actors alike" and hence produce outcomes that are counterproductive (1993: 138). Dominguez and Frankel also point out that by preannouncing limits, policymakers can get speculators to work for rather than against them (1993: 136). And ultimately even Goldstein acknowledges that credibility of target zone commitments could counteract market speculation so that some of his skepticism hinges on whether publicity contributes to credibility (1994: 305).

More to the point of this study, however, is that the emphasis on public and external factors in these proposals is highly reminiscent of Keohane and Nye's discussion of multilateralism in a post-hegemonic complex interdependent setting. In fact it is probably no accident that there are noticeable commonalties, since Bergsten and Henning cite both *Power and Interdependence* and *After Hegemony* in the course of their discussion (1996: 80). Bergsten and Henning go onto argue that extensive policy coordination among the G7 is not necessarily required and that various other mechanisms could achieve optimality when compared to the alternative of unilateral monetary policymaking. As with Keohane and Nye, unilateralism's bottom line is the complete neglect of the external context in which exchange rate issues operate, which would then produce suboptimal outcomes.[26]

The result is that the monetary literature has outlined a standard of functional institutional efficiency in international monetary affairs which comes quite close in content to that implied by the interdependence and regimes literature. Because each element of the proposed system is argued to contribute in interrelated ways to its optimality, the proposals are taken as a whole package and are outlined in table 4.1. This target zone system appears to be consistent with the type of institutional monetary arrangement envisioned by liberal cooperation theory in the post-Bretton Woods period.[27] As such it represents the type of policy coordination that monetary elites should desire and act upon if liberal cooperation theory is correct to posit a causal link between the condition of interdependence, economic elite learning, and international cooperation. And it is used in chapter 5 as the standard by which to assess whether the pattern of post-Bretton Woods American monetary elite behavior conforms to the theory's expectations regarding regime creation.

In other words, if liberal cooperation theory is correct when it posits that functional institutional efficiency is central to cooperative choices in the issue area, then there is good reason to anticipate that this would be the type of institutional arrangement to which policymakers should aspire. American support for, and participation in, the development of such a post-Bretton Woods system would constitute evidence for the theory's propositions about elite learning in conditions of interdependence. Such a system would indicate not only that external consequences had acquired greater saliency for U.S. monetary policymakers, but also that those policymakers had purposefully eschewed unilateral policymaking for coordinated policymaking.

Table 4.1
Anticipated Cooperative Behaviors in Response to Suboptimal Monetary Outcomes

Real exchange rates used as primary indicators triggering action[1]
Jointly-agreed upon target zones with wide bands and soft margins[2]
Publication of agreed-upon target zones
Constant monitoring, surveillance, and data collection of exchange rates and of
    each other's monetary and fiscal policies via the IMF or some other
    institutional mechanism
Public announcements regarding potentially destabilizing government policies via
    the IMF or some other institutional mechanism
Frequent adjustments to agreed-upon target zones ("crawling zones")
Coordinated exchange rate interventions (not fully sterilized) to discourage rates
    from straying[3]
Ongoing and joint public commitment to the target zone system

Source: Based on the international monetary target zone system outlined by Williamson (1985) and Bergsten and Henning (1996).

[1]Williamson is careful to specify that the system is based on calculating "real" or "equilibrium" as opposed to "nominal" or "parity" exchange rates and discusses the means by which real rates may be established (Williamson 1985: 19–22; Williamson and Miller 1987: 55–58).

[2]Williamson argues for bands of 20%, Bergsten and Henning (1996) for bands of 10%.

[3]In a sterilized intervention, official purchases or sales of foreign currencies are offset by domestic transactions so that the monetary liabilities of both the home and foreign authorities remains unchanged. The argument against sterilization is that while it may have a temporary signaling effect on the market, it produces no lasting or substantive effect on exchange rates.

Of course such a system could fail to take shape due to the actions of other nation-states which are beyond the scope of this study to incorporate. We must obviously be careful to examine the development or movement toward such an exchange rate system within the context of U.S. monetary elite behavioral patterns alone. Regardless of what monetary elites from other nation-states were doing, if liberal cooperation theory is correct we should see a pattern of U.S. monetary elite behavior after Bretton Woods which supports the development of such a target zone system. That behavioral pattern must also be progressive because within the parameters of regime creation a target zone exchange rate system represents a functionally efficient ideal toward which monetary elite behavior should be consistently inclined over time. Obviously all of the elements of such a system need not be established at once. Indeed liberal cooperation theory anticipates stages of learning, experimentation, and institutional innovation, so that some elements of the system might develop at different stages as well as be subject to change and modification. How to actually conduct the publicity of target zones or monitor one another's policies might be the subject of some trial and error. Thus the development and transition to such a system need not be smooth, and uneven development would not contradict the theory's expectations.

However, the logic of liberal cooperation theory does indicate that elite behavior may not be regressive. Post-1971 U.S. monetary elites should consistently seek to develop, support, or adjust to an international, publicly announced, target zone exchange rate system. It would be entirely incongruous with the regime creation expectations of liberal cooperation theories, on the other hand, if U.S. monetary elites initially supported and then subsequently sought to subvert, contradict, abandon, or ignore such a system by returning to unilateral policymaking. Even given a time lag in elite learning or unevenness in institutional development, once American monetary elites took the first steps in support of such a system, there is no deductive space within the theory to allow those elites to entirely reject such a system and to engage in outright behavioral backsliding. The process of regime creation may include learning in fits and starts, but it cannot logically allow the complete unraveling of lessons learned.

This point is worth underscoring. According to the theory the reason why elites would want such a system is because they have lost cognitive faith in the efficacy of unilateralism and now recognize the greater efficiency of multilateralism instead. If those multilateral efforts prove to be useful in the resolution of suboptimal outcomes, then a subsequent reversion to unilateralism is logically inconsistent with the theory's expectations. Indeed, such a reversion would indicate that the kind of learning anticipated by liberal cooperation theory and its impact on organizational procedures had failed to occur. A pattern of recidivism following multilateral efforts at regime creation would cast significant doubts on the theory's ability to explain those efforts as a result.

POST-BRETTON WOODS AS REGIME MAINTENANCE
AND SATISFICING STABILIZATION

The central proposition of a regimes maintenance argument supports the expectation that recidivism will not occur as well. This may not be immediately obvious, however, because the behavioral pattern anticipated during a period of regime maintenance in conditions of interdependence is different from that of regime creation. The central difference between the two periods and their associated patterns of behavior lies with the issue of progressive institutional efficiency. If creation implies an ongoing and consistent movement toward a functionally more efficient institutional arrangement within the issue area, maintenance suggests that optimality will not necessarily inform behavior after the initial institutionalizing efforts have been made.

According to Keohane, "Cooperation often builds on itself, but this process is by no means inevitable," and "international regimes tend to maintain patterns of cooperation, but they do not necessarily facilitate innovative expansions of cooperation in response to crisis and change" (1984: 210; see also 103, 215–216). Krasner concurs:

> Basic causal variables may be less important for explaining regime persistence than for explaining regime creation. While the influence of basic casual variables does not evaporate, principles, norms, rules, and decisionmaking procedures come to have their own exogenous impact on outcomes and behavior (1983b: 359).

In other words, functional institutional efficiency in the issue area can only be used as a standard by which to judge the initial cooperative effort; it cannot be used as a means to assess the cooperative effort thereafter. Thus the "more 'efficient' (under given circumstances) a regime would be, the more likely it is to be created," but "regimes *persist* despite the declining satisfaction of their members, precisely because *creating* a regime in the first place is so difficult" (Hasenclever, Mayer, and Rittberger 1997: 37, 38–39; their emphasis).

The implication of this formulation for policymaking behavior is that while elites will initially move toward the creation of a more efficient institutional arrangement, at some point in time progressive movement will cease. The idea of a publicly announced target zone exchange rate system would only inform their initial attempts to address suboptimal outcomes produced by unilateral policymaking. Whatever elites believed had worked in that instance would then be the behavioral standard to which they returned in order to resolve any subsequent suboptimal outcomes. And because the desirability of further institutional development would not necessarily inform their choices and behaviors thereafter, we should not anticipate the progressive development of a target zone exchange rate system. The baseline for a confirmatory behavioral pattern would instead be established by whatever choices, policies, and behaviors were contained in the initial cooperative efforts undertaken to resolve suboptimal outcomes in the issue area.

This difference in the behavioral patterns anticipated in periods of either regime creation or maintenance means that precise dating of the transition from one to the other would be necessary in order to determine when the differing behavioral patterns would apply. Post-Bretton Woods American monetary policymaking would appear to lend itself to such an identification, since 1971 marked the end of a fixed exchange rate system which, as Keohane and Nye had originally proposed, would require a period of elite learning and regime creation. One would anticipate that at some point later in the decade, or perhaps earlier in the next, a cooperative effort would occur in response to suboptimal monetary outcomes which would then establish the behavioral baseline for monetary policy coordination thereafter. Any attempt to empirically assess the theory's propositions regarding regime maintenance would have to identify this behavioral baseline in order to compare subsequent elite behavior to it. After the transition had occurred, consistent movement toward the creation of a target zone exchange rate system would no longer be the standard by which to assess elite behavior. That is, while initial cooperative efforts would have been informed by such a standard, subsequent coordination would not involve its further development. Rather whatever attributes of the system were adopted in the initial attempt would remain the policies and behaviors to which elites returned thereafter.

Remarkably this is *not* how liberal cooperation theorists have proceeded; nor has there been any effort to follow through on such an empirical study in the liberal cooperation literature. The reason for this is because most liberal theorists do not consider the end of Bretton Woods to have required a period of regime creation.[28] It is instead routinely characterized as a period of regime maintenance. Despite his initial interpretation of post-Bretton Woods as a period of regime creation, for example, Keohane later argued in *After Hegemony* that the international monetary regime principles established by the United States simply continued. The end of Bretton Woods was instead the abandonment of specific regime rules:

> Although the rules of the Bretton Woods regimes were altered in 1971–73, the principles of multilateralism and relatively unfettered capital flows were maintained. After the advent of flexible exchange rates, major capital markets continued to become increasingly open, and elaborate cooperative networks, including private and central banks as well as finance ministries, flourished (1984: 208; see also 186–187, 209–210).

He further asserts that the major industrials did not need to learn to abandon unilateral behaviors such as "beggar-thy-neighbor policies in response to dilemmas of collective action" because "the persistence of a regime provided reassurance about others' intentions and practices" (210).

Both Ruggie and Cohen agree with this interpretation of the end of Bretton Woods. Cohen argues, for example, that "no matter how profound the regime's recent change may appear, it does not in fact add up to a transformation of kind" and "at the level of principles and norms, the regime remains very much as it was" (1983a: 317). The end of Bretton Woods was instead an "operational adaptation" in the context of a deeper commitment to "play by the rules of the game" (333). Similarly Ruggie maintains that change in international monetary policymaking after 1971 "has been at the level of instrument rather than norm" and "represent adaptations to new circumstances" (1983b: 228). From this perspective, we should not assess post-Bretton Woods behavioral patterns according to the yardstick of regime creation, in which elites would create progressively more efficient institutions in the issue area. We should instead use the standard of regime maintenance, in which subsequent policymaking behavior would be compared to the existing cooperative baseline, however inefficient that baseline might be.

The problem with this perspective is that the end of Bretton Woods was the destruction of the prior cooperative behavioral baseline and the instruments which accompanied it. It represented a fundamental disjuncture in the exact form which monetary cooperation had taken to that point so that in the early 1970s it is empirically impossible to argue that a cooperative policymaking baseline still existed in the issue area. Certainly there was some continuity in elite communication networks, as well as in international trade and exchange, which indicates that shared capitalist-market principles and norms remained in tact. This may be the intended point, but none of this constitutes continuity of cooperative policymaking within the issue area itself. As Dominguez and Frankel point out, under the Bretton Woods system "intervention was not viewed as a discretionary policy instrument available in government's policy tool kits" (1993: 5), yet coordinated exchange rate interventions were the primary form that post-Bretton Woods monetary cooperation took. As a result there *is* no continuity in the policymaking instruments from one period to the next. When the Bretton Woods decisionmaking rules were abandoned so too were the actual policymaking behaviors whereby any maintenance or preservation of cooperative behavior could be measured and assessed. This has the effect of making the theory empirically unfalsifiable.

In addition, if we accept that the post-Bretton Woods period has been one of regime maintenance in which no learning was necessary, then we would also have to believe that after 1971 American monetary elites cooperated in international monetary affairs because they had vested interests in, and commitments to, the cooperative monetary arrangements which they had just actively, purposefully destroyed. This is obviously a bizarre argument to make since the end of Bretton Woods was a clear repudiation by U.S. elites of the specific multilateral institutional and behavioral forms that international monetary policymaking had taken between 1945 and 1971. As Henning notes, in the final analysis the United States was "fundamentally unwilling to bear the costs of maintaining the regime" (1994: 263), so that the end of Bretton Woods can be read as a relatively straight-forward example of recidivism.[29] When confronted with ongoing suboptimal outcomes, U.S.

decisionmakers engaged in unilateral, neomercantilist policymaking in order to address them. While liberal cooperation theory is still unable to explain why such outright recidivism would occur after several decades of multilateral efforts in the issue area, treating the period which followed merely as one of regime maintenance reduces the theory's explanatory abilities even further. It means, in essence, that unilateral policymaking is perfectly consistent with the behavioral expectations of interdependence and regimes theories.

This is a real problem for these theories since their central premise is that unilateralism and multilateralism are antitheses of one another and that the latter comes about due to the displacement of the former in elite strategic perception and behavior. In order to empirically support such a proposition there must be identifiable differences in what would constitute unilateral and multilateral behaviors. Yet if it is possible to argue that the unilateral policymaking which led to the end of Bretton Woods is consistent with the theory's expectations, then there appears to be no behavioral or institutional changes within the issue area, short of the complete collapse of the international capitalist-market system, which could disprove the theory. It becomes impossible to use actual policymaking activity in the issue area to support *or* contradict the theory. It simply is consistent, we are told, although we have no way of empirically establishing how and in what ways it is so.

The reasons why the regimes maintenance argument is so problematic can be traced to the flaws in its deductive logic and these are explored in chapter 6. For our purposes here, the problem remains the impossibility of operationalizing the argument in any meaningful sense in order to compare it to the empirical record and to assess whether the theory can accurately account for that record. Without identifiable empirical consequences, we cannot compare alternative theoretical accounts of these events. It is for this reason that this study categorically rejects the characterization of the post-Bretton Woods period as merely the continuation of an established monetary regime. This does not mean that it rejects the regime maintenance argument itself, however, or its potential applicability to monetary policymaking at some point after 1971. Rather what is being rejected is the notion that the end of Bretton Woods did not constitute or require a period of regime creation and that what came after it can be characterized simply as a continuation of the established regime in monetary affairs. Since such a characterization makes it impossible to establish the behavioral expectations that would support or contradict the theory's propositions, it is deductively illogical and empirically unsatisfactory.

Given that 1971 events destroyed the prior cooperative behavioral baseline in the issue area, a new baseline to which elites would have vested interests and commitments would have to be established before satisficing behavior would kicked in. In other words, in order for the behavioral patterns anticipated in a period of post-Bretton Woods regime maintenance to be established and delineated, there *must* be an initial period of regime creation which sets the cooperative baseline for the period of regime maintenance thereafter. Keohane and Nye had originally suggested 1976 as the transition year to a new regime in monetary affairs, but given how close to that date they were writing it seems unreasonable to hold the theory to that particular transition date. There should be a wider latitude for dating such a transition, particularly since Keohane later asserted that "the 1980s should provide an appropriate period" for an application of his post-hegemonic regimes argument (1984: 218).

It would also be inappropriate to arbitrarily date a transition that we cannot know a priori actually occurred. The empirical record itself should serve as a guide for determining if and when U.S. monetary elites shifted from optimizing to mere satisficing in their cooperative efforts. Because any subsequent cooperation after the initial efforts could result from the desire to either optimize or satisfice, any given instance of U.S. monetary elite cooperation could be accounted for with either of these behavioral patterns. Thus the historical record must be examined simultaneously for evidence of both behavioral patterns.

OPERATIONALIZING REALIST-CONSTRUCTIVIST EXPECTATIONS

While the behavioral pattern during a regime maintenance period may be different from that of a regime creation period, in neither period is there deductive space for recidivism. Progressive institutional development may not be a characteristic of regime maintenance, but nor is a return to unilateral policymaking and behaviors which directly undermine the initial cooperative baseline. That baseline was still the result of elite recognition that unilateralism had produced suboptimal outcomes and that some form of multilateralism would not. Hence the baseline was initially informed by what was functionally efficient within the issue area and represents a cognitive development which precludes reversion to a unilateralism that contradicts it thereafter. Cognitive satisficing is not, after all, the same thing as cognitive regression. Thus even if subsequent choices are not informed by this same standard of efficacy, a return to unilateral policymaking would not be anticipated and so, as with a period of regime creation, we should not see regression in a period of regime maintenance either. That is, we should not see U.S. monetary elites establishing a cooperative baseline and then subsequently subverting, contradicting, abandoning, or ignoring that baseline in their relations with other major industrials

This type of pattern would be consistent with the realist-constructivist alternative outlined in chapter 3, however. According to that alternative, the individuals who are responsible for making cooperative choices for the group do so as a result, and through the prisms of, the group practices in which they are engaged. Group practices represent a package which obtains the immutable goal of survival for group members; hence that package takes causal precedence for policymakers (both cognitively and institutionally) over an issue area interest as an objective in its own right and in its pursuit independent of the social practices of the group. All issue area interests are in service of the group itself and can only be experienced through the social institutions which glue the group together and constitute it as an entity separate from other groups. Because an issue area interest cannot be experienced separate from group practices, internal decisionmaking institutions take causal precedence in the pursuit of issue area interests.

This means that any attempt to pursue the maximization of wealth on behalf of the group is informed, first and foremost, by the group's social practices and institutions. In fact the pursuit of any goal is evaluated, encouraged, and constrained by that process context, and efficiency of policymaking behavior and choices can only be defined within that context. It cannot matter theoretically or practically to the national policymaker that in conditions of complex interdependence multilateralism would most effectively obtain capitalist-market economic interests. What matters instead are the domestic practices and institutions which make the policymaker a "maker of policy" on behalf of the group in the first place. As a package, these processes serve a purpose entirely different from that of maximization of wealth as a goal in its own right.

Of course it is tempting here to insist that because state interests may be equated with societal interests in modern liberal democracies, societal demands for higher standards of living force state elites to make capitalist profit maximization a primary goal in order to fulfill their own functions and responsibilities. The proposition that societal pressure may be interpreted as the carte blanche for elites to revamp state institutions remains highly dubious, however, since society also participates in the processes which give "elite" its meaning. From a realist-constructivist perspective, society is also cognitively and structurally predisposed to contextualize external, systemic imperatives within group practices and institutions.[30] This means it defines issue area interests within the context of the social practices and institutions which have evolved within the nation-state groupings as well. These practices not only serve the interest in group survival, but also bind subgroups and individuals to one another and balance substrata interests and concerns in ways particular to the group. Thus the extent to which society demands any specific interest or outcome and so is willing to accept the types of dramatic institutional changes implied by standards of functional institutional efficiency in particular issue areas is highly circumscribed.

Nor does "demand from below" change the fact that to act as a state elite is to reify the practices of the state and the differences of governance to which it is attuned. Downs points out, for example, that "although many officials serve the public interest as they perceive it, it does not necessarily follow that they are privately motivated solely or even mainly by a desire to serve the public interest *per se*" (1967: 87). Among the goals which could motivate officials, Downs lists those related to self-interest within the institutional context (e.g., power within the bureau, money income, prestige, and job security) before a desire to serve the public interest (84). While it may be possible to assume that elites are utility maximizers, what they are attempting to maximize is not necessarily the formal social goals for which they are responsible.

In fact, because the institutions of contemporary nation-states embody autonomy as a constitutive principle, they are predisposed to its practice and consider cooperation only within the context of domestic political structures which have a logic entirely their own and in relation to each other. These institutions are objects of subgroup competition in their own right, because they involve the ability to determine resource allocation within the group and because individual participants derive their identities as state elites from them. This means that even when groups pursue wealth and a host of other nonsecurity related interests, the act of transgroup cooperation can only be evaluated within the context of group practices, many of which involve competition for decisionmaking control and jurisdiction within the domestic realm. Since these institutions and practices establish the context within which all choices for the group are made, it is only possible to understand why cooperation occurs as it does by examining the domestic political context in which national policymakers operate.

One broad pattern that can be anticipated from this perspective is that the international cooperation which occurs in interdependent issue areas would not be efficient from the perspective of the issue area. It is hardly a revelation from a realist-constructivist perspective that multilateral management of interdependent issue areas is so frequently "of the wrong kind or is executed poorly" (Gallarotti 1991: 183). If the intent of such multilateral management were the joint maximization of an issue area interest, this would be remarkable news indeed. But since a realist-constructivist alternative assumes that the choice to engage in transgroup cooperation is derived instead from domestic processes, many of which are not informed by the issue area interest and do not have its maximization as their primary goal, functional *in*efficiency from an issue area perspective would actually be the anticipated norm.

So too would be a pattern of ad hoc cooperative efforts which had little lasting effect on the way in which American monetary policymakers went about their business. Public enthusiasm for multilateral efforts would be followed by a reversion to unilateral policymaking, because the source for such efforts would be domestic conditions and not systemic conditions in the issue area in question. State elites would be using cooperation to further their own institutional interests relative to other domestic institutions, and so their commitment would be to their institutional power and autonomy within the group, not to the act of international monetary cooperation itself. And while stabs at multilateral management may do nothing to further the cause of functional institutional efficiency in conditions of complex interdependence, they may be quite effective at obtaining other institutionally-derived goals within the domestic context. These goals could include protecting institutional interests from encroachment by other domestic group's; defending bureaucratic, executive, or legislative jurisdictions and prerogatives; or avoiding policy choices and actions that would undercut parochial constituency support or individual power.

If the initial multilateral effort proved effective at meeting these type of domestic challenges and thereby defusing them, the impetus for moving beyond initial effort to actually affecting substantive changes in policymaking institutions would be defused as well. In fact, the impetus for maintaining *any* multilateral effort would effectively dissipate, which is why the reversion to unilateral policymaking following multilateral efforts would be an anticipated behavioral pattern of the realist-constructivist alternative. Because the efficacy of multilateralism has no meaning beyond domestic processes, nor is it ever intended to by the policymakers who chose it, its efficacy can only be determined within the domestic context. That context ensures that cooperation is chosen not to overcome decisionmaking autonomy from other nation-states but in order to maintain and reinforce it.

RESEARCH DESIGN SUMMARY

There have been periods of particularly intense monetary cooperation among the major industrials during the post-Bretton Woods period, and in each of these periods monetary cooperation took the form of a coordinated exchange rate intervention. It is possible to divide the post-Bretton Woods monetary policymaking record into discreet cooperative events that may be compared and contrasted with the behavioral patterns anticipated during regime creation and maintenance. Thus with each successive cooperative act we must ask not only if it reflects movement toward a functionally efficient institution in the issue area (i.e., a publicly-announced, target zone exchange rate system), but also whether the behavioral baseline established in the last cooperative event was maintained. Since evidence for either pattern in each successive act would be confirmatory evidence for liberal cooperation theory, each period of cooperation in the issue area must be examined in comparison with the last and in light of both behavioral patterns. It is only by proceeding in this comparative, chronological manner that we can establish whether the empirical, historical record supports the evolutionary expectations of liberal cooperation theory.

It is also an appropriate means by which to determine if recidivism occurs instead. According to liberal theory what accounts for policy coordination is the elite's desire to either optimize or satisfice interests in the issue area. This means that once coordination has been put into play, it must continue in one of these two forms in order to support the theory's propositions. And in this context it is important to underscore that not just any evidence of learning will do. The interdependence and regimes literature has some very particular expectations about what it is that policymakers are suppose to learn and what sort of policymaking behaviors they will pursue as a result. One does not really need the assistance of IR theory to anticipate that suboptimal outcomes might occur in the issue area after Bretton Woods and that such outcomes would require a policymaking response. Nor does it seem to be a theoretically contentious observation that American monetary policymakers might engage in some form of regular exchange rate management in response to such outcomes.

What is contentious, however, is whether the management that evolves in the issue area must necessarily involve multilateralism. Liberal cooperation theories insist that the management of monetary policy will require policy coordination with other nation-states. Not all forms of exchange rate management would be consistent with the theory's expectations as a result. Management that involves uncoordinated intervention in exchange rate markets, for example, would still be a form of unilateral policymaking and would therefore not qualify as evidence in support of the theory. In a similar vein, coordinated interventions would support the theory only if there was progressive movement toward their institutionalization (in the form of a target zone system), or if a chronological comparison across interventions revealed behavioral consistencies regardless of their efficiency (thus reflecting satisficing behavior). What would not support the theory, on the other hand, is if coordinated interventions remained ad hoc or exhibited no discernible consistency in their form, timing, or conduct over time. And if subsequent suboptimal outcomes were caused by the active rejection of multilateralism despite prior engagement in it, or if elites selected policies to deal with such outcomes which neither optimized nor satisficed (according to prior behavioral standards), then policymaking regression would have occurred. An increasing tendency for this sort of regressive unilateralism would contradict liberal cooperation theory's behavioral expectations and support realist-constructivist expectations instead.

In other words, it is not enough that when decisionmakers ignore currency values they do so at their own peril, or that they learn from these perils that some form of intervention in exchange rate markets can stabilize currency values. To be consistent with the expectations of the interdependence and regimes literature, policymakers must seek to coordinate their actions with other nation-states, and they must do so in a manner that is informed by a standard either of functional institutional efficiency or of "satisficing" as established by prior coordinations. Decisionmaking behavioral patterns which match neither optimizing nor satisficing expectations after several cooperative plays cast serious doubts on liberal cooperation theory's ability to account for the pattern of post-Bretton Woods American monetary cooperation. It would instead be a pattern consistent with the realist-constructivist alternative that has been proposed here. It is only by comparing events chronologically that it is possible to determine if what occurred from one event to the next was a regression to unilateral policymaking instead of the evolution of optimizing or satisficing behavior.

In summary the research design which informs chapter 5 accepts that both functional institutional efficiency *and* subsequent investiture in post-1971 cooperative monetary efforts might account for U.S. monetary cooperation after Bretton Woods. Even if we find that post-1971 U.S. monetary cooperative efforts do not meet the minimal standard by which efficient coordination would be defined in the issue area, the potential for U.S. elite investiture could make those efforts the standard by which cooperative behavioral patterns would have to be assessed thereafter. It is only decreases in status quo cooperative efforts which would definitively contradict liberal cooperation theory's empirical expectations. That is, the theory's overall ability to account for monetary policymaking patterns after Bretton Woods only becomes suspect if *both* of these conditions fail to hold.

Such a research design works ultimately by a process of elimination. Each successive period of U.S. international monetary policymaking is being compared with the last to determine if one of three potential outcomes occurred. Specifically, each event is being comparatively examined to determine whether there was further development of a functionally efficient international monetary arrangement, whether cooperative policymaking behaviors were maintained from the last event, or whether neither of these outcomes occurred and elites instead reverted to unilateral policymaking. The first two outcomes are consistent with liberal cooperation theory while the last is antithetical to it and is instead consistent with the realist-constructivist alternative.

blank 142

Chapter 5

U.S. International Monetary Cooperation, 1971–1993

Have post-1971 American monetary policymakers behaved in a manner consistent with the expectations of liberal cooperation theory? Have they learned that unilateralism is strategically inappropriate while multilateralism is functionally more efficient at obtaining monetary goals in a world of increasing economic interdependence? Have policymakers translated this lesson into multilateral monetary arrangements which have either evolved progressively or, at the very least, served as a guidepost for continuity in subsequent policymaking? Alternatively, have policymakers pursued cooperation in an ad hoc manner, exhibiting no discernible consistency in cooperative form, timing, or conduct? Have policymakers instead continued to rely on unilateralism, reverting to it despite prior engagement in, and commitment to, multilateral efforts? This chapter seeks to answer these questions by reviewing U.S. policymaking in the post-Bretton Woods era.

"THE DOLLAR MAY BE OUR CURRENCY BUT IT'S YOUR PROBLEM"

The final decision to close the gold window in 1971 was made over the weekend of 13–15 August at a secret Camp David meeting between Nixon and a small group of his top advisers.[1] According to Charles Coombs, who was at the Federal Reserve Bank of New York and was responsible for Treasury and Federal Reserve operations in the gold and foreign exchange markets up until early 1975 when he retired, only Arthur Burns, the Federal

Reserve Chair, was opposed to ending the pegged exchange rate system (1976). Among the participants at the meeting was Treasury Secretary John Connally, who had replaced David Kennedy in February 1971. Connally had made no secret of his skepticism of the IMF or of his conviction that American allies were engaged in unfair trading practices while also refusing to pull their weight under the American defense umbrella.[2] Thus when the task of defending and executing the administration's new monetary policies fell to Connally, it was hardly a surprise that monetary system reform was not high on his list of priorities. As Coombs puts it, "Connally had become the prime spokesman for the doctrine of benign neglect that now reached it fullest flower in the policy slogan: 'The dollar is our currency but your problem.' No American effort would be made to support the dollar through a return to convertibility or even through Federal Reserve operations in the exchange markets" (1976: 219).[3]

That Connally himself was not predisposed to participate in negotiations to reform the international monetary system quickly became obvious to most policymakers at the time. But those same participants assumed that a return to some sort of fixed exchange rate system was inevitable once the crisis had subsided. One of those participants, Robert Solomon, notes that throughout this initial post-Bretton Woods period "no one questioned the desirability of a return to a system of 'fixed parities' " (1982: 193). The idea of reworking the system to include greater policymaking flexibility (e.g., widening the pegging margins) had been the subject of an academic conference and publication in 1970.[4] Even in these earlier explorations, however, it was taken as a given that the monetary system would remain one of pegged exchange rates backed by the U.S. dollar with convertibility into gold.

This assumption was undoubtedly prolonged by the mixed signals emanating from American monetary policymaking itself. Throughout this period American monetary policymakers consistently encouraged and engaged in negotiations to reform the fixed exchange rate system. And, just as consistently, they refused to support those reforms with substantive policymaking actions, even going so far as to pursue policies which completely undercut them at times. According to Odell, this produced the central puzzle of the immediate post-Bretton Woods period in U.S. monetary policymaking: "Why did Washington invest considerable diplomatic effort in reforming and preserving the par value regime, and yet at the same time act in ways that raised question[s] about pegged rates and contributed to the regime's disintegration?" (1982: 293). The Smithsonian Agreement is a case in point.

The Smithsonian Agreement was announced on 18 December 1971 and was the culmination of monetary discussions among the G10 throughout the fall. Immediately following Nixon's August announcement European currency markets had been closed for a week, and market speculation was rampant after they reopened on an uncoordinated basis later in August. The currency markets were the primary subject of discussion at most international meetings and forums (e.g., the G10, IMF and OECD) between September and December. Because European policymakers (particularly the French) anticipated the return to fixed exchange rates, they wanted the United States to agree to a devaluation of the dollar.[5] According to Solomon, there was a widespread conviction among European policymakers that a revaluation of their own currencies absent an American devaluation would simply let the United States "off the hook" (1982: 169). Because the United States had not routinely subjected itself to the same balance of payments discipline it expected of others, it would be given no assistance in avoiding tough choices.

Yet for much of the fall Connally gave the distinct impression that he was in no hurry to reach an agreement, largely because he was not that averse to a floating exchange rate system. In fact with the exception of Burns, none of the major players in U.S. international monetary policymaking were particularly anxious to return to a parity system, which goes a long way in explaining why floating exchange rates came about. By November Nixon signaled to Connally that it was time to reach an agreement on realignment and what followed was the Smithsonian Accord.[6] At a 17–18 December G10 meeting at the Smithsonian Castle in Washington, D.C., the United States and its allies reached agreement on an exchange rate realignment based on an increase in the $35 official gold price by 8.57 percent to $38 per ounce (Coombs 1976: 222). A devaluation of the dollar was accompanied by smaller devaluations of some currencies and upward revaluations by differing amounts for others (the mark and yen included).[7] It was agreed that the trading bands surrounding these new central rates would be widened to 4.5 percent, and Solomon notes about the haggling over precise appreciations relative to the dollar that "whenever the ministers seemed to arrive at an impasse, Secretary Connally would remind them that continued generalized floating was always an alternative to an agreed realignment" (1982: 207).

The widening of the bands specified in the Smithsonian Accord suggests movement toward the kind of target zone exchange rate system that would be anticipated in a period of post-Bretton Woods regime creation. But the Smithsonian Accord would not last long, largely because U.S. monetary policymakers refused to take even the most basic and necessary actions to support it. Exchange markets were initially relieved after the Accord was announced, but this quickly gave way to market anxieties over the fact that the dollar remained inconvertible and that it might be devalued again. Coombs notes that "market concern accordingly focused on the risk that certain foreign central banks might suddenly withdraw from their Smithsonian commitments to defend their currencies at the new upper limits by buying inconvertible dollars in unlimited amounts" (1976: 223).[8] Between January and February 1972 successive waves of speculation drove many currencies up to their official ceilings. Throughout the spring of 1972 pressure had been building on the British pound. In June it was swept off its Smithsonian parity and was floating by the end of the month. Coombs notes that in trying to beat back successive waves of speculation and to defend the pound, Common Market currencies were all driven off their Smithsonian parities as well, and yet simultaneously there was a "total absence of any commitment by the United States to help defend the new structure of parities" (1976: 225; see also Solomon 1982: 217).

As the Federal Reserve official responsible for exchange market operations at the time, Coombs's frustration with the Treasury's international monetary policy is palpable. He complains that his repeated warnings to Treasury officials to intervene forcefully in the exchange rate markets were just as repeatedly ignored (1976: 225). The lack of concern or willingness to engage in operations to support the parities was hardly limited to the Treasury however. Paul Volcker, who was Treasury Under Secretary for Monetary Affairs at the time, observed about Federal Reserve Chair Burns that:

Despite his enthusiastic support of fixed exchange rates, he seemed to me to have a kind of blind spot when it came to supporting them with concrete policies. Certainly, I saw no evidence that the White House was any more committed to preserving the Smithsonian exchange rates (Volcker and Gyohten 1992: 104; hereafter Volcker 1992).

Thus the United States stood by idly while the entire burden for protecting the Smithsonian parities fell on the shoulders of its allies and their central banks. When the Treasury finally did agree to limited resumption of Federal Reserve exchange market operations in defense of the dollar, by reactivating the Federal Reserve swap network on 18 July 1972, Coombs notes in frustration that Treasury officials called the next day to put a stop to any more trading (1976: 226–227).

At the same time tentative steps were being made to reform the international monetary system. As with the Smithsonian, U.S. policymakers played a major role in initiating these negotiations and in setting their agenda. And, as with the Smithsonian, U.S. policymakers would also refuse to take the actions necessary to support the negotiated reforms in which U.S. policymakers themselves had played a major role. The question of systemic reform had already been taken up by a small interagency group organized by Volcker under the direction of his deputy, Jack Bennett. The group had not made much progress on the subject, however, because according to Volcker, "John Connally had not encouraged much reform discussion, thinking it premature" (1992: 118). In March 1972 Connally authorized Volcker to begin consultations over an appropriate forum for reform negotiations, suggesting that the twenty nations which comprised the existing representation of the IMF's Executive Board might be appropriate.[9] Although Connally's views on reform would soon become a moot point, as he was replaced as Treasury Secretary in May, his suggestion did determine the forum in which reform negotiations were eventually conducted. That group was known as the "Committee of 20" (C20) and was drawn from the IMF Board of Governors. After 1974 it would be renamed the "Interim Committee" and continued to serve as a forum for reform discussion.

Connally was replaced by George Shultz, whom Solomon reports was "somewhat of a monetarist, very much a 'free market' man, with a leaning toward floating exchange rates" (1982: 220; see also Odell 1982: 306–311). Upon taking office, Shultz asked Volcker for the U.S. plan on international monetary system reform: "I had to confess they did not exist," says Volcker, "at least not in the sense of a considered position paper that had been internally debated and adopted" (1992: 118). Shultz asked that something be prepared in time to present at the IMF annual meeting in late September. Volcker then worked up an outline of a reformed international monetary system that became known as the "Volcker Plan" and served as the basis for the subsequent negotiations.[10] The suggested system was still one of pegged exchange rates with the United States acting as its guarantor, but it also had wider margins with the option to temporarily float if necessary. An additional innovation was the use of disproportionate gains or losses in reserves as an indicator to guide the adjustment process (Solomon 1982: 226–227).

There was a great deal of optimism expressed at the IMF meeting that year as a result. Although European currencies had been swept off their Smithsonian parities over the summer, market speculation had diminished after July. The Smithsonian Agreement appeared to be holding, and negotiations for a reformed international monetary system were finally underway. The C20 began to meet on a regular basis that fall and would do so in order to hammer out an agreement over the next two years. However the optimism was to be short-lived and the agreed-upon reforms never implemented. Currency speculation began again in earnest at the beginning of 1973, leading the Italians to float the lira on 20 January with the Swiss quickly following suit. The Treasury allowed the Fed to intervene in currency markets in late January and also negotiated a further 10 percent devaluation of the dollar, but by early February the dollar had fallen to its new floor against various currencies. In the face of continued, massive speculation and pressure on the dollar, the Nixon administration still refused to support the Smithsonian parities. Solomon notes with regards to this crisis that, given the choice, policymakers in the Treasury, Federal Reserve, and White House preferred floating currencies to another overt devaluation of the dollar (1982: 231).

The result was that speculation against the dollar continued and markets were closed on 1 March 1973 as the European Economic Community (EEC) and G10 held emergency meetings (Solomon 1982: 231–234). When markets officially reopened on 19 March, a floating currency system had become a reality. Yet the C20 participants continued to negotiate, under the assumption that a pegged exchange rate system was still desirable, and tended to view the March 1973 currency floats as "a temporary departure from normality" (334). From March 1973 to early 1975 the value of the dollar would swing wildly in what Coombs characterizes as "roller coaster progress":

> For my own part, I had become increasingly concerned over the absurd and damaging gyrations of the dollar against the Continental European currencies during the previous two years. Over that 24 month span the dollar rate against the mark first plummeted by 31 percent, rebounded by 30 percent, slumped again by 17 percent, rose once more by 12 percent, and fell off again by 10 percent (1976: 234–235).

The Treasury remained largely unconcerned with these gyrations and, according to Coombs, it always took pleading from the Fed before the Treasury would allow it to participate in coordinated interventions. Such interventions remained relatively rare as a result, so that between March 1973 and February 1975 the United States only participated in two.[11]

The first occurred in July 1973 when speculative pressures produced such disorderly trading conditions that a number of New York banks were refusing to quote rates for the major European currencies (Coombs 1976: 231). With exchange trading essentially grinding to a halt, the Treasury authorized Federal Reserve representatives to reach an agreement on a coordinated intervention while they were attending a BIS meeting in Basel. The Fed's intervention totaled slightly more than $270 million, but the extent and nature of the intervention was considerably less than Coombs had hoped. Solomon observes about the intervention that "when the Treasury did agree, it apparently did so grudgingly. And it kept Coombs on a short leash. He reported to the Federal Open Market Committee (FOMC) on 17 July that he had been unable 'to secure Treasury agreement to anything more than secret intervention through commercial bank agents'" (Solomon 1982: 338). Nor did the operation signal a new willingness to participate in coordinated interventions on an ongoing basis. Subsequent U.S. currency market interventions were unilateral, "remained limited to no more than day-to-day smoothing operations," and the next coordinated intervention would not occur until February 1975 (Coombs 1976: 233).

Meanwhile the reform efforts of the C20 had continued, but were to be irrevocably damaged by the October 1973 oil embargo of the Organization of Petroleum Exporting Countries (OPEC). As Solomon notes, no one was willing to commit to a par value when the impact of the oil crisis on their future balance of payments was so uncertain (1982: 258–259). Even French policymakers, who had been the staunchest supporters of a par values system, began to suggest that the world might have to reconcile itself to floating exchange rates. Yet the C20 deputies continued to meet, and Solomon compares their continued diligence in attending to the technical details "to the twitching of an animal's lower extremities after its head had been cut off" (261). The C20 made its final report public in June 1974, but the world of floating exchange rates into which it was introduced made the report's central concerns over par values and convertibility irrelevant.

While the failure for the reform exercise could hardly be placed entirely on the American doorstep, its consistent refusal to support the values agreed upon at Smithsonian or act to stabilize the value of the dollar certainly played a major role. U.S. policymakers behaved as if the dollar's exchange rate value was simply not an issue and that they had no responsibility for encouraging its stability in currency markets. It may have been that the Watergate hearings, which had begun in May 1973, were a major distraction for the Nixon administration throughout this period. But the fact remained that the goal to which the C20 reform exercise was committed was not one shared by the majority of U.S. monetary policymakers. Indeed, Volcker notes that "my personal disappointment that we had failed to create a new Bretton Woods amidst all the turmoil was not widely shared in the United States government. Those content with floating currencies felt no urge to keep the negotiations alive" (1992: 123).

While the preference for clean floating was moderated in both the Nixon and Ford administrations over time by a willingness to manage the currency's volatility to some extent, multilateralism was never an essential element of that management. Federal Reserve interventions into currency markets continued to be limited in scope and unilateral in nature. The wild gyrations of the dollar which continued throughout 1974 left Treasury officials relatively unfazed, as they "allowed the dollar-mark rate to roll back and forth like loose cargo on a ship" (Coombs 1976: 236).[12] In early 1974 the Fed resumed currency market interventions but these were uncoordinated and daily amounts were kept modest. According to Coombs,

> throughout 1974 the Trading Desk of the New York Federal remained confined by the straitjacket of administration policy limiting intervention to no more than braking an excessively sharp decline of

the dollar on any single day. Total intervention by the Federal during all of 1974 came to no more than $1 billion (234).

In addition, "U.S. Treasury spokesmen had continued to voice publicly their opposition to anything more than daily smoothing operations in the exchange markets . . . for fear of seeming to buck fundamental trends" (235).

Another episode of coordinated intervention would not occur until February 1975. Coombs reports that at the time he "made a particularly strenuous appeal to Burns for more forceful exchange market operations in support of the dollar, and he secured the necessary policy clearances within Washington" (1976: 236).[13] Over the next six months the Fed would intervene to the tune of $1 billion and managed to reverse the dollar's slide by the summer of 1975. Thereafter the dollar would fluctuate within a relatively narrower band for the next two years, and neither the Ford administration nor the early Carter administration would pursue coordinated interventions as a major component of U.S. monetary policymaking. In fact, as we shall see, the early Carter administration actually encouraged dollar instability as a means to put pressure on its allies for other macroeconomic adjustments.

There were no other attempts to reform the pegged exchange rate system either. In early 1974 Shultz had been replaced as Treasury Secretary by William Simon, and Jack Bennett became the Under Secretary for Monetary Affairs. Solomon notes that both Simon and Bennett were much more public and explicit than their predecessors about their support for floating exchange rates (1982: 269). In this they were supported by some members of Congress who disliked the C20 report and wanted floating to remain a long-term option as well. The result, as Henning puts it, is that the Nixon and Ford administrations were relatively "content with floating exchange rates, and willing to let the effort to reform the international monetary system in the C20 negotiations lapse inconclusively" (1994: 269). The Carter administration (and all subsequent administrations) did nothing to revive those efforts.

The exchange rate system which had emerged and was legitimized at the Rambouillet summit in November 1975 could be characterized as "dirty" floating. The summit statement acknowledged that restoring fixed parities was no longer a G10 objective, that floating was a legitimate option, and that central bank interventions were an acceptable means to prevent "erratic fluctuations" and to maintain orderly currency markets. The G5 countries, along with Italy, agreed to set up a system of consultation for this purpose, with their central banks conferring daily and finance ministers meeting quarterly. The Rambouillet statement was given a formal IMF stamp of approval at the Interim Committee's early January 1976 meeting in Jamaica. Due in part to the fact that 1976 was also a presidential election year, there were no other significant developments in U.S. monetary policymaking until 1977 when Carter took office.

Yet as Volcker notes of the Rambouillet statement, "the call for close collaboration to achieve the 'orderly underlying conditions . . . for financial and economic stability' did not offer any real guidance as to how the requisite cooperation would be achieved" (1992: 143). As he puts it,

> Stability in exchange rates, while devoutly to be desired, would have to emerge from "orderly underlying economic and financial conditions" rather than from any specific government decision to determine an appropriate rate. Nations were to avoid "manipulating" exchange rates, and the IMF itself was to exercise firm surveillance efforts so that efforts to distort the market through intervention or otherwise would be discouraged (141).

At the same time, however, Solomon points out that the French had given up on a fixed exchange rate system in return for what they had believed was an "agreement by the United States to accept greater responsibility for the movement of its exchange rate in the market" (1982: 274). Exactly what constituted "manipulation" versus "appropriate management" depended on where one sat. As Solomon goes onto observe, "the interpretation of this principle raises thorny questions and, in later years, created a considerable amount of acrimony." Indeed one could argue that Carter monetary policymakers would in fact take management responsibility for the movement of the dollar, but only so they could manipulate its value for other American economic goals.

Ultimately there is not much supporting evidence for regime creation during this period. The Rambouillet summit set up the consultative networks between the relevant policymakers for the purposes of coordinating interventions into exchange rate markets. Yet U.S. monetary policymakers had demonstrated no commitment or inclination to support coordinated interventions as an ongoing monetary policymaking mechanism. The establishment of those networks was a good example of what Solomon notes is a basic maxim of politics: "When politicians cannot agree on substance, they will always come up with an agreement on procedure" (1982: 257). As we shall see, it is a maxim repeated in international monetary affairs throughout the post-Bretton Woods period. And while the Treasury appeared to have learned during this period that some form of exchange rate intervention was necessary in order to avoid suboptimal outcomes, coordination was not considered a necessary component of dollar management. Market interventions were unilateral, governed by short-term perspectives, and coordination was grudgingly authorized.

It may have been that the Federal Reserve was more predisposed than the Treasury to multilateral efforts and coordinated interventions. Coombs observed in 1975 that "although Burns and the New York Federal disagreed on many things, we shared an acute distaste and distrust of free floating exchange rates, and market experiences over the past two years had thoroughly vindicated our judgment" (1976: 236). Yet from Volcker's perspective at the Treasury, Burns did not appear to be any more enthusiastic about or supportive of coordinated interventions. Indeed, Coombs is forced to admit that the need for coordination with others "seemed to be lost on most Washington officialdom" (238). And in any case the Federal Reserve did not control international monetary policymaking, the Treasury did, and it was clearly indisposed to pursue coordinated efforts to stabilize the international monetary system.

Nowhere is this lack of commitment to multilateralism more apparent than in the work of the C20. Having used a proposal from a member of the U.S. Treasury itself as the basis for two years of monetary negotiations, the committee's final report turned out to be superfluous. And it was made so because that same bureaucracy, and the administration it represented, had no substantive interest in reforming the international monetary system along the lines specified by its original proposal. Reform was a rhetorical exercise, leaving Volcker to observe, "I don't know how many speeches and toasts my counterparts and I delivered over the 1960s and 1970s to the god of international cooperation, but coordination was another matter" (1992: 144). This too would be a pattern repeated throughout the post-Bretton Woods period. It is difficult to find any evidence for regime creation in U.S. international monetary policy between 1971 and 1976 as a result. That policymakers had to learn how to live in a world without a pegged exchange rate system and made policy adjustments accordingly is undeniable. There is little evidence during this period, however, that policymakers were also learning that some form of multilateralism was efficacious and so should be a component in those policy adjustments.

"IN A BOAT WITH AN ELEPHANT"

When Carter assumed the presidency in January 1977 the need for macroeconomic coordination was an administration theme from the start. Before January had even ended Vice President Mondale was dispatched to tour various allied countries and encourage them to accelerate growth. This was the so-called locomotive strategy which was primarily the product of various American think tanks and posited that if nation-states running payments surpluses stimulated their own economies, they would act as "locomotives" in spurning world economic growth. The locomotives in question were Germany and Japan, neither of which took too kindly to pressure from the United States to adopt domestic stimulus packages. Yet the call for stimulus emanated from a variety of quarters (not just American), and it was given impetus by the recession recovery slowdown in the latter half of 1976.[14] In early February 1977 the Carter administration adopted its own stimulus package to the tune of $30 billion and called again on Germany and Japan to follow suit. U.S. economic performance subsequently improved, while Germany and Japan's did not which further fueled American requests for stimulus.

The adoption of expansionary policies was a theme the Americans harped on at the London summit in 7–8 May 1977 (Putnam and Bayne 1987: ch. 4). They wanted Germany and Japan to commit to specific growth targets, and the statement issued after the summit indicated that the G5 were jointly committed to the idea of targets. But no target numbers were actually listed and Germany and Japan continued to resist the adoption of domestic stimulus packages in practice. In order to prompt their compliance, U.S. Treasury Secretary Michael Blumenthal began to use the dollar as a macroeconomic weapon. As Volcker describes this, beginning on 25 May 1977 Blumenthal, "in the first of a series of comments widely interpreted as an attempt to talk down the dollar, assert[ed] that Germany and Japan have agreed not to resist market pressures for the appreciation of their currencies" (1992: 350). Similar comments by Blumenthal after the Paris OECD meeting in June singled out the exchange rates of Germany and Japan for possible appreciation (Solomon 1982: 345–346). Thus "as time passed, the Carter team's desire for an appreciation of the yen and the mark to help make the [locomotive] strategy work by increasing U.S. trade competitiveness became increasingly explicit; it was widely interpreted in financial markets as a certain insouciance about the fate of the dollar" (Volcker 1992: 146).

Not surprisingly, the currency markets responded to this insouciance so that in the fall of 1977, after two years of relative dollar stability, the dollar began to depreciate. Between September 1977 and October 1978 the dollar's effective rate fell 17.1 percent, which Solomon noted was the largest exchange rate movement since rates had begun to float in March 1973 (1982: 344). That U.S. monetary policymakers had prompted the slide and did little to arrest it throughout this period produced considerable consternation among its European allies who, as Solomon observed, were still "in a boat with an elephant" (358). Blumenthal would later argue that his comments had been misinterpreted, that he had not anticipated such a dramatic depreciation, and Volcker characterizes Blumenthal's statements as "less guarded comments" (1992: 146). Solomon also argues that U.S. policymakers tried "with actions as well as words to dispel the widespread notion that it was indifferent to what was happening to exchange rates" (1982: 347).

Yet the impression that Blumenthal and the Carter administration were pleased to see dollar depreciation was reinforced by America's own behavior in the currency markets. In early January 1978 the Treasury and Federal

Reserve announced that they would undertake coordinated interventions with other central banks in order to check the speculation and reestablish stability in the foreign exchange markets.[15] Yet Volcker characterizes these interventions as "gestures" with "little follow through," and the dollar continued to slide throughout 1978 (1992: 149). The fact remained that U.S. policymakers still had an incentive to let it do so. Japan had agreed to a 7 percent growth target on 13 January, and in return the United States had pledged "in principle" to reduce oil imports and control inflation. But U.S. policymakers had made no commitment to stabilizing the dollar because they were suspicious of Japan's real commitment to the growth target. Meanwhile Germany had remained recalcitrant and it was not until the G7 Bonn Summit in July that it finally agreed to increase government spending by 1 percent GNP in return for the end of oil price controls in the United States (Putnam and Bayne 1987: ch. 4). At the summit Japan also tried to reassure the United States that it would indeed adopt the measures necessary for domestic expansion.

There was no discussion of the exchange rate at Bonn, however, and the dollar continued to depreciate after July with U.S. policymakers paying little attention to its performance. This meant, as Volcker observes, that the dollar's behavior in exchange markets was effectively undercutting any positive effects of the Bonn summit (1992: 149). By October 1978 the dollar had reached record lows against the mark and yen, driven there primarily because according to Volcker the markets could "sense that for the Carter administration a stable dollar was a much lower priority than growth and jobs." Carter's own stature in the markets took a beating throughout the month of October. On the 15 October Congress passed a modified version of his energy package which did not include the decontrol of oil prices agreed to at Bonn, and on the twenty-fourth Carter announced an anti-inflation program which was so poorly received by the markets that the dollar's slide actually accelerated. Although the Fed and other central banks intervened heavily in exchange rate markets over the next four days, the dollar-mark rate still went from 1.81 to 1.71 and the dollar-yen from 181 to 178 (Marston 1988: 101). "Again the insistent question arises whether it would have been more appropriate to have paid attention much earlier to the warning signal sent by a falling exchange rate" (Volcker 1992: 151).

Up until this point, then, the treatment of the dollar had been similar in kind across three presidential administrations. The dollar had not been the subject of activist policymaking because its value was not considered a high priority and was treated instead "as the residual of domestic macroeconomic policies" (Henning 1994: 306). The behavior of Carter administration officials *after* October 1978, however, does conform in some respects to the behavior one might anticipate during a period of regime creation in the issue area. After having encouraged an exchange rate misalignment which led to suboptimal market outcomes, the Carter administration then switched to a more activist exchange rate policy on 1 November 1978, and this activism included a greater emphasis on multilateral efforts. They announced that the discount rate would be raised and that an unprecedented package of $30 billion in foreign currency resources had been assembled for the purpose of currency market intervention.[16] Over the next several weeks the Fed, German, Swiss, and Japanese central banks would intervene repeatedly in an attempt to strengthen the dollar.[17]

At roughly the same time, officials from the Treasury and Fed encouraged the initiation of international monetary negotiations to set up a "Substitution Account" in the IMF. The idea behind the account was that it could serve as a receptacle into which foreign central banks would deposit the "dollar overhang" in their portfolios. Its proponents argued that it would enhance exchange market stability because it would allow foreign central banks to reduce their dollar reserves without having to sell them on the open market, thereby putting further downward pressure on the dollar's value (Gowa 1984).

It was the Managing Director of the IMF, Johannes Witteveen, who had first proposed the idea of such account during the spring of 1978 and at a time when the dollar had been consistently depreciating. But, with the exception of Treasury Under Secretary Anthony Solomon, the rest of the Carter administration had shown little interest in the idea. This disinterest was due in part to the administration's continued use of the dollar as leverage against Japan and Germany, and in part because "it had all the earmarks of an official bailout for the dollar" (Solomon 1982: 285). Anthony Solomon had remained its advocate, however and, after the "dollar rescue package" in November "he was able to push for the proposal without arousing suspicion that he was currently worried about the value of the dollar" (286). Momentum within the Carter administration for initiating negotiations grew during the fall of 1978 and reflected a relatively more activist policy stance toward the exchange rate. Negotiations began in the Interim Committee in late 1978 and continued until April 1980.

Ultimately, however, the Interim Committee's efforts to create a substitution account would not bear fruit. In a pattern highly reminiscent of the C20 reform exercise, the Interim Committee would be unable to produce substantive agreement, and a large part of the reason was that U.S. policymakers were not committed to its creation. Treasury enthusiasm for the project waned overtime due to several factors. In her detailed analysis of the negotiations, Gowa points out that under particular circumstances the account would incur financial losses, and the issue of who would act as a guarantor made most participants balk (1984: 671). Thus the G5 could not resolve differences over how to divide burden sharing.[18]

Subsequent international political and market conditions would also affect the desirability of such an account. Even as the negotiations were beginning in the fall of 1978, events in the Middle East were unfolding that would by 1980 make the problem of dollar overhang superfluous. OPEC oil prices began to rise in December as the Iranian revolution began to affect world supplies. When the Shah fled in mid-January 1979 an oil crisis ensued, and OPEC raised oil prices again in late March. This oil crisis erased Japan's accounts surplus and spontaneously reversed the dollar decline, which had actually fallen back to 1.828 to the mark and 194.40 to the yen in late December 1978. Thus throughout 1979 the dollar appreciated. Volcker notes that there was little interest in the subject of monetary coordination at the June 1979 Tokyo summit and no significant monetary agreements were reached (1992: 352). External political and market conditions had taken away the necessity to make tough choices in order to implement monetary coordination, which would have been a hard sell domestically in any case.

This last issue was the final strike against the substitution account because the Carter administration was by this time facing considerable domestic difficulties. In early August 1979 Carter came back from a Camp David soul-searching trip to fire a number of his Cabinet members and deliver what would become known as his "malaise speech." Blumenthal was replaced as Treasury Secretary by G. William Miller (who had to this point been Federal Reserve Chair), and Paul Volcker took over Miller's position at the Fed.[19] Solomon writes that when Miller began to examine the proposed details of the substitution account, he realized that the idea of burden sharing was a losing proposition domestically. The task would have been impossible during the upcoming election year:

> And even after the election, the task was not an appealing one. How does one persuade a Congressman from the Midwest, say, that dollars deposited in a little-understood account should be guaranteed by the United States when American citizens' savings were being eroded by inflation and carried no such guaranty? Secretary Miller's political instincts apparently led him to reject the notion of a guaranty completely. . . . (Solomon 1982: 292)

According to both Solomon and Gowa, that rejection effectively deadlocked negotiations on the substitution account so that by April 1980 the account would be "dead in the water" (Gowa 1984: 667). As with the prior C20 negotiations, the bureaucracy which had encouraged the initiation of negotiations now proved to be unsupportive of their purpose when given the choice between the status quo or supporting the reform effort through coordinated policy adjustments.

That status quo did not reflect much concern with institutionalizing monetary coordination either. From November 1978 through 1980 the Treasury and Fed remained active in currency markets and intervened on a regular basis, frequently in coordination with other central banks. But as with Treasury policy under the Nixon and Ford administrations, these were limited to daily smoothing operations. Thus there was no movement toward the creation of a target zone exchange rate system and, by the fall of 1979, even some complaints from European quarters that the United States was neglecting the dollar again (Volcker 1992: 168). Certainly the Carter administration had other things than the currency markets to worry about by late 1979, which were relatively stable at that point in any case. The hostage crisis had begun in early November 1979, and consumer reaction to a new inflation-fighting program Carter announced in March 1980 sent the economy into a recession (172–173, 352). The discussions at the June 1980 G7 Venice Summit were about fighting inflation and oil conservation, not systemic monetary reform as a result.

Given a chronological comparison with the international monetary policymaking of the Nixon and Ford administrations, it seems that the Carter administration made a qualitative transition in its approach to the dollar in late 1978. Henning notes that initially it had pursued policies similar to its predecessors, such as "pressing others for faster growth and refusing to undertake adjustment or substantial intervention on its part," but that "by late 1978, U.S. authorities were cooperating with foreign central banks and governments and accepting part of the burden of coordination" (1994: 269). That acceptance did not extend very far, as the failed substitution account negotiations demonstrated, but the administration did appear willing to use the consultative networks established at Rambouillet for the purpose they were intended. That is, after the fall of 1978 it was willing to participate in coordinated interventions to try to stabilize the dollar in currency markets and to iron out "erratic fluctuations." In other words, the Carter administration had begun to pursue a goal which it had originally eschewed, and it engaged in coordinated policies in support of that goal.

There are elements in the late Carter administration's international monetary policymaking which conform to liberal cooperation theory expectations as a result. The Carter administration did initially invoke the "god of cooperation" (to use Volcker's expression), but it expected others to do the adjusting and attempted to unilaterally force its preferences onto others via the exchange rate. This produced suboptimal market outcomes, and in response its policymakers turned to multilateralism in the form of coordinated interventions. These interventions do not exactly match what would be anticipated in a period of regime creation, since there was no attempts to establish a target zone exchange rate system. Certainly the substitution account negotiations were informed by concerns with functional institutional efficiency in the issue area, but their complete failure underscores the lack of movement toward regime creation.

However the fact that coordinated interventions did seem to be accepted as a behavioral norm after 1978 suggests that Carter's monetary officials learned from their mistakes in a way that Nixon and Ford officials had not (Cohen 1983b). While the timing of these interventions were not prescribed according to any established formula, from a regime maintenance perspective they may have become the standard by which subsequent policymaking behavior in the issue area would be guided. That is, having learned that dollar instability could produce suboptimal market outcomes, U.S. monetary policymakers would continue to rely on coordinated interventions as a means to stabilize currency markets. This interpretation can only be sustained by examining the next phase of U.S. monetary policymaking. If the propositions of liberal cooperation theory are correct, we would anticipate that *either* U.S. policymakers would continue to stabilize the dollar via coordinated exchange rate interventions *or* they would go further in seeking to develop a more efficacious policymaking arrangement in the issue area. As we shall see, however, decisionmakers did neither. Instead, U.S. monetary policymakers engaged in one of the starkest examples of exchange rate neglect the post-World War II period had ever witnessed.

"THE MAGIC OF THE MARKETPLACE"

The seeds for potential exchange rate chaos had been sown before Ronald Reagan took office in January 1981. The expansionary policies adopted at the 1978 Bonn summit collided with the contractions caused by the 1979 oil shock. Global inflation rates shot up to an annual peak of 15.7 percent in 1980 and a recession of unprecedented severity ensued (Volcker 1992: 351). In October 1979 the Fed adopted a more overt anti-inflation stance and restrictive monetary policies. Other central banks pursued similar policies; however none of them coordinated their actions with each other. As Dobson observes, the aggregate restrictive effect of these policies deepened the ensuing recession in the early 1980s more than any single institution had intended (1991: 16). Between August 1980 and January 1981 the dollar regained 20 percent in value from its previously depressed levels, but the exchange markets remained relatively stable during this period (Volcker 1992: 352). That was about to change.

In order to promote recession recovery after 1981, the major industrials adopted different macroeconomic policy mixes. The Reagan administration wanted to bring down inflation with a restrictive monetary policy that did not involve raising taxes. Henning points out, "this was exactly the opposite approach to that taken by conservative governments abroad, which were determined that significant tax cuts would be enjoyed only *after* spending was reduced" (1987: 13; his emphasis). Japan and Germany both pursued policies of restrictive fiscal consolidation, and when the U.S. government switched to an expansive monetary policy in 1982, sluggish world economic growth ensued. According to Dobson,

> The result of this constellation of national policies was three fold: persistent high real interest rates worldwide, lasting long after the beginning of the recovery; rapid appreciation of the US dollar during the 1980–85 period; and buildup of the US current account deficit in the 1980–87 period (1991: 39).

Their opposing policy mixes would become the primary source of macroeconomic conflict among the major industrial between 1981 and 1983. Because the Europeans were concerned primarily with inflation, they did not want to see their currencies depreciate against the dollar. Yet calls for coordinated currency interventions during this time fell on unreceptive American ears.

This was because the economic policies followed by the first Reagan administration were entirely domestic in focus. As Henning puts it, "international considerations were an afterthought for the supply-siders, monetarists and orthodox fiscal conservatives who vied to dominate administration policy" (1994: 271). The Reagan administration focused almost exclusively on domestic economic problems from the start, and it was vigorous in its unilateral pursuit of all aspects of economic policy.[20] In a throwback to the early Carter administration's attitudes, Reagan monetary decisionmakers expected others to adjust to America's macroeconomic policies and not vice versa. Nowhere was this lack of interest or concern with the international impact of American behavior more obvious than in the administration's exchange rate policies. In fact it would be more accurate to say that in a very real sense the administration had *no* exchange rate policy. It took no responsibility for the dollar's value in currency markets and even disdained the very notion that intervention in such markets was appropriate.

In April 1981 the new Treasury Secretary, Donald T. Regan, and his Under Secretary for Monetary Affairs, Beryl W. Sprinkel, announced that the Treasury would halt all currency interventions. Their announcement applied to both coordinated and unilateral interventions, and the latter would occur only in extraordinary circumstances which they expected to be rare, since they offered, by way of example, the buying of dollars after the March 1981 shooting of the president. They also renounced all the traditional mechanisms which had been used to signal in what direction the Treasury wanted the dollar's value to go. This meant they would renounce changes in monetary and fiscal policy, capital controls, and even declaratory policy with the intent of affecting the dollar. According to Dominguez and Frankel,

> The policy was noninterventionist in the general sense that the move-ment of the dollar was not seen as requiring any sort of government response, or indeed to be a problem. The policy was also noninter-ventionist in the narrower sense that the authorities refrained from intervening in the foreign exchange market—that is, from the selling (or buying) of dollars in exchange for marks, yen, or other foreign currencies (1993: 8).

In fact, the Treasury would not even develop an internal view of what level for the dollar might be justified by market fundamentals (Henning 1994: 273).

Regan and Sprinkel meant what they said. In December 1981 the Fed-eral Reserve Bank of New York announced that it had not bought or sold any foreign currencies from May to October. Funabashi notes, "it was the first six-month period in almost a decade that monetary authorities had not con-ducted exchange market intervention" (1989: 68). In their detailed study of currency market interventions, Dominguez and Frankel point out that there were, in fact, a number of occasions between 1981 and 1984 when the Fed did intervene in currency markets (1993: 9). But these interventions were always small in magnitude, unilaterally conducted, and rarely publicized. The inclination to intervene was so slight that instead of covering the 1984 IMF quota increase with SDRs, Sprinkel used the mark and yen reserves he had inherited from the Carter administration. The extent of exchange rate neglect under the Reagan administration was even greater than that of the late Nixon and Ford administrations, and it was to last from 1981 to 1985.

The administration's exchange rate policy was partly a response to what it perceived to be the constant complaints of trading partners to realign the dollar's value in the late 1970s, as well as the Carter administration's respon-siveness to these complaints (Funabashi 1989: 66–67). But what also lay behind this "hands-off" approach to the exchange rate was the conviction that the marketplace was better equipped than governments to determine the true value of a currency. European requests for joint interventions were viewed "as an attempt to circumvent the 'magic of the marketplace' " (Henning 1987: 15), and the zeal with which Reagan's monetary policymakers applied these ideals contributed more than any other factor to the currency misalignment that was to come. Unanticipated market forces played a part as well since, as Destler points out, few policy-makers anticipated that the movement of world capital would swing into high gear during the 1980s (1986: 53). When it did, exchange rates came to be driven increasingly by factors unrelated to trade transactions.

As long as the United States had pursued inflationary policies in the late 1970s, the dollar had usually moved in the direction of depreciation. This was because such policies reduced the real returns on dollar assets as well as the dollar's value, and money tended to flow out of the United States as a result. However when the United States moved to a mix of economic policies that raised real interest rates in 1981, funds poured into dollar assets enticed by favorable returns, and the magnitude of these investments was enormous.[21] The United States needed these foreign funds to finance its deficit, since the Reagan administration had made it abundantly clear that it would not raise taxes for this purpose, but the dollar began to appreciate as a result. Although it may have been unreasonable to expect Regan or Sprinkle to anticipate the size and mobility of capital flows in the 1980s, their failure to recognize the direct link between the dollar's value and American trade competitiveness can certainly be faulted. Both consistently and publicly argued that the exchange rate had little direct impact on the budget deficit, interest rates, and trade imbalances. Yet because the dollar's relative price is the single most important determinant of U.S. producer trade competitiveness, the dollar's appreciation had by 1985 produced a ballooning U.S. trade deficit (Destler 1986: 51).

Sprinkel was a monetarist, however, and a true believer in Milton Friedman's arguments with respect to the virtues of a free market.[22] And while Regan could not be characterized as such, he was fiercely loyal to the president and rigorously defended Reagan's macroeconomic policies. Volcker recounts one speech Regan delivered to the Interim Committee in which he "aggressively... almost shouting" asserted that "they had it wrong and we had it right" (1992: 193). America's economic relationship with its allies in the early 1980s was, as Volcker puts it tactfully, "not a high point for the niceties of international diplomacy."[23] The Reagan administration's free market philosophy and its exchange rate policymaking specifically were a bone of contention at almost every summit in the early 1980s. The Europeans repeatedly asked the Americans to participate in coordinated interventions and were just as repeatedly rebuffed on the grounds that interventions were ineffective. This claim even became a point of public disagreement between Sprinkel and his French counterpart, Michel Camdessus, during preparations for the 1982 G5 Versailles summit (Putnam and Bayne 1987: 133). In a classic example of Solomon's maxim, the G5 agreed to have their deputies produce a report that examined whether or not exchange rate intervention was really the useful tool which the French kept insisting it was.[24]

The "Jurgensen Report," as it became known, was presented at the Williamsburg summit in late May 1983. It argued that coordinated interventions might be beneficial in some cases but could not prevail against ingrained market sentiment. The report was moderate enough in its attempt to reach a compromise between diametrically opposed perspectives, but Volcker notes,

> Secretary Regan went to a press conference immediately afterward and said in effect that he could hardly imagine a situation where intervention would in fact be helpful. That seemed to me totally inconsistent with the spirit of the communiqué. But it had the virtue, I suppose, of making it clear there would be no change in the hands-off policy of the United States (1992: 237).

The Americans at Williamsburg also continued to deny that there was any connection between their expansionary policies and the rising dollar. Instead, they encouraged the G5 deputies to enact a process of "multilateral surveillance" which might be useful in the fortuitous event that its allies suddenly wanted to adjust their macroeconomic policies in accordance with American preferences. Multilateral surveillance would be resurrected again in 1986 as yet another instance when agreement on process was in reality "a second-best substitute for agreement on policy coordination" (Henning 1987: 36; see also Cohen 1993; Dobson 1991).

According to Henning and Destler, then, "the pervasive attitude was that if foreign governments disliked the depreciation of their currencies against the dollar, they should adjust their macroeconomic policies to better emulate those of the US" (1988: 321). And depreciate they did! According to Federal Reserve Board statistics collected by Cohen, the dollar appreciated by 94 percent between the middle of 1980 and late February 1985 (1988: 206–207). It increased approximately 150 percent against the French franc, 125 percent against the British pound, 90 percent against the German mark, and 17 percent against the Japanese yen. In 1984 the dollar had risen above 2.60 marks and was in the 220–260 yen range. When it peaked in February 1985 it was at 3.47 marks and 265 yen, respectively.

The result was an astounding trade deterioration. The U.S. trade deficit nearly quadrupled between 1980 and 1986 from $36 billion to $148 billion (Cohen 1988: 207). In the years 1983, 1984, and 1985 it jumped respectively from $67 billion to $114 billion to $124 billion (Destler 1986: 54). Total U.S. imports increased by almost 50 percent from $257 billion in 1980 to $362 billion in 1985, and manufactured imports nearly doubled during this period, rising from $257 billion in 1980 to $362 billion in 1985 (Cohen 1988: 207). These figures had overwhelming implications for American exporters:

> From its trough in 1980 to its peak in late February 1985, the trade-weighted value of the dollar rose an incredible 70.2 percent. At this point, the dollar was roughly 40 percent above the level that would

have brought balance to the US current account. This meant that American producers of internationally traded goods faced a 40 percent cost disadvantage in relation to foreign rivals in the US and overseas markets (Destler 1986: 51–52).

At the same time, Japan's external surplus had turned positive again in 1981 and rose annually to reach $94 billion in 1986.

Despite these staggering figures, the Treasury remained adamant that its "hands-off" exchange rate policy was appropriate. Business leaders who complained to the Treasury were continually rebuffed, and Destler reports that "some were told, in essence, that they were crybabies and should stop asking for government help against the workings of the marketplace" (1986: 106). The administration even continued to cheer the currency upward as it reached unimagined levels. Regan extolled the benefits of a strong currency to the press throughout 1984 and early 1985, and over the summer both he and the president continued to argue publicly that the trade deficit was not harmful.[25] The Treasury and the Fed were privately at odds over the policy as well. Volcker disagreed with the Treasury's perspective on the efficacy of interventions and thought that "sooner or later . . . there would all too likely be a sickening fall in the dollar," but despite his private reservations he did not seriously entertain the idea of intervention without Treasury approval (1992: 180–181; Melton 1985: 174–175).

The Treasury did permit the Fed to intervene in small quantities when the dollar was peaking at the beginning of 1985, but it continued to ignore the dollar thereafter, even as political pressure for policy change had become particularly intense. Having received no satisfaction from the administration, the pressure of manufacturing, exporting, and agricultural sectors had subsequently shifted to Congress. Congressional pressure on the administration had, in turn, reached a fever's pitch by the summer of 1985. There was an eruption of proposed legislation to deal with the trade problem, and approximately 100 bills designed to impede imports in some way were introduced in the Ninety-ninth Congress of 1985–1986 (Cohen 1988: 211). As Funabashi puts it, "by September 1985, four years of the Reagan administration's 'benign neglect' of international economic policy had resulted in a soaring dollar, high interest rates, a bloated current account deficit, raging protectionism in the US Congress, and exasperation on the part of America's trading partners" (1989: 9).

Clearly this period of U.S. international monetary policymaking provides no evidence for either regime creation or regime maintenance. U.S. monetary elites verbally and behaviorally renounced multilateralism in both its more efficacious and status quo forms. The administration actively ascribed to the argument that coordinated interventions were not effective or necessary and thus refused to participate in them. Its hostility to the concept of intervention itself was so great, in fact, that it even refused to unilaterally intervene in exchange rate markets. There was no movement toward the kind of managed exchange rate system that would be anticipated if functional institutional efficiency in the issue area is the primary motivation for policymaker behavior. Nor is it possible to sustain the argument that this was simply a period of regime maintenance in which policymakers relied on prior cooperative behavioral standards for policymaking in the issue area. Whatever the Carter administration had learned about the efficacy of a stable dollar and coordinated interventions to that end, those lessons did not translate to the next administration which unequivocally repudiated both the goal and the behavior.

This does not mean that evidence for regime creation or maintenance could not still occur in subsequent American monetary policymaking. But in taking stock of the first fifteen years of American behavior in the issue area after Bretton Woods, there is clearly more evidence for the recidivism anticipated by the realist-constructivist alternative than for either of the patterns of behavior anticipated by liberal cooperation theory. In comparison to the coordinated interventions of the late Carter administration, monetary policymaking behavior during Reagan's first term in office was starkly regressive in its unilateral tendencies and preferences. Its policymakers returned to the kind of dollar neglect which had been present for most of the 1970s, with the only difference being that the Reagan administration pursued its policies of neglect with fanatical enthusiasm.

However while the chronological comparison lends no support to liberal expectations regarding cooperation, what is consistent with interdependence and regimes theory is that unilateral policymaking produced suboptimal market outcomes that the administration would eventually have to address. By foreswearing interventions of any kind, Reagan monetary policymakers managed to produce "the most severe and protracted currency misalignment that the postwar had ever seen" (Destler 1986: 52). It is the sort of crisis that should be conducive to elite learning and regime creation, and so evidence for liberal cooperation theory may still emerge depending on how American policymakers responded to the misalignment. In responding cooperatively, there is also the potential to generate a new cooperative behavioral baseline to which subsequent policymaking might conform thereafter. Events after the summer of 1985 are examined in light of these two potentialities.

"COWBOYS AT THE HOTEL"

In September 1985 the Reagan administration's noninterventionist exchange rate policy came to an end with the announcement of the Plaza Accord.

Under the initiative of the new U.S. Treasury Secretary, James A. Baker III, the G5 met in New York's Plaza Hotel and following the meeting issued a statement indicating their intention to coordinate an exchange market intervention in order to accelerate the decline of the dollar. The dollar had already depreciated by 13 percent from its peak in February, but the communiqué noted that G5 ministers and governors felt "some further orderly appreciation of the main nondollar currencies against the dollar is desirable," and they stood "ready to cooperate more closely to encourage this when to do so would be helpful" (Dominguez and Frankel 1993: 12–13). As one European described the Accord to Funabashi, "the cattle were already moving in the right direction. Then Baker summoned the cowboys at the hotel and shot off his gun" (1989: 218).

Although the details of the G5 meeting have never officially been made public, Funabashi conducted a number of subsequent interviews which revealed that the total amount of intervention was set at $18 billion to be conducted over a six-week period in denominations of dollars, yen, and marks (1989: 16–21).[26] They agreed that the intervention should occur on a day-to-day basis in order to prevent the dollar's subsequent rise, that daily intervention amounts would be $300–$400 million, and that occasionally the United States would be prepared to purchase pounds and francs if others would too. The G5 also agreed to a target of 2.54–2.59 for the dollar-mark rate, 214–218 for the dollar-yen rate, and the proportion of intervention action between the countries (United States 30 percent, Federal Republic of Germany 25 percent, Japan 30 percent, United Kingdom 5 percent, France 10 percent).

The Plaza announcement had an immediate effect on world currency markets. The dollar began to rapidly depreciate and, whenever it showed signs of rebounding during the next six weeks, the central banks intervened to sell dollars with the heaviest interventions being conducted by the Federal Reserve and the Bank of Japan (BOJ). According to Funabashi, "the dollar ended October some 13 percent down from the level at which it had traded during the week before the G5 meeting in relations to the yen, 10.5 percent down in relation to the deutsche mark, and 8 percent down in relation to the pound sterling" (1989: 23). Another coordinated intervention occurred on 7 November when the dollar began to rise again, but it began to fall thereafter, and at the next G5 meeting held in January 1986 in London the finance ministers expressed their satisfaction with the depreciation progress of the dollar.

One of the factors most often cited in the literature for the reversal in American exchange rate policy at the Plaza was the Baker-Regan job switch. In January 1985 Baker had moved to the Treasury while Regan had taken Baker's old job as White House Chief of Staff. At the same time Sprinkel had left the Treasury to become Chair of the Council of Economic Advisers

(CEA), while Baker's aide, Richard G. Darman, became Deputy Secretary at the Treasury and essentially took over the portfolio that had been held by Sprinkel as Under Secretary for Monetary Affairs. The personalities of Regan and Baker (as well as Sprinkel and Darman) couldn't have been more different. While Regan was dogmatic and unyielding, Baker was more pragmatic and accommodating. Dominguez and Frankel even date the change in the administration's exchange rate policy at the job switch rather than the Plaza Accord, because the dollar had begun depreciating on its own after February and this may have been due to market anticipation that Baker and Darman were more receptive to intervention (1993: 11–12).[27]

And, unlike Regan, Baker appeared to personally enjoy international negotiations and to be more amenable to the idea of multilateral efforts in general. At the April 1985 OECD meeting, Baker had offered to host an international conference to consider reforms of the international monetary system. His thoughts on the subject may have been informed by a private memo from Darman which, according to Funabashi, suggested the promotion of a target zone exchange rate system (1989: 197–202). Funabashi points out that Darman's own thinking had, in turn, been directly influenced by a luncheon with Williamson, Bergsten, and other target zone supporters at the Institute for International Economics in May. The Deputy Assistant Secretary of the Treasury, Charles Dallara, was also amenable to considering the idea, although at the time none of them made their opinions public because there was still a great deal of resistance to exchange rate management among the monetarists in the Reagan administration. The April 1985 memo had discussed other proposals as well, such as indicator mechanisms, policy coordination, and intervention strategies. These elements were to comprise a package of multilateral policy initiatives described by Funabashi as the "Plaza Strategy" which Baker and Darman would gradually unveil over the next two years (1989: 213).

During the summer of 1985 Treasury officials began to seriously explore a change in the hands-off policy and began consultations (first with Japan and then with the other G5 members) on the idea of a coordinated intervention (Funabashi 1989: 11–14). Given the administration's refusal to intervene in currency markets up to September 1985, the Plaza Accord was a relatively dramatic and public way to demonstrate that a change in policy had occurred with regards to both intervention and coordination. Baker continued to encourage the idea of macroeconomic coordination in the G5 thereafter, although he introduced other elements of the "Plaza Strategy" besides the target zone proposal first. At the Tokyo summit in May 1986 he and Darman suggested that the G5 be expanded to a G7 with the inclusion of Canada and Italy. They also proposed reviving the "multilateral surveillance" process and expanding it into an "indicators approach" for the purposes of macroeconomic policy adjustment. Each nation-state would agree to work toward specific performance goals. A series of indicators (e.g., growth, inflation, budget performance, and exchange rate) would be used to assess performance and guide coordinated policy adjustments in order to meet agreed-upon goals.

These proposals have led to the common assertion within the scholarly literature that "the differences in the priorities and values of two successive Treasury Secretaries . . . provided the main impetus in 1985 for a fundamental shift in U.S. exchange rate policy" (Cohen 1988: 166). This is significant in the context of this analysis because it suggests that Baker may have been predisposed to the type of strategic learning and cognitive changes that liberal cooperation theory anticipates during a period of regime creation. Indeed, Iida makes this argument specifically, contending that Baker's "preferences were different from those of his predecessors" and that "another crucial difference between Baker and his predecessors was his willingness to learn" (1993: 450–451; see also Volcker 1992: 240–242). This willingness or predisposition may have led Baker to the realization that U.S. unilateral policymaking had produced suboptimal market outcome and that it would be more efficacious for the United States to pursue multilateral efforts instead. Given the jurisdictions and prerogatives of the U.S. Treasury, Baker was also in a position to steer U.S. international monetary policymaking in a more cooperative direction.

However it is difficult to sustain this interpretation during the year which immediately followed the Plaza Accord. For all the claims made regarding Baker's greater ability to learn and his predisposition to multilateralism, his behavior during 1986 reflected a continued tendency toward unilateralism in the making of U.S. international monetary policy. Whatever Baker may have learned, it did not immediately translate into behaviors which supported macroeconomic coordination or even coordinated interventions in currency markets. While a policy change had clearly occurred, in that Baker would consistently use declaratory policy to signal where he wanted the dollar to go, as Henning points out, "the new activism quickly became aggressive" (1994: 281). In a replay of the "dollar weapon" strategy adopted by the early Carter administration, Baker repeatedly "talked the dollar down" in the press as a means to induce Germany and Japan to stimulate their economies. Throughout 1986 policymakers from both countries pleaded with Baker to help them resist the appreciation of their currencies, but Baker's monetary policymaking during that year remained a classic example of "brinkmanship diplomacy" (Funabashi 1989: 180).

The result was that by the Tokyo Summit the macroeconomic indicator of most concern to Germany and Japan was the exchange rate. Support for dollar depreciation had begun to evaporate in both countries as the dollar continued to fall, their currencies began to appreciate, and their own net exports shrank. By March 1986, for example, the yen had appreciated another

12 percent to 176 to the dollar, and it took another jump in April (Henning 1987: 39). German and Japanese policymakers hoped that Baker would agree to stabilize the dollar, but the summit focused instead on his rather rancorous suggestions for a revised process of macroeconomic coordination. There were a number of reasons why the proposals proved to be so controversial.

While Canada and Italy had been attending G5 meetings as observers for sometime, the G5 central bankers disliked the idea of including them in delicate monetary policy discussions. And although, as Funabashi points out, both "multilateral surveillance" and an "indicators approach" were hardly new ideas with the latter going back to the "Volcker Plan" and the C20 negotiations (1989: 131), central bankers balked at the idea of sharing this kind of data with them. In fact, the entire proposal elicited considerable concerns among the central bankers that the use of national indicators as a surveillance device would mean greater ministerial interference into central bank independence.[28] Small wonder, then, that Baker's proposals would upset the other G5 members and were even referred to in Japan as *Baker shokku* (Baker's shock) (Funabashi 1989: 142).

The proposals that Baker floated at the May 1986 summit were also not about an American commitment to undertake macroeconomic adjustments itself, but about a process of coordination designed to force others to adjust instead. The indicators approach was a mechanism to "help that country in a deficit position, namely, the United States, while placing the burden of adjustment on the surplus countries, namely, West Germany and Japan" (Funabashi 1989: 232, 239; see also Volcker 1992: 276–279). It was hardly surprising that Germany and Japan would find the indicators approach so unpalatable as a result. As with the Williamsburg summit, where the process of "multilateral surveillance" had last been encouraged by the United States, the formalization of an "indicators approach" would have been useful to the United States in the fortuitous event that Germany and Japan would once again agree to adjust their macroeconomic policies in accordance with American preferences.[29] Baker's refusal to stabilize the dollar while touting the multilateral surveillance scheme reinforced the suspicion among its allies that, in a familiar pattern of behavior, the United States was attempting to shift the responsibility for adjustment onto others in order to avoid hard choices itself. *The Economist* would remark later about U.S. attitudes toward the G7, "All along, economic cooperation among the G7 has really been a matter of helping America to avoid changing its fiscal policy, rather than the opposite" (1988: 71).

And while there were dangers in the strategy of talking down the dollar as Volcker and others began to express as time when on, it was still a relatively painless way for the United States to force others to adjust their macroeconomic policies while avoiding adjustments of its own. In a statement to the

Interim Committee in September 1986, for example, Baker linked the indicator's approach to the dollar as a weapon by suggesting that if others did not pursue the stimulative policies the United States desired, it would continue to talk the dollar down.[30] Thus the extent to which Baker's "multilateral surveillance" proposals were also a behavioral commitment to multilateralism is questionable. Certainly those proposals were part of a larger reform package that was consistent with liberal cooperation theory's expectations about efficacious learning in the issue area. Yet as Cohen observes about the Tokyo summit, "declaring a collective commitment to policy cooperation seemed innocuous enough when no real compromises of national interests were required" (1993: 141).

In a negotiation exercise similar to the C20 reform and "substitution account," the G5 deputies worked diligently to systematize a surveillance process which would never be utilized for the purposes of macroeconomic policy adjustment (Dobson 1991: 132; Henning 1987: 36). Solomon's maxim remained as pertinent as ever to U.S. international monetary policymaking, as procedures instead of substance became formalized and as the "god of cooperation" was toasted yet again. In fact Volcker noted that, having had "personal experience in developing a far simpler indicators proposal" during the 1970s, he "had no faith in the workability of the proposals" and "was delighted not to be asked to defend them" (1992: 278–279).

The fact that the United States did not engage in a single instance of currency market intervention from November 1985 to the end of January 1987 underscores just how aggressively Baker used the dollar as a weapon. It also suggests that the Plaza Accord was an ad hoc, one-shot play of monetary policy coordination. The extent to which it represented the kind of learning anticipated by liberal cooperation theory is questionable as a result, although it may have been a necessary first step. But as Japan and Germany frantically attempted to cap their currencies in the year following the Plaza, the U.S. Treasury did nothing to arrest the dollar's continued depreciation. By September 1986 the dollar-yen rate had declined from its peak of about 260 to 154, and by early 1987 the dollar had fallen approximately 36 percent against the mark and the yen since the Plaza Accord, and 47 percent and 42 percent, respectively from its late February 1985 peak (Henning 1987: 39). A 1986 Bundesbank Report noted that whenever it had attempted to intervene in support of the dollar, "these efforts were in vain not least because statements by US officials repeatedly aroused the impression on the markets that the US authorities wanted the dollar to depreciate further" (quoted in Dominguez and Frankel 1993: 15).

Even after Baker appeared to be shifting to the goal of dollar stabilization in the fall of 1986, he continued to use the dollar as a weapon to force Japanese compliance with the stimulus package it had agreed to in October

1986. The United States and Japan had announced a deal that month in which Finance Minister Kiichi Miyazawa would introduce a stimulus package into the Diet, and in return Baker would stop talking down the dollar. But as Funabashi points out, "the 'Baker-Miyazawa Accord' proved not to be carved in stone" (1989: 161). When the yen began to appreciate again at the end of 1986, the Treasury still did not intervene to stop it and actually resumed the talk down strategy.[31] It was not until after Miyazawa rushed to Washington in January 1987 to reassure Baker that the stimulus package would be adopted that the Treasury authorized an intervention in order to stop the dollar's fall. It was the first intervention the United States had conducted in over a year.

Thus the year following the Plaza Accord actually involved the kind of macroeconomic conflict between the United States, Japan, and Germany that had existed in the early Carter administration. And it was similar because U.S. monetary policymakers were pursuing a similar exchange rate strategy for a similar macroeconomic purpose. The crisis that had prompted the Plaza Accord may have encouraged the Reagan administration to rediscover the virtues of currency market activism. But that activism involved the use of declaratory policy in order to keep the dollar's value unstable. It did not include coordinated or unilateral currency market interventions. If we compare U.S. monetary policymaking between September 1985 and January 1987 to the expectations of liberal cooperation theory, it is still difficult to find confirmatory evidence for its propositions.

The concept of regime maintenance can have no application at this point since all forms of currency market interventions and responsibility for the dollar had been repudiated in the four years prior to the Plaza Accord. There simply was no cooperative behavioral standard guiding policymaking behavior. Of course one might argue that the Plaza Accord was the resurrection of the cooperative interventionist policies of the prior administration and that those policies served as "satisficing" guidelines for Baker's own policymaking behavior. In order for this argument to hold, however, one would have to demonstrate that Baker had vested interests, either personally or institutionally, in the late Carter administration's monetary policies. This would be an exceedingly bizarre argument to make, since Baker was a loyal member of the Republican administration which had been so active in discrediting those very policies. Nor does it appear that there were any domestic institutional constraints on the Reagan administration's ability to fully discredit and abandon them.

If a direct empirical linkage cannot be established between Baker's monetary policymaking and that of the Carter administration, then arguing that the Plaza Accord was merely regime maintenance would be a good example of the deductive problems noted in the chapter 4. It would be an assertion of cooperative continuity despite the fact that the intervening period (1981–

1985) represented recidivism when compared to the late Carter administration. Such an assertion would essentially make neoliberal institutionalism's claims regarding regime maintenance empirically unfalsifiable, since it would amount to an assertion that even a period of unilateral regression was consistent with the theory. Alternatively there are a number of elements in this period which do initially appear to be consistent with the expectations of regime creation. U.S. unilateral policymaking in the issue area did produce a crisis and the Treasury did eventually address the crisis with a coordinated effort. There was talk of a target zone exchange rate system within the Treasury, and clearly the "mutual surveillance indicators approach" floated at the Tokyo summit would have been efficacious had it ever been implemented.

Yet the latter was proposed not because U.S. policymakers were committed to obtaining functional institutional efficiency in the issue area, but as a means of pressuring others to make policy adjustments so that the United States could avoid adjustments itself. The lack of support for a regime creation interpretation is underscored by the absence of any U.S. currency market interventions in the year which followed the Plaza Accord. The pattern of U.S. monetary policymaking behavior immediately after the Plaza Accord is simply not consistent with the expectations of regime creation either. Given the subsequent Louvre Accord, however, it may be possible to argue that in retrospect the Plaza Accord was a necessary first step, both institutionally and cognitively, in an ongoing process of regime creation.

"REMEMBER, IT WAS ONLY DINNER CONVERSATION"

Unlike prior periods of U.S. international monetary policymaking, the behavior of American monetary officials from February 1987 to August 1988 is consistent with the behaviors that would be anticipated during a period of regime creation. Although Baker and Darman had not acted on the target zone idea in the year following the Plaza Accord, and in fact pursued dollar policies which were in direct contradiction to it, that changed with the G5 Louvre meeting of February 1987.[32] By then U.S. officials were satisfied with Japan's commitment to a stimulus package and had managed to elicit a promise of tax cuts from German officials. The reward was an agreement to support currency stabilization and the form this support would take was the adoption of a target zone exchange rate system.

Preparations for the Louvre meeting began among the G5 deputies in late January 1987, and Darman, along with French officials, now pushed the idea of adopting target zones. There was considerable discussion at the ministerial meeting over how the zones would work and precisely what it was that the G5 were committing themselves to. In Darman's view,

Each country would undertake to keep rates within a range of plus or minus 2.5 percent; a divergence beyond plus or minus 2.5 percent would signal the desirability of intervention. Cooperative efforts would be expected to intensify up to plus or minus 5 percent, beyond which the only obligation was consultation on policy adjustment and realignment (Funabashi 1989: 185).

Yet the German and Japanese representatives hesitated over the idea of defending their currencies at current values. The Germans argued that arbitrarily establishing an exchange rate baseline would create market distortions, and Miyazawa wanted the yen to be defended at a higher level. Ultimately it was agreed that the midpoint rates would be provisional and reassessed at the upcoming Washington G5 meeting in April. This tended to assuage the concerns some participants had over the agreement. "Remember," said one of them to Funabashi later, "it was only dinner conversation" (1989: 204).

But the American willingness to support the zones with currency market interventions throughout the spring of 1987 indicates that this was not a sentiment shared by Treasury officials. The final agreement had specified the midpoint rates of 1.8250 marks and 153.50 yen, respectively to the dollar. Voluntary, mutual intervention would occur at the plus or minus 2.5 percent point around these rates. Intervention efforts were expected to intensify between 2.5 percent and 5 percent, and at the latter point consultation on policy adjustment was to be obligatory. In order to support the zones until the April meeting, the G5 agreed to $4 billion as the total intervention amount, with the United States, Japan, and Europe each responsible for about a third (Funabashi 1989: 187). Although the Louvre Accord never actually mentioned target zones, nor were the ranges ever publicized, it referred to the G5's belief that their currencies were "within ranges broadly consistent with underlying economic fundamentals" and that they were ready to intervene to stabilize exchange rates "around current levels." Despite protestations to the press that no ranges had been adopted, much of the Accord's language managed to signal to the currency markets that ranges were in operation, and subsequent interventions led to fairly accurate guesses about what they were.

Between February and April 1987 the Fed engaged in the largest currency market interventions since the Carter administration. When the dollar reached the upper level of the Louvre range against the mark (1.8745) on 11 March, the Fed intervened by $30 million. Funabashi points out, "it was the first demonstration of the US monetary authorities' commitment to defense of the range" (1989: 187). In mid-March the dollar began to move below 150 yen and, in coordination with the BOJ and European central banks, the Fed began to intervene almost daily from late March to early April. Its operations in defense of the yen during this period totaled about $3 billion, and between

March and May the Fed bought almost $4 billion against the yen alone in an effort to stabilize the dollar.

Despite these interventions, the yen was 146 by the early April G5 meeting in Washington. This meant it was outside the Louvre baseline, having appreciated 7 percent above it, and Miyazawa wanted an agreement to get the yen back to that baseline. The Europeans refused, however, and Baker suggested instead that the target zones be rebased to reflect the yen's value at that moment. That meant the yen's target zone would then have been a 2.5 percent margin of 142.43–149.65 and a 5 percent band of 139.04–153.30 (Funabashi 1989: 189). Total intervention amounts were also raised to $15 billion, with the same apportionment of a third each. When the yen continued to appreciate against the dollar after the meeting, the Fed participated in additional coordinated intervention to stop its progress, which hit bottom on 27 April at 137.25 to the dollar, but then began to reverse and stabilize.

U.S. policymakers would demonstrate their support for the target zones again later in the year. Volcker had retired in August 1987 and, after Alan Greenspan's appointment as Federal Reserve Chair, the discount rate was unilaterally raised in early September despite Baker's urgings that Greenspan consult with other central bankers before doing so (Destler and Henning 1989: 62–63; Volcker 1992: 281–282). A round of uncoordinated foreign interest rate hikes ensued in the early Fall, putting further depreciation pressure on the dollar, and Baker criticized the Bundesbank and BOJ for violating the spirit of the Louvre Accord. Baker had stopped using declaratory exchange rate policy as a weapon after February, but now he suggested that the dollar might have to depreciate again if Germany did not comply with American preferences for lower foreign interest rates. The recriminations between Baker and the Bundesbank during this period were not the only cause for the stock market crash of 19 October, but as Destler and Henning remark they "put the market in the mood to crash" (1989: 63).[33]

Yet the American commitment to defending the Louvre target zone system survived "Black Monday." It may have been true, as one G5 participant noted, that "so shocked was the U.S. administration over the crisis, it did not give a damn about the Louvre for two weeks after the crash" (Funabashi 1989: 211). Yet in order to support the dollar which was under heavy selling pressure, coordinated currency interventions began almost immediately. And after the shock wore off, Baker turned to the target zone exchange rate system to try to stop further dollar depreciation. The crash had effectively rebased the mark to the 1.60–1.80 range and the yen to the 120–140 range. In a late December telephone exchange with the other G7 finance ministers, Baker obtained their commitment to defend these new zones. The 22 December communiqué which accompanied the "Telephone Accord" reaffirmed their commitment to the Louvre Accord and reiterated their common interests in exchange rate stability. The statement's emphasis on the dollar's rise was taken as "a deliberate signal that the group wanted to put a floor under the dollar at its current level" (Dominguez and Frankel 1993: 19).

However the dollar continued to slide against the yen and mark. At the time of the "Telephone Accord" the dollar was at 1.63 mark and 126 yen respectively, and in the week following the announcement it dropped to 1.56 mark and 120 yen respectively. In response, the Treasury organized what was called a "Bear Trap" or "Bear Squeeze" in which, in order to signal a determined effort to support the dollar and to place a firm floor under it, the Treasury organized a series of round-the-clock coordinated interventions on the first trading day of 1988 (Destler and Henning 1989: 66–67). During the first week of January the total intervention for the G7 countries was almost $3 billion, with the U.S. share at $654 million. This effectively caught the market by surprise and brought the mark back up to 1.65–1.70 and its rebased zone, while the yen was in the upper 120s. The dollar rebounded and in March Baker indicated satisfaction with the dollar's value as well as his belief that further decline would be counterproductive (*Financial Times*, 2 March 1988).

The G7's commitment to exchange rate stability was reiterated in the statements issued after the Tokyo economic summit in mid-June 1988. In the month following the summit the dollar reached 1.90 marks and 135 yen respectively, and the United States intervened unilaterally by about $3 billion. In August the mark pierced the 1.92-level, over the upper level originally agreed upon at Louvre, and in response the United States took part in coordinated interventions to stop the dollar's continued rise. Between 27 June and 23 August 1988 the United States conducted its largest purchase of foreign currency ever on the open markets when it sold $4.7 billion for marks. Clearly as Henning points out, "by early 1988, the second Reagan administration completed its transition from confrontational to cooperative activism in international monetary policy" (1994: 288). Baker ended the practice of using the dollar as a weapon, he and Darman encouraged the adoption of a target zone exchange rate system, and U.S. monetary authorities subsequently intervened in unprecedented amounts to support that system.

The Louvre Accord and U.S. international monetary policymaking from February 1987 to August 1988 provides a near textbook example of the behaviors one would anticipate in a period of regime creation. U.S. decisionmakers encouraged the adoption of precisely the kind of target zone exchange rate system one would anticipate if their goal was functional institutional efficiency in the issue area. While Volcker could argue with some skepticism that "it added up to the mildest possible form of exchange rate targeting—limited, temporary, and unacknowledged" (1992: 282), that system clearly served as a guide to American international monetary policymaking in the year following Louvre. The second Reagan administration undertook numerous and substantial interventions into currency markets in order to defend the target zone ranges, thereby promoting dollar stability in a way that it had never done prior to February 1987. Dominguez and Frankel found that throughout 1988 the exchange rate levels were generally consistent with the target zones agreed upon at Louvre (1993: 79–80). And the fact that first the yen and then the mark were rebased, and then defended within those ranges, is consistent with the crawling zones envisioned by Williamson.

The target zone system still lacked some essential elements, with the need for publication being the most obvious, but this too could be consistent with regime creation expectations since public acknowledgment could always have come later. Indeed, many of the Louvre participants believed they would openly commit to the system at a later date and that "the details could be published as part of a gradual process of institutionalization" (Funabashi 1989: 203). Thus the second Reagan administration even surpassed the cooperative monetary policies of the late Carter administration. Coordinated interventions were conducted according to a preestablished formula that specified in a relatively precise manner the suboptimal outcomes to be avoided as well as the primary means of avoiding these outcomes. This preestablished formula had been determined through multilateral agreement, and it prescribed when interventions were to occur rather than conducting them in an ad hoc manner as had been the case in post-Bretton Woods U.S. monetary policy to that point. Henning is hardly overstating the case in arguing that "when Baker agreed to the Louvre Accord, U.S. international monetary policy crossed an extraordinary threshold," because "not since the final days of the Bretton Woods regime had the United States entertained such a strict notion of desirable limits to exchange rate fluctuation" (1994: 285, 286).

The question remains, of course, whether this pattern would hold. At this point it is a good sign for liberal theories of cooperation that the empirical record should reveal the creation of the type of exchange rate system anticipated in a period of regime creation. Yet as we saw with regards to events after the late Carter administration, that revelation is not enough. In order to support the theory's propositions regarding international cooperation there must be some evidence for behavioral continuity in post-1988 American international monetary policymaking. That continuity can be reflective of either regime creation, in that the target zone exchange rate system is further institutionalized, or of regime maintenance, in that some elements of the system and its goals are preserved regardless of their inefficiencies. In other words, there must be evidence that the target zone system continued to serve as a guide for continuity in subsequent American exchange rate policymaking. The record of American international monetary policymaking after 1988 does not, however, favor liberal cooperation theories.

"ONCE IN A WHILE I THINK ABOUT THOSE THINGS, BUT NOT MUCH"

The decline of the target zone exchange rate system and the goal of stabilization it was meant to obtain was gradual to be sure, but by 1990 it was possible to assert unequivocally that target zones were no longer relevant to U.S. exchange rate policymaking. Bush and his new Treasury Secretary, Nicholas F. Brady, signaled a more complacent attitude toward the dollar almost immediately. The dollar began to depreciate in the fall of 1988 and in November it was in the 121–123 yen and 1.73–1.75 mark ranges respectively. Bush reaffirmed his commitment to "policy coordination and exchange rate stability," but also admitted, "once in a while I think about those things, but not much" (*Washington Post*, 15 November 1988). Along similar lines, Brady commented about the dollar's value, "Markets go up and down. I don't really worry about it very much."[34]

The dollar and currency markets in general stabilized at the end of the year, but in the spring of 1989 the dollar began to appreciate. In May it rose above 150 yen and 2.00 marks respectively, which was well above the Louvre's upper limit for the latter. A yen rate of 150 was consistent with both the original Louvre and April 1987 rebase, yet the 1987 October crash had effectively rebased it again so that the United States had been defending it in the 120–140 range throughout 1988. Thus both currencies were at a 2½ year high, and the White House issued a statement in May reaffirming the desirability of stable exchange rates and its commitment to the G7 coordination process (*New York Times*, 23 May 1989). The Treasury and Fed also intervened in record quantities in May and June, selling more than $7 billion against the yen and $4.7 billion against the mark. These were the largest intervention magnitudes of the 1980s, as Dominguez and Frankel point out (1993: 20).

But the intervention operations in early summer were not coordinated, in part because the Bundesbank initially refused to participate in them, and so no declaratory statements were made in order to reinforce them. By the July G7 summit meeting the dollar had fallen to 140 yen and 1.9 marks respectively. This meant the mark was still above and the yen just at the upper levels which had been established after "Black Monday." The summit communiqué repeated the G7's support for the Plaza and Louvre Accords and exchange rate stability in general, but Brady revealed after the summit that neither the dollar nor the need to strengthen, modify, or maintain exchange rate coordination had been discussed. Brady remained complacent about the lack of G7 coordination progress in general, commenting on MacNeil-Lehrer, "Why change the throttle settings when we've had seven years of economic progress?"[35]

The dollar continued to rise and in late September 1989 the G7 issued a statement indicating their belief that this was "inconsistent with long run economic fundamentals" and that they had agreed to "cooperate closely in exchange markets" to correct the situation (quoted in Henning 1994: 291). U.S. monetary officials participated in a series of coordinated interventions and, according to Henning, spent another $5.8 billion in the currency markets between mid-August and mid-October (1994: 291). Yet to most observers the process of G7 coordination seemed to be breaking down and another G7 collective intervention into the currency markets would not occur until January 1991. The Bush administration took no major steps to repair the coordination process or to restore market confidence in it. Exchange rate stability was less of a priority than it had been under the second Reagan administration and, "in the absence of real coordination, the verbal support that the Treasury now offered for the G7 process had a platitudinous ring" (Destler and Henning 1989: 72).

By end of 1989 the dollar had pierced the upper boundary of the Louvre target range for the yen and had stayed there. Meanwhile it had pierced the upper range against the mark, at 2.00, then had fallen back through the lower boundary, at 1.70, although the latter was still consistent with the October 1987 rebase. Dominguez and Frankel are undoubtedly correct that through 1989 the mark-dollar exchange rate did not exhibit the same wild fluctuations that it had during the Plaza Accord period (1993: 79–81). Yet the dollar was still beginning to behave a bit like Coombs's "loose cargo on a ship" again. Certainly there was no dramatic break with the "Plaza Strategy" during the first year of the Bush administration, and Destler and Henning point out that "there was rhetorical continuity and some intervention" (1989: 79). However they also note that as the zones were pierced during 1989,

> The Treasury confronted the policy choice of whether to disband or restore the target ranges and, if the latter, whether to mount a new effort to reunify the G7 in its commitment to the old target ranges or to revise them. The Treasury chose to intervene in moderate quantities and to reiterate statements of commitment in a moderate tone, but declined to take stronger action. Coupled with monetary policy changes that were essentially cooperative but that took place outside of any framework of deliberate coordination, the Treasury's response raised the specter of a policy retreat—if not the laissez faire exchange rate policies of the first Reagan administration, then at least away from the highly activist approach taken by the second (79–80).

U.S. monetary policymakers under Bush made no effort to reach a G7 agreement on rebasing the zones as a result, nor did they even feel obligated to consult with their G7 partners about the zone breaches or about the possibility of coordinated policy adjustments. As usual, Volcker managed to capture the essence of the situation:

> The Plaza Agreement raised the large question of how profoundly American attitudes had change, whether the Plaza would be first step toward a more managed system of exchange rates, and whether, in support of that effort, the governments of the world were ready to devote any real effort to the systematic coordination of their economic policies on a continuing basis. That is the fundamental question. . . . And the answer, I fear, was not really (1992: 229–230).

There was no progressive movement toward institutionalizing the target zone exchange rate system, as one might have anticipated if this were still a period of regime creation.

While the administration appeared to be comfortable with letting lapse any further progress in the coordinated exchange rate effort, the zones did appear to serve as a minimal guide to the Treasury's exchange rate policymaking during its first year in office. That is, the piercing of the zones did tend to generate intervention responses from the administration and these were relatively substantial in size. It may be possible to argue, then, that a shift to regime maintenance had occurred during this period. Yet any semblance of continuity in U.S. international monetary policymaking was about to be confounded when the Louvre target zones were permanently breached in 1990, and thereafter the administration allowed them to be dismembered by degrees.

The directions of the yen and the mark had begun to diverge by the end of 1989. The yen weakened against the dollar, and in February and March the United States spent $1.68 billion in coordinated interventions to stop the yen's further depreciation. But by late spring the yen had continued to depreciate against the dollar so that over the summer it was at 125 again. Some Treasury officials were becoming increasingly concerned. Darman had left the Treasury in April 1987, but David Mulford, who had participated in the Louvre Accord negotiations as a deputy, had remained and provided some policy continuity during the transition from Baker to Brady.[36] Mulford was the Treasury Assistant Secretary for International Affairs during most of 1988, and was later promoted to Under Secretary, while Charles Dallara became the Assistant Secretary. By the time of the G7 Paris meeting in April 1990 he and Dallara made their concerns over currency instability public, yet Brady effectively contradicted them by arguing that a weak yen was no cause for concern.[37] The Japanese had hoped that the United States would agree to support the yen at the meeting, just as they had supported the dollar from the

Plaza Accord on, but Brady and the other G7 members refused to make any specific commitments to do so.[38]

The mark, on the other hand, had begun to strengthen against the dollar beginning in November 1989 when the Berlin Wall fell. In July 1990 the Fed and Bundesbank conducted a concerted intervention to try to hold the mark at the 1.70 level, but the dollar continued to depreciate against the mark. By the end of the year it was past the 1.50 range and in record low territory. This level was well outside the ranges agreed upon at both Louvre and after "Black Monday," yet Henning observes that "in contrast to the previous encounter with these levels, immediately before the Louvre Accord, the administration and Fed were complacent" (1994: 297). No interventions were taken to halt the dollar's decline and, according to Henning, Brady "announced that, because the decline had been orderly, he was not overly concerned about it."

By January 1991 the Treasury had begun to feel that perhaps the depreciation had gone too far, and for the first time in over a year the G7 conducted a coordinated intervention to put a floor under the dollar at 1.45 marks. Yet by summer the dollar had become too strong so another G7 coordinated intervention occurred just before the London G7 summit in mid-July in order to cap the dollar at around 1.80 mark and 140 yen respectively. Although Dominguez and Frankel note that these rates fell within the original Louvre ranges and renewed talk that the target zones might still be in effect (1993: 25), the coincidence was not a matter of conscious policy. As Henning points out, because the "Brady Treasury continued to pursue its ad hoc approach to limiting exchange rate fluctuations," the ranges were simply no longer serving as a guide to continuity in American international monetary policymaking (1994: 299).

This was amply illustrated by the U.S. intervention patterns which Dominguez and Frankel document up to 1991 and in which they found that it was impossible to predict the timing of interventions:

> The argument is made that the exchange rates prevailing at the time of the Louvre in February 1987 did not incorporate a sufficiently depreciated dollar to be sustainable for long but that by the beginning of 1988 the exchange rate (the mark-dollar rate, at least) had fallen to a level that was sustainable. In retrospect, however, it is no easier to identify a target zone, even a relatively broad one, into which the dollar was confined during the period starting in 1988, than during the period starting a year earlier at the Louvre (1993: 78).

Thus despite the Louvre's preestablished intervention formula for avoiding suboptimal monetary outcomes, there was no predictability or continuity to

U.S. currency market interventions by 1991. In fact, the policymaking pattern which emerges in the last year of the Bush administration and in the early Clinton administration is remarkably similar to the "benign neglect" of prior periods of post-Bretton Woods U.S. international monetary policymaking. There was little activism with regards to the exchange rate; the dollar's value was either intermittently ignored, used as a weapon, or managed via unilateral interventions, and coordinated interventions occurred on an ad hoc, unpredictable basis.

With the United States in a recession and peaking unemployment numbers during the 1992 presidential election year, Bush began to "toast the god of cooperation" again. In a pattern of behavior which should by now look familiar, the Treasury allowed the dollar to depreciate while Bush called upon the other G7 members to stimulate their economies. Brady pressed the idea throughout the spring of 1992 and at the July G7 summit in Munich declared that everyone was in agreement. Just days later, however, the Bundesbank raised interest rates thereby illustrating that the G7 was not in accord, and the dollar sank to a new low of 1.44 against the mark. U.S. authorities participated in several coordinated interventions during this time but the amounts were modest, and in August Brady would unequivocally repudiate the Louvre Accord when, in a disagreement with German officials over interest rates, he rejected a proposal to put a floor under the bilateral exchange rate.

The result was that "by August 1992, even the broader limits hypothesized by some had been breached, as the dollar fell through its all-time nominal low against the mark and the yen" (Dominguez and Frankel 1993: 137). As the Fed reduced interest rates and as the dollar continued to slide, it had by early September 1992 reached record lows against the mark and yen, at 1.3865 and 118.60 respectively. By the time Bush left office the Treasury had allowed the dollar to fluctuate well outside the zones that had been agreed upon at Louvre and at the 1987 rebasings. Those zones had been relatively large, with a 120–150 range for the yen and 1.60–1.90 for the mark, yet during the Bush administration the dollar had fluctuated between 119–163 for the yen and 1.39–2.05 for the mark (Henning 1994: 303). As we shall see in a moment, the yen's margin was about to get even wider.

According to Henning, by 1992 it had become clear that "the G7 process of macroeconomic policy coordination and exchange rate stabilization had completely broken down" (1994: 303). While other G7 members surely shared the blame, it was also clear that during Bush's term in office "the G7 coordination process received only weak support from the secretary of the Treasury, the president, and the rest of the administration." Exchange rate stability had not been pursued or supported because it was a low priority for both Bush and Brady. The result was that after 1988 American exchange rate policy was informed neither by a standard of functional institutional efficiency nor by the cooperative policies and behaviors that had been established in the issue area from 1987 to 1988. In the transition from the second Reagan administration to the Bush administration, there was no progression of, or continuity to, U.S. monetary policymaking or to the G7 cooperative effort. Policymaking regressed to "benign neglect" and that regression could be seen in the early Clinton administration's exchange rate policymaking as well.

In February 1993 the new Treasury Secretary, Lloyd Bentsen, suggested to the press that yen appreciation might be in order and Clinton did the same in mid-April. In light of negotiations over the continued bilateral trade imbalance between the United States and Japan, yet one more American administration decided to use "dollar weaponry" to put pressure on its trading ally to comply with its preferences. The administration's statements helped drive the yen into new territory and, although the United States intervened in currency markets in late April, the yen continued to climb. The United States took no other intervention action until mid-August when the yen was at the 100-level. If anyone was still in doubt as to whether the target zones were guiding U.S. exchange rate policy, the level of the yen and the Clinton administration's response to it was clear enough. Not only did Treasury officials avoid any public discussion of what range might be desirable for the yen, but Henning notes that in the May and November 1993 Treasury reports to Congress, its officials repeatedly argued that "manipulation" of exchange rates was inappropriate (1994: 305). Bergsten and Henning have since argued that the yen's appreciation against the dollar from 1992 on was the "most conspicuous failure" of the deteriorating G7 coordination process (1996: 30).[39] What this failure means for liberal explanations of international cooperation, and why realist-constructivism may better account for it, is the subject of the remaining chapters.

blank 182

Chapter 6

Why Liberal Theories Fail to Account for the Empirical Record

A review of post-Bretton Woods American international monetary policymaking reveals little evidence for the propositions of liberal cooperation theory. This chapter underscores that conclusion by considering the cooperative episodes which did occur and the patterns which emerge when these episodes are examined as a chronological package. It seeks to pinpoint what within the empirical record refused to conform to the behavioral expectations derived from theories of interdependence and regimes. On this basis it considers why liberal theories of cooperation cannot adequately account for the cooperative phenomenon, and it argues that the reasons for this inadequacy may be traced to flaws in the deductive logic of these theories.

There are at least three major errors of deductive logic embedded in the theoretical frameworks of liberal explanations for cooperation. The first two errors are specific to the complex interdependence and neoliberal institutional explanatory variants, because they result from the effort to avoid identity transformation issues altogether. That effort makes it impossible for these variants to provide any logically sound accounting of the historical economic policymaking record and, in order to explain why cooperation is maintained, an implicit identity transformation has to be smuggled into their causal chains. The third error in deductive logic is shared by all variants of liberal coopera-tion theory because it results from the presumption that interdependence has the capacity to generate a functionally efficient institutional response. Such a presumption requires the existence of a social vacuum which constructivism has convincingly argued cannot exist in either a theoretical or empirical sense. While other IR theorists may be willing to excuse these errors as conceptual slips (or sleights) of hand, the actual behavior of policymakers and the empirical record itself has not been so accommodating.

REVELATIONS FROM THE EMPIRICAL RECORD

If the late Carter and second Reagan administrations are considered in isolation, policymaking during those periods comes closest to approximating the expectations of liberal cooperation theory. In both instances monetary officials engaged in unilateral policymaking which generated suboptimal market outcomes that they then attempted to address with multilateralism. The Baker Treasury went farthest in institutionalizing these efforts along the lines anticipated in a period of regime creation. Those efforts may also have served as a minimal guide for policymaking behavior during the Bush administration's first year in office, thus conforming to the expectations of regime maintenance. However, when these periods are examined within the larger historical context for the *patterns* of U.S. policymaking, it becomes apparent that there is no evidence to support the proposition that post-Bretton Woods American exchange rate policymaking is consistent with the expectations of either regime creation or regime maintenance. Functionally efficient institutions were neither created nor were even minimal cooperative efforts maintained.

On the other hand, the pattern of behavior which has been consistently present since 1971 is the one pattern that confounds liberal cooperation theory and that supports the realist-constructivist alternative. That pattern has been a tendency toward recidivism, usually with the start of each new administration but often in the aftermath of crisis as well. Whatever Carter administration officials had learned about unilateralism and suboptimal outcomes in interdependent conditions, those lessons did not translate to the first Reagan administration. That would prove to be the case between the second Reagan, Bush, and Clinton administrations as well. When compared to the policymaking which preceded and followed, the multilateralism of the late Carter administration and the second Reagan administration appear to be ad hoc, single-play cooperative efforts in response to crisis. That they were crisis-driven as a result of unilateral policymaking may be consistent with liberal cooperation theory, but in neither case were cooperative efforts developed progressively or maintained as behavioral baselines thereafter. Instead those efforts were abandoned by subsequent policymakers so that once the crisis generated by unilateral policymaking had passed, American policymakers simply reverted to unilateralism again.

Henning has noted this pattern to U.S. international monetary policymaking as well. He argues that it is a cyclical pattern in which there are three distinct stages:

in the first instance, [officials] treated the exchange rate (or the balance of payments) as the residual of domestic macroeconomic policies. . . . Such neglect inevitably led to exchange rate misalignments or payments imbalances with deleterious domestic consequences. American officials initially responded to the external problems by seeking adjustment on the part of foreign governments, typically through expansionary macroeconomic policy, a strategy that usually proved to be internationally confrontational. . . . When the limits of that strategy were reached, the US administration would settle with its foreign counterparts on multilateral cooperative arrangements on payments and exchange rates. . . . Senior US officials gave priority to international monetary matters, however, only so long as those issues were proximate constraints on the achievement of basic economic objectives. Once external threats abated, the administration and Federal Reserve would become uninterested in external monetary policy again, beginning the cycle anew (1994: 306).[1]

During these periods of reversion the majority of U.S. decisionmakers were neither aware of nor did they particularly care about the potential problems of unilateral policymaking or the failure to maintain an external perspective on exchange rates. This pattern of behavior has contributed to what Cohen observes is the "distinctly episodic quality" of G7 monetary cooperation, which has "tended to ebb and flow cyclically like the tides" (1993: 134).

Yet it is also the case that we have seen instances in post-Bretton Woods U.S. policymaking when particular monetary policymakers were personally and ideologically committed to cooperative efforts. Some of them, such as Mulford, remained active participants who tried to keep the spirit of cooperation alive even during periods of regression to exchange rate neglect. Others were clearly aware of the standards for functional institutional efficiency in the issue area and were active in encouraging multilateral negotiations to those ends. Coombs's early encouragement of coordinated interventions, Volcker's role in the C20 reform exercise, Solomon's efforts on behalf of the substitution account, and Darman's enthusiasm for the target zone exchange rate system are all cases in point. The latter is particularly interesting since it is possible to establish a direct link between Williamson's exchange rate system and Darman's knowledge of it. Thus there were efforts at liberal economic regime creation and maintenance among American policymakers themselves. Yet obviously it takes more than conviction to have a lasting impact on the cyclic pattern of U.S. international monetary policymaking.

That observation leads us to the crux of the empirical problem for liberal theories of cooperation. Even when particular policymakers do appear to learn the lessons anticipated by such theories, those lessons are rarely translated into policy. And when they are, such as the "Plaza Strategy," they do not thereafter determine a pattern of policymaking behavior consistent with the theory's propositions. There is no progressive tendency to develop more efficacious institutions involving multilateralism in the issue area, nor are even minimal stabs at multilateralism in response to crisis maintained. Instead there is a regular tendency toward unilateral recidivism, which could only occur if the lessons anticipated by liberal cooperation theory were never learned or institutionally encoded. As Levy had argued, one can only posit organizational learning if a process has occurred in which individual learning leads to changes in organizational procedures and behaviors and that then serve as a feedback loop to reinforce individual learning (1994: 288). The process can be blocked at each stage, so that individual learning may ultimately have no impact on organizational behavior.

This appears to be the case for American international monetary policy-making, since there is evidence that some of the participants involved in monetary policy were acquainted with standards of functional institutional efficiency in the issue area. The problem does not appear to be one of learning, then, but of institutionalization. Or as Cohen has put it, "the issue is not myopia: policymakers surely are not unaware of the impacts of their behavior on market expectations, . . . and would stick to their commitments if that seemed desirable" (1993: 152). The review of post-Bretton Woods American monetary policymaking undertaken here suggests that two domestic institutional factors are relevant in this regard. Neither of these have received much attention in the liberal cooperation theory literature, but they are central to the realist-constructivist explanatory alternative.

First, the pattern of neglect and activism noted by Henning can be correlated with the advent of presidential administrations. Recidivism is particularly obvious at the beginning of each new president's term in office, while activism (if it occurs at all) is typically associated with the latter half of the administration. This does not appear to be a pattern correlated with party politics since it is present in both Republican and Democratic administrations, but presidential electoral politics and cycles do appear to play a role in that they produce changes in Treasury personnel and also (presumably) a tendency to reject the policies of one's predecessors.[2] It may be the case, then, that with each new crop of administrators the lessons of interdependence must be relearned precisely because they have not been institutionalized (Cohen 1983b).

Second, policymakers who consistently favor multilateral efforts in the issue area are usually below the rank of Treasury Secretary and are allowed to pursue these efforts only at the discretion of the Secretary. Such allowances do not necessarily signal the Secretary's commitment to the final product of the negotiations, however, and frequently it is the case that the Secretary does not share the same commitment to multilateral efforts. In fact, the ebb and flow of commitment can often be matched to a change in Treasury Secretary personnel, as the differences in multilateral commitments (and even interest) between Connally and Shultz, Blumenthal and Simon, Regan and Baker, and Baker and Brady can all attest. Contrary to liberal cooperation theory's expectations, U.S. policymakers do not feel institutionally bound to the multilateral policies of their successors and appear to encounter no institutional barriers to abandoning these polices for unilateralism again. Certainly that abandonment might then produce suboptimal market outcomes, but that possibility in itself does not serve as an inhibition to complete policymaking regression.

All of this undoubtedly suggests to some scholars that what is needed is more learning, more institutionalization, and more structural adjustment to the realities of interdependence. Gallarotti argues, for example, that "international bureaucrats and national policymakers . . . need to be more sensitized to the complexity of the effects of IO when considering optimal responses to international problems" (1991: 221–220). Presumably this means that Treasury secretaries must be better acquainted with these complexities before they take office, and that the regular upheaval in administrative personnel, which is the hallmark of the American executive branch and presidential politics, should be modified as well. Because the idiosyncrasies of the American federal bureaucracy (in which one-third of the upper echelon are replaced with each new administration) is inefficient and undesirable in a world of complex interdependence, American civil servants should instead be allowed to rise up in the ranks, as they do in Japan or Great Britain, which would give decisionmakers below the rank of Secretary the chance to have a long-term impact on American international monetary policymaking. International efficiency must be emphasized over domestic accountability when international economic affairs are marked by complex interdependence.[3]

While there is undoubtedly a grain of truth to these arguments from the perspective of the issue area itself, what they imply is nothing less than a fundamental reordering of American domestic processes and institutions. This is, of course, what liberal cooperation theories are all about. The external environment of complex interdependence forces internal changes that then leads to a greater acceptance and emphasis on multilateral efforts in national policymaking. Yet according to the interdependence and regimes arguments such reordering ultimately depends on the development of particular cognitive predispositions among decisionmakers who, as the last chapter has revealed, exhibit no inclination to reorder the American domestic space according to liberal theoretical expectations.

This disinclination is true not only for Treasury secretaries but also among those Treasury personnel who can be identified as enthusiastic about multilateral commitments. There is no evidence that any of them attempted to circumvent or to flout the authority of the Secretary in international negotiations or in other settings. Nor did they attempt to change the domestic institutional structures in which they were working in order to bind their successors. In fact, during international negotiations they consistently protected American interests even when to do so meant the certain failure of the multilateral effort all together. Thus Henning found in his review of the institutional changes which had evolved in American international monetary policymaking since the end of Bretton Woods that these were minimal at best and "primarily changes on the margin" (1994: 307).[4] Why, then, does the empirical record fail to match the expectations of the interdependence and regimes literature? There are at least three major errors of deductive logic embedded in the theoretical frameworks of liberal explanations for cooperation, and it is to the first of these errors that we now turn.

ECONOMIC POLICYMAKERS IN HISTORY

As with the other strands of liberal cooperation theory, the interdependence and regimes literature assumes that decisionmaker identity will reflect the issue area to which they have been assigned and that their primary motivation will be to maximize a particular interest in that issue area. In the case of capitalist-markets, policymakers are assumed to be motivated by the desire to maximize profits on behalf of their societies.[5] In order to do so, however, exchange must be efficiently organized; hence policymakers will be motivated to adopt whatever methods will most efficiently maximize profits. As noted earlier, where the interdependence and neoliberal institutional strands part company with other variants of liberal cooperation theory is in their attempt to hold identity constant and treat the perceptions that are inhibiting cooperation as if they resulted not from elite identity but from elite behavior. This can be compared to neofunctionalism and functional-constructivism, in which the components of identity from which the perceptions and behaviors of autonomy are derived *must change* in order for the cooperative outcome to be realized. In other words, according to these other variants elites seek to maximize the interests of their issue areas, but political loyalties and the parameters of self-identification have to be altered in order for cooperation to be realized.

Alternatively the perceptions inhibiting cooperation are treated by the interdependence and regimes literature as byproducts of behavior rather than of identity, and so they result from the methods or strategies that elites have been employing to obtain assigned interests. The policymaker is assumed to already have an identity and interests which are not only compatible with multilateralism as a strategy but even predisposed to it. What has not kept pace, however, are the perceptions on the part of policymakers that their own behavior and cognitive preconceptions are inhibiting their ability to obtain their assigned interests. Changing the level and nature of elite interaction reveals the inefficiency of their own behavior, which then leads to simple learning in which strategic perceptions and behaviors are changed as well. Hence cooperation does not require a functional identity transformation, only a strategic realization that multilateralism is comparatively better at obtaining interests than is unilateralism. And if state decisionmakers remain reliant on unilateralism it is not interest-driven but out of perceptional and cognitive habit.

Yet why are economic decisionmakers wedded to the practices of unilateralism? We have seen in their treatment of autonomy that interdependence and regime theorists provide a general, historical answer to this question. Autonomy, unilateralism, and independence used to be efficient at obtaining interests, but in conditions of interdependence they are no longer efficient and so the rationale for maintaining them has disappeared. These were the policies of economic mercantilism pursued by European states between the sixteenth and eighteenth centuries, which associated "the possession of industry with economic self-sufficiency and political autonomy" and that attempted to "protect the economy against untoward external economic and political forces" (Gilpin 1987: 33). While the interdependence and regimes literature does not specify what it assumes about the relationship between mercantilist policies, economic interests, and elite identities during this period, its separation of strategic behavior from identity suggests that neither mercantilism nor liberalism are derivable from elite identities. The constant is instead the incentive to maximize profits, while the adoption of either strategy is a function of which ever will most efficiently obtain profits in the given systemic conditions. Economic elites in both the past and the present would then have no loyalty to any particular strategy, but would adopt whichever maximizes profit instead.

Because systemic attributes are what ultimately determine which strategy would be most efficient, the application of liberal policies would have to await systemic conditions more appropriate to their implementation. This would be consistent with the "logic of discovery" perspective on ideas that, as Woods notes, "new economic ideas emerge and compete in a marketplace of knowledge in which the best ideas for a new set of circumstances prevail" (1995: 166). Rosecrance asserts, for example, that the trading world had precursors prior to the twentieth century and first made its "debut" in Britain and in other continental European states during the nineteenth century so that "apostles of free trade and international cooperation" were present in these states (1986: 95). The incentive to maximize profits had apparently always been present, but what brought it to the fore was that state decisionmakers began to maximize profits on behalf of developing liberal societies rather than monarchs. These budding liberal elites were unable to prevent recidivism, however, because socio-economic and political conditions were not yet conducive.

The problem with invoking the historical record in this way is that when conditions are finally supposed to be favorable later in the twentieth century, economic decisionmakers had apparently forgotten the lessons of Adam Smith and David Hume. The time period that has been of most concern to interdependence and regime literature is the 1970s and beyond. It was a decade in which, according to Smith, we could begin to "talk of interdependence as an empirical phenomenon" that had been "occurring incrementally through the 1950s and 1960s, giving rise to a qualitative change in international relations in the 1970s" (1984: 67).[6] Yet support for free trade and cooperation were not automatic because, we are told, the state's economic decisionmakers had reinternalized mercantilism's cognitive and perceptual barriers. According to Rosecrance the "recognition dawned gradually" after 1945 that interdependence was a "fundamental and unchangeable feature" and that "the United States may perhaps have been the last to acknowledge it" (1986: 141; see also Keohane and Nye 1989: 236). Thus it was not strategic choice which kept the practice of unilateralism alive in American economic bureaucratic circles, nor did security-oriented or other parochially-minded elites step in to prevent cooperative economic policies. Rather it was that the *perceptions* of economic policymakers themselves prevented them from recognizing when conditions were finally ripe for liberal policies again.

As Woods points out, however, "very few ideas are very new," and certainly liberal economic ideas could not claim to be so in the 1970s (1995: 168). Given the dominance of liberal economic ideology in the major industrial societies, why wouldn't post-1970 economic elites already be aware of the argument that multilateralism had the potential to efficiently maximize profit? The historical record indicates that there were ample opportunities throughout the twentieth century to learn the basic lessons of economic liberalism. Depending on how one measures interdependence, for example, it is possible to argue that it began to increase and reached significantly high levels among industrializing nation-states prior to, and certainly earlier in, the twentieth century.[7] If this is the case, then economic policymakers would have had the opportunity to learn the appropriate lessons and to adopt more efficient strategies much earlier than the 1970s.

Even if the condition of interdependence did not provide for dramatic levels of interaction until after World War II, the Great Depression looms large as a seminal economic event which by most popular accounts led to significant learning on the part of economic elites who then left a decisive mark on the post-war international economic order. The planning by American and British economic policymakers during the war involved a conscious attempt to force the abandonment of mercantilist policies and to replace them with institutional arrangements which would promote and encourage liberal open markets and cooperative policies (Ikenberry 1992). One could even argue that this planning was an example of the type of simple, behavioral learning derived from conditions of interdependence that liberal cooperation theory seeks to explain and predict. Rosecrance actually does cite the Great Depression as having promoted social learning and asserts that today "political economists have finally begun to understand the long-term effects of protectionism" because, "having experienced the disasters of the 1930s, they do not wish to repeat them in the 1990s" (1986: 213).

But ready agreement to this formulation makes the practice of unilateralism and autonomy among American and British economic decisionmakers post-1930s all the more puzzling. Why is there a sixty-year gap between the seminal event and the cognitive, practical recognition of its lessons? If the theory is correct about the constancy of elite economic interests and about the need for only simple learning, then why didn't the lessons of the Great Depression translate into the complete abandonment of mercantilist strategies by economic policymakers in these states? Why did these practices continue when the Great Depression had supposedly already forced these policymakers to recognize their inefficiency and undesirability?

One answer provided by the regimes literature is that U.S. hegemony between 1945 and the 1971 served as a kind of intervening variable in the interdependence-cooperative learning process, by making active adjustment by both American and non-American economic elites unnecessary during that time period. The hegemon's decline then acted as the systemic trigger for a period of learning in the 1970s. Yet here too it is not clear why autonomy is still a cognitive barrier to cooperation given the assumptions about state policymakers and economics interests upon which regimes theory relies. Given that the policymakers in the hegemonic state had been instrumental in establishing post-World War II multilateral economic institutions and had actively participated in and supported them, why would they need a period of learning which involved rediscovering the efficacy of multilateralism? Why wouldn't the hegemon's policymakers instead be the first to promote cooperative efforts?

The failure on the part of American economic decisionmakers to learn these lessons cannot be due to uneven learning, because neoliberal institutionalism aspires to explain more than single-shots of cooperation. As Keohane has argued, liberal cooperation theory "does not view cooperation atomistically as a set of discrete, isolated acts, but rather seeks to understand patterns of cooperation in the world political economy" (1984: 56). Ultimately the learning and application of appropriate lessons depends on generational and organizational accumulation; otherwise cooperation would be neither a pattern nor predictable. It would depend instead on the personal vagaries and idio-syncrasies of each decisionmaker and could not be a choice derived from the roles they occupied as economic elites within the state. But then how does such accumulated learning take place when, as Levy has argued, "organiza-tions do not literally learn in the same sense that individuals do. They learn only through individuals who serve in those organizations, by encoding in-dividually learned inferences from experience into organizational routines" (1994: 287). If institutional encoding is required for cognitive lessons to stick, then why weren't the lessons of multilateralism encoded into organizational routines in the American case?

Actually, one could argue that they were encoded, since service in mul-tilateral forums became a part of the post-World War II job description for the state's economic decisionmakers. But then this simply returns us to the question with which we began. If one argues that circa-1945 American eco-nomic policymakers recognized and attempted to encode organizational rou-tines in order to promote multilateralism, then why were post-1970 American economic policymakers still cognitively predisposed to behave autonomously? Why did they still need to learn the basic lessons of economic liberalism? The theory does not specify how accumulation of knowledge works in practice, or how much interaction time and opportunity economic elites need before the comparative efficiency of multilateralism over unilateralism is both perceived and applied. Is forty years too little or too much time? Would five more years make a difference?

And as for secondary states, Keohane argues that American hegemony depended on the perception by policymakers in secondary states that they were benefiting from acquiescence to U.S. economic preferences (1984: 45, 137). When the hegemon declined these same policymakers had to learn that they would benefit from the continued support and promotion of cooperative practices among themselves. If, however, economic elites have always been predisposed to adopt the strategy most efficient at profit maximization, and if the hegemon actively encouraged such strategies as well as provided the institutional and economic conditions conducive for their implementation, then why is unilateralism still a cognitive barrier to cooperation within the decisionmaking structures of these states after the hegemon declines? Under American tutelage the policymakers in secondary states participated in coop-erative liberal economic institutions for roughly twenty years. One might assume that this would have predisposed them to understand the importance of promoting higher levels of interaction, cajoling their counterparts in other departments to abandon parochial methods and perceptions, binding them-selves and their successors to multilateral commitments, substituting regime for unilateral rules of thumb, and so on. Yet what is argued instead is that after the hegemon declines these policymakers still do not have a cognitive appreciation of the virtues of multilateralism and so they must undergo a learning period in which they will discover that unilateralism is inefficient.

The historical record raises considerable problems for interdependent and regime explanations of international economic cooperation as a result, and these problems may be traced to the fact that these explanations ignore some of the theoretical implications of their own assumptions about interests and behavior. They appear to work backward from the empirical facts, acknowledging that the practice of unilateralism and autonomy were indeed still virulent among state decisionmakers in the 1970s and that this was a barrier to functionally efficient cooperation among them. Yet this acknowledgment fails to recognize that the continued existence of these cognitive barriers is not a puzzle to be explained *with* neoliberal institutionalism but a problem *for* it. That economic policymakers in the major industrials would still be practicing mercantilist policies after almost two centuries of influential liberal free trade argument and a century of developing interdependency and multilateral institutions suggests that such policies cannot be treated merely as functions of behavioral strategic choice.

If one considers mercantilist policies to result from elite identity, their continued virulence throughout the twentieth century and beyond would be more explicable. As part of the decisionmaker's internal measuring stick for efficacy itself, mercantilist policies would inhibit choice even when systemic conditions no longer made them appropriate. Of course this is precisely how the interdependence and regimes literature does not want to proceed. But by assuming that policymakers have an interest in efficient profit maximization, that the systemic context is one of complex interdependence, and that autonomy is merely a behavioral perception unrelated to the given interest and in direct contradiction to the specified systemic context, liberal cooperation theory overdetermines the possibility of cooperation while underdetermining the extent to which autonomy will be a barrier.

In so doing the theory also cuts at its own justifications for treating autonomy as a cognitive barrier when conditions of complex interdependence exist. Without some reference to identity transformation, neoliberal institutionalism has no means of explaining why the practice of autonomy continues to hobble a decisionmaking context in which decisionmakers are predisposed to practice whatever strategies will efficiently maximize profit and in an issue area that has been characterized as having already obtained a systemic condition in direct contradiction to that practice. The theory's own deductive logic implies that the continued existence of these cognitive barriers in antithetical systemic conditions would be inexplicable. Hence it establishes a theoretical puzzle for itself which it cannot deductively solve. It is a puzzle of the present which should, according to its own logic, be a puzzle of the past.

THE SHIFT FROM REGIME CREATION
TO REGIME MAINTENANCE

The second deductive flaw in the interdependence and regimes framework is that an identity change is actually required in order to explain the shift from regime creation to maintenance. In other words, even as practitioners of liberal cooperation theories claim to hold identity constant, an implicit identity transformation must eventually be smuggled into their posited causal chain in order to explain why regimes are maintained. That such smuggling is deductively inconsistent with exogenous interests is worth underscoring from the start. In attempting to explain how the barrier of autonomy is overcome, the interdependence and regimes literature posits that the pursuit of cooperation and the abandonment of autonomy does not necessitate a change in interests. What changes are "states' *conceptions* of their interests, and of *how* their objectives should be pursued," not the content or nature of the interests themselves which are assumed to remain constant (Keohane 1984: 245; my emphasis). This presumption of exogenous interests excludes the *necessity* of identity transformation in order for cooperation to occur and it even excludes its *possibility*, at least in the short-term.

It is because liberal cooperation theory treats behaviors, but not interests or identities, as endogenous to interaction that only simple rather than complex learning is required. As Wendt puts it, "interests are formed outside the inter-action context, and then the latter is treated as though it only affected behavior. This can be merely a methodological presumption, but given its pervasiveness in the current debate it may also be seen as an implicit hypothesis about world politics: systemic interaction does not transform state interests" (1994: 384). This is also the reason why neoliberal institutionalism has been the target of constructivist criticism. From a Wendtian constructivist perspective the presumption of exogenous interests means that liberal cooperation theory is all about structure with little room for agency or the capacity to change structures via agent interaction. By insisting upon bracketing the formation of interests, liberal cooperation theory "also brackets an important line of argument against realists namely, that through interaction, states might form collective identities and interests" (384). Ruggie seconds this perspective, arguing that such a neoutilitarian approach "has no analytical means for dealing with the fact that the specific identities of specific states shape their perceived interests and, thereby, patterns of international outcomes" (1998: 14).

In its definitions of structure, however, the interdependence and regimes literature is not that far removed from Wendt's claim that "institutions are fundamentally cognitive entities that do not exist apart form actors' ideas about how the world works" (1992: 399). Keohane and Nye, for example, readily acknowledge that the very designation of an issue area is a cognitive act shaped by what elites are already doing (1989: 65). The self-interested actor's freedom of choice is always embedded in the larger social practices of capitalist-markets as well as in other shared norms, principles, and institutions which have developed and are associated with it. That social practice undergirds his entire regimes argument is also acknowledged by Keohane, because in order to explain cooperation,

> we need to examine actor's expectations about future patterns of interaction, their assumptions about the proper nature of economic arrangements, and the kinds of political activities they regard as legitimate. That is, we need to analyze cooperation within the context of international institutions, broadly defined, . . . in terms of practices and expectations (1984: 56; see also 1993: 289).

And a decidedly constructivist note is struck when he goes onto argue on the same page that "any act of cooperation or apparent cooperation needs to be interpreted within the context of related actions, and of prevailing expectations and shared beliefs, before its meaning can be properly understood." Because elite choices are embedded within prevailing regime practices, the interdependence and regimes literature essentially concurs with what Wendt labels the "fundamental principle of constructivist social theory . . . that people act toward objects, including other actors, on the basis of the meanings that the objects have for them," and that "it is collective meanings that constitute the structures which organize our actions" (1992: 396–397).

These affinities may arise because liberal IR theory and constructivism share a "process-based" ontology. What this means is that their practitioners share the metatheoretical commitment to human interaction as the sole component to social reality.[8] The terms *institution, structure,* and *process* are frequently used interchangeably in the liberal literature to denote the "particular human-constructed arrangement(s)" which "involve persistent and connected sets of rules (formal and informal) that prescribe behavioral roles, constrain activity, and shape expectations" (Keohane 1989: 162–163; 1990: 175). Processes are the collective practices, both formal-material and ideational, which groups of human beings create and propagate in order to achieve particular goals and to interact with one another. "Liberalism's strength," according to Keohane, "is that it takes political processes seriously," because it "stresses the role of human-created institutions in affecting how aggregations of individuals make collective decisions [and] emphasizes the importance of changeable political processes rather than simply of immutable structures" (1990: 175; 1989: 10). The processes in which human engage can be endlessly varied, according to liberal theory, and can run from the formal and precise, such as types of governments, economic systems, and technological advancements, to the informal and more diffuse, such as the sharing of norms, principles, and discursive practices (Zacher and Matthew 1995: 119).

In order to put a process-based ontology into perspective, it may be helpful to momentarily compare it to the differing ontology of realism. For realism, anarchy is an external environment separate from what human beings do. It is not simply a void to be filled with human interactions and institutions, but a particular type of environment with its own characteristics that have acted as selection mechanisms in encouraging species-wide reproductive adaptations such as group formation. As such, realism treats anarchy as a physical reality that is separate from yet affecting human activity and social reality. Choice is still filtered through human perception and differing perceptions of environment create differences in choice, but environment cannot be changed by what human beings do or by the processes they create within it. Thus when realism attempts to explain why human activities change, are created, or disappear, it makes reference not only to the processes which human beings have created as they interact with one another, but also to a causally constraining force external to human activity.

Anarchy in either liberal IR theory or constructivism, on the other hand, is not an environment external to human activity, but a reflection of human activity and particular types of human processes. Those processes may become structural and materially causal, but their ontological basis is still humanist rather than environmental, natural, or physical. Such an ontology allows for much wider latitude in the capacity of human interaction and social practices to affect changes in identity, interests, and behavior. Liberals argue that environment-based theories such as realism, on the other hand, "fail to pay sufficient attention to the institutions and patterns of interaction created by human beings that help to shape perceptions and expectation, and therefore alter the patterns of behavior that take place within a given structure" (Keohane 1990: 175). The difference ultimately rests, however, on whether there is something causal which lies beyond or outside of human processes and that is relevant to explanations of human social behavior. An environment-based ontology posits that there is, while a process-based ontology does not.

Because they share a process-based ontology, there are some theoretical affinities between constructivism and liberal IR. Thus it comes as no surprise that so many constructivists would be attracted back to older variants of liberal functional theorizing. Wendt points out that "despite important differences, cognitivists, poststructuralists, standpoint and postmodern feminists, rule theorists, and structurationists share a concern with the basic 'sociological' issue bracketed by rationalists—namely, the issue of identity- and interest-formation" (1992: 393). Because functionalism and its "neo" variant were also concerned with how particular processes encouraged interaction that could potentially change identities and interests, constructivists such as Wendt have used them as a basis from which to consider how nation-state identities and interests might be endogenous to and hence transformable through intrastate interaction (1994).

Of course one of constructivism's contributions to IR theoretical debates has been to highlight the basic problem in regime analysis that, as Kratochwil and Ruggie put it succinctly, "epistemology contradicts ontology" (Ruggie 1998: 95). They have been joined by a number of other scholars who note the inherent tension between a process-based ontology and the dominant positivist epistemology in the social sciences, with the latter assuming a clear separation of subject and object, demanding empirical validation of hypotheses, and giving actors priority over rules.[9] Constructivists argue that this essentially privileges human agency over the social structures in which their choices and behaviors are embedded. As a result, it fails to recognize that individual choices are influenced by the processes in which they are already engaged and so are structurally shaped prior to any given moment of choice. For example, Hasenclever, Mayer, and Rittberger observe with regards to the regimes argument that

> While it appears to be accepted that states are ultimately constituted by the fundamental norms and rules of an international society, the same states are expected to proceed as utility-maximizers once they have to decide on the creation and maintenance of international regimes. To put it differently: socialization sets states free to engage in rational behavior when it comes to solving collective action problems, and as long as the deep normative structures of an international society remain unchanged they will not have any further impact on particular choices (1997: 161).

This sort of sequential causal ordering is present in the interdependence literature as well and effectively separates any understanding of the codeterminant relationship between structures and agents which constructivists are striving to examine.[10]

Alternatively constructivists argue that greater attention must be given to how social practices and structures shape choice and action, as well as how agency interaction can affect change to those practices and structures. Striking a causal balance between agent and structure is obviously a formidable epistemological and philosophical task within the context of a process-based ontology.[11] Dessler refers to the difficulties of developing theory that successfully meets both demands because, as Marx had put it, "people make history but not in conditions of their own choosing." As a result, the agent-structure problem emerges in social theory "from two uncontentious truths about social life: first, that human agency is the *only* moving force behind the actions, events, and outcomes of the social world; and second, that human agency can be realized only in concrete historical circumstances that condition the possibilities for action and influence its course" (Dessler 1989: 443; my emphasis). What disturbs constructivist critics about neoliberal institutionalism is that, despite its process-based ontology, its assumption of exogenous interests places an exclusive bet on immutable structures over the interactive capacity of agency to change identities and interests.

Or does it? That is, does liberal cooperation theory ultimately make no room for interaction among agents to change their identities and interests? Obviously the explicit presumption of exogenous interests would appear to preclude such a possibility, but upon closer examination it becomes clear that the causal chain connecting interdependence and regimes to international cooperation actually contains an implicit identity transformation. The point in the causal chain at which liberal cooperation theory definitively strays into constructivist territory is when it shifts from explaining regime creation to regime maintenance. Maintenance involves a commitment to the cooperative effort itself which cannot be derived from the original premise that elites are motivated to adopt new strategies which are more efficient at maximizing national profits within a given systemic context. Hence in order to explain why regimes are maintained, neoliberal institutionalism implicitly assumes that successive acts of cooperation have the potential to affect intersubjective meanings and identities.

The idea that long-term participation in regimes has the potential to induce more than simple learning and changes to perceptual, strategic behavior is built into the liberal theoretical framework from the start. According to Keohane it is a "fact that people adapt their strategies to reality" and that "adaptive strategies of institution-building can also change reality, thereby fostering mutually beneficial cooperation" (1984: 30). And Keohane and Nye argue this is because while there is a "wide latitude for choice, decision, and multiple-level bargaining," it is also the case that "a regime creates a bargaining process which leads to a pattern of outcomes" and these patterns do "influence actor's ability to use [their] capabilities" overtime (1989: 54–56). Thus regimes themselves are social institutions, which raises the possibility that "in the long run, one may even see changes in how governments define their own self-interest in directions that conform to the rules of the regimes" (259). More specifically "the principles and norms of regimes may be internalized by important groups and thus become part of the belief systems which filter information" as well as "alters the way key participants in the state see cause and effect relationships" (266).

What this means is that iterated acts of cooperation can lead to an internalized commitment to the social practice of cooperation itself. This is actually Keohane's argument in *After Hegemony*, because the value of existing regimes lies not in their efficiency but in the difficulties of having obtained some level of multilateralism to begin with. Thus "international regimes embody sunk costs, and we can understand why they persists even when all members would prefer somewhat different mixtures of principles, rules, and institutions" (1984: 102; also 210, 215). Stein also argues that "regimes actually change actor preferences," because actors develop vested interests in them and so "their very existence changes actors' incentives and opportunities" (1983: 138–139). Actors "who previously agreed to bind themselves out of self-interest may come to accept joint interests as an imperative." Such an internalization stands in marked contrast to the theory's initial treatment of interests as exogenously-given and strategic behavior as separate from identity. Policymakers were assumed to commit to policy on the basis of its ability to efficiently maximize their utility function within a given systemic context. At some point in time, however, it appears that continued interaction also has the capacity to induce a commitment to multilateralism in whatever form it has taken and regardless of its efficiency.

In arguing that state decisionmakers commit to the practice of cooperation in this way, liberal cooperation theory strays from its own separation of exogenous identities/interests and endogenous strategic behavior. Economic elites were originally motivated to cooperate because they believed it was the most efficient means of maximizing economic interests. Yet eventually interest efficiency is dropped as the evaluative yardstick for strategic behavior. Instead economic policymakers continue to commit to the multilateral practices left by the hegemon because the practices are themselves effecting how policymakers define efficiency. Different forms of multilateralism are no longer being judged according to the originally posited motivation, and this could only be the case if an identity transformation had occurred due to increased cooperative interaction and contact among state decisionmakers. The upshot is that the interdependence and regimes literature actively implies a possibility consistent with a constructivist explanation for cooperation:

> Even if not intended as such . . . the process by which egoists learn to cooperate is at the same time a process of reconstructing their interests in terms of shared commitments to social norms. Over time, this will tend to transform a positive interdependence of outcomes into a positive interdependence of utilities or collective interest organized around the norms in question (Wendt 1992: 417).

In fact, the IO world structure of "governance without government" envisioned by liberal cooperation theorist can only occur because international cooperation as a social practice begins to reshape intersubjective meanings and hence state policymaker identities and interests. Policymakers develop a commitment to cooperative practices which cannot be derived from the initial assumptions about identity and which could only develop if cooperative practices had an impact on identity instead. Policymaker identities are eventually reconstituted by the established practices and rules of cooperation.

It is for these reasons that the constructivist critique of neoliberal institutionalism misses the mark. The two theories actually share the same commitment to combining agent and structure within the parameters of a process-based ontology. Neoliberal theorists agree with constructivists that cooperation is the outcome of both choice and the structures in which those choices are embedded. It is just that neoliberalism chooses to arrange structure and agency in chronological order rather than analyzing them, as constructivists have recommended, in terms of a "codetermined irreducibility" (Wendt and Duvall 1989: 59). Structure is originally taken as a given, but eventually repetitive agency choice becomes social practice itself and goes onto transform the structures initially held constant. As economic policymakers interact and choose cooperation, multilateralism becomes a causal institution in its own right which then reshapes policymaker identities and interests so that cooperation becomes the normative precondition to policymaker identity, interests, and hence rational choice and strategic behavior thereafter. Identity is held constant only to a point because, after iterated acts of cooperation, identity transformation is not only possible and expected, but also the only means by which cooperation's "maintenance" is explicable.

Thus at a key moment in the causal chain, the interdependence and regimes literature drops its positivist epistemological commitment to exogenous interests and sides with constructivists in favor of their common process-based ontology instead. That the maintenance of cooperation results is only because the theory simultaneously maintains its epistemology with regards to the practice of autonomy. The fact that this particular error in deductive logic occurs at the point in the liberal causal chain when the regime is no longer being created but instead simply maintained also suggests an interesting connection between the development of liberal theorizing about international cooperation and the empirical record in American monetary policymaking.

The error may have arisen from the fact that the initial premises of regime creation never held for actual policymaking behavior in an issue area that had earlier on been selected as most conducive to it. Positing regime creation might explain discreet episodes of post-1971 American monetary cooperation, but the overall historical pattern of U.S. policymaking in the issue area could in no way be characterized as efficient. Rather than abandoning the liberal theoretical framework entirely, however, the regimes maintenance argument was introduced as a means to salvage it. Now each of these episodes could be theoretically linked together into a pattern involving not efficiency but a commitment to whatever cooperative effort had preceded it. The problem with this proposition is not only that the empirical record has not supported such linkages, however, but that in the final analysis it also contradicts the very logic with which the interdependence and regimes literature had begun.

INTERDEPENDENT DEMAND AND FUNCTIONALLY EFFICIENT SUPPLY

Both of these flaws in the more contemporary variants of liberal cooperation theory are caused by the attempt to avoid the issue of identity transformation entirely. The more modest ambitions of the interdependence and regimes literature led it to propose that cooperation could be obtained in the absence of an identity transformation and with simple learning alone. The breakdown in logic of these strands of liberal cooperation theory coupled with their inability to account for patterns in the empirical policymaking record point to an obvious conclusion already suggested by the neoclassical realist-constructivist combination. Simple learning about new environmental conditions has no capacity to affect the necessary behavioral changes anticipated by the interdependence and regimes literature. Transformation of policymaker identities would have to be involved if cooperation is to be causally accounted for from a systemic interdependent basis. In other words, if one is going to argue that economic interdependence has the capacity to generate cooperative policymaking choices, it appears that the transformation of policymaker identity is going to have to remain a central link in the causal chain between the two phenomena, as it was in earlier functionalist theorizing and as it is today in functional-constructivism.

As soon as this is acknowledged, however, we are back to the very rock upon which neofunctionalism and functionalism before it had floundered. It is not simply that the practice of autonomy is well ingrained both cognitively and institutionally and so may be more difficult to change than some liberal cooperation theories anticipate. This would imply that it was still a matter of discovering the correct interactive mechanisms that would overcome this ingraining. The problem lies instead with the very notion that economic interdependent conditions demand functionally efficient institutions and have the capacity to create that supply, which is in turn premised on the assumption that the territorial nation-state's representatives may be considered capitalist market representatives for the sake of analysis. According to every strand of liberal cooperation theory, it is the difficulty or complete inability to obtain desired capitalist goals according to the territorial limitations of the nation-state that leads its own elites to abandon the functional logic of the state.

It is because the two forces which are motivating the economic policy-maker—capitalist profit and the state—are mutually exclusive that the policymaker must choose between them. We return, as a result, to the philosophical theme described by Gilpin:

> Whereas powerful market forces in the form of trade, money, and foreign investment tend to jump national boundaries, to escape political control, and to integrate societies, the tendency of government is to restrict, to channel, and to make economic activities serve the perceived interests of the state and of powerful groups within it (1987: 11).

This means the elite can either be a good capitalist who maximizes profits in interdependence, or she can maximize profits on behalf of a particular state and society. What she cannot do is maximize profits according to both the systemic condition of interdependence and the social practices which reify the difference between another nation-state and her own. It is, after all, the differences among existing social and governing practices which "diverge considerably from the path of economic efficiency" and make the pursuit of profits inefficient (Garrett and Lange 1996: 52). Capitalist interests may have initially been obtainable with autonomous and insular state institutions and domestic social practices. But eventually the process of capitalism itself demands expansion, and as markets grow these same institutions and social practices become functionally inefficient at obtaining profit.

It is no coincidence that Bergsten and Henning list differences in party control, policy preferences, and national institutions as some of the "practical barriers" (!) to international monetary coordination (1996: 144–145). Nor is it coincidental that in making the case for regimes Keohane suggests that states are willing to substitute multilateral for unilateral rules of thumb because "they need to simplify their own decisionmaking processes in order to function effectively at all" (1984: 115). The nation-state is quite explicitly to blame according to Rosecrance because "ultimate success" in ventures such as "economic growth for societies and individual self-improvement" fundamentally "depend on moving beyond the national state as the limit of economic and political horizons" (1986: 225).

According to liberal theories of cooperation, then, state policymakers must shed the practices of governance in which they have been engaged. They must in essence become better capitalists for the society's that they represent. This means reorienting national economic practices in accordance with systemic opportunities and constraints, and so they must insist upon multilateralism and adopt farsighted perspectives because that is what will maximize economic interests in complex interdependent conditions. But in doing so, state policymakers essentially have to change the very practices of governance which connect their own state and society and which differentiate their nation-state from other nation-states. It is impossible to retain these differences and at the same time efficiently maximize capitalist interests in conditions of complex interdependence. As a result the policymaker is faced with a fundamental contradiction in the pursuit of *self-interest*, which is captured by the very use of the term in an economic interdependent context. While the "self" is defined as a collective entity separate from other such entities, the interest in capitalist profit is unobtainable if such separations are maintained. The state policymaker can behave according to what is functionally efficient either within the context of the state social practices and institutions in which she is engaged or within the context of economic interest, but she cannot behave according to both logics equally and simultaneously since they are incompatible.

Liberal cooperation theory resolves this dilemma theoretically by privileging the functional efficiency of the interest in its systemic context over the constitutive principles which differentiate units. It is not the social practices of governance that make cooperation the most efficient course of action for the policymaker, but the interest in profit maximization in a world of expanding, integrated capitalist markets. Hence economic policymakers are exhorted to abandon their "purely domestic" illusions and accept "collective economic security as a principle for the conduct of international economic policy" (Keohane and Nye 1989: 232). They are told that "maintaining unrestrained flexibility can be costly," because it "makes a government an undesirable partner for others" in the international economic setting (Keohane 1984: 259). And we are assured that although the "conception of each state-unit acting like a little atom, self-sufficient and autonomous" has "continued to capture the imagination of statesmen and peoples," it is actually "belied by recent history and it cannot last much longer" (Rosecrance 1986: 190). The solution to commonly shared global problems lies with "conscious human action" (Keohane 1990: 172), and what is required is "the active leadership of a few individuals or states who feel a serious need for change" (Axelrod and Keohane 1986: 253).

What motivates policymakers in all of these accounts is the experience of the nation-state's opposite. Efficiency is defined according to function within the nonterritorial space, not according to function within the territorial space. Because the interest in capitalist efficiency is not territorially defined while the policymaker's responsibility for it is, the interest and the policymaker's responsibility are set in functional, spatial opposition to one another. And it is in the experience of the nonterritorial functional space that policymakers come to recognize the inefficiencies of the practices in which they have been engaged. This space not only does not conform to the practices of autonomy, but it also contains the problems that escape its capacities. There the elite comes to understand the functional inefficiency of autonomy and so chooses its functional opposite. In other words, the practices which promote autonomy are eventually transcended because particular interests and problems can only be obtained or resolved in the systemic interdependent context by adopting autonomy's functional opposite.

The tension between territorial and nonterritorial functional space as a premise for cooperation shows up in the functional-constructivist literature on IO as well. The path-dependencies of existing state social practices are transcended by experiencing their functional opposites or what is outside or beyond their own constitutive principles and abilities to address.[12] Ruggie argues, for example, that "the emergence of multiperspectival institutional forms," such as regimes and common markets, "unbundle territoriality" (1998: 197). Such forms represent "postmodern tendencies in the world polity" and differ from modernity in that they reflect "holism and mutual dependence of parts" rather than "territoriality and its accouterments" (192, 196):

> In sum, *nonterritorial functional space* is the place in which territorial rulers situate and deal with those dimensions of collective existence that they recognize to be irreducibly transterritorial in character. It is here that international society is anchored, and in which its patterns of evolution may be traced (191; my emphasis).

This international society derives from the paradox of having established mutually exclusive, territorially-fixed states to begin with (what Ruggie calls "absolute individuation") which could not then deal with problems irreducible to territorial solutions.

As with the functional-constructivist variant, other strands of liberal cooperation theory argue that the constitutive principles of the modern international system may be unbundled by state decisionmakers who experience interests and problems that are irreducibly transterritorial in character. Such an experience is reinforced by ongoing interaction that makes decisionmakers aware of the inefficiencies of their present social practices while also providing the incentive to adopt more efficacious patterns of behavior. Decisionmakers choose cooperation because they learn through interaction with one another that it is the most efficient means to obtain the interest over which they have responsibility. Or as Mitrany put it, "the essential principle is that activities would be selected specifically and organized separately—each according to its nature, to the conditions under which it has to operate, and to the needs of the moment" (1943: 42). Cooperative processes displace autonomous processes because they are functionally more efficient at obtaining particular interests.

The problem with accounting for change in this way is that it treats what is external to the practices of autonomy as if it were a cognitive vacuum that cannot theoretically exist. If "social identities and interests are always in process during interaction" then, as Wendt points out, "choices may not be experienced with meaningful degrees of freedom" (1994: 386; 1992: 411). And if, as all of these cooperative theoretical variants acknowledge, autonomy and interdependent cooperation should be arranged chronologically, then the existing social practices of autonomy inform the perception of interests in their external contexts. Given that policymakers derive their identities from social practices that create and reify the territorial space, it would be theoretically impossible for these same policymakers to freely experience what was functionally efficient within the context of the nonterritorial space.

In fact, functional efficiency itself would be meaningless absent the processes in which policymakers were already engaged. To define functional efficiency according to the interest alone is to posit an "objective" standard for behavior that can have no meaning in the context of existing intersubjective understandings and expectations. Nor should it have any meaning in the context of a process-based ontology, since according to Ruggie "constitutive rules define the set of practices that make up any particular consciously organized social activity—that is to say, they specify *what counts as* that activity" (1998: 22; his emphasis; see also Jackson 1998: 25–29). It makes no theoretical sense to subsequently argue that a logic inherent to the social activity itself can be experienced absent the set of territorially-defined practices which specify that it counts as an activity. Ruggie himself argues elsewhere that "functional contexts do not exist apart from particular configurations of actor attributes in relation to any given issue" (1998: 46), which makes all the more curious his argument that the experience of transterritoriality in a functional context has the potential to subvert territoriality. Because state policymakers would have no capacity to experience the nonterritorial space absent or separate from the territorial space from which their own identities and interests are derived, the nonterritorial space is not and cannot be "an unproblematic empty space in which a peace-loving humanity can be erected" in a postmodern world (Folker 1996: 13).[13]

The implications of this for liberal explanations of international cooperation is that economic policymakers would have no capacity to cognitively appreciate what is functionally efficient with respect to economic interests and in the absence of the practice of autonomy. Without this capacity policymakers would be unable to recognize the flaws of their own governing practices and hence would have no incentive to modify them in accordance with an alternative logic. Instead policymakers experience the logic of the marketplace *through* the logic of the state, not separately or in opposition to it. Not only does the state predispose economic policymaker preferences to

the "inefficient," but the state, as a collection of ideational and formal practices, blocks the economic policymaker's ability to recognize what a standard
of efficiency would look like absent its logic.

It cannot matter to choice, then, that the maximization of profit is most
efficiently obtained via multilateralism, because the practices and institutions
from which economic policymakers derive their identities do not give priority
to the interest by itself but instead embed it within a contradictory logic.
Ultimately policymakers would be cognitively *in*disposed to modify the structures of the state according to multilateralism, because doing so would destroy
the very institutions which give their own roles and perceptions meaning in
the first place. In the self-perpetuating cycle to which Wendt refers,
policymakers could not and would not conceptualize the pursuit of the capitalist interest absent the governing practices that differentiate their state and
society from others. The posited mechanism of functional institutional
efficiency simply could not impact this self-perpetuating cycle in the manner
specified by liberal cooperation theories.

The result is that according to the parameters of these theories the choices
made by policymakers cannot be derived from existing policymaking institutions and are not guided by their imperatives. Such institutions do not even
serve as a guide for what the policymaker would consider rational behavior.
When Keohane and Nye assert that a "sophisticated" version of liberal IR
theory examines "the way interactions among states and the development of
international norms can interact with the domestic politics of the states," they
do not mean "domestic" politics in any form that an Americanist or
comparativist would recognize (1989: xi). "Domestic politics" boils down to
the pursuit of capitalist wealth which is assumed to be a timeless interest not
bound by domestic institutions or governing practices. In this context Keohane
and Nye's call for domestic politics to be incorporated into the study of
complex interdependence because "as long as we continue to regard preferences as exogenous, our theories will miss many of the forces that propel
changes in state strategies," takes on a particularly hollow ring (258).

Small wonder, then, that the empirical record does not support liberal
expectations. It is difficult to see how it could, since as Gelber notes "the
transnational organizations and elites which appear to supersede national
structures, nevertheless have these same national structures as the only legitimate and politically defensible bases of their own authority" (1997: 231).
Proponents of liberal cooperation theories are offering what Hoffmann observes is "advice to state agents on how to transcend the limits of the game
which it is however these agents' role and duty to perpetuate" (1995: 234).
And Volcker, a proponent of multilateralism himself, once again manages to
hit the nail on the head in his explanation for why international coordination
of macroeconomics remains so difficult for the policymakers involved:

To a politician, that all implies some loss of sovereignty. Academics can dance around that philosophically in emphasizing quite correctly that participation in an open world economy necessarily implies a loss of autonomy, and that external influences on policy are bound to become larger as the volume of international trade and investment increases. Nonetheless, to those politically responsible for decisionmaking in the real world, the idea of coordination invades very sensitive political territory (1992: 145).

That territory involves domestic political institutions and practices which continue to exert more immediate weight on policymaking behavior and outcomes than does the condition of interdependence and the strategies necessary to maximize economic outcomes in its context.

Not surprisingly, then, we find that among American monetary policymakers since 1971 the Treasury secretaries did not recognize or care about what was institutionally efficient according to the marketplace. And while there was some concern along these lines within the lower ranks of the Treasury, such officials were incapable of affecting long-lasting institutional changes, nor did they seek to subvert the authority of the Treasury Secretary in order to do so. Given the Treasury's institutional structure, it would seem irrational to expect lower-ranking officials to do anything but abide by the Treasury Secretary's wishes. After all, Coombs, Volcker, Solomon, Darman, and Mulford were bureaucrats working within particular administrative structures which had their own standard operating procedures, lines of advancement, and mechanisms for punishing institutional disloyalties. These administrative structures operate within a larger hierarchy and political context which could reward and punish as well. Given their temporary appointment status, each of these decisionmakers could always be removed from office. The translation of individual learning into organizational learning confronts the logic of the state at every turn, and expecting lower-ranking U.S. Treasury officials to behave otherwise would seem wishful indeed.

Yet for some scholars this is precisely where liberal cooperation theories derive their strength. Their value lies less in the realm of explanations for international cooperation and more in the realm of prescriptions for policymaking action. Choice is derived not from constitutive principles within the theoretical parameters specified, but from alternative principles which are out of context to those parameters. The result is that actual policymaking behavior is not explained; rather the policymaker is encouraged to be guided by principles that are preferred by the theorist, and not by the principles and parameters which give the activity of policymaking its meaning in the first place. Keohane admits as much when he argues, "liberalism holds out the prospect that we can affect, if not control, our fate, and thus encourages both better theory and improved practice. It constitutes an antidote to fatalism and a source of hope for the human race" (1990: 194).

This tendency to evaluate liberal IR theory in terms of hopeful prescription rather than rigorous explanation may be encouraged to some extent by the very nature of process-based theorizing. Because a process-based ontology considers nothing external to human social practices and institutions to have an independent effect on human identities, interests, and behaviors, the purposes of such processes must lie in qualities particular to the processes themselves. That is, there is nothing external to process which may explain why institutions such as bureaucracies, political parties, interests groups, democracies, and capitalist markets, would be created, maintained, or abandoned. Creation may largely be a matter of historical accident, but once created social practices take on a life of their own in Wendt's cycle of self-perpetuating path-dependencies. Processes are sustained because they *are* processes which determine identities and interests, and not because something external to human social practices has had an affect on human behavior, choices, and adaptation.

Yet by treating social practices and institutions as ends in themselves, rather than as means to an end within a given environment, such theories have difficulty explaining not only why processes would develop at all but also how they would ever change. The selection mechanism is so underspecified that, as Weber points out, there is "no clear reason to expect any particular institution to emerge," and a supplemental argument is required to explain "why one set of knowledge claims 'wins' and why others are left behind" (1997: 240). As with creation, random acts of chance might account for change, but when the goal is to account for and predict a particular type of outcome, such as interdependent cooperation, chaos is inevitably dispensed with as a causal variable and social practices are instead causally prioritized.[14]

Such a strategy for explaining change might appear to make sense because the only causal variables available in a process-based theory are other processes. The problem is, however, that there is no means by which one could prioritize social practices in order to determine when institutions which are already informing identities, interests, and behaviors would stop being causal so that entirely different practices could inform identity and interests instead. Hasenclever, Mayer, and Rittberger put this problem in the language of agent-structure invoked by Wendtian constructivism itself. Because the theory still fails to specify when and why "the identity-forming capacity of structures triumph over the structure-transforming power of agents and vice versa," then "the agent-structure problem, which has driven constructivist theory-building to such a large extent has not been solved but has merely reemerged in a different (though certainly fascinating) guise" (1997: 191–192). The theorist must ultimately smuggle something ontologically external into the explanatory equation in order to explain why some practices will be more causal than others.

The mechanism that has been favored by functionalists, interdependence and regime theorists, and now many constructivists is the assumption of functional institutional efficiency which is defined by comparing one social practice to another. Yet within the context of the given ontology, functional efficiency can have no comparative meaning other than that accorded it by the theorist. The only possible source for defining it comparatively and for then using it as a basis for prioritizing processes is the personal predispositions of the theorist. Even if the definition of efficiency is consistent with standard liberal economic expectations, the causal prioritization of capitalist-market practices over other institutions would still amount to the substitution of personal preference for explanation. As a result the practices of autonomy are considered of lesser causal weight not because epistemological and ontological orientations indicate this is the case. In fact, as I have sought to demonstrate repeatedly, it should be autonomy that is overdetermined on the basis of such orientations, not cooperation. If, however, the social practices of autonomy are indeed path-dependent, then cooperation becomes a much more difficult phenomenon to explain and predict. In its failure to grasp the thorny nettle of competing process causality, liberal cooperation theories continue to divert our attention from the more credible explanation of post-Bretton Woods U.S. international monetary cooperation to which we now turn.

blank 210

Chapter 7

Explaining U.S. International Monetary Cooperation with Realist-Constructivism

One of the interesting implications which can be drawn from a review of post-Bretton Woods U.S. international monetary policymaking is that cooperation can occur even when there has been no cognitive or institutional displacement of unilateral practices. According to liberal theories of cooperation, policymakers are faced with a cognitive tradeoff between what is efficacious within an issue area characterized by complex interdependence and almost every other domestic political process in which they are engaged. While bureaucratic, electoral, and budget politics engender role-specific interests and concerns that contrast with and frequently contradict issue area efficacy, the logic of liberal cooperation theories is that such processes are all potential inhibitors to cooperation. This means they could not simultaneously be causes of it.

As the pattern of post-Bretton Woods U.S. monetary policymaking reveals, however, these processes continue to hold sway even as decisionmakers cooperate with their international counterparts. Treasury policymakers who pursued multilateral efforts, such as in the late Carter or second Reagan administrations, did so despite the fact that the domestic administrative structures and parochial political contexts in which they operated had in no way been supplanted. This has serious implications for liberal theories of cooperation because it indicates not only that the condition of complex interdependence cannot displace the social practices and institutions which reify unilateralism, but also that these theories are incapable of explaining why cooperation even occurs when it does. As it turns out, it is not necessary for the decisionmaker's faith in unilateral policymaking to be dislodged and supplanted with a new found faith in multilateralism in order for cooperation to occur. Decisionmakers instead retain their misplaced unilateral perspectives and, even as they engage in multilateralism, their policymaking behavior continues to be informed and reinforced by the domestic institutions within which they operate.

Why does cooperation occur if the dichotomous tradeoff between unilateralism and multilateralism anticipated by liberal theories is not necessary and does not explain it? Part of the answer is obvious. It is only a dichotomy if we concur with liberal theories that cooperation must be the result of issue area interests and functional efficiency in the context of complex interdependence. Alternatively we could argue that the simultaneous occurrence of international monetary cooperation and issue area efficacy are accidental and that this is true even when the decisionmakers involved are aware of ideas about institutional efficiency in the issue area. In other words, something other than issue area efficacy is causing the cooperation to occur, and the fact that tendencies toward autonomy and unilateralism continue to dominate American international monetary policymaking suggests a possible answer. The choice of cooperation may be prompted by, and derived from, the processes of autonomy themselves. An entirely different standard of efficiency would then inform the cooperative choice, making it an extension of (rather than competitor to) unilateralism and a reinforcement (rather than deposer) of autonomous tendencies in policymaking.

This is where the neoclassical realist-constructivist alternative gains its explanatory strength and capacities, of course, since it would anticipate that the logic of the state would continue to take causal precedence even in changing economic systemic conditions. The starting point for this alternative explanation involves the selection pressures emanating from the anarchic environment, which have encouraged the formation of groups as a fundamental parameter of human existence and activity. As the most recent incarnations of human groupings, nation-states have developed internal decisionmaking structures that are specific to each of them and that embody the practice of decisionmaking autonomy relative to other nation-states. And because resource allocation decisions necessary for the survival and reproduction of individual group members involves a process that is internal to each nation-state, each nation-state is to some degree internally obsessed with itself. Its internal decisionmaking institutions serve as both avenues for, and sources of, competition within, thereby becoming prizes in their own right for competing subgroups.

This means that there is an internal logic by which domestic decisionmaking practices and institutions operate that involves and has been informed by intragroup resource allocation battles. This does not mean that groups are unresponsive to external circumstances, since available resources would be affected by the presence and activities of other nation-state groupings as well. But it does indicate that foreign policy choices in general and the choice to engage in international cooperation specifically must be derived from the nation-state's own internal logic. From this perspective monetary cooperation occurs not because policymakers wish to maximize issue area interests and doing so in interdependent systemic conditions requires multilateralism, but because cooperation is sometimes useful in the pursuit of interests derived from role-specific domestic processes that have little if nothing to do with issue area interests and everything to do with internal political power struggles. International cooperation can be just one more tool or instrument available to the policymaker for expanding and protecting bureaucratic jurisdictions, promoting or defending executive policies and prerogatives from legislative encroachment and electoral challengers, and deflecting both legislative and media scrutiny.

As it turns out, then, the choice of cooperation can have everything to do with the very processes of autonomy that liberal cooperation theory insists must be displaced in order for cooperation to occur. Institutions and social practices within the nation-state that reify national identities and the pursuit of policies in service of the national group *as a group* can account for cooperative instances in post-Bretton Woods American monetary policymaking instead. The cooperative choice can be driven by parochial interests and perspectives that find cooperation to be useful for purposes *other than* issue area efficacy in systemic conditions of interdependence. That condition provides policymakers with the opportunity to pursue cooperation with their transnational counterparts, but it does not serve as the impetus for that pursuit. The fact that cooperation might also be objectively efficacious within the issue area is then spurious and not causal, so it is hardly surprising that liberal cooperation theory cannot provide a satisfactory account of U.S. international monetary affairs. In their account of international cooperation, liberal theorists have consistently confused objective efficiency in the issue area for what policymakers are actually doing and why.

An examination of policymaking in the issue area supports the realist-constructivist alternative in general, since it reveals that presidential politics encourages policymaking recidivism, individual learning does not translate into institutional encoding, and decisionmakers do not substitute multilateral rules of thumb for unilateral decisionmaking. Levy's observation that "unless new knowledge is institutionalized, it will not endure, and a change in personnel would immediately result in unlearning" (1994: 289) is clearly pertinent here and connected to Quandt's observation that "experience and power, as well as the time and inclination to deal with foreign affairs, are tied to the rhythms of the electoral cycle" (1988: 89). The ongoing prevalence of recidivism in U.S. international monetary policymaking suggests that for national policymakers the game *is* domestic electoral politics and control over national decisionmaking institutions, and this affects their foreign policy choices and how they respond to external events. While American monetary policymakers frequently turn to multilateralism when there is a crisis (typically of their own making), such cooperation serves merely as a quick fix that is abandoned shortly after the crisis passes, thereby leaving no lasting impression on American policymaking in the issue area (Cohen 1993). The disinterest in the progressive development of efficacious multilateral institutions and the failure to maintain even minimal cooperative behaviors are precisely the types of outcomes and patterns which a realist-constructivist approach would anticipate and make explicable.

However while the empirical record supports realist-constructivist expectations in general, the burden of proof for a realist-constructivist explanation of international cooperation must also shift from periods of unilateralism to the cooperative efforts themselves. That is, while realist-constructivism would anticipate unilateralism to remain the norm, highlighting the pattern of recidivism in the empirical record is the easy task for such a perspective. The more pressing theoretical chore is to establish whether this alternative can also explain why U.S. monetary policymakers choose to cooperate when they do. Is it possible to explain post-Bretton Woods U.S. monetary cooperation without any reference to functional institutional efficiency in the issue area? Can it be explained instead (and exclusively) as a result of domestic institutional interests competing with one another over resources and the allocation of decisionmaking jurisdictions within the nation-state? Can intragroup competition over the levers of power within the group serve as the source for the cooperative choice?

The answer provided in this chapter is yes. The goal is to demonstrate how the approach can be applied empirically to the choice of cooperation itself and in so doing underscore why it provides a superior account of the cooperative phenomenon. In the context of realist-constructivist propositions, the most confounding instance of cooperation in the empirical record is what Funabashi called the "Plaza Strategy" of the mid-1980s. The policies pursued by Baker during Plaza and extending to the Louvre Accord came closest to the type of cooperation anticipated by the interdependence and regimes literature. Thus if the argument against liberal cooperation theory and for realist-constructivism is to be empirically supported, it is particularly important to demonstrate that the "Plaza Strategy" was initiated and pursued for reasons other than issue area interests and their efficacious achievement. A realist-constructivist approach to cooperation would anticipate that the processes of autonomy themselves encouraged the choice of cooperation in that instance, that they did so without being displaced by the act of cooperation, and that cooperation actually reinforced the practices and processes of national autonomy as a result.

RETURNING TO THE HOTEL

Why did James Baker encourage the "Plaza Strategy" if not to obtain more efficient outcomes in international monetary affairs? This is the central question which a realist-constructivist explanation for post-Bretton Woods U.S. international monetary cooperation must address. Between 1971 and 1993 it was the cooperative episode which appears to be most inconsistent with realist-constructivist expectations. And it was an American cooperative effort which came closest to institutionalizing the forms of multilateralism that one would anticipate if functional institutional efficiency in monetary affairs was the goal of national decisionmakers. That strategy was outlined in Darman's spring 1985 memo to Baker, in which Darman proposed a number of multilateral mechanisms in order to resolve the currency crisis and including coordinated interventions, a target zone exchange rate system, and a multilateral surveillance system. These proposals served as the basis for U.S. international monetary policymaking between September 1985 and November 1988. In addition there is evidence that Darman had been directly exposed to suggestions regarding how a target zone exchange rate system could achieve greater efficiency in the issue area. Thus the causal link between functional institutional efficiency and subsequent policymaking behavior in the issue area appears to be quite strong.

Although this time period ultimately does not confirm to liberal cooperation theory propositions when it is examined in a chronological context that documents overall policymaking patterns, in isolation the Plaza Strategy appears to confound realist-constructivist expectations and to confirm liberal expectations. As a result it is particularly important that the alternative approach to cooperation proposed here be capable of accounting for it. In order to do so such an account must rely solely on domestic institutional interests which are distinguishable from issue area interests, such as the maximization of wealth or their efficient pursuit in an interdependent context. It must be able to demonstrate that when American monetary policymakers were confronted with a monetary crisis of their own making, they resorted to multilateralism for domestic institutional reasons which differed fundamentally from those that would be anticipated by liberal cooperation theories. It must establish that policymakers were not seeking to maximize interests in the issue area on behalf of their nation-state and thus (re)discovered the virtues of multilateralism in complex interdependence. It must instead reveal that they were seeking to maximize other institutional interests which could only have meaning to decisionmakers in the domestic political context. What, then, was this context and what were these interests?

As noted earlier, the Reagan administration's "hands-off" policy toward the dollar had produced an unprecedented currency crisis and trade imbalance by the summer of 1985. The dollar's appreciation against the currencies of all of its major trading partners had a direct effect on the trade competitiveness of American exporters. Yet domestic pressure did not build on exchange rate policymakers until 1984 because the administration's macroeconomic policies worked fairly well in the short-term. Henning and Destler point out, for example, that inflation fell, growth surged, and the administration managed to avoid hard budget choices and to maintain domestic consumption by borrowing from abroad (1988: 328–329). When the economy seemed to be recovering in 1983 and 1984 there was no immediate reason for the Treasury to change its nonintervention policy. In addition, growth in employment and the GNP offset deteriorating U.S. international competitiveness. This tradeoff shifted the burden of adjustment onto blue-collar workers while directly benefiting traditional Republican constituencies (Funabashi 1989: 70). The strong dollar harmed manufacturing and agricultural sectors, but it was helping the financial and services sectors and consumers.

When the recovery slowed after Reagan's reelection in late 1984, however, the overvalued dollar and the deteriorating U.S. trade balance became increasingly difficult to offset or ignore. American manufacturing and agricultural groups began to vocalize their opposition to exchange rate neglect in ever-increasing numbers. The National Association of Manufacturers, the Chamber of Commerce, and farm lobbies sought out their representatives in the executive branch such as Secretary of Commerce Malcolm Baldrige, U.S. Trade Representative (USTR) William E. Brock, and Secretary of Agriculture John R. Block. These Cabinet members began to argue in favor of intervention for dollar depreciation, but the Treasury merely reaffirmed its basic faith in market mechanisms and called for additional federal spending cuts as a means to reduce the budget deficit. There was little that other executive departments or agencies could do directly, since they were jurisdictionally excluded from exchange rate policymaking.

Frustrated that their direct petitions to the White House fell on deaf ears, American business and agricultural groups began by early 1985 to shift their attention to Congress. This angered members of Congress since the executive branch had traditionally acted as a buffer to protectionist pressures.[1] By the middle of 1985 Congress was seething at the categorical refusals of the administration to admit that anything was seriously amiss with the balance of payments or the exchange rate. Like the Commerce and Agricultural departments in the executive branch, Congress had no direct control over exchange rate policymaking and now the Treasury's jurisdictional autonomy over international monetary policymaking became a focal point for congressional ire and frustration. While the decision to solve the currency misalignment with international cooperation was made by the Treasury, the motivation for the decision was the growing pressure from Congress. It wanted the

Treasury to do *something* about the trade imbalance but it did not particularly care whether this involved multilateralism, because as far as Congress was concerned it was Treasury neglect of exchange rates that had created the trade imbalance in the first place. When the Treasury proved to be recalcitrant during the spring of 1985, Congress used one of the immediate weapons at its disposal—a spate of protectionist legislation which the administration had neither requested nor desired.

Approximately one hundred bills designed to impede imports in some way were introduced in the Ninety-ninth Congress of 1985–1986 (S. D. Cohen 1988: 211). Many of them would have forced the executive branch to negotiate a better deal for U.S. producers or to impose retaliatory barriers. The first bill was introduced in March 1985 and was specifically directed at Japan. Both houses passed a nonbinding concurrent resolution that branded Japan an unfair trader and instructed the president to take action to rectify the situation. The binding version of the resolution was passed by the Senate Finance Committee in April 1985, although it never made it to the floor for full Senate approval. Yet it was clear from the start that Japanese trade surpluses were not really the issue for Congress. As one aide to a Senate Republican put it, "The target isn't the Japanese; its the White House!" (Destler 1986: 105–106). Congress wanted to force the administration to recognize the linkage between monetary and trade issues because, as Sen. John C. Danforth (R-MO) put it later, "no trade policy can work if the exchange rate problem is not resolved" (Funabashi 1989: 74). The introduction of protectionist bills was meant to cajole a committed free trade administration into finally doing something about the currency misalignment.

Yet because it was widely viewed as the main culprit in the crisis, Congress also targeted the powers and prerogatives of the Treasury specifically. For the first time since floating exchange rates had been introduced in the early 1970s, Congress threatened to revoke the Treasury's control over exchange rate policymaking and to exercise congressional oversight in the issue area instead. This previously ignored area of legislation now became a prime target and by mid-1985 Congress had, according to Destler and Henning, "fired several warning shots over the Treasury's bow" (1989: 107). The first shot came in May when the Senate passed a resolution sponsored by Sen. Bill Bradley (D-NJ) that called on the Treasury Department and the Federal Reserve to cooperate with the G5 to lower the dollar. Then in mid-July three prominent democrats, Sen. Lloyd Bentsen (D-TX), and Rep. Dan Rostenkowski (D-IL) and Richard Gephardt (D-MO), introduced legislation which imposed an import surcharge on target countries running large bilateral trade surpluses with the United States. The "Trade Emergency and Export Promotion Act," as it was called, also required the Treasury Secretary to develop a plan for multilateral coordination to reduce exchange rate volatility and to specify both a schedule and the institutional arrangements necessary for implementation.

In early August Senator Bradley submitted a piece of exchange rate legislation which would have created a Strategic Capital Reserve (SCR) similar to the ESF. The Act would have required the Treasury to use the SCR to purchase at least $3 billion in foreign currency each quarter when the previous four quarters' current account deficit exceeded 1.5 percent of GNP and the dollar was at least 15 percent above the level required to balance the current account. At the same time, Sens. Daniel Moynihan (D-NY) and Max Baucus (D-MT) submitted a similar bill which would have directed the Treasury and Federal Reserve to develop a Strategic Foreign Currency Reserve account to use in moderating the dollar's value. Both bills called for essentially the same thing—mandatory intervention along guidelines predetermined by Congress—with the only difference being that Bradley's bill would not have allowed for sterilized interventions. All three senators argued that mandatory intervention was necessary given the Treasury's recent record of behavior. At the same time, Reps. Stan Lundine (D-NY) and John J. LaFalce (D-NY) were cooperating on similar legislation in the House Banking Committee.

By the end of 1985 seven different bills in both Houses contained sections on exchange rate policy and were being actively supported by many different members.[2] All of these bills attempted to reduce Treasury discretion in intervention decisions and to render the Treasury more accountable to the relevant congressional committees in international monetary policymaking. This was an unprecedented threat to the Treasury's jurisdiction and control over the issue area. Destler and Henning point out that "over the course of the 1980s Congress held more hearings that raised the exchange rate issue than in any previous decade. It was a topic in more than 130 hearings and was given in-depth treatment in at least one-third of these" (1989: 101). It is undoubtedly true that Congress did not really want to set exchange rate policy, but it did want the Treasury to do something and it was angry enough to threaten Treasury prerogatives and powers to get some action.

WHY TOAST THE GOD OF COOPERATION?

The Plaza Accord was the Treasury's response to this congressional pressure, but why a multilateral effort? Did the Treasury choose cooperation as a means to resolve the currency crisis because cooperation satisfied domestic institutional interests which were independent of issue area efficiencies? Or did the Treasury choose cooperation because it recognized that currency interdependencies rendered unilateral decisionmaking inefficient while multilateral efforts would best resolve the problem? Certainly standard economic logic supports the proposition that a coordinated intervention would have had an impact on currency markets and so help resolve the crisis. Yet a number of other potentially viable policy options were available to the Treasury in the summer and fall of 1995 which could have also addressed congressional concerns and resolved the trade imbalance.

For example, the United States could have indirectly driven the dollar down by lowering interests rates, raising taxes, and reducing the budget deficit. While the exchange rate may have been of immediate concern, its misalignment was due to deeper structural economic problems that the Reagan administration's own macroeconomic policies had exasperated. Instead of a coordinated exchange rate intervention, the U.S. government could have addressed these underlying problems directly. However President Reagan had already made it clear that he did not want to raise taxes or engage in actual deficit cutting. Multilateral coordination was, in Gallarotti's words, "a way of escaping necessary and costly adjustments in government spending: bringing down the dollar through intervention was preferred to bringing down the dollar by cutting the budget, which would have brought interest rates down" (1991: 202). This made international cooperation a convenient way to avoid making hard domestic choices which would have been economically more efficient in the long-term, but would have negatively affected the president's popularity and primary constituency support in the short-term.

A second option the Treasury could have pursued was a direct but unilateral intervention in foreign currency markets. The dollar had been dropping on its own since the peak it had reached in February, and even a unilateral declaratory policy and a modest intervention would have had a dramatic impact on the dollar's value. Henning and Destler argue, for instances, that

> It would have been possible to hold a well-staged press conference to announce that the dollar was overvalued and should depreciate, and that the U.S. would aggressively purchase foreign currencies (a good buy at rates prevailing at that time) until exchange rates reached more reasonable levels. . . . Without a doubt, such a unilateral declaration would have produced a sensation in the foreign currency markets (1988: 325).

It would have done so because it would have been a dramatic reversal of the "hands-off" dollar policies that the Reagan administration had pursued so fanatically to that point. In addition, while an exchange rate intervention is assumed to be more effective when other central banks participate, many international economists remained wholly unimpressed by the intervention quantities at the time and described the Plaza Accord as a "nonevent" that fulfilled no real purpose (Funabashi 1989: 217–218). From this perspective the coordinated intervention simply prodded a depreciation which the market was already determining on its own. For all these reasons the rationale for a multilateral approach is less than obvious or compelling.

The variable most often cited for the cooperative choice is, of course, the Regan-Baker job switch. Baker and his advisers were simply predisposed to multilateralism and learning in a way that Regan was not, so the argument goes. As noted in chapter 5, however, it is difficult to sustain this interpretation for the year between the Plaza and Louvre accords when Baker's policymaking behavior was decidedly unilateral and aggressive in character. And even if we accept that a mental epiphany occurred with the Louvre, inconsistencies in Baker's behavior still remain thereafter which suggest that he still did not really understand the necessity for multilateralism. His public disagreement with the German Bundesbank and renewed talk of "dollar weaponry" that contributed to the October 1987 stock market crash are frequently attributed to his "erroneous assumptions" about market behavior in interdependent conditions (Gallarotti 1991: 196). If it is possible that Baker still did not understand that multilateralism would solve the problems of interdependence after over a year of encouraging it, then why precisely had he been pursuing it?

The alternative explanation is that Baker understood market inefficiencies well enough, but that they had never been his primary motivation for encouraging international cooperation. Multilateralism was instead a useful cover for obtaining multiple domestic interests. It avoided raising taxes and budget cutting which would have actually been more economically efficient (but, of course, politically more painful), it deflected immediate congressional pressures on both trade policy and Treasury jurisdictions, and it relied upon traditional areas of Treasury autonomy which avoided interagency consultation and debate. Because the Treasury controlled access to the G5, it was a useful forum through which a transnational coalition could be established for the purpose of protecting the interests of the Treasury and the White House in the domestic political setting. The efficient maximization of issue area interests were secondary to the endeavor, because what motivated the "Plaza Strategy" were institutional parameters determined by the domestic political setting and jurisdictional infighting within it.[3]

Precisely how was multilateralism a useful cover for obtaining particular domestic interests, and whose interests was Baker obtaining? First and foremost Baker was loyal to the president who, by the spring of 1985, was witnessing a congressional assault on his free trade policies and wanted something done about it. Yet President Reagan had also made it clear that he did not want to raise taxes, cut the deficit, or lower interest rates. This considerably narrowed the range of options left to the Treasury and provided strong incentives for it to rely on the one policy option that the Treasury alone controlled—a direct manipulation of the exchange rate. It was, as Henning and Destler put it, "something Treasury *could* dominate . . . a matter on which Treasury had the 'lead,' and on which it could act alone: privately through intervention in public exchange markets; publicly through official statements" (1988: 323–324, their emphasis).

In this context the relevance of the Regan-Baker job switch becomes much more debatable. Due to presidential preferences there were few other options besides international cooperation left for the Treasury by the summer of 1985. Cooperation became an option only because the administration's parochial domestic policy preferences had already closed off all other policy options which would have obtained greater efficiencies in the long-term. In addition Regan had left the Treasury before the spring offensive against free trade and exchange rate policymaking had even begun. Baker, on the other hand, faced considerably greater pressure to do something about the currency misalignment. Henning and Destler point out that

> even Baker would probably have seen little value in adopting a new exchange rate policy had the trade deficit and tradable sector interests not created a political "market" for it. And even Regan, who had responded fitfully to this market from time to time, would have been unlikely to resist policy change indefinitely had he retained the Treasury portfolio (1988: 330).

In fact, from his new position as White House Chief of Staff Regan approved of the Plaza Accord when it was announced, and Henning suggests that Regan may have wanted the job switch so that he could avoid the necessity of publicly repudiating his own monetary policies (1987: 72–73). Thus it is not at all clear that it was the difference in personal preferences between the two secretaries which accounts for the shift in strategy. What varied instead was the increased congressional pressure by the spring of 1995, while at the same time the Treasury continued to face domestic constraints on its policy options.

What also varied was the type of pressure the Treasury was under, and here lay the second domestic institutional interest which Baker sought to obtain through a strategy of multilateralism. The Treasury and its Secretary derive considerable power from the Treasury's jurisdictional control over international economic and monetary policymaking, yet this control was under direct congressional threat for the first time in mid-1985. This was no small matter to the Treasury which, like all other bureaucratic departments, derives policy tools, resources, power, and security within the administrative hierarchy from policymaking autonomy over an issue area.[4] The congressional threats to exchange rate autonomy constituted threats to the security of the department itself, and so they threatened the source from which the department's bureaucrats and leaders derive their own powers, prestige, and ultimately job security and promotion. This type of threat tends to generate fierce departmental loyalties on the part of its members because, as A. Downs has observed, "all officials exhibit relatively strong loyalty to the organization controlling their job security and promotion" (1967: 211).[5] While Baker may have been assured another prestigious job within the administration even if the Treasury lost control over the exchange rate, as long as he was Treasury Secretary his subordinates expected him to protect departmental prerogatives, he derived considerable power from those prerogatives, and so he had an incentive to protect the Treasury against congressional oversight.[6]

A multilateral effort had the potential to effectively deflect congressional threats to the Treasury's exchange rate control in several ways. By shifting his decisions to an international forum, Baker could exclude other domestic actors from the decisionmaking process. Access to, and discussions with, the G5 were dominated by Treasury representatives, so that negotiations could be informed by the preferences of the Treasury, not by Congress or other bureaucratic agencies. According to Destler and Henning, an exclusionary strategy was reflected in Baker's policymaking behavior in general:

> Although he raised the *sensitivity* of the Treasury to broad economic considerations in pursuing international adjustment, Secretary Baker discouraged greater *openness* of the policy process. Simply being more responsive to trade concerns in exchange rate policy determination did not make the process more participatory; Baker in fact vigilantly guarded Treasury's formal authority in this area from encroachment by other agencies, as Treasury Secretaries generally do. He used the interagency Economic Policy Council, which he chaired, to address trade policy, but he kept exchange rate matters within his own small circle (1989: 74, their emphasis).

In addition the secrecy surrounding the negotiations and the Plaza Accord itself allowed the Treasury to shape the accord so that it highlighted the Treasury's essential and decisive role in bringing the crisis to an end and in protecting American interests abroad.

From this perspective, the criticism that the Plaza Accord was merely a publicity stunt, "a staged theater" according to one critic since the dollar was already dropping, miss the entire point of the accord (Funabashi 1989: 218). The publicity value was precisely the reason to go multilateral. In a dramatic public fashion, the Treasury could announce a breakthrough international agreement which *it* had negotiated as the U.S. representative in monetary global affairs. The Treasury could take complete and immediate credit for the policy change, since no other domestic actors had been involved, and in so doing demonstrate that it was effectively handling exchange rate policymaking. Such a maneuver would undercut congressional critics and the need for congressional oversight. Without the presence of other domestic actors in the process, the Treasury could also avoid questions regarding the accord's effectiveness on the markets or even its necessity.

The Treasury clearly expected the Plaza Accord to undercut congressional action on both trade and exchange rate policies. On the day of the Plaza announcement, Senator Bradley happened to meet Baker and Darman at the airport in Washington as they came back from the Plaza meeting. When Bradley inquired about the Accord, Darman reportedly quipped, "You can take your bill out of the hopper" (Funabashi 1989: 85). According to Destler and Henning, "the Treasury argued that the Plaza Agreement obviated exchange rate legislation on the grounds that it was now pushing against an open door" (1989: 109). Baker and Darman had also originally wanted to hold the Plaza meeting just before Labor Day so that it would coincide with the return of Congress and transmit a clear message of Treasury commitment to change (Funabashi 1989: 231).

A multilateral agreement arranged without involvement by other domestic actors and about which they had no information would also reinforce the impression that international exchange rate policy was a abstruse arena over which only the Treasury had sufficient command. By addressing the crisis behind the international screen of the G5, it appeared that the Treasury's traditional expertise in international monetary affairs was indispensable and so should be left unassailed. The impression that the crisis was generated by interdependencies that could only be solved by engaging in multilateral efforts actually worked to the Treasury's own institutional advantage in this regard, since it implied that only the Treasury had the sufficient expertise in international economic forums to negotiate a solution. Far from being motivated by these interdependencies to eschew unilateral decisionmaking, then, Baker used them as a cover to pursue a multilateral effort intended primarily to obtain particular interests in the domestic institutional context. In doing so, he was protecting unilateral decisionmaking structures and ensuring that the Treasury would maintain exchange rate policymaking autonomy from both domestic and international decisionmaking structures.

POST-PLAZA POLITE "DINNER CONVERSATION"

The brinkmanship behavior in which Baker engaged between Plaza and Louvre, as well as the multilateral efforts at Louvre and beyond, also become explicable within the context of domestic institutional interests and concerns. While the Plaza Accord was welcomed by Congress as a step in the right direction, the threat of exchange rate and protectionist legislature remained pertinent as long as the U.S. trade deficit with Japan remained so high through-out 1986. By September 1986 the trade-weighted value of the dollar had dropped 29 percent from its February 1985 peak and against the Japanese yen it had fallen even further (from 262 to 154). Yet as Destler points out, "even this major drop would only bring the U.S. trade deficit a bit below $100 billion by 1988" (1986: 52). Thus there was a domestic incentive throughout 1986 for Baker to talk the dollar down in currency markets, as well as to float the idea of a multilateral surveillance system at the 1986 Tokyo summit. Both were part of a continuous strategy to soften congressional anger by appearing to be both internationally conciliatory and disciplined, while attempting to force American trading partners to respond in kind.[7]

In other words concerns over functional institutional efficiency in the issue area did not motivate the Plaza Strategy. Rather what induced the pursuit of cooperation was a combination of the particular constraints placed on macroeconomic policymaking by presidential preferences, the prerogatives and jurisdictions which the Treasury enjoyed, and the nature of the domestic threat itself. What shaped the cooperative pursuit, then, were domestic insti-tutions and social practices which encouraged short-term, parochial perspec-tives, interests, and concerns. This explains why the Tokyo summit, along with so many of the other cooperative monetary proposals floated by the Americans since 1971, turned out to be about procedure rather than sub-stance and involved negotiations that U.S. policymakers did nothing to sup-port or implement in practice. Working out the details of a procedure was what the Treasury found most useful about international cooperative efforts, because doing so appeared to send such clear signals to other domestic insti-tutions that it was actively engaged in something of importance (yet ulti-mately of little lasting institutional effect) in the international realm. It was the perspectives and perceptions of other domestic actors, themselves unin-formed or uncaring about standards of efficiency in monetary affairs, which ultimately mattered the most to the decisionmakers in the issue area. Thus as the crisis subsided, new problems arose, and domestic attention was diverted, the impetus on the part of the Treasury to continue to look internationally involved subsided as well.

The Louvre Accord and U.S. monetary policymaking through 1988 con-forms to this general pattern and perspective. Henning and Destler point out that fears over domestic inflation played a major role in Baker's decision to shift from dollar weaponry to dollar stabilization by early 1987 (1988: 329). At the same time, however, a major trade bill was working its way through Congress. The Treasury worked diligently to contain the potential legislative damage to the administration's free trade policies as well as to the Treasury's own control over exchange rate policymaking. Thanks largely to its G5 efforts the latter threat proved containable, so that when the Omnibus Trade and Competitiveness Act was finally passed in 1988 it left jurisdictions and prerogatives untouched. It required only that the Treasury report annually to Congress on exchange rate and international economic policy.[8] The trade problem and protectionist threat remained unresolved, however, even as inflation increasingly became a concern so that, according to Henning, "Baker struggled to find a balance between the two threats over the course of the year" (1994: 285).

The exchange rate system adopted at the Louvre Accord was intended to strike this balance, which means that once again the primary impetus for U.S. enthusiasm over G5 multilateralism was not the resolution of currency market inefficiencies but rather a concern with the interests and potentially threatening behaviors of a particular institution within the domestic realm. Market efficiencies were entirely secondary to the choice of multilateralism. In fact, beyond dealing with the immediate repercussions of the October stock market crash, it is not clear that concerns over market efficiency played *any* role in American international monetary policymaking during 1987 and 1988. Henning points out that it was Baker's continued concern over congressional reaction which led him to so publicly repudiate the fall 1987 foreign interest rate increases (1994: 286). Thus while Baker is frequently criticized for having failed to recognize the impact his statements would have on the markets, the efficacy of his behavior can only be evaluated within the domestic institutional context which he himself was most concerned. To evaluate it in any other manner is to confuse what his motivations actually were with what his motivations should have been according to the issue area.

Destler and Henning also note that because 1988 was an election year, with the vice president of the incumbent administration running for the presidency, the desire to prevent international economic instability from intruding on Bush's chances of winning could explain Baker's support for the target zones through 1988 (1989: 69–70). If this were part of the motivation, then the Bush administration's subsequent repudiation of the target zone system and the Louvre Accord's failure to make any lasting impression on U.S. international monetary policymaking both become more understandable. Since the primary motivation for supporting the zones from late 1987 through 1988 was derived from a combination of congressional protectionist threat and from the American presidential electoral cycle itself, it was that cycle which determined the pattern of American participation in international monetary cooperative efforts, rather than the issue area and concerns over market inefficiencies. By 1988 the trade deficit and congressional legislative threat had largely subsided, so that after it had won office the new administration had no domestic political incentive to remain committed to dollar stability or to maintain an international cooperative effort. The result was that the target zone system and multilateralism under G7 auspices were allowed to lapse accordingly. Clearly, then, it is quite possible to explain both the Plaza and Louvre accords without any reference to functional institutional efficiency in the issue area and instead according to domestic institutional competition involving resources and the allocation of decisionmaking jurisdictions within the nation-state.

DIRECTIONS FOR FUTURE RESEARCH

As this book has sought to repeatedly reveal, we as a field have done a pretty poor job of explaining international cooperation. The central reason for this poor showing is the inability of most theorists who study the phenomenon to get past the mentalities which license the condition of complex interdependence, and what constitutes functionally efficient institutional choices within its parameters, as the primary cause of international cooperation. Yet because cooperative efforts so *in*frequently reflect standards of functional institutional efficiency and are consistently followed by recidivism, the empirical policymaking record is filled with more puzzles than revelations for the liberal theoretical strands which dominate the study of cooperation. Why, for example, did U.S. policymakers propose and take part in negotiations for the "Volcker Plan" if they had no intention of supporting those proposals? Why did the U.S. Treasury repudiate all forms of currency market interventions in the early 1980s, after regular engagement in coordinated interventions in the late 1970s? Why did Baker pursue dollar-brinkmanship throughout 1986, after organizing the Plaza Accord in 1985? Why did the United States subsequently repudiate the target zone exchange rate system which it encouraged the G7 to adopt? Why do G7 cooperative efforts, as Cohen has observed, ebb and flow like the tide?

Despite having earlier on selected international monetary policymaking as exemplary of interdependence-driven multilateralism, the reality is that the record of post-Bretton Woods U.S. international monetary policymaking confounds the expectations of liberal cooperation theories. Patterns basic to the issue area become anomalies because such theories have continually insisted that issue area concerns determine actual policymaking. In fact, however, issue area concerns are secondary to the domestic institutions and social practices in which U.S. monetary policymakers are engaged. It is only from a theoretical perspective which recognizes why domestic institutions and practices remain primary to policymakers that it is possible to understand why the pattern of American monetary policymaking looks as it does, as well as to understand the regular role that international cooperation has played in that pattern. Reliance on multilateralism has actually assisted U.S. monetary policymakers in maintaining the domestic institutional status quo. Thus it has helped reify their continued reliance on autonomous policymaking relative to other nation-state in the issue area.

Because we have misunderstood much of what we have seen when policymakers engage in international cooperation, a major overhaul in our own licensing mentalities is in order if we are to appropriately understand the cooperative phenomenon. At the very least we must become more cautious about beginning analysis at a systemic level and then simply theorizing causality downward to the policymakers involved. Domestic institutions and the agents who participate in them are not empty vessels but causal variables in their own right. Nor is the choice between levels-of-analyses mutually exclusive; rather each level brings something to the causal table and it is the interaction between them which produces outcomes. All this implies that a great deal more empirical legwork at the domestic and individual levels-of-analysis will be required of cooperation theorists, particularly since positing a systemic condition and then claiming its causal impact on the basis of systemic data and correlation alone has been one of the more troubling aspects of the interdependence and regimes literature.

Including nonsystemic institutions and actors also means taking the nation-state seriously and without normative bias. This does not mean that the nation-state is immutable, but it does mean that our accounts of cooperation in the present global system must recognize that nation-states are the institutional prisms through which the choice of *international* cooperation occurs. This recognition may prove to be impossible within the parameters of liberal cooperation theory, however, since beginning with Mitrany every strand of liberal theory has shared a suspicion of the nation-state and a certain conviction that it is the primary obstacle to functionally efficient cooperation on a global scale. Yet as Barnett and Finnemore argue, such normative evaluations "should be an empirical and ethical matter, not an analytic assumption" (1999: 727; see also Gruber 2000). One way to counter this normative bias is to demonstrate, as I have attempted to do in this work, that a theoretical alternative which takes the nation-state and its institutions seriously can actually be more explanatory for the cooperative phenomenon. My hope is that those scholars who might be persuaded on the basis of deductive logic and empirical evidence alone will find it a plausible alternative even if they are not realists themselves.

The fact that the neoclassical realist-constructivist approach outlined in chapter 3 has sweeping explanatory implications might also underscore the ongoing need to break down the explanatory barriers that we as a field continue to reify between the phenomenon of cooperation and that of conflict. Certainly the realist-constructivist perspective may be applied to and tested against a host of other contemporary cooperative economic issues, such as the development of the Euro, Chinese-U.S. economic relations, and globalization patterns in general. In fact the comparative development literature already supports the proposition that there is no one-size-fits all development model (despite what yet another group of liberal theorists would have us believe), precisely because economic strategies may be imitated yet simultaneously are layered onto domestic institutions with causal impact in their own right. That causal impact should be as pertinent in situations of interstate conflict and violence as it is in economic and cooperative situations, since domestic institutions and social practices are the prisms through which each nation-state grouping makes decisions relative to other nation-states in general. How the United States approached the war in Bosnia-Herzegovina, for example, and its involvement in North Atlantic Treaty Organization (NATO) peacekeeping after 1995 could be as much about domestic institutional infighting as systemic variables and consequences.[9]

Because I would argue that a realist-constructivist framework is capable of explaining patterns of behavior and outcomes for *both* cooperation and conflict, there is a strong case to be made here that this alternative meets what Dessler argues are the criteria of "scientific realism" for claiming superiority over theoretical rivals (1989). As he puts it, "a theory's explanatory power comes from its ability to reduce independent phenomena—that is, to show how apparently unconnected phenomena are actually products of a common ontology," and "the greater the number of independent phenomena a theory reduces, the better that theory is" (446). The deductive framework of the neoclassical realist-constructivist approach meets this criteria and is derived from an ontology that makes it empirically transportable within the present global system as well as historically across global systems. Far from being out of reach to realist analysis, the subject of systemic change and historical difference may only be sufficiently elucidated from an ontological basis that is fundamentally realist in character.

However it is also the case that the specific explanation for international cooperation which I have derived from the realist-constructivist approach has limitations. One of those limitations is it exclusive focus on the role of state institutions and actors in the process of cooperative policymaking itself.[10] That focus is a function of the deductive challenge I have leveled here against liberal cooperation theories, which all place the burden of adjustment to systemic interdependent conditions on the shoulders of particular state policymakers (as chapter 2 documents). In order to demonstrate that policymakers chose to cooperate for other reasons, the explanation for cooperation that I provide at the end of chapter 3 also focuses on the role of state decisionmakers and in an issue area which has traditionally involved state institutions. And within the American state decisionmaking context, the particular bureaucratic department charged with responsibility over the issue area, in this case monetary policymaking and the Treasury, also had sole control over decisionmaking in the issue area.

Yet a great deal of the cooperation we see in the global system today involves nongovernmental actors and occurs in issue areas that are relatively recent (e.g., transnational environmental pollution or human rights). Such issues were not historical arenas for state activity and therefore do not have established and clearly defined institutional counterparts within the state. In many cases this has resulted in shared responsibilities across existing bureaucratic departments and overlapping decisionmaking jurisdictions. The opportunity to control access to multilateral forums and thereby to use transnational counterparts for specific institutional interests in the domestic arena would undoubtedly be affected by these overlaps. This means that the type of bureaucratically-driven cooperation that I argue explains patterns in U.S. monetary policymaking may not be applicable in other issue areas, because the specific mechanisms and avenues by which it occurs are not present either. Certainly the explanation for cooperation that I have derived from realist-constructivism does not exhaust the potential causes for, and explanations of, cooperation, some of which may have their dynamic sources in other venues within the domestic or systemic arenas. But given the larger deductive framework of realist-constructivism and the flaws inherent to liberal cooperation theories, it remains a highly dubious proposition that functionally efficient choices in interdependent conditions would be the causal explanation for cooperation in other issue areas.

Along similar lines, it is impossible to generalize from the American monetary policymaking case study to the monetary policymaking patterns of other nation-states without additional empirical research. That is, whether policymakers in other G7 nation-states have cooperated in monetary affairs for similar domestically-derived institutional interests can only be established through careful examination and documentation of the domestic political arenas in each case. Obviously such a comparative study has not been undertaken in this instance,[11] but it is also at this juncture that some tension begins to emerge between the expectations of realism and Wendtian constructivism as alternative approaches. A constructivist perspective suggests that each nation-state's institutions will be specific to it, and so it may be the case that the United States remains relatively unique in its internal institutional design, its isolationist tendencies, and its protectiveness of autonomous decisionmaking. While it is certainly possible to think of other nation-states which have been similarly protective (e.g., France comes to mind), it may not be a universal phenomenon. Alternatively a realist perspective suggests that because social practices are developed and maintained in the service of groups, internal decisionmaking structures would inevitably develop within each group so that the practice of autonomy could be considered a universal phenomenon.

The point of combining realism and constructivism is to try to strike a theoretical balance between the excesses to which each tends. Throughout human history there has been an obvious pattern of group formation and institutional similarity across them. This needs some type of explanation other than random chance in order to be theoretically convincing. Alternatively no group defines its interests or pursues them in exactly the same manner precisely because intragroup institutions and social practices are causal and also vary quite dramatically. These variances do indeed make a decisive difference to behavior and outcomes. Although I do not address the ontological basis upon which realism and constructivism may be coherently combined here (see instead Sterling-Folker 2002), bringing them together allows one to identify historical patterns of behavior across groups yet simultaneously insists that those patterns are bounded by institutions and social practices specific to each group. What is produced from this combination is a realism that recognizes clear boundaries for what can be generalized from intergroup interaction and its capacity to produce specific ahistorical outcomes, and a constructivism that recognizes clear boundaries for what can be generalized about social activity and its capacity to produce infinite change and variation. One broad and important implication derivable from the combination and which deserves some attention in this final section is what the realist-constructivist alternative suggests for world order and for its future.

COOPERATION AND THE POSSIBILITY OF FUNDAMENTAL SYSTEMIC CHANGE

Given that realist-constructivism explains international cooperation in a very different manner from liberal cooperation theories, its implications and expectations for fundamental systemic transformation are very different as well. Almost any cooperation in complex interdependent issue areas is treated by liberal cooperation theorists as if it were evidence for national policymaking adjustment to new systemic conditions. When subjected to theoretical and empirical scrutiny, however, it is clear that these patterns, as well as specific instances of cooperation, do not support such a conclusion. Cooperation is not necessarily reflective of national policymaking adjustments to new interdependent conditions. Yet the tendency to assume that there is a connection remains quite strong in the liberal literature because there is a fundamental tendency in liberal IR theorizing to treat international cooperation as a normatively positive development in and of itself. International cooperation is considered to be something to encourage despite its inefficiencies, because it is assumed to be a step in the right direction, or as Barnett and Finnemore observe, "a peaceful way to manage rapid technological change and globalization, far preferable to the obvious alternative—war" (1999: 701).

Keohane, for example, justifies multilateralism among the major industrials on the grounds that "cooperation, however imperfect, appears likely to have positive overall effects on the stability of the world political economy and the welfare of individuals within the advanced industrialized countries" (1984: 252–253). Elsewhere he argues that "the strength of liberalism as moral theory lies in its attention to how alternative governing arrangements will operate in practice, and in particular how institutions can protect human rights against the malign inclinations of power holders" (1990: 194). Along similar lines, Zacher and Matthew contend that "peace, welfare, and justice are realized significantly through international cooperation," which is being driven by a number of "modernization" processes with complex interdependence being one of them (1995: 117). Such positive evaluations only make sense if international cooperation actually serves as a steppingstone to the transformation of parochial perspectives and institutions, which is what liberal theories of cooperation ultimately assume.

According to realist-constructivism, however, multilateralism has no such capacity and, far from transforming parochial perspectives and institutions, the choice and subsequent act of international cooperation may actually assist in their maintenance. If the game *is* domestic politics for national policymakers then all international choices are evaluated in its context, even responses to external threat and economic policymaking in conditions of complex interdependence. Of course liberal cooperation theories disagree with this assertion, arguing that as a systemic condition interdependence has the capacity to end the game of domestic politics itself. But since this capacity actually relies on the policymaker's ability to objectively perceive it, and since theoretically she could not do so given the nature of existing domestic processes, there is, in fact, no avenue by which the transformative capacities of interdependence could be felt or acted upon.

Instead what drives the cooperative choice in complex interdependent conditions are institutional interests within the context of the group, and so cooperation is used for purposes other than the pursuit of issue area interests in the context of the systemic condition. Far from transposing the practice of autonomy and unilateral policymaking, cooperation in interdependent conditions can serve merely as an avenue for policymakers to continue business as usual. In the case of the "Plaza Strategy," for example, cooperation was a way for particular subgroups to protect their domestically-derived institutional interests and to avoid compliance with demands for institutional change from other subgroups. Multilateralism actually contributed to the maintenance of the very status quo, in both its cognitive and institutional manifestations, which liberal cooperation theory posits must be changed if multilateralism and its systemic transformative effects are to occur. In a dichotomous twist, the condition of complex interdependence and the existence of regimes allows the act of multilateralism to occur, but that act then reifies rather than trans- poses the institutional and cognitive tendencies toward parochialism, unilateralism, and the practice of autonomy in international affairs.[12] Because the normative assessment of cooperation is based on an assumption about transformative capacities that the act of multilateralism does not actually have, it is difficult to maintain the conviction that international cooperation is, in the abstract and on aggregate, a good thing in and of itself.

Functional-constructivists may yet see a glimmer of hope in the approach to anarchy and group dynamics I have proposed here, however, in that social practices have such an important causal role to play in the argument. In accepting that interests are embedded in social practices, the door appears to be open to Wendt's assertion that the only counterargument realism can muster against constructivism is actually consistent with it and should there- fore lead realists to accept that the anarchic environment does not make self- help inevitable (1992: 411–412). This implies that by accepting the importance of social practice to interests, behaviors, and outcomes, realists have conceded that the barrier to fundamental transformation lies primarily in the present crop of social practices and institutions themselves rather than in anything objectively separate and obvious about the anarchic environment. If we live in a world of self-help, it is due to some historical accident that put us on a trajectory reified daily by the practices in which the majority of us remain engaged. But if we could turn back time or wipe the process slate clean, anarchy and our social practices might no longer be self-help in quality.

This conclusion would fundamentally contradict realist theory writ large, because it suggests that the only barrier to the kind of outcomes anticipated by liberal IR theory are the practices in which we have already engaged. If, on the other hand, those practices could be removed there would at least theoretically be the potential to engage in massive, purposeful social engi- neering by engaging in the "right" sorts of processes and social institutions, such as capitalist free trade or democracy. In doing so it might be possible to create a world which, even if it didn't precisely approximate liberal expecta- tions, would at least put an end to self-help behaviors such as violence and the kind of group differences and divisions which I have argued are an essen- tial element of realist theorizing. One could also derive from this the conclu- sion that the real problem with liberal cooperation theory is not its logic but that it simply pins its hopes for fundamental systemic transformation on a particular set of agents who cannot so freely affect the structures in which they participate.

Yet while it is the case that neoclassical realism has the deductive space to recognize constructivist insights such as the path-dependency of domestic institutions and the importance of history to current outcomes, its perspective on anarchy indicates that some patterns of behavior are ahistorical and would be rediscovered even if we could wipe the process slate clean. Group formation and transgroup competition are such patterns. Hence it anticipates that the human capacity to socially engineer human processes and outcomes remains within a band prescribed by the anarchic environment in which human beings exist. Even with a clean slate, neoclassical realism would anticipate that forms of self-help behavior such as group formation, transgroup competition, and the practice of autonomy would all be reinstitutionalized, although the precise form any of these took would certainly be path-dependent. Thus we could not predict that upon replaying the tape of history the United States and the Soviet Union would engage in a Cold War in the latter half of the twentieth century. But neoclassical realists could expect that groups would form, that they would compete over resources, that particularly powerful groups would be obsessed with one another, and that they would pursue balance-of-power politics as a means to their own survival and propagation. Engagement in particular types of processes does not give human beings the capacity to deny and ignore the ongoing selection pressures of their anarchic environment.

Thus the problem with relying on participation in particular types of processes to posit desirable outcomes, as liberalism does, is threefold from a realist-constructivist perspective. First, these processes are still a function of the most powerful groups in the system and they can only cause benign outcomes if they are practiced by the powerful. Second, because anarchy's pressures are immutable, there is an ongoing incentive for group competition which causes shifts regarding which groups are most powerful at any particular moment in time (Layne 1993; Mastanduno 1997). The social practices of the powerful might provide a context for relatively peaceful imitative change only to the extent that they remain powerful, but anarchic selection pressure on groups provides an ongoing dynamic which ensures they cannot remain powerful forever. Once again, social practices are not causal because of any logic inherent to themselves, but because they exist within a particular environment which exerts its own logic upon them.

The third problem, which has been the primary focus of discussion here, is that processes such as democracy and capitalism are adopted by, and imitated in, service of groups. This means that they are still sources for intergroup competition. Their layering on top of existing group social practices and institutions produces unintended consequences which makes it difficult to draw conclusions about their benign effects on the system as a whole overtime. And the extent to which any type of social practice can serve as a steppingstone to overcome group boundaries is severely prescribed by the anarchic environment in which human beings as a species have attempted to survive and reproduce. Because social practices and institutions have been the means to a particular end for human beings in such an environment, they reify group boundaries even when several groups imitate and engage in those same practices at once. As Mercer observes, "a closer examination of intergroup relations suggests that nature trumps process" (1995: 236). Multilateralism in complex interdependent conditions is as affected by this dictum as are other processes singled out by the liberal IR literature for their purported transformative capacities. The very collective practices and institutions in which we as human beings engage reflects the continued primacy of our environment. Anarchy trumps us with every social act, and knowledge that this is the case does not make it any less so.

Notes

CHAPTER 1. EXPLAINING INTERNATIONAL COOPERATION

1. See Sewell's observations that Mitrany relied on evolutionary laws specified by Lamarck in order to explain by analogy the growth of functional unions (1966: 67–68); the liberal literature on cooperation does not hesitate to cite functionalism and neofunctionalism as relevant theoretical predecessors. Keohane and Nye acknowledge their indebtedness to Deutsch and E. B. Haas in their afterword to the second edition of *Power and Interdependence* (1989: 247–248); Keohane relies on prior functional theorizing in *After Hegemony* (1984: 7–8, 66–67); Adler, Crawford, and Donnelly explicitly use neofunctionalism and Haas's "cognitive evolution" in their explanation for "progress" (1991: 25–29; the book is even dedicated to Haas); and Lebow and Jervis rely on Deutsch and presumptions of cognitive evolution (1994: 269–277 and 1991/92: 55 respectively), to name only a few examples.

2. The term *governance without government* is taken from the title of an edited volume of the same name by Rosenau and Czempiel (1992). Other examples of this post-Cold War "governance without government" literature includes Adler and Crawford (1991); Czempiel and Rosenau (1993); Goldgeier and McFaul (1992); Hobbs (2000); Jervis (1991/92); Jessop (1997); Lebow (1994); Cerny (1995); and Rosecrance (1996).

3. Flier for "Conflict and Peacemaking in an Evolving World: College and University Faculty Seminar," U.S. Institute for Peace, Washington DC, 13–19 July, 1998. A similar symposium was held in 24–25 September, 1993 at the College of William and Mary with the theme "Beyond the Nation-State: Transforming Visions of Human Society." According to this symposium's announcement, "The nation-state has been the defining political institution of the modern age. Today, however, it is confronted by unparalleled challenges from within and without. While no other institution has emerged to overturn the ideological underpinnings of the nation-state, almost everywhere the legitimacy and authority of existing nation-states are being questioned." As a final example, the theme of the International Studies Association's 1998 Annual Convention was "The Westphalian System in Global and Historical Perspective," and its theme panels focused on sovereignty and its assumed or projected decline at the turn of the century. These sorts of pronouncements are hardly limited to academic circles. In a *New York Times Magazine* article, Altman declared that "The global markets are the most powerful force the world has ever seen, capable of obliterating governments almost overnight" (1998, 34).

4. The earlier theoretical study of the EU included two other strands which are not as relevant to this particular discussion but deserve mention. Federalism argued that dismantling national institutions was a prerequisite to successful supranational cooperation, while transactionalism focused on the attitudinal effects of trade, communication, and other transaction flows. The work of Deutsch remains the best example of transactionalism, while examples of federalism include Spinelli (1966), and Hay (1966). Debates among these alternative theoretical perspectives involved the methods by which regional cooperation would be achieved and whether it was possible or necessary to specify the institutional structures of integration in advance. Federalism and neofunctionalism offered alternative perspectives in this regard, but because national institutions were not dismantled after the war federalism was quickly left with no empirical grounding. The theory clearly had an influence on European policymakers, proponents of European institutional structures, and on competing functional theorists, but of the two it was functionalism which had the greater subsequent theoretical impact. Transactionalism, on the other hand, was compatible with either theory since it was open-ended with regards to the outcome of interaction and focused instead on the role of changing attitudes to cooperation (which was important to neofunctionalism as well). Rochester provides a useful review of these alternative regional integration theories (1986: 784–791), while Little provides an alternative way of tracing the common threads which bind the "pluralist" literature (1996).

5. This is a term which E. B. Haas himself used to describe the work of regional integration scholars in the 1960s and 1970s (1970). Rosenau also used this term and defined it as "an early step toward explanation of specific empirical events and a general orientation toward all events, a point of view or philosophy about the way the world is. Ideally pretheories would be limited to the former meaning, but this requires that a field be in general agreement about the 'proper' orientation toward its subject matter" (1966: 41).

6. Along similar lines, Bailey argued that "the modern state is brought into contact with other states in almost every aspect of its national existence," and that "the strands of modern international relations spread to every nook and cranny of the government machine" (1930: 273); see also Rappard (1927: 818). I would like to thank Joe Grieco for calling my attention to the Bailey article.

7. E. B. Haas (1958: 16); see also Lindberg (1971).

8. (E. B. Haas 1975; 1976). Tranholm-Mikkelsen provides a good review of the criticisms, revisions, and eventual abandonment of neofunctionalism (1991). See also Webb (1983); Cornett and Caporaso (1992); Groom (1978); and Haggard (1991: 427–431). In addition, those who continue to work with neofunctionalism as a theoretical framework have attempted to substantially revise its parameters. For example, Carlsnaes (1992) and Corbey (1995).

9. Works on interdependence from the late 1960s and 1970s other than those already mentioned include Brown (1974); Cooper (1968; 1972); Hanrieder (1971: ch. 7), Morse (1970; 1976); Rosenau (1967; 1969; 1980); and Young (1969). For a useful review of the interdependence literature and arguments, see McMillan (1997).

10. Another interesting commonality is the list of countries characterized as "major industrials," which Hanrieder identified as "the United States, Canada, Japan, and Western and Northern Europe" (1978: 1283). This list has changed little over the

years so, for example, Goldgeier and McFaul identify them in a footnote as "the industrialized states of Western Europe, North America, and Japan" (1992: 469), and Jervis as "United States, Western Europe, and Japan" (1991/92: 46). Perhaps the list is determined by empirical phenomenon, yet its unchanging nature raises questions regarding how to test propositions associated with regimes and interdependence. Buzan has noted, for example, that "if the liberal economic system is only partially applicable to the international system as a whole, its ability to explain a period of relative harmony [such as 1945 to the present] must be correspondingly limited" (1984: 604; see also Jones and Willetts 1984: 11). An alternative explanation for such harmony, as Buzan points out, is the larger context of balance-of-power politics. Such a conclusion might be avoided by examining the behavior of states which are not defined as "major industrial," which began to trade later, and which did not share the same security concerns. Yet such a tack is rarely taken, despite the fact that definitions of interdependence generally do not include caveats that their applicability is limited to particular states. Thus the tendency to apply the concept exclusively to states which were part of the American Cold War alliance system, and to draw generalizable conclusions about interdependence from their relationships, already rests upon shaky deductive grounds.

11. Alternatively Kowert and Legro refer to it as a "sociological turn" (1996). The works Checkel reviews include Finnemore (1996); Katzenstein (1996); and Klotz (1995). Other examples of constructivism include Adler (1997); Dessler (1989); Carlsnaes (1992); Kratochwil (1982); Kubálková, Onuf, and Kowert (1998); Ruggie (1998); and Wendt (1987; 1992; 1994). Other reviews of constructivism include Copeland (2000); Hopf (1998); Jackson and Nexon (1999; 2001); Keohane (1988); and Haggard (1991).

12. Quotes are from Ruggie (1998: 14); Finnemore (1996: 2); and Wendt (1994: 384) respectively.

13. Ruggie claims, for example, that constructivism "has no direct antecedent in international relations theory," and although he acknowledges a personal theoretical debt to neofunctionalism, he also insists that his own collection of constructivist arguments effectively jettisons its core assumptions (1998: 11, 42, 46–47, 131). In a similar vein, Finnemore is careful to differentiate her constructivist explanation for the diffusion of norms from a functionalist or demand-driven explanation. As she puts it, "in the cases I investigate, state officials were not responding to any pressing demands or obvious crises. They were not looking for a solution to a problem" (1996: 12). See also March and Olsen (1998: 948–954); Finnemore (1996: 28–31); and Finnemore and Sikkink (1998: 908, 912–913). On the other hand, some constructivists explicitly rely upon functionalism, for example, Wendt (1994; 1992: 425); Dessler (1989: 468–473); Zacher and Matthew (1995: 136); and Carlsnaes (1992: 263).

14. Powell (1994: 317). See also Jervis (1988); Ruggie (1998); Wendt (1992, 1994); and the review provided by Hasenclever, Mayer, and Rittberger (1997: ch. 5).

15. But as Little observes, by then the damage had already been done and "because of the book's prominence . . . the confusion has been transmitted through the discipline" (1996: 80). In a more recent article on complex interdependence, Keohane and Nye again manage to replicate the confusion, referring to how to "change perceptions of self-interest" (1998: 94).

16. Yet hereto Keohane manages to generate some confusion in arguing that what constitutes "perceptions of self-interest" are expectations about behavioral consequences and fundamental values (1984: 63). This means that changes in perceptions of self-interest could involve changes in expectations but not necessarily values. However Keohane does not preclude the possibility that regimes could affect values. When he refers, for example, to the "malleability of interests" (8), to the redefinition of self-interest (99, 123–124), and to the possibility that self-interest may become "less myopic and more empathetic" (257), it is unclear whether these are merely changes in expectations or in values as well.

17. For similar assertions and examples see Keohane (1984: 115, 258–259); Keohane and Nye (1971: 371, 375; 1998: 94); and Rosecrance (1986: 22–24, 190). Kratochwil and Ruggie point out that this separation is basic to "instrumentalism" in the presumption "that it is always possible to separate goals (presumably expressed in principles and norms) from means (presumably expressed in rules and procedures), and to order them in a superordinate-subordinate relationship" (Ruggie 1998: 99).

18. These arguments are developed more extensively in Sterling-Folker (2000).

19. Copeland (1996a); Gasiorowski (1986); Knorr (1977).

20. Buzan (1984); Gowa (1989; 1994); Gowa and Mansfield (1993).

21. Crawford (1996); Grieco (1990; 1993); Haggard and Simmons (1987); Hasenclever, Mayer, and Rittberger (1997); Keely (1990); Kratochwil and Ruggie (1986); Mearsheimer (1994/95); Rochester (1986); Strange (1983); Young (1986; 1989b).

22. See, for example, Martin (1992a; 1992b; 1992c); Oye (1986); Snidal (1985); Stein (1991); Yarbrough and Yarbrough (1987); and Young (1989a).

23. See also Axelrod and Keohane (1986: 249). In his studies of global management networks, Hopkins lays causality squarely at the decisionmaker's cognitive doorstep, arguing that "The new frontiers of international politics . . . lie within the minds of the world's effective elites. The expectations and identifications of these people will determine to a great extent how and what decisions are taken" (1978: 42). Other liberal references to perception and its centrality to the cooperative choice are provided in chapter 2.

24. Gourevitch also highlights the importance of studying domestic politics in order to understand and predict international cooperation, noting in his review of work by Simmons and Eichengreen that "the credibility of international arrangements continues to rest on the convergence of domestic interests and politics," and "international cooperation on policy survives so long as the political forces committed to its continuation within each country are able to prevail" (1996: 372, 371).

25. See Hopkins (1976; 1978) and Dickerman (1976). A notable exception to this trend has been the work of Garrett (1995); Garrett and Lange (1991; 1996); Karvonen (1987); and Karvonen and Sundelius (1990). Yet none of these more recent studies have focused on the proposition that interdependence produces an increased tendency for multilateral coordination, nor have they discovered any evidence for this proposition.

26. Other examples that misuse systemic data are Held (1996) and Zacher with Sutton (1996).

27. See also Thomson and Krasner (1992: 314–321). Along these same lines, *The Economist* ran a series of "Schools Brief" between October and December 1997 which took direct issue with the aggregate data on globalization, as well as with some of the predictions based upon it. The briefs examined various types of measurement indicators for globalization and found that the extent of globalization (and the claim to unprecedented levels) was frequently exaggerated. I would like to thank John Walko for drawing my attention to these briefs and for sharing them with other members of our IO seminar at the time. Equally suspect is the tendency to treat high levels of compliance with regulatory regime treaties as evidence that collective problem-solving can occur in the absence of enforcement (Downs, Rocke, and Barsoom 1996).

28. In fact in their contribution to the volume Garrett and Lange explicitly make this point in a footnote, stating that "in this paper, we do not explore collective attempts among governments to change the structure of the international economy, which has been the subject of much scholarly attention the past decade" (1996: 263). They then go onto raise serious questions about the policy convergence hypothesis, which suggests that even when explorations are limited to the first loop of interdependent causality, there is only limited and highly qualified evidence to support it. See also Pauly and Reich (1997).

29. See also Keohane and Nye (1989: 232). Even with regards to the claim of declining policy autonomy, the evidence presented in the volume is highly questionable. Keohane and Milner single out Garrett's and Frieden's chapters as providing "the strongest evidence" for this outcome (1996: 248). It is certainly true that each chapter provides evidence that the range of policy choices has become more limited, yet those policy choices and instruments that do remain available to governments are still wielded autonomously. It is not at all clear that "efficacy" of particular types of macroeconomic policies and "autonomy" of macroeconomic policymaking are the same thing, yet Keohane and Milner consistently equate the two by taking evidence for the first as confirmation for the second (247–249).

30. Also Garrett and Lange (1991; 1996); Garrett (1995); Gelber (1997); and Weber (1994).

31. For example, Cowhey (1990); Mayer (1992); Oatley and Nabors (1998); and Weatherford and Fukui (1989). The literature on two-level games also raises questions regarding the compatibility of domestic level variables and interdependence-regimes expectations (Putnam, 1988; Evans, Jacobson, and Putnam 1993).

32. Copeland (2000; 1996b); Grieco (1990; 1993; 1995); Glaser (1994/95); Gruber (2000); Sterling-Folker (1997; 2000).

33. The realists whom Rose cites as neoclassical realists include Christensen, Schweller, Wohlforth, and Zakaria. To this list I would add Friedberg, Mercer, Taliaferro, and myself. This variant obviously rejects the assertions made by realism's critics that either "the analyst must go outside the paradigm and look at the determining influences of domestic politics, belief systems, and learning" (Lebow 1994: 268), or that incorporating such influences is the hallmark of a degenerating paradigm (Vasquez 1997; Legro and Moravcsik 1999; Rosecrance and Stein 1993; Russett 1995). Even among realists there is disagreement over whether systemic realism can be used as a basis for theorizing about foreign policy behavior. See, for example, the debate between Elman

and Waltz in the 1996 issue of *Security Studies;* De Mesquita and Lalman (1992); Diehl and Wayman (1994: 248); Snyder (1991); and Zakaria (1992; 1998: ch. 2). Variance also exists among neoclassical realists because some focus on the filtering role of domestic institutions while others concentrate on cognitive or even biological filters such as the in-group/out-group distinction, emotions and perceptions, and risk aversion. Reviews of other realist variations include Brooks (1997); Jervis (1998; 1999); Schweller (1998); Spirtas (1996); and Zakaria (1992).

34. As suggested, the variant of constructivism utilized here is based on the early work of Wendt (1987; 1992; 1994) and in particular his discussions of the reification of intersubjective meanings through practice. Although Wendt himself has tended to focus on and favor those aspects of his constructivism which explain change, his variant also recognizes that "for both systemic and 'psychological' reasons . . . intersubjective understandings and expectations may have a self-perpetuating quality, constituting path-dependencies that new ideas about self and other must transcend" (1992; 411). It is the anticipation of those self-perpetuating qualities which makes Wendtian constructivism relevant to this study and, while other variants of constructivism exist (see, e.g., Ruggie's classification [1998: 35–36] or Jackson and Nexon's "relationalism" (1999: 2001), they are not the focus here.

35. They credit Vinod Aggarwal for employing such a method (as well as for coining the term) and he, in turn, cites the work of Alexander George.

CHAPTER 2. LIBERAL COOPERATION THEORY

1. As they also make clear, other regimes arguments exist besides Keohane's and may be categorized according to whether they are interest-based (Keohane, Young, and game theory arguments); power-based (Krasner, Grieco, and hegemonic stability arguments); or knowledge-based (P. M. Haas, Wendt, and Cox). Some of these arguments are irrelevant to this critique, however, since my focus is on those regime arguments which specifically assume interdependence as a permissive condition for cooperation. Generally it is the interest-based theories that adopt this assumption, while power-based arguments and most (although not all) knowledge-based arguments do not.

2. Additional discussions on defining interdependence may be found in Baldwin (1980); Cooper (1985: 1196–1200); Crawford (1996: 50–53); Jones (1984); Little (1996); McMillan (1997); and Milner (1991).

3. Jones provides a discussion of cost as "the ambiguous cornerstone of interdependence" (1984: 25–29). As he points out, one of the problems with including cost as a core component of the definition is that costs (however defined themselves) are not constants: "given sufficient time, ingenuity can be allowed to flourish and long-term policies brought to fruition. It is improbable, then, that it will prove impossible to find some avenue of escape from what once appeared to be daunting vulnerability" (27). On a slightly different note, it is interesting to consider the theoretical source for treating costs as a central component of interdependence. While the condition of interdependence is supposed to be applicable across issue areas, the emphasis on costs is consistent

with a core tenet of liberal *economic* theorizing that "every decision involves an opportunity cost, a tradeoff among alternative uses of available resources. The basic lesson of liberal economics is that 'there is no such thing as a free lunch'; to get something one must be willing to give up something else" (Gilpin 1987: 29). This suggests that even as the concept of interdependence is applied to military-security issue areas, it is ultimately derived from a perspective that is fundamentally about liberal economics (as Gilpin notes, "what Marxists call orthodox or bourgeois economics," [28]).

4. There is considerable disagreement over the degree to which nation-states ever controlled events within their borders, however, as well as the extent to which realism makes this assumption. Interdependent arguments have been challenged by a number of authors (many of them realists) for "tacitly assuming that states have, in some golden age in the past, been able to effortlessly control transborder movements" (Thomson and Krasner 1992: 312). See Gelber (1997); Gourevitch (1978: 882, 907–911); Mann (1997); Krasner (1995/96); Smith (1984: 76–77); Thomson (1995: 216); and Thomson and Krasner (1992). It should also be noted that skepticism of this presumed preinterdependent "golden age" for state decisionmaking is hardly new. In fact Keohane and Nye's statements in *Transnational Relations* regarding prior centralization were in direct response to Kaiser's suggestion that world politics had never actually approximated a state-centric model and that transnationalism could not be considered a new phenomenon (1971: 371; see also Waltz 1970). Little's review of the links between pluralist thought and the interdependent concept also provide insights on this point (1996: 76–77).

5. Goldgeier and McFaul also assert that "from the eighteenth to the early twentieth century, many of the assumptions of structural realism seem valid. The actors could be considered unitary for the purpose of developing theory, since the policies of a France, Russia, Prussia, Austria, or Germany were largely made by individual leaders or their foreign ministers even if pressures existed for one policy or another from small groups of elites" (1992: 472). Another excellent example of this liberal perspective on the "preinterdependent world," when states could pursue their self-interests with little regard for the impact it had on others, may be found in Scott (1982: ix).

6. The belief in relational imposition is hardly limited to the liberal literature. According to Buzan, Jones, and Little, "interaction capacity" may be considered a systemic variable in that "the evolution of technology continuously raises the absolute capability for interaction available within the system" (1993: 69). Ruggie offers a similar concept of "dynamic density" based on the work of Durkheim (1983a: 281).

7. For a similar perspective on the diminished but continuing ("legitimacy") role of the state in interdependence, see Cerny (1995); Jessop (1997: 573–576); and Rosenau (1988).

8. Adler, Crawford, and Donnelly note, for example, that "security is the paramount international objective of nearly all states, at nearly all times," so that other objectives "will be pursued only to the extent that they do not appear to interfere with their security" (1991: 21). And Keohane and Nye acknowledge that "military power dominates economic power in the sense that economic means alone are likely to be ineffective against the serious use of military force" (1989: 16).

9. Two of the most frequently cited forces are nuclear weapons, which are argued to have shifted the cost-to-benefit ratio in favor of peace, and the increased number of democracies, which have tended not to fight one another. Other factors include economic interdependence, public opinion and cognitive revulsion to wars, hegemonic stability, and bipolarity. For each of these forces an extensive literature about its causal role has developed, but works that discuss them as a package include Goldgeier and McFaul (1992); Jervis (1991/92); Rosecrance (1986, part 2); Zacher and Matthew (1995); and Zacher (1992). According to these authors, "the forces for peace among the developed countries are so overwhelming that impulses which under other circumstances would be destabilizing will not lead to violence" (Jervis 1991/92: 54). For dissenting opinions see Layne (1993); Mastanduno (1997); Mearshiemer (1990); and Waltz (1993).

10. Lipson, Oye, and Axelrod and Keohane all argue that military-security issues can also be characterized by increasing-sum games, particularly when a common security threat exists, so that "security issues share significant common features with economic issues" (Lipson 1984: 13). Yet ultimately the association between zero-sum games and military-security issues holds even among theorists who caution against it, because the dimensional contexts of mutual interests, iteration, and shadow of the future are not very decisive when security interests are at stake. Thus Axelrod and Keohane acknowledge that "economic issues usually seem to exhibit less conflictual payoff structures than do those of military security," that "the dimension of the shadow of the future seems to differentiate military from economic issues," and that sanctioning problems "tend to be more severe on military-security than on political-economic issues" (1986: 231, 232, 236). And Lipson notes that "the tendency to convert variable-sum games into constant-sum struggles is a persistent feature of security issues," and that "the crucial differences" between security and economics "appear to lie in the costs of betrayal, the difficulties of monitoring, and the tendency to comprehend security issues as strictly competitive struggles" (1984: 15, 18). For discussion of zero-sum, increasing-sum, and mixed-motive games, the outcomes associated with them, and the context dimensions, see Grieco (1990: 35–50); Keohane (1984: 67–68); Lipson (1984); Oye (1986: 4–11); and Stein (1983: 134).

11. Of course an alternative explanation for iteration (and for the small number of players) in nonsecurity issue areas is the presence of a hegemon, such as the United States during the Cold War. After all, if it were merely iteration one could have expected interdependence to have had a similar impact on nonwestern states during that period. Yet no interdependence scholar argues this point (at least not prior to the end of the Cold War), and it is interesting to note that Rosecrance studiously avoids attributing the trading world's development to the presence of the United States. It is the result instead of "many nations" (by which he means Europe and Japan) that "began the quest for a new and peaceful means to national advancement" after World War II (1986: 70–71). The United States, on the other hand, remained a "recalcitrant nation" which refused to adopt this new philosophy and continued to pursue a military-political strategy (191). While such a perspective may be consistent with his theory, it essentially denies the United States's well-documented historical role in creating and supporting post-World War II liberal economic institutions and conditions. Furthermore, the suggestion that Japan and Germany were responsible for promoting trade

as a strategy is a glaring misrepresentation of their relationship with the United States (and with American occupational forces) in the decade immediately following the war.

12. As Stein goes onto assert, "it is in their interests mutually to establish arrangements to shape their subsequent behavior and allow expectations to converge, thus solving the dilemmas of independent decisionmaking (1983: 127)." Similarly Oye claims that in situations of mutual benefit, "the capacity of states to cooperate under anarchy, to bind themselves to mutually beneficial courses of action without resort to any ultimate central authority, is vital to the realization of a common good" (1986: 6). And Keohane insists that "as long as the situations involved are not constant-sum, actors will have incentives to coordinate their behavior, implicitly or explicitly, in order to achieve greater collective benefits without reducing the utility of any unit" (1983: 171).

13. Keohane provides a similar definition in *After Hegemony:* "Issue areas are best defined as sets of issues that are in fact dealt with in common negotiations and by the same, or closely coordinated, bureaucracies, as opposed to issues that are dealt with separately and in uncoordinated fashion" (1984: 61). Distinguishing interests according to issue areas is an accepted methodological practice in the discipline and is frequently couched in the language of high versus low politics. High politics are issue areas involving military, security, and political interests, which realists have argued predominate over low politics issue areas involving economic, environmental, health, and energy interests (to name a few). In keeping with this distinction, for example, Waltz argues that for a systems theory to be a success it "has to show how international politics can be conceived of as a domain distinct from the economic, social, and other international domains that one may conceive of" (1979: 79). Buzan, Jones, and Little use the term *sectors* instead and define them as "views of the whole system through some selective lens that highlights one particular aspect of the relationship and interaction among all of its constituent units" (1993: 31). Yet as they point out, despite an accepted reliance on sectoral distinctions for the purpose of analysis, the practice has not itself been much scrutinized, and it is questionable whether a theory can be constructed within sectors that does not inevitably confuse the sector with the system (30). In an attempt to avoid such confusion, scholars who write about interdependence and regimes are usually careful to distinguish between issue areas when discussing outcomes.

14. Their discussion of these points is confusing and contradictory. Early in the book, for example, Keohane and Nye claim that "the difference between traditional international politics and the politics of economic and ecological interdependence is *not* the difference between a world of 'zero-sum' (where one side's gain is the other side's loss) and 'nonzero-sum' games. Military interdependence need not be zero-sum. . . . Conversely, the politics of economic and ecological interdependence involve competition even when large net benefits can be expected from cooperation" (1989: 10; their emphasis). Yet this caveat is largely belied by an earlier association they make between military force and the maximization of power (8) and their later discussion in which wealth is differentiated from power on the basis of absolute gains.

15. Keohane and Nye, for example, also cite ecological issues and include as one of their case studies the politics of the oceans. And Rosenau provides a list of what he calls "the newer issues of interdependence," which include "oceans, exchange rates,

pollution, agricultural production, population size, energy allocation," and which presents new problems, "from those involving monetary stability to those associated with food-population ratios, from the uses of the ocean to the abuses of the atmosphere, from the discovery and distribution of new energy sources to the redirection of trade and the reallocation of wealth" (1976: 43, 37, 40).

16. Keohane refers to this as "issue density" and argues that it is a feature of high levels of interdependence (1983: 155–157; 1986: 79–80). Rosenau argues that most of the new issues of interdependence "encompass highly complex and technical phenomena," and "overlap so thoroughly that proposed solutions to any one of them have important ramifications for the others, thereby further complicating their highly technical character" (1976: 40–41). And Zacher comments that solutions to environmental damage impinge upon the economic activities of nation-states and hence involve complex tradeoffs if both ecological and economic objectives are to be realized (1992: 76–80).

17. Hanrieder concurs that to obtain social and economic objectives, "the modern state is compelled to interact with other states in ways which, although not lacking in conflict and competition, demand cooperation, acceptance of the logic of interdependence, and a willingness to condone restraints on state behavior and sovereign prerogatives" (1978: 1276). And in describing the transformation of the Westphalian system, Zacher asserts that its source is "the growing interdependencies in economic, social, and environmental areas" and that, "what is occurring in the world is not a serious demise of states as the central actors in the system . . . but rather their acceptance that they have to work together in controlling a variety of interdependencies" (1992: 67). See also Adler, Crawford, and Donnelly (1991: 21) and Scott (1982).

18. Iteration is argued to be important because future expectations affect calculations of gain in the present and provide the opportunity to develop strategies of reciprocity, while the number of actors involved can produce collective action problems such as freeriding or defection identification and sanctioning. See Axelrod (1981; 1984); Keohane (1984: 67–78, 75–78); Oye (1986: 12–22); Schelling (1978); and Snidal (1985; 1991a; 1991b).

19. That this is in fact the case is amply demonstrated in the literature devoted to these subjects. Oye argues, for example, that "the effectiveness of strategies of reciprocity hinges on conditions of play—the ability of actors to distinguish reliably between cooperation and defection by others and to respond in kind" (1986: 15). Yet he goes onto acknowledge that in IR nation-states will define cooperation and defection differently, governments may not be able to detect one another's violations, and "internal factions, organizational, and bureaucratic dysfunctions may limit the ability of nations to implement Tit-for-Tat strategies" (16). All of these problems are a function of the established differences between autonomous nation-states, and they become even more intractable as the number of nation-states involved increases. In the context of market failure, Keohane recognizes the connection between the problem of uncertainty and existing nation-state structures. He observes that "governments contemplating international cooperation need to *know* their partners, not merely know about them" and that cooperation depends "not merely on interests and power, or on

the negotiating skills of diplomats, but also on expectations and information, which themselves are in part functions of the political structures of governments and their openness to one another" (1983: 163; his emphasis). He notes elsewhere that "in world politics, sovereignty and state autonomy mean that transaction costs are never negligible, since it is always difficult to communicate, to monitor performance, and especially to enforce compliance with rules" (1989: 166–167). What this means is that the solutions to international cooperation identified by the collective action literature (trustworthy reputations, greater transparency, unbiased information, and better communication) remain contingent on nation-state autonomy and ultimately its intractability.

20. Stein argues, on the other hand, that liberal cooperation theory has not made explicit the theory of state-society relations upon which it relies (1993; see also Litfin 1997). Although there is some truth to this claim, it is nonetheless possible to deduce from the liberal literature a recognizable reliance on a model of economic pluralism.

21. Hanrieder observes, for example that "in each country powerful juridical, political and ideological traditions have developed which circumscribe the proper role of government in the economy and society" so that different governments might respond in different ways to the same external pressures (1978: 1285). Rosenau also recognizes a variety of societal barriers, including social cohesion and "the images underlying the adaptive capacities of states derive from the functioning of their communication systems, the viability of their value frameworks, the flexibility of their political ideologies, and the dynamics of their educational systems, as well as the structure of their public bureaucracies" (1976: 48–49). And Rosecrance acknowledges that societal constituents negatively affected by international competition and openness will have to develop a "relatively high level of popular understanding of the situation in which the nation finds itself" (1986: 220–223, 40).

22. In fact almost *all* liberal theoretical treatments of international cooperation assume that the perception of interdependence is essential to subsequent acts of cooperation. Lipson lists it as the first requirement for iterated mixed-motive games to produce stable cooperation (1984: 7). Axelrod and Keohane summarize their findings with regards to cooperation under anarchy by noting the fundamental role that perception plays in decisionmaking (1986: 247). Milner notes that strategic interdependence involves a focus on state expectations and perceptions (1991: 84). And both Jervis (1991/92) and Jonsson (1993) cite it as the cognitive prerequisite for international cooperation. See also Adler, Crawford, and Donnelly (1991: 24–27).

23. In this regard Bergsten and Henning provide an interesting appendix to their Group of Seven (G7) study which lists (briefly) the reasons why coordination is necessary in economic policymaking, the obstacles to coordination, the methods to overcome them, and the empirical significance of coordination (1996: 144–147).

24. In a similar vein, Jervis states with regards to economic interdependence, "if statesmen examine the situation with any kind of *sophistication*, they will be concerned not about the size of the flows of trade and capital, but rather with what will happen to their states' welfare if these flows are halted" (1991/92: 49; my emphasis). And Keohane and Nye argue that "actor's strategies, and their *cleverness* in implementing them, can substantially affect the evolution of international regimes" (1989: 57, also 241; my emphasis).

25. See also Keohane (1984: 94); Rosenau (1976: 45); and Adler, Crawford, and Donnelly (1991: 28–89).

26. This is, of course, the same logic which underpins more recent work on epistemic communities, about which the work of P. M. Haas remains most seminal (1990; 1992).

27. Discussions (and critiques) of this definition may be found in Crawford (1996: 53–56); Hasenclever, Mayer and Rittberger (1997: ch. 2); Rittberger (1993); Rochester (1986); and Strange (1983).

28. Nye's definitions are frequently equated with E. B. Haas's use of the terms *adaptation* and *learning*. See Hasenclever, Mayer, and Rittberger (1997: 146) and Jonsson (1993: 218).

29. In fact Jonsson even finds it necessary to defend an exploration of cognitive factors in regime dynamics, despite the fact that, as he notes, the regimes definition itself includes the term *actor expectations* (1993: 202–203). On this point see also Kratochwil and Ruggie (1986: 764) and Hasenclever, Mayer, and Rittberger (1997: 162–163).

30. However regimes may be treated as part of the condition of interdependence confronting countries not classified as major industrials and who have sought to adopt capitalist-market in place of centrally-planned economies or join cooperative efforts already in progress. In these instances some authors have suggested that regimes may actually be capable of changing interests as well as methods and so contribute to the pressure on states to adjust their interests in accordance with the liberal economic order. See Biersteker (1992); Krasner (1983b: 362–363); Oye (1986: 11); and Stein (1983: 139, footnote 32). However, the extent to which one could attribute causality to regimes and not other variables in such cases, such as power, domestic political change, or threat, is highly questionable. The problem of correct causal attribution is one which already plagues much of the liberal economic development literature, as numerous critics have pointed out. See, for example, Colclough and Manor (1991) and Wade (1992; 1996).

31. It is on this basis that Axelrod and Keohane argue that "states are often dissatisfied with the structure of their own environment," and that "governments have often tried to transform the structures within which they operate so as to make it possible for the countries involved to work together productively" (1986: 253). In accounting for the state's commitment to cooperative institutions, they are actually even more specific. States have been "groping toward new institutions and norms" because "decisionmakers themselves perceived (more or less consciously) that some aspects of the situations they faced tended to make cooperation difficult. So they worked to alter these background conditions" (248–249).

32. Zacher asserts, for example, that the decline of the Westphalian system will be "uneven and gradual" (1992: 100), Keohane and Nye that patterns of adjustment could be "inconsistent and incoherent" (1989: 238) and that "our view of the future is less sanguine" (229), and Axelrod and Keohane that cooperation "proceeds by fits and starts" and that "there is always danger that prior achievements will come unstuck" (1986: 253). Keohane and Nye even complain in the afterword to *Power and Inter-dependence* that "our warning at the beginning of chapter 2 was forgotten by many

readers who treated our discussion of complex interdependence as if it were our description of the real world rather than our construction of a hypothetical one" (1989: 249–250). It is difficult to take this complaint seriously, however, given the number of times they themselves assert that complex interdependence has been realized in some portions of the globe. They claim, for example, that the characteristics of complex interdependence "are fairly well approximated on some global issues of economic and ecological interdependence and that they come close to characterizing the entire relationship between some countries" (25), and that "there are reasons to expect that significant aspects of world politics will continue to approximate the conditions of complex interdependence. In some issue areas and some country relationships, complex interdependence is deeply rooted" (227, see also 161, 223). In their revisitation of the concept, they again assert that while it is still an accurate description of some aspects of the current international system, its realization is not yet "complete" (1998: 84).

CHAPTER 3. A REALIST-CONSTRUCTIVIST ALTERNATIVE

1. Schweller and Priess have argued that Mearsheimer's views do not reflect traditional realist theorizing about international institutions, yet while they do underscore the greater subtleties to the realist approach to institutions, ultimately institutions remain dependent variables in their discussion as well because they "reflect the interests of the dominant, established powers" and are the "brass ring" over which revisionist states want control (1997: 12–13). See also Jervis (1998; 1999; 1988).

2. See, for example, Gilpin (1981) or Snyder (1991). I would like to thank Miriam Fendius Elman for drawing my attention to this point.

3. Keohane states, for example, that liberal cooperation theory is "not simply an alternative to neorealism, but, in fact, claims to subsume it" (1989: 15). Similar claims are made by Axelrod and Keohane (1986: 227); Niou and Ordeshook (1994: 232); and more recently by Legro and Moravcsik (1999). Analyses which are critical of the concept of anarchy in IR theorizing in general include Powell (1994: 329–334) and Milner (1991).

4. In this regard my arguments differ from those of Buzan, Jones, and Little (1993). We are in agreement that realism's structural determinacy has been misunderstood and mischaracterized by its critics, but their subsequent attempt to revise the theory by adding interaction capacity as an independent systemic variable is, as I argue in the next section, problematic and ultimately unnecessary.

5. This American "Enlightenment" context generated a near-universal commitment within the academy to the notion that, as Somit and Peterson have put it, "social behavior was, for all meaningful purposed, learned behavior" (1999: 42). There are striking parallels, in fact, between a Lamarckian approach to evolutionary biology and liberalism in that both emphasize the idea that human beings are shapers of the environment or least control their own evolution within it to a large extent. On the other hand, realism clearly has more parallels with Darwinism in that both emphasize the idea that human beings are shaped by an environment external to them. Given

these similarities and the vehement attacks to which Darwinism has also continually been subjected to in America (see Bowler 1984 and Dennett 1995), it seems reasonable to conclude that the American social sciences have never been a hospitable atmosphere for theories which refuse to subscribe to a humanist, progressive ontology. Aspects of this argument are developed further in Sterling-Folker (2001; 2002).

6. Waltz (1979: 126); Grieco (1990: 38); Mearsheimer (1990: 12); my emphases.

7. I would like to thank Dan Nexon, Yale Ferguson, Patrick Jackson, and the other participants at the International Studies Association—Northeast Annual Meeting's Northeast Circle in November 2000 for elucidating this problem for me.

8. See also Der Derian who notes, "Realism in general refers to a belief or doctrine that a physical world exists as a reality independent of how we might perceive or conceive of it" (1995: 393), or Onuf who says of realism, it "holds that the world exists independent of ourselves and the things within it await our naming" (1989: 37).

9. Mercer cites a wealth of studies in this regard, but several appear particularly pertinent to his arguments including Hogg and Abrams (1988) and Tajfel and Turner (1986). The in-group/out-group distinction is gradually finding its way into IR theorizing, for example, Ignatieff (1996); Falger (1994: 123–127); Kowert (1998); and D. Smith (1996).

10. See also Buzan, Jones, and Little (1993: 9, 116); Lapid (1996: 139–140); Mercer (1995); and the list of cites provided by Schweller and Priess (1997: 6).

11. This does not mean, however, that isolation allows one to argue that group-formation and intergroup biases are merely social constructs as well. Wendt attempts this in his example of "ego and alter" who, in encountering each other for the first time have no "biological or domestic imperatives for power, glory, or conquest" so that the nature of their interaction cannot be assumed a priori (1992: 404). Yet if ego and alter are not infants, then they have survived because they are members of groups, even if those groups are simply families as Bloom has pointed out. This means they would already make cognitive distinctions between in- and out-groups which would affect how they categorized the unfamiliar, and their group's social practices would be the prisms through which they gauged one another's behavior. Regardless of the precise nature of those practices, ego and alter would be predisposed to view one another as members of alternative groups and hence as potential competitors. This point is actually consistent with Berger and Luckmann's arguments on social construction, despite the fact that Wendt cites them in support of his own perspective (405, footnote 53). Elias has also noted that the tendency to theorize about adults who were never children is common to philosophers and abstract thinkers (1991).

12. Most scholars who discuss "interaction capacity" reach the alternative conclusion, including Buzan, Jones, and Little, who assert that higher levels of interaction "could pave the road for an eventual deep structural shift to hierarchy" (1993: 78–79). Similarly Wendt assumes that "the possibility of predation does not in itself force states to anticipate it a priori with competitive power politics of their own," so that "social threats are constructed, not natural" (1992: 405). It is then possible to imagine an international system based on entirely different intersubjective meanings which could result from changes in the level and quality of unit interaction. And it is, of course, a fundamental tenet of liberal IR theory that higher levels of interaction will

make a difference to the policy choices nation-states make with regards to one another. Keohane and Nye, for example, argue that "variations in the capacity to communicate" are an aspect of "systemic process" which "liberals have traditionally emphasized," and they foreshadow Buzan, Jones, and Little in noting that Waltz ignored this because he equated system with structure (1989: 262). Higher levels of interaction supposedly have the capacity to promote the communication and hence trust necessary for greater levels of international cooperation.

Yet as with Keohane's theory of regimes, Buzan, Jones, and Little attempt to use realist logic in order to reach nonrealist conclusions, arguing that realism's pessimistic predictions regarding the cyclic inevitability of international conflict can be contradicted with its own logic. The problem with their approach, as with Keohane's earlier attempt, is that their definition of anarchy does not include the most fundamental component identified by systemic realism—death and a tendency for group formation. Interaction capacity is instead defined according to capability (made possible with technology) and incentive, which is provided by shared norms and organizations among the units in the system (1993: 69–71). Thus the one motivation which is primary to any systemic realist explanation for change is not even acknowledged by Buzan, Jones, and Little, yet it makes a tremendous difference to the types of conclusions one would draw about interaction capacity in anarchy. In addition, Buzan, Jones, and Little consistently substitute adjacency for technological capacity and shared norms when discussing subsystems that exhibited these behavioral patterns (75–76), which suggests the alternative explanation that it is group competition over shrinking resources, rather than willingness and capability, which is promoting the imitation.

13. There is, then, some common ground between systemic realism and postmodernism in that the social practices in which groups engage represent ideologies that serve as interpretative frameworks providing intersubjective meanings that do not, in themselves, represent an objective truth *per se* (see, e.g., Folker 1996). That is, they both treat discourse as interpretation, but part ontological company with regards to whether an objective reality actually exists beyond those interpretations.

14. Ray's discussion of the abolition of slavery and its implications for the end of international war provides a good example in this context. Consistent with the "logic of discovery," Ray argues that "the notion from the Enlightenment that all men are created equal undermined the credibility of the invidious comparisons between categories of human beings on which slave systems were based" (1989: 423). Yet these enlightenment values were practiced by the most powerful states in the system, and from a realist perspective the abolishment of the international slave trade could have resulted not from common values and hence spreading repugnance at its practice, but because other groups viewed the imitation of such values as a means to an entirely different end. That the powerful would have such norms is not entirely inconsistent with realist logic either, since anarchy's indeterminancy regarding how to obtain survival and the process-layering produced by imitation could account for differences in social practices. See Schweller and Priess (1997); Resende-Santos (1996); and Thomson (1992).

15. See Gurr (1988); Hintze (1975); Rasler and Thompson (1989; 1994); and Tilly (1975). Desch provides a good overview of other relevant works, and points out that

these can often be categorized according to "theories that emphasize economic factors (the English school) and those that point to military factors (the German school)" (1996: 241). There is an obvious affinity between the latter types of state-formation theories and realists, whom often draw theoretical support from the fact that war is universally regarded as having played a critical role in the development of states. Yet there is still a chicken-and-egg disagreement over whether war was the means to a military-political or economic end. So, for example, Spruyt distinguishes his explanation for state-formation from that of Tilly's by arguing that its greater efficiency at garnering economic revenues accounted for the sovereign state's selection (1994: 30, 83–84).

Ultimately, however, Spruyt mixes and matches environment and social practices inconsistently, recognizing on the one hand that "as in all evolution, death is the final arbiter" and that it was a cause for the emergence of the territorial state (1994: 84), but asserting, on the other hand, that economic efficiency was the standard by which imitative selection led to the triumph of the state. Given the first causal attribute of the environment he identifies, why would profit as a process by itself then become the standard for selection? In the final analysis, Spruyt is using economic efficiency as the standard by which the sovereign state is judged against its competitors, which means he adopts assumptions of comparative institutional efficiency that are consistent with liberal rather than realism's environmentally-based explanations for change.

16. For example, it is difficult to understand why Spruyt claims his logic of unit transformation is different from that of Waltz. Spruyt argues that "units are faced with the necessity of competitive efficiency and effectiveness," and that "the unit that is best able to capitalize on environmental changes . . . exerts a competitive, marketlike pressure on the others" (1994: 15). This is entirely consistent with Waltz's discussion of anarchic competition, since it is because some of the units "succeed in providing a wanted good or service more attractively and more cheaply that others do" that "either their competitors emulate them or they fall by the wayside" (1979, 76–77). Spruyt's argument that institutional forms are selected by "mutual empowerment of actors" (1994: 15) and that this is inconsistent with systemic realism is also odd. The concept of anarchic socialization involves the creation of, and pressure for, conformity to common norms among the units. These arise because the units are interacting with one another: "Each is playing a game, and they are playing the game together. They react to each other and to the tensions their interactions produce" (Waltz 1979: 75).

17. These issues are explored more fully in Falger (1997; 1994); Guzzini (1998); Shimko (1992); and Sterling-Folker (2001; 2002). If one argues that there is indeed a biological, genetic, or physiological foundation for these characteristics, then one interesting implication would be how medical or genetic manipulation might affect realist theorizing. Eventually human beings might be able to manipulate their genetic or physiological composition in such a way that these particular behavioral characteristics could be altered and/or the horizon of death nullified to such an extent that its pressure as a selection mechanism no longer operated on the species as a whole. This would have a potentially confounding effect on realist theorizing.

18. This observation may appear to be similar in form to two-level games arguments that decisionmakers are caught between the international and domestic and are forced to balance interests at both levels when making international agreements with other states (Putnam 1988; Evans, Jacobson, and Putnam 1993). However, that ap-

proach remains primarily a method by which the constraints and opportunities of international negotiations and bargaining may be examined, rather than a theory in its own right. And upon closer examination, it is clear that it falls well within a liberal theoretical framework for the study of international cooperation. It does not begin with a realist conception of an unchanging anarchic environment and instead examines domestic processes only after the theorist has identified a situation which he or she believes should have the potential for cooperation. As Caporaso puts it, "two-level games are uniquely appropriate for situations in which there are at least two distinct governments at odds over some issue, but where negotiations could in principle yield joint gains" (1997: 585). Thus it leaves unexplored the reasons why negotiators would be motivated to cooperate in the first place.

19. See also Barnett (1990) and Barnett and Levy (1991).

20. See, for example, Desch (1996); Gurr (1988); Hintze (1975); Rasler and Thompson (1994; 1989); and Tilly (1975).

21. Essays by Ashley and Connolly in Der Derian and Shapiro (1989); Biersteker and Weber (1996).

22. Mann (1997: 479); Wade (1996); Gilpin (1996b: 18–26). In its school brief on the role of multinational corporations in globalization, *The Economist* found that the average multinational firm produced more than two-thirds of its output and located two-thirds of its employees in what it designated as its home country (1997a; see also 1997b).

23. In their discussion of Congress and foreign affairs, Kegley and Wittkopf note that it tends toward parochialism because, unlike the presidency, its members do not have a national constituency. In addition, because committee assignments are the primary means of servicing constituency demand, those which involve foreign relations are less desirable, and in several instances the Chair of the Senate Foreign Relations Committee has been defeated for reelection for being too involved in foreign rather than domestic affairs (1991: 421). They also observe that "if there is a charge that is unique to State, it is that the department is insensitive to domestic politics," and that Presidents often feel it works counter to their own political needs as a result (371).

24. Although Webb's observations in this regard are dated, they still manage to capture an ongoing dynamic of EU politics:

> Commission officials have discovered to their cost that national officials who might be expected to be collaborators in a transnational administrative network are often instinctively protective and conservative of their national procedures, autonomy, and competence. This tendency has little or nothing to do with the prevailing attitude of the political leadership in any state towards the Community. Rather it seems to persist irrespective of the national political climate, whenever national civil servants see their positions threatened by the Commission's desire to enlarge its competence and authority (1983: 19–20).

25. For example, see the interviews with two financiers and former members of the Clinton administration in "White House Externs," *New York Times*, 3 February 1999, C1+.

26. Within this context, Downs argues that the struggle for autonomy is the primary motivational force for bureaucratic behavior: "No bureau can survive unless it is continually able to demonstrate that its services are worthwhile to some group with influence over sufficient resources to keep it alive," which means that "it must impress those politicians who control the budget that its functions generate political support or meet vital social needs" (1967: 7).

27. Other constructivists have also tended to bracket domestic processes or included them as causally pertinent only in the initial stage of institutional preference innovation. Bracketing occurs in Finnemore (1996: 53–55), while initial stage use occurs in Ruggie (1998: 72, 126–127) and in Finnemore and Sikkink (1998: 896–899). Finnemore and Sikkink even go so far as to argue that "a government's domestic basis for legitimation and consent and thus its ability to stay in power" derives from a domestic desire to be internationally legitimate, which implies that domestic governance structures have no independent causal weight of their own absent their relation to collective systemic interests (903). Because they ignore domestic political processes as causal in their own right, all of these constructivist accounts end up overdetermining either the possibility of fundamental systemic transformation or the causality of systemic processes.

28. See also Druckman (1994); Duckitt et al. (1999); Ignatieff (1996); D. Smith (1996); and Mercer (1995).

29. This does not mean that transgroup relations cannot be transformed in fundamental ways. It is possible for groups to merge into a larger unit and to do so by choice rather than by imposition (as the American colonies did). However the circumstances whereby such merger occurs are necessarily restrictive in the realist argument. Obvious security interdependencies must exist, those interdependencies must be ongoing and demonstrably successful at obtaining each group's survival (in comparison to going it alone), and the cognitive barriers that social practices and institutions intentionally create and nurture in order to maintain and insure group unity must be overcome. While the last conditions may be subject to some agency-intent, the first two conditions are merely fortuitous. Thus according to realism, the conditions for willingly expanding group identities are rarely met in global politics.

CHAPTER 4. EMPIRICAL PROPOSITIONS AND THE BRETTON WOODS MONETARY REGIME

1. The attempt by Jones to define and identify interdependence according to particular empirical measurements and data sets remains one of the best examples of the difficulties inherent to the interdependence literature. In many cases complex aggregations of data are needed in order to substantiate the phenomenon of interdependence and its particular impacts, yet most indicators are indirect at best (1984: 33, 61). He concludes that "empirical indicators remain, to an extent, arbitrary measures of phenomena that have been imbued with significance by some theory of reality. Such theoretical direction of empirical analysis is nowhere more clear than in the case of the 'contested concept' of interdependence, where diverse definitions emphasize different measures and indicators" (18).

2. International monetary policymaking is one of two issue areas examined by Keohane and Nye (1989), and is one of three examined by Keohane (1984). Frieden's examination of U.S. monetary policymaking in the *Internationalization and Domestic Politics* volume is cited by Keohane and Milner as one of two chapters which provide "the strongest evidence" that "internationalization especially in the form of capital mobility, reduces the autonomy and efficacy of governments' macroeconomic policy choices" (1996: 248).

3. Lindeman suggests that because congressional confidence in the State Department's economic abilities were quite low at the time, the House Banking and Currency Committee also wrote Treasury leadership into law as a means to prevent the State Department from assuming control over post-war foreign financial affairs (1963: 524–525).

4. For example, because Japan did not assume advanced-country status in the IMF until 1964, the conduct of its monetary affairs during the 1950s was shared by its Ministry of Foreign Affairs and by its Ministry of International Trade and Industry. This division of responsibility was an historical legacy of the American occupation and, according to Johnson, Japan's move to industrialized status in the early 1960s triggered intense bureaucratic infighting because it mandated that the Ministry of Finance (MOF) assume policymaking control for an issue area over which it had no prior responsibility (1977; 1982). Johnson also points out that it was not until 1961 that MOF officials met with U.S. Treasury officials for the first time, and that the MOF did not even have a bureau for international financial affairs until 1964. The subsequent increase in the MOF's status within the Japanese executive branch is frequently noted by scholars who study Japanese economic policymaking, for example, Horne (1985); Rosenbluth (1989); and Angel (1991). This suggests an interesting twist on the proposition that it is the increasing interdependence and technicality of issue areas which has led to the increase of elite communication networks among the major industrial nations in the post-World War II period. Although this proposition is not the subject of dispute here, it is possible to surmise a counterproposition based on the historical record that, at least with regards to their form and content, these networks are instead the result of processes of autonomy specific to America and Great Britain which were then institutionally imposed on other nation-states. The parochial bureaucratic jurisdictions and idiosyncrasies of the American and British Treasury departments in the 1940s go a long way in explaining why post-World War II international monetary networks developed as they did.

5. For the exact process see Dominquez and Frankel (1993: 65) and Volcker and Gyohten (1992: 233–235).

6. However they also point out that another reason why such attempts fail is because central banks jealously guard their independence from one another and so resist pressures for greater coordination (Bergsten and Henning 1996: 87). See also Dobson (1991).

7. The best example of attempts at evasion throughout this period was Great Britain, which suffered a series of Sterling crises during the mid- to late-1960s due to the pound's use as a reserve and to the balance overhang between the government's gold reserves and foreign exchange. Yet Britain viewed devaluation as so disastrous that it preferred to borrow from the IMF, and Gowa notes that the British aversion

was echoed in the U.S. government as well. In both cases there appeared to be a cognitive association between reserve currency status and world power, with the accompanying conviction that devaluation would destroy both simultaneously (1983: 132). Because it was so frequently the case that states did not make policy adjustments until balance of payment disequilibriums had reached crisis proportions, as Weinstein observes "fixed exchange rates provide only an illusion of stability. Rate changes are infrequent, but when they do come, they can hit with the force of a bomb" (1998: C8). Spero and Hart note that the policy choices within a fixed exchange rate system included the ability to "finance the imbalance or impose exchange controls, . . . either change the value of their currencies—devalue or revalue them—or alter domestic fiscal or monetary policy" (1997: 17–18). Because alterations to currency values or fiscal and monetary policy entailed domestic political costs, it is hardly surprising (at least from a perspective other than liberal cooperation theory) that "political leaders were often reluctant to take politically risky measures to address structural imbalances."

8. This suspicion may have derived in part from the belief that, as Makin describes it, the BIS "was really like a club for central bankers and has often been characterized as such. Beleaguered heads of central banks could meet there—in privacy, or some would say secrecy, since until 1977 the entrance to the BIS was an unmarked doorway next to Frey's Chocolate Shop across from Basel's railway station—and count on sympathetic ears to listen to complaints about pressures from national treasuries to print more money" (1983: 169).

9. Strange points out in legal or formal terms that it was not an agreement at all, but rather a public statement of the future intentions of central bankers (1976: 84–85).

10. Switzerland became an eleventh member despite the fact that it was not a member of the IMF. Camps and Gwin point out that at least initially the bureaucratic participants from Germany and Sweden were their central bankers and not their treasuries, and they also provide details about the GAB negotiations (1981: 223–224).

11. There were at the same time other forums in which monetary affairs were discussed. Besides existing organizations such as the General Agreements on Tariffs and Trade (GATT) and the Organization for Economic Cooperation and Development (OECD), the OECD's Economic Policy Committee had also developed a "Working Party 3" in 1961 which was informal and composed of Finance Ministry and central bank representatives from OECD countries. The representatives would meet every six to eight weeks in Paris and, according to Strange, "would present prepared statements tending usually to explain away or to play down the importance of any recent movement in their external payments positions" (1976: 148–149). While the Working Party 3 became increasingly more frank and useful as a forum for the exchange of information, Strange notes that it did not have the staff that the IMF possessed to conduct multilateral surveillance (129), and that the G10 continued to dominate as the negotiating forum for monetary affairs.

12. According to Solomon, "the logistics of the meetings were such that there were 20 deputies around the table—a senior treasury and a central bank official from each of the members of the Group of Ten—plus observers from the Swiss National Bank, the IMF, the OECD, and the BIS. Behind the deputies of each country sat two

or three advisers, and there were also five 'secretaries,' officials from countries that were members of the group" (1982: 66).

13. They also continued to exclude the IMF to a large degree. Dobson noted that while the IMF Director began each G5 meeting with a presentation, the Treasury ministers did most of the talking thereafter and then the Director was expected to depart so that the ministers and central bank governments could discuss confidential business (1991: 43). This was the case even at meetings of the Treasury deputies. The IMF Economic Counselor was allowed to attend some portion of the meeting, but had to leave the room before certain aspects of business were discussed.

14. Camps and Gwin, for example, claim that economic summitry preempted center stage and replaced the G5 (1981: 226), and Dobson asserts that summitry preceded the real heyday of the G5 (1991: ch. 1).

15. Angel has noted this phenomenon within the Japanese context as well: "Issues related to international monetary affairs are perceived by the general public, the communications media, the business community, politicians, and even the rest of the economic bureaucracy, as highly technical and difficult to understand. An objective examination of the principles of international monetary affairs fails to justify that reputation, but whether justified or not, only ordained international monetary specialists in Japan were considered qualified even to discuss the subject" (1991: 270).

16. The relationship between the G5, Helmut Schmidt, and Giscard D'Estaing is particularly complicated in this regard, since they were founding members with firsthand experience and personal knowledge of the intricacies of international monetary policymaking at the ministerial level, and yet later became heads of their national governments.

17. Levy (1994) and Woods (1995) discuss various research designs that track learning and ideas causality.

18. Whether this pre-1971 reliance on the hegemon among secondary state elites amounted to an example of strategic misperceptions regarding autonomy's efficacy is really an open question. It may have been the case that it was simply strategically efficient to remain relatively autonomous from one another as long as the hegemon was coordinating the cooperative effort and allowing access to its markets.

19. One need only compare the role which practical obstacles play for Cooper, who argues that a common currency for all the major industrials would be best (1984; 1992), with Williamson, who argues that exchange rate intervention target zones would be sufficient as long as they were publicly announced (1985; and with Miller in 1987), and with Goldstein, who argues that neither target zones nor publicity is necessary (1994), to realize the difficulties of establishing a standard by which actual behavior in the issue area could be evaluated as "efficient" and thus in operationalizing the concept empirically. See also Gallarotti (1991).

20. Or as Williamson describes this, an exchange rate "floats 'freely' or 'cleanly' if the authorities do not take any actions designed to influence the behavior of the exchange rate" (1985: 64). The complete absence of a policy response would have to be the equivalent to unilateral policymaking since, regardless of its announced justification, it would also effectively serve as a refusal to even attempt policy coordination in the issue area.

21. A similar schematic for examining alternative exchange rate arrangements historically as well as across the present global economic system is offered by Kenen, although he breaks down each category in a slightly different manner (1994: 147), and by Marston (1988).

22. These sentiments have been expressed in a variety of quarters, often in response to particular events and in support of freely floating exchange rates. See, for example, Henning's discussion of the groups which vocalized concerns over a target zone exchange rate system after the October 1987 stock market crash (1994: 287); Gallarotti (1991); and Dominguez and Frankel (1993: 18).

23. Williamson and Miller (1987: 62–63) note that Frenkel (1987; and with Goldstein 1988) is similarly skeptical of depending on the exchange rate as the standard for target zones and the trigger for action.

24. In support of this position, Bergsten and Henning note that U.S. Federal Reserve Board research reveals that it was the exchange rate which acted as the primary conduit through which changes in U.S. monetary policy had an impact on its economy in the 1980s (1996: 106).

25. In a similar vein, Dominguez and Frankel argue that intervention has an important effect on the exchange rate only *when* it influences expectations, which implies that intervention activities and goals must be publicly known in order to be effective. They also point out, however, that this would require a major policy change and attitude shift in how central banks conduct currency market interventions, since most central banks are secretive not only about intervention amounts but also over whether an intervention has even occurred, leaving scholars and traders alike to infer them by matching up contemporary wire serve reports with official bank numbers released at the end of the quarter (1993: ch. 5, 60–61, 70–71).

26. Bergsten and Henning also argue repeatedly that monetary policymaking must develop a greater sensitivity to external circumstances and that a public focus on the exchange rate is the best means of doing so (1996: 86, 104–108, 128–129). Besides the need for commonly agreed-upon and publicly announced exchange rate target zones, Bergsten and Henning suggest additional cooperative measures that would avoid suboptimal monetary outcomes. These include greater surveillance of one another's monetary and fiscal policies, and an early warning system in which potentially destabilizing government policies would be publicly and internationally revealed. They also argue that both of these measures would be most effective if the IMF were given the organizational responsibility for them (134–137), which is similar to Keohane's recommendation. See also Williamson (1985: 72–73).

27. It is also generally consistent with Cooper's early discussions of a post-Bretton Woods monetary system in which he argued for "a system of closely managed floating, with rules governing central bank intervention, or a system of exchange rate parities with strong presumptive rules for 'gliding' the parities" (1975: 96). Cooper moved away from such a system in his later writings (1984; 1992).

28. As Kratochwil and Ruggie have noted, whether or not the end of Bretton Woods was the end of a regime in the issue area should be a fairly straightforward empirical question, but that there is deep disagreement within the liberal cooperation theory literature over this point (Ruggie 1998: 95). However they do not see this

disagreement as one which has serious deductive implications and consequences for neoliberal institutionalism and for whether it can be empirically falsified. Alternatively I believe the disagreements on this point indicate problems in the deductive logic of neoliberal institutionalism which are so severe that it is undermined as an empirical and theoretical explanation for international cooperation. This argument is developed further in chapter 6.

29. Henning also observes that "the United States supported the Bretton Woods regime . . . only so long as the costs of doing so remained fairly small in terms of domestic priorities. . . . When the rules of the regime threatened to constrain American monetary policy, the United States jettisoned the regime" (1994: 262). Gowa (1983) and Odell (1982) support this perspective as well.

30. In fact demand from below may actually put more pressure on state elites to behave autonomously rather than cooperatively. Druckman notes that in studies done on the individual's role as representative of a group, the pressure to "prove" one's loyalty is particularly intense and leads to considerable inflexibility regarding problem-solving (1994: 54–55). Another problem with depending on society's demand for higher standards of living to account for elite choices is that it imputes a monolithic motivation which, upon closer examination, cannot even be maintained for the economic sector, let alone for the rest of society. If countervailing interests to the maximization of wealth exist within society, then some segments of society may be vehemently opposed to the abandonment of autonomy regardless of its effects on aggregate wealth.

CHAPTER 5. U.S. INTERNATIONAL MONETARY COOPERATION, 1971–1993

1. Solomon (1982: ch. 11) provides an excellent overview of the international economic events which led up to the Camp David meeting, as does Odell (1982: ch. 4).

2. Solomon reports, on the other hand, that Connally initially made a good impression on the Europeans and describes him as being more of a nationalist than an idealist with regards to monetary policy (1982: 191). But he also notes that this good impression quickly vanished with post-August events, and that Connally was dubbed "Typhoon Connally" by the Japanese press (200). And relations between the IMF's Managing Director and Connally were particularly rancorous during this period. Southard recounts the first meeting between the two men in May 1971 at which Schweitzer and Connally consistently disagreed over whether broader parity changes would be necessary: "Following that one exchange of views with Secretary Connally, Schweitzer's working contacts with U.S. financial officials were chiefly with Under Secretary Volcker. Secretary Connally made it obvious that he personally did not intend to continue a consultative relationship with the IMF" (1979: 37–38). Coombs also observes about Connally's first visit to the IMF, that he treated it "as a museum in which anything that wasn't already stuffed ought to be" (1976: 219). See also Odell's account of Connally (1982: 245–263), and Connally's own description of his international policymaking goals: "My basic approach is that the foreigners are out to screw us. Our job is to screw them first" (quoted in Odell, 263).

3. The doctrine of "benign neglect" to which Coombs refers is a characterization with a long history in the study of U.S. monetary policymaking. It refers to particular periods, in what Henning and others have noted are cycles of neglect and activism in U.S. international monetary policymaking, when U.S. policymakers ignore the dollar's value and its ramifications for U.S. economic interests. See Odell's discussion of the term (1982, 191–199), and Solomon, who uses it with regards to the pre-1971 American attitude toward its balance of payments. For sources which document and discuss these cycles of neglect and activism, see those cited by Henning (1994: 263).

4. The conference was held in early 1969 and was comprised of professors and bankers who became known as the "Burgenstock group," while the published proceedings came out in 1970 (Solomon 1982: 169).

5. The French preference for a return to fixed exchange rates was so unequivocal for most of this period that it must be singled out. Solomon recounts a comment made by a European official about a European Economic Community (EEC) meeting at which the French were insisting upon a return to par values: "eight of the nine EEC members were isolated on this issue" (1982: 269).

6. According to Odell (1982: 280–283) and Solomon (1982: 200–201), pressure on Connally to reach agreement came from a variety of corners, including Kissinger, Burn, and even Congress which suggested replacing Connally with Burns as spokesperson in the negotiations. Connally had three objectives immediately following the 1971 August decision: realignment of exchange rates, a reduction of foreign trade barriers, and more equitable defense burden sharing. Under pressure from Kissinger, the latter was eventually dropped as a demand in Connally's negotiations (191). Solomon also provides details on the various meetings and negotiations which proceeded the Smithsonian meeting, such as the November G10 meeting in Rome (29 November–1 December) and the meeting between French President Pompidou and Nixon in the Azores, 13–14 December (where the actual figures for realignment were agreed upon). See Volcker's account of this period as well (1992: 80–90).

7. The pound and franc remained at their previous gold parities while the Canadians decided to let their dollar continue to float. Solomon notes of their decision, "while Canada was treated as something of a pariah at that time, its decision to float appeared considerably more respectable later" (1982: 208).

8. Solomon discusses other factors which led to currency instability after Smithsonian, and why the initial results of the realignment were expected to be perverse (1982: 209–211). He also covers the crumbling of the Smithsonian agreement between 1972–73 in greater detail (ch. 13).

9. According to Volcker, this was suggested because Connally perceived the G10 to be too dominated by Europeans (1992: 115–116).

10. Actually this was not the first plan for systemic reform drawn up or publicly presented by a U.S. monetary policymaking official. Burns had laid out the elements of a reformed monetary system at a May 1972 conference in Montreal, but was rebuked by Volcker in a press conference afterward, who noted that Burns did not speak on behalf of all U.S. officials. Volcker provides considerable detail on the C20 negotiations in his capacity as a participant (1992: 114–135), as does Solomon who also participated (1982: ch.14).

11. There may have been a third incident, although the evidence as to whether it actually took place is sketchy. Coombs writes that at the May 1974 BIS meeting, he and representatives from the German and Swiss central banks reached tentative agreement on a coordinated intervention to counter speculation against the dollar (1976: 234). Word of this agreement leaked to the press that very day, and both the mark and Swiss franc fell 4 percent against the dollar (Solomon 1982: 340). Coombs notes satisfaction with these results, suggesting that the leaked story alone had the intended impact and might have made the actual currency market intervention superfluous. Dominguez and Frankel do not include the incident in their documentation of the major episodes of post-Bretton Woods U.S. currency intervention (1993).

12. The oil embargo initially reversed the dollar's depreciation, so that by mid-January 1974 the German mark and the Swiss franc had fallen by roughly 23 percent from their peak levels of July 1973. By mid-May 1974 the dollar had fallen 21 percent below its January high against the mark. Then in August the dollar rose against the mark again to a level 10 percent above the lows reached in early May. Over the 1974–1975 winter the dollar would crest and then plunge again into a new slide (Coombs 1976: 233–234).

13. The details of this coordination are provided by both Coombs (1976) and Solomon (1982: 341). Agreement was reached between Burns, Coombs, and representatives from the German and Swiss central banks at an impromptu meeting in a hotel room at Heathrow airport. Solomon also notes that, when questioned by the press afterward, Burns denied the agreement was an attempt to peg rates, and "declined even to discuss 'possible numerical targets for levels of exchange rates in the short run' " (341).

14. Economists at the Brookings Institution and at the Trilateral Commission were the chief proponents of the strategy, although the OECD would also make similar recommendations (see Solomon 1982: 310 and Volcker 1992: 146, 349).

15. They would use $4.7 billion of the Treasury's ESF and $2.2 billion in central bank swap lines (Volcker 1992: 350). See also Solomon (1982: 346–347).

16. The discount rate was raised by 1 percent to $9^{1/2}$ percent, both of which Marston points out were unprecedented highs at the time (1988: 101). And the $30 billion in resources consisted of $15 billion in swaps with foreign central banks, $5 billion in drawing on the IMF and sales of SDRs, and $10 billion in "Carter bonds," which were U.S. Treasury notes denominated in marks and Swiss francs to be sold abroad. For details regarding how the package was assembled and by whom within the administration, see Campbell (1986: 120) and Solomon (1982: 349–350).

17. The New York trading desk bought over $600 million on 1 November, and would conduct another operation of similar proportions in December. The U.S. intervention totals for the months of November and December respectively were more than $3.5 billion and $3.1 billion.

18. And also reminiscent of the C20 negotiations was the fact that "in initial discussions of the substitution account, the Europeans and Japanese sought to make the United States behave more like an 'ordinary' state by demanding that the United States restrain its overseas spending if the account was established" (Gowa 1984: 673). The United States showed no inclination to do so, however, and Gowa's central argument is that the entire substitution account episode serves as an excellent example

of the hegemonic stability theory proposition that small groups will not cooperate in the absence of hegemonic leadership.

19. Blumenthal's popularity within the administration had not been very high for sometime because, according to Campbell, it had been Charles L. Shultze, Chair of the Council of Economic Advisers (CEA), and not Blumenthal, who had been primarily responsible for organizing the November 1978 dollar rescue package (1986: 120). This did not sit well with other Treasury officials, who wanted the Treasury to retain the lead on such matters (139, 150).

20. The emphasis on domestics was apparent in some of Reagan's administrative appointments as well. Campbell notes that the Treasury's International Monetary Affairs Deputy (in the Office of the Assistant Secretary for International Affairs) traditionally had a strong relationship with the Office of the Under Secretary for Monetary Affairs but this was not the case in the Reagan administration. Beryl Sprinkel, as the Under Secretary for Monetary Affairs, was more concerned with the regulation of the banking and securities communities and managing government debt. Campbell also points out that the Assistant Secretary for International Affairs during Reagan's first term was a lawyer, Marc E. Leland, and that this was a departure from the practice of appointing someone who had experience in the global aspects of monetary affairs (1986: 129).

21. Investors sought the most immediate and short-term favorable returns based on factors such as comparative real interest rate returns, anticipated currency values, and the political strength and stability of governments, rather than trade transactions. The rapidity with which funds could be shifted had an impact as well, so that by 1984, world trade in goods and services was about $2 trillion, while global capital transfers reached $20–$30 trillion (Garten 1984: 453).

22. These arguments are best illustrated by Sprinkel's own characterization of the new "hands-off" policy: "It means that when I work in the office, the markets will take care of the exchange rate and not the Treasury and the Federal Reserve" (quoted in the *New York Times,* 5 May 1981, D13).

23. The Reagan administration was suspicious of multilateral institutions in general, and Bowring notes of its relationship with the IMF and the World Bank that it ranged from "cool to caustic" (1981).

24. Although this can be a subject of disagreement among scholars as well (see, e.g., Dominguez and Frankel 1993), much of the disagreement between Sprinkel and Camdessus revolved around the issue of sterilization, which is when official purchases or sales of foreign currencies are offset by domestic transactions so that the monetary liabilities of both the home and foreign authorities remains unchanged. Sprinkel argued, from a monetarist perspective, that sterilization had only a temporary signaling effect on the market but produced no lasting effect on exchange rates.

25. See, for example, articles in the *New York Times* on 1 February, 23 February, and 5 June 1984; White House press release, "News Conference by the President," 17 September 1985; and Funabashi (1989: 65).

26. Funabashi refers to the G5's discussion of its intervention strategy as a "nonpaper" (1989: 17–19), which was apparently drafted by David C. Mulford, who was Assistant Secretary for International Affairs at the Treasury during this period.

27. Destler and Henning point out that at Baker's January 1985 confirmation hearings he had suggested that the hands-off policy was "obviously something that should be looked at" (1989: 41–42). Both he and Darman were also at the G5 meeting in January 1985 at which the United States agreed to intervene in modest amounts, and Funabashi reports that Baker later concurred that the change in policy began at that meeting (1989: 10–11).

28. Central bankers have always tended to believe that monetary policy coordination was too sensitive a topic to discuss in the presence of finance ministers (Funabashi 1989: 46). When he was in the Treasury in 1975, Volcker noted the preference for secrecy among both finance ministers and central bankers, but "central bankers, I later came to understand, would not be averse to dropping finance ministers out of the equation when it came to dealing with monetary policy!" (1992: 139). Volcker also observed that bureaucratic tensions between the Treasury and Fed reduced the procedural efficiency of U.S. currency market interventions, in that the staff on both sides tended to be overly protective of their bosses and suspicious of jurisdictional encroachments (235).

29. There was little chance of this happening, however, since their agreement to expand during 1978 would be viewed as costly mistakes by both Japan and Germany after the oil shock occurred. Bergsten and Henning note with regards to Bonn that while "many American analysts view the agreement as a prototype, perhaps even the zenith, of international policy cooperation. . . . By contrast, most Germans (and some Japanese) view the agreement as a disaster" (1996: 57, 78). See also Lincoln (1988: 91–92) and MOF interviews by Funabashi (1989: 94–95).

30. Statement of the IMF Interim Committee, Washington, 28 September 1987. See also Funabashi's discussion of Baker's appearance on *This Week with David Brinkley* on the same day (1989: 158).

31. For details on these events see Funabashi (1989: 155–167) and Dominguez and Frankel (1993: 15). Miyazawa was particularly eager to reach an agreement because during the elections in July 1986 he had been an outspoken critic of the prior Finance Minister's policies. In return for stabilizing the dollar, Miyazawa agreed to submit a supplementary budget to the Diet in order to stimulate the Japanese economy by 3.6 trillion yen (as well as to cut the discount rate and initiate tax reform). The deal was agreed to in September but not announced until the end of October. In the interim the yen depreciated, which made the Treasury suspicious that the MOF was attempting to manipulate its value in order to lock in a favorable rate. Lincoln also points out that upon closer inspection the U.S. Treasury discovered that the supplementary budget which Miyazawa pushed through the Diet in the fall of 1986 was a lot less stimulative than they had been led to believe (1988: 288). When the United States demanded additional expansion, Miyazawa argued that he could not incorporate any more changes into the 1987 fiscal budget because it had been drawn up the summer before he was appointed and he was obligated to support it—an explanation which did not sit well with the U.S. Treasury.

32. Although membership had been expanded at the Tokyo summit, Italian participation continued to be a sore subject and the G5 officials refused to let them take part in their meetings held the day before the G7 conference was scheduled. In

reaction to this affront, the Italian representatives returned to Rome in protest and did not participate in the accord (Funabashi 1989: 180–181; Volcker 1992: 281–282).

33. One of the causes cited by some economists for the crash was the target zone exchange rate system itself. Dominguez and Frankel note that the market may have feared that the Fed would deliberately raise interest rates in order to keep the dollar from falling through the baselines set at Louvre. See also Henning (1994: 287) and Volcker's commentary on Martin Feldstein's criticisms (1992: 285).

34. *Wall Street Journal*, 21 November 1988; see also "Brady Avoiding Critics as Group of 7 Gathers," *New York Times*, 2 February 1989, D1.

35. Quoted in Destler and Henning (1989: 72). They also point out that there is some evidence for an internal debate within the Treasury during the spring over whether to maintain or abandon the zones, and cite Kilborn (1989) and Rowen (1989). Another factor that undoubtedly played a role in these internal debates was the acrimonious relationship which developed during the Bush administration between the White House and Treasury on the one hand and the Fed on the other. Henning discusses these disputes at length (1994: 292–298), noting that in its efforts to protect its independence from political pressure, the Fed became increasingly resistant to undertaking foreign exchange rate interventions at this time, going so far as to challenge the legal basis for the Treasury's use of the ESF for that purpose, and refused to comply with interest rate coordinations suggested by the Treasury. The House Banking Committee would convene hearings on the subject in 1990, and in 1992 the White House held up Fed appointments while Brady endorsed a review of Fed structures as a means of continued pressure.

36. Darman later became Director of the Office of Management and Budget under Bush. Funabashi includes numerous examples of Mulford's role in the process of the "Plaza Strategy" (1989: 11–14, 156–157, 160–162).

37. For Mulford and Dallara statements see *Washington Post*, 20 April 1990. For Brady statements see *New York Times*, 25 March 1990 and the IMF's press review, 18 April 1990.

38. At the time the Treasury was engaged in talks with Japan over financial market liberalization and Brady may have withheld his support as a means of pressuring the Japanese to come to an agreement in those talks (Henning 1994: 165–167, 296). Thus this may be yet another example of "dollar weaponry," although Brady's use of it was certainly less obvious than that of Blumenthal's and Baker's.

39. The yen would go on to reach remarkable levels, and by early 1995 the dollar was actually above 80 yen. Although post-1993 events are not covered in this study, Bergsten and Henning provide a detailed discussion of the G7's reaction to the yen and attempts at intervention from 1994 to 1995 (1996: 32–34).

CHAPTER 6. WHY LIBERAL THEORIES FAIL TO ACCOUNT FOR THE EMPIRICAL RECORD

1. For other discussions of this pattern see Henning (1987); Bergsten and Henning (1996); and Destler and Henning (1989).

2. In this context it is interesting that Odell recognizes the importance of administration change yet still insists it may be characterized as a cognitive rather than domestic political variable. He argues, for example, that "changes in the general predispositions of the governing leadership and in their specific perceptions and calculations explain the 1971 choice of diplomatic strategy," because the change in governing leadership led to "the disappearance of old attitudes toward the Bretton Woods system" in the White House and Treasury (1982: 240–241). Yet those ideas would not have arrived at the White House (either in 1971 or in later periods) without a regular four-year cycle of electoral politics to put them there. It is difficult to see how the relevance of ideas could be used as a counterargument to the relevance of domestic processes and institutions as a result. It may simply be the case that Odell is defining domestic political variables narrowly (e.g., to indicate political parties, rather than the domestic institutional context in general), and his detailed study of ideas in U.S. international monetary policymaking certainly provides a great deal of evidence to contradict liberal cooperation theory expectations. It reveals that the content or substance of the ideas themselves ran directly counter to those which liberal cooperation theory would anticipate decisionmakers to learn in conditions of complex interdependence.

3. The potential discrepancy between interdependence and democratic control over foreign policy was noted much earlier by Kaiser (1971), and what work has been done on the "democratic deficit" is usually related to the study of the EU, although Keohane and Nye do note the potential conflict in their more recent consideration of complex interdependence (1998). The potential incompatibilities between democratic forms of governance and interdependence deserves further study, particularly since the liberal IR literature tends to lump them together as compatible causes for international cooperation, for example, Goldgeier and McFaul (1992); Jervis (1991/92); Zacher (1992); and Zacher and Matthew (1995).

4. These changes include the activation of private interest groups concerned with exchange rate policymaking and biannual reports by the Treasury to the Congress on international monetary affairs.

5. See Keohane (1984: 24); Keohane and Nye (1989: 40); Rosecrance (1986); and Weber's discussion of the ahistorical nature of this particular assumption in liberal theorizing (1997: 246–248).

6. It should be noted that to the non-American and/or later political scientist, the obsession with that decade and its centrality to the interdependence and regimes literature is peculiar. While certain seminal events did occur in the 1970s, it is simply not clear to "other" observers by what standards scholars at the time could argue that international politics in the 1970s was fundamentally different from prior (and certainly subsequent) decades. The concern with the 1970s may have been less the result of social scientific endeavor and more a function of other factors such as nationality, generational expectations, and the immediacy of the events themselves. As British scholars Jones and Willetts observe "there are those who see the adoption of interdependence as an intellectual response to the practical setbacks experienced by the United States of America during the later 1960s and early 1970s. Interdependence, in this vein, may thus be viewed as a *rationalization* of failure in Vietnam and the enforced abandonment of dollar convertibility into gold" (1984: 2; my emphasis).

Strange makes a similar argument about the American tendency to exaggerate the "shocks" of the 1970s and its subsequent "faddish" influence on regimes scholarship (1983: 338–342; see also Northedge 1976). If these observations are correct, then the most unfortunate aspect of this 1970s obsession is the impact it had on the ensuing development of cooperation theory.

7. See Thomson and Krasner (1992: 314–321); Jones (1984); and *The Economist* (1997a).

8. For an excellent discussion of this commitment and its alternative, see Jackson and Nexon (1999).

9. Hasenclever, Mayer, and Rittberger (1997: 162); P. Rosenau (1990); Smith (1996).

10. On the other hand, it has been observed by Checkel (1998) and Jackson and Nexon (1999: 9) that this temporal-sequential resolution of the agent-structure problem is also common to the constructivist literature.

11. Kratochwil and Ruggie discuss a number of epistemological options and ultimately recommend that one adopt the more interpretive epistemological methods utilized by Alker, Ashley, Cox, Der Derian, and Ernst Haas (to name only a few), such as privileging consensual knowledge or the shifting intersubjective frameworks of human discourse and practice (Ruggie 1998: 96). Yet these methods are drawn from critical theory in the humanities, particularly the study of literature and language, and have occasioned considerable theoretical debate within those disciplines. Their application in any discipline is not contention-free, and one of the most glaring difficulties, given that critical theory derives from the study of texts, is determining what constitutes a "text" in the context of IR (other than the work of fellow theorists). For essay collections which attempt to apply discourse analysis to IR, see Der Derian and Shapiro (1989) and Beer and Hariman (1996). Although critical theory is not the subject of critique here, much could be said about the potential pitfalls of utilizing its epistemological methods in the field of IR. See, for example, P. Rosenau (1990); Hasenclever, Mayer, and Rittberger (1997); Folker (1996); Lapid (1989); and Biersteker (1989).

12. One interesting parallel here is that the juxtaposition of opposites is what a postmodern epistemology implies is necessary in order to discover the imposed hegemony of ideas as well. In the foreword to Der Derian and Shapiro's collection, Donna Gregory notes that the deconstructive theorist "tackles the fiction that a thing can be known only by what it is not" and so "observes that a particular text or argument depends on an opposition structuring," that terms have been "differently weighted, one having more power than the other," and that the paired concepts have been structured as "inevitably opposed and as opposed in a zero-sum relation" (1989: xv–xvi; see also P. Rosenau 1990 and Lapid 1989). Given that many constructivists draw upon postmodern insights, it is remarkable that, as Folker has observed, "constructivists have been generally inclined to affirm something like the millennial end product of the liberal project" (1996: 13). Schlesinger notes as well that all postmodern theories have had a tendency to insert into the empty space beyond the hegemonic discourse a possibility for tolerance of the "stranger" (1994: 317).

13. In fact from the perspective of psychology, the individual's reaction to the nonterritorial space is more likely to be what Schlesinger has called "identity panic"

in which the nation-state is cognitively clung to as the focus of identification even more rigorously (1994: 318; he is citing Etienne Balibar in his use of the phrase). See also Bloom (1990: 35–53).

14. Chaos plays a central role in most liberal cooperation theories as a result. Actors encountering one another for the first time have no preconceptions about one another, and, because environment is not causal, it is instead the "first social act [which] creates expectations on both sides about each other's future behaviors" (Wendt 1992: 405). The quality of that first encounter is accidental, so that according to Jervis, "the flow of international politics is, in significant measure, contingent or path-dependent," there is "a large role for chance and accident," and for every event "one can imagine a variety of policies and outcomes, each of which would have produced a quite different world" (1991/92: 42–43). Yet the adoption of an historical contingency approach seems to be fundamentally at odds with behavioral positivism. It suggests that there is no way to predict if one type of practice (say cooperation) would ever displace another (e.g., autonomy), because one cannot assume there are underlying governing laws or truths which are reflected in behavior or outcomes. Since it would be difficult to rely on historical contingency and remain a political "scientist," it is hardly surprising that the use of historical contingency has been haphazard and inconsistently mixed with postivistist epistemologies in order to explain outcomes such as international cooperation. Jervis, for example, argues strongly for an historical contingency approach but then only applies it to the processes of self-help, while the liberal processes of capitalism and democracy are apparently immune from its implications since they reflect the "triumph of interests over passions" and so are "irreversible" (52, 55). For a dissenting opinion regarding the use of historical contingency in American political science, see Kowert and Legro's discussion of it (1996: 489, footnote 92).

CHAPTER 7. EXPLAINING U.S. MONETARY COOPERATION WITH REALIST-CONSTRUCTIVISM

1. As S. Cohen observes about this type of constituency pressure and expectations, "The Congress does not cherish this role. Throughout the first nine months of 1985, it increasingly wanted protection from protectionist demands. The executive branch had ceased performing its traditional buffer role as lightning rod, absorbing and deflecting the heat of protectionist demands away from elected members of Congress" (1988: 209).

2. For greater detail regarding these proposed exchange rate bills, see Destler and Henning (1989, 101–9) and S. Cohen (1988: 74–75).

3. One could argue that Baker would rely on multilateralism as an instrumental and domestically-motivated tactic again when he built the Gulf War coalition in the fall of 1990, since it was a useful domestic and international political cover for what was essentially an American operation.

4. Such policymaking autonomy may be defined as "the extent to which an organization possesses a distinctive area of competence, a clearly demarcated clientele or membership, and undisputed jurisdiction over a function, service, goals, issue, or

cause" (Clark and Wilson 1961: 157). Clark and Wilson go onto note on the same page that "organizations seek to make their environment stable and certain and to remove threats to their identities. Autonomy gives an organization a reasonably stable claim to resources and thus places it in a more favorable position from which to compete for those resources. Resources include issue and causes as well as money, time, effort, and names."

5. And not coincidentally, Downs called this the "Law of Self-Serving Loyalty" (1967: 211).

6. By way of comparison, consider Carter's first Treasury Secretary, Michael Blumenthal, who was particularly unpopular within the Treasury precisely because he failed to protect the Treasury as an institution relative to other bureaucratic agencies. Campbell notes that it was Shultze and the CEA which organized the November 1978 dollar rescue package, not Blumenthal, and that among Treasury officials the Carter administration was considered a low point with regards to the internal coordination of U.S. economic policymaking because Blumenthal frequently let other agencies take the lead in economic affairs (1986: 120, 139, 150).

7. Throughout this period jurisdictional tensions between central bankers and finance ministers (and the Fed and the Treasury in particular) were frequently apparent as well. At a BIS meeting in February 1986 Volcker worked out an agreement to coordinate a round of interest rate cuts in March 1986 with other central bankers. The Fed was indignant when the Treasury later took credit for these cuts as part of its G5 Plaza strategy. In trying to reverse the public impression that the Treasury had anything to do with them, the Federal Reserve Spokesperson, Joseph Coyne, flatly told the press that the cuts had "no direct relationship with any G5 meetings or discussion" and that "consultation has been entirely among the central banks" (*Wall Street Journal,* 10 March 1986). The Treasury's behavior must have been particularly irritating for Volcker, whose preference for coordinated cuts was almost overruled by two new Reagan-appointed Fed governors who wanted unilateral cuts instead and nearly prompted him to resign. For a fuller discussion of the so-called "Palace Coup" of February 1986, see Funabashi (1989: 47–49) and Henning (1994: 284).

8. The Treasury did so for the first time in October 1988. The Act also mandates that the Treasury Secretary testify personally on the substance of the report.

9. I have already tentatively explored this argument and believe that there is a great deal of evidence to support the proposition that the nature of U.S. involvement in that conflict is inexplicable without an analysis of domestic institutional relationships, such as the Clinton administration's heated battles with Congress and the Department of Defense, as well as the electoral learning curve which occurs for most presidents during their first year in office (Sterling-Folker 1998).

10. I would like to thank Eric Leonard and Craig Murphy in particular for bringing this point to my attention at the International Studies Association—Northeast Annual Meeting's Northeast Circle in November 2000.

11. Although hereto it is a subject which I have explored in other venues. In my dissertation completed at the University of Chicago in 1993, I examined Japanese monetary policymaking during the Plaza Accord, as well as British and German Agricultural Ministry cooperation in the Common Agricultural Policy and Foreign

Ministry cooperation in the European Political Cooperation during the 1970s and early 1980s. In every case there is evidence that the departments under examination choose to cooperate not because it was functionally efficient to do so in the issue area, but because it promoted the department's institutional interests vis-à-vis other domestic institutions and deflected jurisdictional threat emanating from them.

12. In his study of globalization and state regulation of economic activity, Gelber reaches similar conclusions: "Not only do such international connections not weaken the nation-state, but in many and perhaps most cases they require the state and its machinery to be strengthened" (1997: 232).

blank 268

Bibliography

Adler, E. 1997. "Seizing the Middle Ground: Constructivism in World Politics." *European Journal of International Relations* 3:319–363.

Adler, E. B., and B. Crawford, eds. 1991. *Progress in Postwar International Relations.* New York: Columbia University Press.

Adler, E., B. Crawford, and J. Donnelly. 1991. "Defining and Conceptualizing Progress in International Relations." In *Progress in Postwar International Relations,* edited by E. Adler and B. Crawford. New York: Columbia University Press.

Ainley, E. M. 1979. *The IMF: Past, Present and Future.* Bangor, North Wales: University of Wales Press.

Allison, G. 1971. *Essence of Decision: Explaining the Cuban Missile Crisis.* Boston: Little, Brown.

Almond, G. A. 1989. "The International-National Connection." *British Journal of Political Science* 19: 263–289.

Altman, R. 1998. "The Nuke of the 90s." *New York Times Magazine,* 1 March, 34–35.

Angel, R. C. 1991. *Explaining Economic Policy Failure: Japan in the 1969–1971 International Monetary Crisis.* New York: Columbia University Press.

Art, R. J. 1973. "Bureaucratic Politics and American Foreign Policy: A Critique." *Policy Sciences* 4(December): 467–490.

Axelrod, R. 1981. "The Emergence of Cooperation Among Egoists." *American Political Science Review* 75(June): 306–318.

———. 1984. *The Evolution of Cooperation.* New York: Basic.

Axerold, R., and R. O. Keohane. 1986. "Achieving Cooperation Under Anarchy: Strategies and Institutions." In *Cooperation Under Anarchy,* edited by K. A. Oye. Princeton, New Jersey: Princeton University Press.

Bailey, S. H. 1930. "Devolution in the Conduct of International Relations." *Economica* 10:259–274.

Baldwin, D. A. 1980. "Interdependence and Power: A Conceptual Analysis." *International Organization* 34:471–506.

Barnett, M. N. 1990. "High Politics Is Low Politics: The Domestic and Systemic Sources of Israeli Security Policy, 1967–1977." *World Politics* 42(July): 529–562.

Barnett, M. N., and M. Finnemore. 1999. "The Politics, Power, and Pathologies of International Organizations." *International Organization* 53(Autumn): 699–732.

Barnett, M. N., and J. S. Levy. 1991. "Domestic Sources of Alliances and Alignments: The Case of Egypt, 1962–73." *International Organization* 45(Summer): 369–395.

Barrington, L. W. 1997. "Nation and Nationalism: The Misuse of Key Concepts in Political Science." *PS: Political Science and Politics* 72:712–716.

Beer, F. A., and R. Hariman, eds. 1996. *Post-Realism: The Rhetorical Turn in International Relations.* East Lansing: Michigan State University Press.

Bergsten, C. F., and C. R. Henning. 1996. *Global Economic Leadership and the Group of Seven.* Washington, DC: Institute for International Economics.

Biersteker, T. J. 1989. "Critical Reflections on Post-Positivism in International Relations." *International Studies Quarterly* 33:235–254.

———. 1992. "The 'Triumph' of Neoclassical Economics in the Developing World: Policy Convergence and Bases of Governance in the International Economic Order." In *Governance Without Government: Order and Change in World Politics,* edited by J. N. Rosenau and E.-O. Czempiel. Cambridge, England: Cambridge University Press.

Biersteker, T. J., and C. Weber, eds. 1996. *State Sovereignty as Social Construct.* Cambridge, England: Cambridge University Press.

Bloom, W. 1990. *Personal Identity, National Identity, and International Relations.* Cambridge, England: Cambridge University Press.

Bowler, P. J. 1984. *Evolution: The History of an Idea.* Berkeley: University of California Press.

Bowring, P. 1981. "Watershed in Washington." *Far Eastern Economic Review* 9(October): 58–60.

Branson, W. H., J. A. Frenkel, and M. Goldstein, eds. 1990. *International Policy Coordination and Exchange Rate Fluctuations.* Chicago: University of Chicago Press.

Brooks, S. G. 1997. "Dueling Realisms." *International Organization* 51(Summer): 445–478.

Brown, S. 1974. *New Forces in World Politics.* Washington DC: Brookings Institution.

Bryant, R. C. 1995. "International Cooperation in the Making of National Macroeconomic Policies: Where Do We Stand?" In *Understanding Interdependence: The Macroeconomics of the Open Economy,* edited by P. B. Kenen. Princeton, New Jersey: Princeton University Press.

Bueno De Mesquita, B., and D. Lalman. 1992. *War and Reason: Domestic and International Imperatives.* New Haven, Connecticut: Yale University Press.

Buzan, B. 1984. "Economic Structure and International Security: The Limits of the Liberal Case." *International Organization* 38(Autumn): 597–624.

Buzan, B., C. Jones, and R. Little. 1993. *The Logic of Anarchy: Neorealism to Structural Realism.* New York: Columbia University Press.

Campbell, C. 1986. *Managing the Presidency: Carter, Reagan, and the Search for Executive Harmony.* Pittsburgh: University of Pittsburgh Press.

Camps, M., and C. Gwin. 1981. *Collective Management: The Reform of Global Economic Organization.* New York: McGraw-Hill.

Caporaso, J. 1997. "Across the Great Divide: Integrating Comparative and International Politics." *International Studies Association* 41(December): 563–592.

Cargill, T. F. 1989. *Central Bank Independence and Regulatory Responsibilities: The Bank of Japan and the Federal Reserve.* New York: Salomon Brothers Center for the Study of Financial Institutions, New York University.

Carlsnaes, W. 1992. "The Agency-Structure Problem in Foreign Policy Analysis." *International Studies Quarterly* 36(September): 245–270.

Cerny, P. G. 1995. "Globalization and the Changing Logic of Collective Action." *International Organization* 49(Autumn): 595–626.

Checkel, J. T. 1998. "The Constructivist Turn in International Relations Theory." *World Politics* 50(January): 324–348.

Christensen, T. J., and J. Snyder. 1990. "Chain Gangs and Passed Bucks: Predicting Alliance Patterns in Multipolarity." *International Organization* 44(Spring): 137–168.

Clark, P., and James Q. Wilson. 1961. "Incentive Systems: A Theory of Organizations." *Administrative Science Quarterly* 6(September): 129–166.

Cohen, B. 1983a. "Balance-of-Payments Financing: Evolution of a Regime." In *International Regimes*, edited by S. D. Krasner. Ithaca, New York: Cornell University Press.

———. 1983b. "An Explosion in the Kitchen? Economic Relations with Other Advanced Industrial States." In *Eagle Defiant: United States Foreign Policy in the 1980s*, edited by K. A. Oye, R. J. Lieber, and D. Rothchild. Boston: Little, Brown.

———. 1993. "The Triad and the Unholy Trinity: Lessons for the Pacific Region." In *Pacific Economic Relations in the 1990s: Cooperation or Conflict?* edited by R. Higgott, R. Leaver, and J. Rowenhill. Boulder, Colorado: Lynne Rienner.

Cohen, S. D. 1988. *The Making of United States International Economic Policy: Principles, Problems, and Proposals for Reform.* 3rd ed. New York: Praeger.

Colclough, C., and J. Manor, eds. 1991. *States or Markets? Neoliberalism and the Development Policy Debate.* New York: Oxford University Press.

Connor, W. 1994. "A Nation Is a Nation, Is a State, Is an Ethnic Group, Is a . . . " In *Nationalism,* edited by J. Hutchinson and A. D. Smith. New York: Oxford University Press.

Coombs, C. A. 1976. *The Arena of International Finance.* New York: Wiley.

Cooper, R. N. 1968. *The Economics of Interdependence: Economic Policy in the Atlantic Community.* New York: McGraw-Hill.

———. 1972. "Economic Interdependence and Foreign Policy in the Seventies." *World Politics* 24(January): 158–181.

———. 1975. "Prolegomena to the Choice of an International Monetary System." *International Organization* 29(Winter): 63–97.

———. 1984. "A Monetary System for the Future." *Foreign Affairs* 63(Fall): 166–184.

———. 1985. "Economic Interdependence and Coordination of Economic Policies." In *Handbook of International Economics,* vol. 2, edited by R. W. Jones and P. B. Kenen. Amsterdam: North-Holland.

———. 1992. "What Future for the International Monetary System." In *International Finance Policy: Essays in Honor of Jacques J. Polak,* edited by J. Frankel and M. Goldstein (Washington, DC: International Monetary Fund).

Copeland, D. 1996a. "Economic Interdependence and War: A Theory of Trade Expectations." *International Security* 20(Spring): 5–44.

———. 1996b. "Why Relative Gains Concerns May Promote Economic Cooperation: A Realist Explanation for Great Power Interdependence." Paper presented at the Annual Meeting of the Northeast International Studies Association, Boston, 14–16 November.

———. 2000. "The Constructivist Challenge to Structural Realism: A Review Essay." *International Security* 25(Fall): 187–212.

Corbey, D. 1995. "Dialectical Functionalism: Stagnation as a Booster of European Integration." *International Organization* 49(Spring): 253–284.

Cornett, L., and J. A. Caporaso. 1992. " 'And Still it Moves!' State Interests and Social Forces in the European Community." In *Governance Without Government: Order and Change in World Politics*, edited by J. N. Rosenau and E. Czempiel. Cambridge, England: Cambridge University Press.

Cowhey, P. F. 1990. "The International Telecommunications Regime." *International Organization* 44(Spring): 169–200.

Crawford, R. M. A. 1996. *Regime Theory in the Post-Cold War World: Rethinking Neoliberal Approaches to International Relations*. Brookfield, Vermont: Ashgate.

Czempiel, E., and J. N. Rosenau, eds. 1993. *Global Changes and Theoretical Challenges*. Lexington Books.

David, S. R. 1991. "Explaining Third World Alignment." *World Politics* 43(January): 233–256.

Dennett, D. C. 1995. *Darwin's Dangerous Idea: Evolution and the Meanings of Life*. New York: Simon & Schuster.

Der Derian, J. 1989. "The Boundaries of Knowledge and Power in International Relations." In *International/Intertextual Relations: Postmodern Readings of World Politics*, edited by J. Der Derian and M. J. Shapiro, eds. New York: Lexington Books.

———. 1995. "A Reinterpretation of Realism: Genealogy, Semiology, Dromology." In *International Theory: Critical Investigations*, edited by J. Der Derian. New York: New York University Press.

Der Derian, J., and M. J. Shapiro, eds. 1989. *International/Intertextual Relations: Postmodern Readings of World Politics*. New York: Lexington Books.

Desch, M. C. 1996. "War and Strong States, Peace and Weak States?" *International Organization* 50(Spring): 237–268.

———. 1998. "Culture Clash: Assessing the Importance of Ideas in Security Studies." *International Security* 23(Summer): 141–170.

Dessler, D. 1989. "What's at Stake in the Agent-Structure Debate?" *International Organization* 43(Summer): 441–473.

Destler, I. M. 1986. *American Trade Politics: System Under Stress*. Washington, DC: Institute for International Economics.

Destler, I. M., and C. R. Henning. 1989. *Dollar Politics: Exchange Rate Policymaking in the United States*. Washington, DC: Institute for International Economics.

Dickerman, C. R. 1976. "Transgovernmental Challenge and Response in Scandinavia and North America." *International Organization* 30(Spring): 213–240.

Diehl, P. F., and F. W. Wayman. 1994. "Realpolitik: Dead End, Detour, or Road Map?" In *Reconstructing Realpolitik*, edited by F. W. Wayman and P. F. Diehl. Ann Arbor: University of Michigan Press.

Dobson, W. 1991. *Economic Policy Coordination: Requiem or Prologue?* Washington, DC: Institute for International Economics.

Dominguez, K. M., and J. A. Frankel. 1993. *Does Foreign Exchange Intervention Work?* Washington, DC: Institute for International Economics.

Downs, A. 1967. *Inside Bureaucracy.* Boston: Little, Brown.

Downs, G. W., D. M. Rocke, and P. N. Barsoom. 1996. "Is the Good News about Compliance Good News about Cooperation?" *International Organization* 50(Summer): 379–406.

Druckman, D. 1994. "Nationalism, Patriotism, and Group Loyalty: A Social Psychological Perspective." *Mershon International Studies Review* 38(April): 43–68.

Duckitt, J., S. Paton, M. Machen, and G. Vaughan. 1999. "Minimal Intergroup Bias and Real-World Prejudice." *Politics, Groups and the Individual* 8:111–121.

The Economist. 1988. "The Dollar's Berlin Wall," 1 October: 71–72.

———. 1997a. "One World?" 18 October: 79–80.

———. 1997b. "Worldbeater, Inc," 22 November: 92.

Elias, Norbert. 1991. *The Society of Individuals,* edited by M. Schrvter, translated by E. Jephcott. Cambridge, Massachusetts: Basil Blackwell.

Elman, C. 1996. "Why *Not* Neorealist Theories of Foreign Policy." *Security Studies* 6(Autumn): 7–53.

Evans, P. B., H. K. Jacobson, and R. D. Putnam, eds. 1993. *Double-Edged Diplomacy: International Bargaining and Domestic Politics.* Berkeley: University of California Press.

Falger, V. S. E. 1994. "Biopolitics and the Study of International Relations: Implications, Results and Perspectives." *Research in Biopolitics* 5:115–134.

———. 1997. "Human Nature in Modern International Relations. Part 1. Theoretical Backgrounds." *Research in Biopolitics* 5:155–175.

Finnemore, M. 1996. *National Interests in International Society.* Ithaca, New York: Cornell University Press.

Finnemore, M., and K. Sikkink. 1998. "International Norm Dynamics and Political Change." *International Organization* 52:887–918.

Folker, B. 1996. "Wordsworth as Romantic Realist and the Poetics of Constructivism." Paper presented at the Annual Meeting of the International Studies Association-Northeast, Boston; 14–16 November.

Frankel, B. 1996. "Restating the Realist Case: An Introduction." In *Realism: Restatements and Renewals,* edited by B. Frankel. London: Frank Cass.

Frenkel, J. A. 1987. "The International Monetary System: Should it Be Reformed?" *American Economic Review.* 77(May): 205–210.

Frenkel, J. A., and M. M. Goldstein. 1988. "Exchange Rate Volatility and Misalignment." In *Financial Market Volatility Federal Reserve Bank of Kansas City.*

Frieden, J. A. 1996. "Economic Integration and the Politics of Monetary Policy in the United States." In *Internationalization and Domestic Politics,* edited by R. O. Keohane and H. Milner. Cambridge, England: Cambridge University Press.

Fukuyama, F. 1989. "The End of History?" *National Interest* 16(Summer): 3–18.

Funabashi, Y. 1989. *Managing the Dollar: From the Plaza to the Louvre.* 2nd ed. Washington, DC: Institute for International Economics.

Gaddis, J. L. 1986. "The Long Peace: Elements of Stability in the Postwar International System." *International Security* 10:99–142.

———. 1987. "How the Cold War Might End." *Atlantic Monthly* 260(November): 88–100.

Gallarotti, G. M. 1991. "The Limits of International Organization: Systemic Failure in the Management of International Relations." *International Organization* 45(Spring): 183–220.

Garrett, G. 1995. "Capital Mobility, Trade, and Domestic Politics of Economic Policy." *International Organization* 49(Autumn): 657–687.

Garrett, G., and P. Lange. 1991. "Political Responses to Interdependence: What's 'Left' for the Left?" *International Organization* 45(Autumn): 539–564.

———. 1996. "Internationalization, Institutions, and Political Change." In *Internationalization and Domestic Politics,* edited by R. O. Keohane and H. Milner. Cambridge, England: Cambridge University Press.

Garten, J. E. 1984. "Gunboat Economics." *Foreign Affairs* 63:453.

Gasiorowski, M. J. 1986. "Economic Interdependence and International Conflict." *International Studies Quarterly* 30(March): 23–38.

Gelber, H. G. 1997. *Sovereignty Through Interdependence.* The Hague, The Netherlands: Kluwer Law International.

Gilpin R. 1981. *War and Change in World Politics.* Cambridge, England: Cambridge University Press.

———. 1984. "The Richness of the Tradition of Political Realism." *International Organization* 38: 287–304.

———. 1987. *The Political Economy of International Relations.* Princeton, New Jersey: Princeton University Press.

———. 1996a. "Economic Evolution of National Systems." *International Studies Quarterly* 40(September): 411–431.

———. 1996b. "No One Loves a Political Realist." In *Realism: Restatements and Renewal,* edited by B. Frankel. London. Frank Cass.

Glaser, C. L. 1994/95. "Realists as Optimists: Cooperation as Self-Help." *International Security* 19(Winter): 50–90.

Goldgeier, J. M., and M. McFaul. 1992. "A Tale of Two Worlds: Core and Periphery in the Post-Cold War Era." *International Organization* 46(Spring): 467–491.

Goldstein, M. 1994. "Improving Economic Policy Coordination: Evaluating Some New and Some Not-So-New Proposals." In *The International Monetary System,* edited by P. B. Kenen, F. Papadia, and F. Saccomanni. New York: Cambridge University Press.

Gourevitch, P. A. 1978. "The Second Image Reversed: The International Sources of Domestic Politics." *International Organization* 32(Autumn): 881–911.

———. 1996. "Squaring the Circle: The Domestic Sources of International Cooperation." *International Organization* 50(Spring): 349–373.

Gowa J., and E. D. Mansfield. 1993. "Power Politics and International Trade." *American Political Science Review* 87(June): 408–420.

Gowa, J. 1983. *Closing the Gold Window: Domestic Politics and the End of Bretton Woods.* Ithaca, New York: Cornell University Press.

———. 1984. "Hegemons, IOs, and Markets: The Case of the Substitution Account." *International Organization* 38(Autumn): 661–684.

———. 1989. "Bipolarity, Multipolarity, and Free Trade." *American Political Science Review,* 83(December): 1245–1256.

———. 1994. *Allies, Adversaries, and International Trade*. Princeton, New Jersey: Princeton University Press.

Grieco, J. M. 1990. *Cooperation Among Nations: Europe, America, and Nontariff Barriers to Trade*. Ithaca, New York: Cornell University Press.

———. 1993. "Understanding the Problem of International Cooperation: The Limits of Neoliberal Institutionalism and the Future of Realist Theory." In *Neorealism and Neoliberalism: The Contemporary Debate*, edited by D. A. Baldwin. New York: Columbia University Press.

———. 1995. "The Maastricht Treaty, Economic and Monetary Union and the Neorealist Research Programme." *Review of International Studies* 21:21–40.

———. 1999. "Realism and Regionalism: American Power and German and Japanese Institutional Strategies During and After the Cold War." In *Unipolar Politics: Realism and State Strategies after the Cold War*, edited by E. B. Kapstein and M. Mastanduno. New York: Columbia University Press.

Groom, A. J. R. 1978. "Neofunctionalism: A Case of Mistaken Identity." *Political Science* 30:15–28.

Gruber, L. 2000. *Ruling the World Power Politics and the Rise of Supranational Institutions*. Princeton, New Jersey: Princeton University Press.

Gurr, T. R. 1988. "War, Revolution and the Growth of the Coercive State." *Comparative Political Studies* 21:45–65.

Guzzini, S. 1998. *Realism in International Relations and International Political Economy: The Continuing Story of a Death Foretold*. London: Routledge.

Haas, E. B. 1958. *The Uniting of Europe: Political, Social, and Economic Forces, 1950–1957*. London: Stevens.

———. 1961. "International Integration: The European and the Universal Process." *International Organization* 15:366–392.

———. 1970. "The Study of Regional Integration: Reflections on the Joy and Anguish of Pretheorizing." *International Organization* 24(Autumn): 607–646.

———. 1975. *The Obsolescence of Regional Integration Theory*. Research Series, no. 25, Institute of International Studies. Berkeley: University of California.

———. 1976. "Turbulent Fields and the Theory of Regional Integration." *International Organization* 30(Spring): 173–212.

Haas, P. M. 1990. *Saving the Mediterranean: The Politics of International Environmental Cooperation*. New York: Columbia University Press.

———. ed. 1992. Special Issue of *International Organization* 46.

Haggard, S. 1986. "The Newly Industrializing Countries in the International System." *World Politics* 38: 343–370.

———. 1991. "Structuralism and Its Critics: Recent Progress in International Relations Theory." In *Progress in Postwar International Relations*, edited by E. Adler and B. Crawford. New York: Columbia University Press.

Haggard, S., and B. A. Simmons. 1987. "Theories of International Regimes." *International Organization* 41(Summer): 491–517.

Hanrieder, W. F. 1971. *Comparative Foreign Policy*. New York: McKay.

———. 1978. "Dissolving International Politics: Reflections on the Nation-State." *American Political Science Review* 72:1279–1280.

Hasenclever, A., P. Mayer, and V. Rittberger. 1997. *Theories of International Regimes.* Cambridge, England: Cambridge University Press.

Hay, P. 1966. *Federalism and Supranational Organizations: Patterns for New Legal Structures.* Urbana: University of Illinois Press.

Held, D. 1996. "The Decline of the Nation State." In *Becoming National: A Reader,* edited by G. Eley and R. G. Suny. New York: Oxford University Press.

Henning, C. R. 1987. *Macroeconomic Diplomacy in the 1980s: Domestic Politics and International Conflict Among the United States, Japan, and Europe.* Atlantic Paper, no. 65. London: Croom Helm.

———. 1994. *Currencies and Politics in the United States, Germany, and Japan.* Washington, DC: Institute for International Economics.

Henning, C. R., and I.M. Destler. 1988. "From Neglect to Activism: American Politics and the 1985 Plaza Accord." *Journal of Public Policy* 8(July/December): 317–333.

Hintze, O. 1975. "Military Organization and the Organization of the State." In *The Historical Essays of Otto Hintze,* edited by F. Gilbert. New York: Oxford University Press.

Hobbs, H. H., ed. 2000. *Pondering Postinternationalism: A Paradigm for the Twenty-First Century?* Albany, New York: State University of New York Press.

Hoffmann, S. 1995. "An American Social Science: International Relations (reprint)." In *International Theory: Critical Investigations,* edited by J. Der Derian. New York: New York University Press.

Hogg, M., and D. Abrams. 1988. *Social Identifications: A Social Psychology of Intergroup Relations and Group Processes.* New York: Routledge.

Hopf, T. 1998. "The Promise of Constructivism in International Relations Theory." *International Security* 23(Summer): 171–200.

Hopkins, R. F. 1976. "The International Role of 'Domestic' Bureaucracy." *International Organization* 30(Summer): 405–432.

———. 1978. "Global Management Networks: The Internationalization of Domestic Bureaucracies." *International Social Science Journal* 30:31–46.

Horne, J. 1985. *Japan's Financial Markets: Conflict and Consensus in Policymaking.* London: George Allen & Unwin.

Huysmans, J. 1995. "Post-Cold War Implosion and Globalisation: Liberalism Running Past Itself?" *Millennium: Journal of International Studies* 24:471–487.

Ignatieff, M. 1996. "Nationalism and Toleration." In *Europe's New Nationalism: States and Minorities in Conflict,* edited by R. Caplan and J. Feffer, eds. New York: Oxford University Press.

Iida, K. 1993. "Analytic Uncertainty and International Cooperation: Theory and Application to International Economic Policy Coordination." *International Studies Quarterly* 37(December): 431–457.

Ikenberry, G. J. 1992. "A World Economy Restored: Expert Consensus and the Anglo-American Postwar Settlement." *International Organization* 46(Winter): 289–321.

Ishida, T., and E. S. Krauss, eds. 1989. *Democracy in Japan.* Pittsburgh: University of Pittsburgh Press.

Jackson, P. T. 1997. Personal E-mail correspondence, Columbia University. 22 August.

———. 1998. "On the Cultural Preconditions of Political Actors." Paper presented at the Annual Meeting of the American Political Science Association, Boston, 3–6 September.

Jackson, P. T., and D. H. Nexon. 2001. "Whence Causal Mechanisms? A Response to Jeffrey W. Legro, 'Whence American Internationalism.' " *Dialog-International Organization* (mitpress.mit.edu/io).

———. 1999. "Relations Before States: Substance, Process, and the Study of World Politics." *European Journal of International Relations* 5: 291–332.

Jacobsen, J. K. 1995. "Much Ado about Ideas: The Cognitive Factor in Economic Policy." *World Politics* 47(January): 283–310.

James, A. 1989. "The Realism of Realism: The State in the Study of International Relations." *Review of International Studies* 15:215–229.

Jervis, R. 1983. "Security Regimes." In *International Regimes,* edited by S. D. Krasner. Ithaca, New York: Cornell University Press.

———. 1984. *The Illogic of American Nuclear Strategy.* Ithaca, New York: Cornell University Press.

———. 1988. "Realism, Game Theory, and Cooperation." *World Politics* 40(April): 317–349.

———. 1991/92. "The Future of World Politics: Will it Resemble the Past?" *International Security* 16:39–73.

———. 1998. "Realism in the Study of World Politics." *International Organization* 52(Autumn): 971–991.

———. 1999. "Realism, Neoliberalism and Cooperation: Understanding the Debate." *International Security* 24(Summer): 42–63.

Jessop, B. 1997. "Capitalism and Its Future: Remarks on Regulation, Government, and Governance." *Review of International Political Economy* 4:561–581.

Johnson, C. 1977. "MITI and Japanese International Economic Policy." In *The Foreign Policy of Modern Japan,* edited by R. A. Scalapino. Berkeley: University of California Press.

———. 1982. *MITI and the Japanese Miracle: The Growth of Industrial Policy, 1925–1975.* Stanford, California: Stanford University Press.

Jones, R. J. B. 1984. "The Definitions and Identification of Interdependence." In *Interdependence on Trial: Studies in the Theory and Reality of Contemporary Interdependence,* edited by R. J. B. Jones and P. Willetts. New York: St. Martin's.

Jones, R. J. B., and P. Willetts, eds. 1984. *Interdependence on Trial: Studies in the Theory and Reality of Contemporary Interdependence.* New York: St. Martin's.

Jonsson, C. 1993. "Cognitive Factors in Explaining Regime Dynamics." In *Regime Theory and International Relations,* edited by V. Rittberger. Oxford: Oxford University Press.

Kahler, M. 1997. "Inventing International Relations: International Relations Theory After 1945." In *New Thinking in International Relations Theory,* edited by M. W. Doyle and G. J. Ikenberry. Boulder, Colorado: Westview Press.

Kaiser, K. 1971. "Transnational Relations as a Threat to the Democratic Process." In *Transnational Relations and World Politics,* edited by R. O. Keohane and J. S. Nye Jr. Cambridge: Harvard University Press.

Karvonen, L. 1987. *Internationalization and Foreign Policy Management.* Aldershot, England: Gower Publishing Company.

Karvonen, L., and B. Sundelius. 1990. "Interdependence and Foreign Policy Management in Sweden and Finland." *International Studies Quarterly* 34(June): 211–228.

Katzenstein, P., ed. 1996. *The Culture of National Security: Norms and Identity in World Politics.* New York: Columbia University Press.

Keely, J. F. 1990. "The Latest Wave: A Critical Review of Regime Literature." In *World Politics: Power, Interdependence and Dependence,* edited by D. G. Haglund and M. K. Hwes. New York: Harcourt.

Kegley, C. W. Jr. 1991. "The New Containment Myth: Realism and the Anomaly of European Integration." *Ethics and International Affairs* 5:99–114.

Kegley, C. W. Jr., and E. R. Wittkopf. 1991. *American Foreign Policy: Pattern and Process.* 4th ed. New York: St. Martin's.

Kenen, P. B. 1994. "Floating Exchange Rates Reconsidered: The Influence of New Ideas, Prioritiesl, and Problems." In *The International Monetary System,* edited by P. B. Kenen, F. Papadia, and F. Saccomanni. New York: Cambridge University Press.

Kennedy, P. 1987. *The Rise and Fall of the Great Powers: Economic Change and Military Conflict From 1500 to 2000.* New York: Random.

Keohane, R. O. 1983. "The Demand for International Regimes." In *International Regimes,* edited by S. D. Krasner. Ithaca, New York: Cornell University Press.

———. 1984. *After Hegemony: Cooperation and Discord in the World Political Economy.* Princeton, New Jersey: Princeton University Press.

———. 1988. "International Institutions: Two Approaches." *International Studies Quarterly* 32(December): 379–396.

———. 1989. *International Institutions and State Power: Essays in International Relations Theory.* Boulder, Colorado: Westview Press.

———. 1990. "International Liberalism Reconsidered." In *The Economic Limits to Modern Politics,* edited by J. Dunn. Cambridge, England: Cambridge University Press.

———. 1993. "Institutional Theory and the Realist Challenge After the Cold War." In *Neorealism and Neoliberalism: The Contemporary Debate,* edited by D. A. Baldwin. New York: Columbia University Press.

———. 1994. "Comment." In *Managing the World Economy: Fifty Years After Bretton Woods,* edited by P. B. Kenen. Washington, DC: Institute for International Economics.

———. 1998. "International Institutions: Can Interdependence Work?" *Foreign Policy* (Spring): 82–96.

Keohane, R. O., and L. Martin. 1995. "The Promise of Institutional Theory." *International Security* 20(Summer): 39–51.

Keohane, R. O., and H. Milner, eds. 1996. *Internationalization and Domestic Politics.* Cambridge, England: Cambridge University Press.

Keohane, R. O., and J. S. Nye, eds. 1971. *Transnational Relations and World Politics.* Cambridge: Harvard University Press.

———. 1989. *Power and Interdependence.* 2nd ed. Glenview, Illinois: Scott, Foresman.

———. 1998. "Power and Interdependence in the Information Age." *Foreign Affairs* 77(September/October): 81–94.

Kilborn, P. T. 1989. "New Strategy on the Dollar." *New York Times,* 22 May, D1.

Klotz, A. 1995. *Norms in International Relations: The Struggle Against Aparthied.* Ithaca, New York: Cornell University Press.

Knorr, K. 1977. "Is International Coercion Waning or Rising?" *International Security* 1(Spring): 92–110.

Koh, B. C. 1989. *Japan's Administrative Elites.* Berkeley: University of California Press.

Koslowski, R., and F. V. Kratochwil. 1994. "Understanding Change in International Politics: The Soviet Empire's Demise and the International System." *International Organization* 48(Spring): 215–248.

Kowert, P. 1998. "Agent Versus Structure in the Construction of National Identity." In *International Relations in a Constructed World,* edited by V. Kubálková, N. Onuf, and P. Kowert. Armonk, New York: M. E. Sharpe.

Kowert, P., and J. Legro. 1996. "Norms, Identity, and Their Limits: A Theoretical Reprise." In *The Culture of National Security,* edited by P. Katzenstein. New York: Columbia University Press.

Krasner, S. D. 1983a. "Structural Causes and Regimes Consequences: Regimes as Intervening Variables." In *International Regimes,* edited by S. D. Krasner. Ithaca, New York: Cornell University Press.

———. 1983b. "Regimes and the Limits of Realism: Regimes as Autonomous Variables." In *International Regimes,* edited by S. D. Krasner. Ithaca, New York: Cornell University Press.

———. 1985. *Structural Conflict: The Third World Against Global Liberalism.* Berkeley: University of California Press.

———. 1995/96. "Compromising Westphalia." *International Security* 20(Winter): 115–151.

Kratochwil, F. 1982. "On the Notion of 'Interest' in International Relations." *International Organization* 36(Winter): 1–30.

———. 1993. "The Embarrassment of Changes: Neorealism as the Science of Realpolitik Without Politics." *Review of International Studies* 19:63–80.

———. 1994. "Preface." In *International Organization: A Reader,* edited by F. Kratochwil and E. D. Mansfield. New York: HarperCollins.

Kratochwil, F., and J. G. Ruggie. 1986. "International Organization: A State of the Art on an Art of State." *International Organization* 40(Autumn): 753–776. Reprinted in Ruggie (1998).

Kratochwil, F., and Y. Lapid. 1996. *The Return of Culture and Identity in IR Theory.* London: Lynne Rienner.

Kubálková, V., N. Onuf, and P. Kowert, eds. 1998. *International Relations in a Constructed World.* Armonk, New York: M. E. Sharpe.

Lapid, Y. 1989. "The Third Debate: On the Prospects of International Theory in a Post-Positivist Era." *International Studies Quarterly* (33): 235–254.

———. 1996. "Nationalism and Realist Discourses of International Relations." In *Post-Realism: The Rhetorical Turn in International Relations,* edited by F. A. Beer and R. Hariman. East Lansing: Michigan State University Press.

Layne, C. 1993. "The Unipolar Illusion: Why New Great Powers Will Rise." *International Security* 17(Spring): 5–51.

Lebow, R. N. 1994. "The Long Peace, the End of the Cold War, and the Failure of Realism." *International Organization* 48(Spring): 249–278.

Legro, J., and A. Moravcsik. 1999. "Is Anybody Still a Realist?" *International Security* 24(Fall): 5–55.

Levy, J. S. 1994. "Learning and Foreign Policy: Sweeping a Conceptual Minefield." *International Organization* 48(Spring): 279–312.

Lincoln, E. J. 1988. *Japan Facing Economic Maturity.* Washington, DC: Brookings Institute.

Lindberg, L. 1971. *The Political Dynamics of European Integration.* Stanford, California: Stanford University Press.

Lindeman, J. 1963. "Political and Administrative Arrangements Affecting Foreign Financial and Credit Operations." In *Fiscal and Debt Management Policies,* edited by the Commission on Money and Credit. Englewood Cliffs, New Jersey: Prentice-Hall.

Lipson, C. 1984. "International Cooperation in Economic and Security Affairs." *World Politics* 37(October): 1–23.

Litfin, K. T. 1997. "Sovereignty in World Ecopolitics." *Mershon International Studies Review* 41(November): 167–204.

Little, R. 1984. "Power and Interdependence: A Realist Critique." In *Interdependence on Trial: Studies in the Theory and Reality of Contemporary Interdependence,* edited by R. J. B. Jones and P. Willetts. New York: St. Martin's.

———. 1996. "The Growing Relevance of Pluralism?" In *International Theory: Positivism and Beyond,* edited by S. Smith, K. Booth, and M. Zalewski. Cambridge, England: Cambridge University Press.

Makin, J. H. 1983. *The Global Debt Crisis: America's Growing Involvement.* New York: Basic.

Mann, M. 1997. "Has Globalization Ended the Rise and Rise of the Nation-State?" *Review of International Political Economy* 4:472–496.

March, J. H., and J. P. Olsen. 1984. "The New Institutionalism: Organizational Factors in Political Life. *American Political Science Review* 78:734–749.

———. 1989. *Rediscovering Institutions: The Organizational Basis of Politics.* New York: Free Press.

———. 1998. "The Institutional Dynamics of International Political Orders." *International Organization* 52:919–942.

Marston, R. C. 1988. "Exchange Rate Coordination." In *International Economic Cooperation,* edited by M. Feldstein. Chicago: University of Chicago Press.

Martin, L. L. 1992a. *Coercive Cooperation: Explaining Multilateral Economic Sanctions.* Princeton, New Jersey: Princeton University Press.

———. 1992b. "Institutions and Cooperation: Sanctions During the Falkland Islands Conflict." *International Security* 16(Spring): 143–178.

———. 1992c. "Interests, Power, and Multilateralism." *International Organization* 46(Autumn): 765–792.

Mastanduno, M. 1997. "Preserving the Unipolar Moment: Realist Theories and U.S. Grand Strategy After the Cold War." *International Security* 21(Spring): 49–88.

Mayer, F. W. 1992. "Managing Domestic Differences in International Negotiations: The Strategic Use of Internal Side Payments." *International Organization* 46(Autumn): 793–818.

Maynes, C. W. 1989. "Coping With the '90s." *Foreign Policy* 74(Spring): 42–62.

McKinnon, R. I. 1971. *Monetary Theory and Controlled Flexibility in the Foreign Exchanges.* Princeton Essays in International Financ, no. 84. Princeton, New Jersey: International Finance Section, Department of Economics, Princeton University.

———. 1984. *An International Standard for Monetary Stabilization, Policy Analyses in International Economics.* Washington, DC: Institute for International Economics.

McMillan, S. M. 1997. "Interdependence and Conflict." *Mershon International Studies Review* 41(May): 33–58.

Mearsheimer, J. J. 1990. "Back to the Future: Instability in Europe After the Cold War." *International Security* 15: 5–56.

———. 1994/95. "The False Promise of International Institutions." *International Security* 19(Winter): 5–49.

———. 1995. "A Realist Reply." *International Security* 20(Summer): 82–93.

Melton, W. C. 1985. *Inside the Fed: Making Monetary Policy.* Homewood, Illinois: Dow Jones-Irwin.

Mercer, J. 1995. "Anarchy and Identity." *International Organization* 49:229–252.

Milner H. 1991. "The Assumption of Anarchy in International Relations Theory: A Critique." *Review of International Studies* 17: 67–85.

———. 1997. *Interests, Institutions, and Information: Domestic Politics and International Relations.* Princeton, New Jersey: Princeton University Press.

———. 1998. "International Political Economy: Beyond Hegemonic Stability." *Foreign Affairs* (Spring): 82–96.

Mitrany, D. 1943. *A Working Peace System: An Argument for the Functional Development of International Organization.* London: Royal Institute of International Affairs.

———. 1945. "Problems of International Administration." *Public Administration* 23:2–12.

———. 1948. "The Functional Approach to World Organization." *International Affairs* 24:350–363.

———. 1959. "International Cooperation in Action." *International Associations* 11:644–648.

Morrow, J. D. 1993. "Arms Versus Allies: Tradeoffs in the Search for Security." *International Organization* 47(Spring): 207–234.

Morse, E. S. 1970. "The Transformation of Foreign Policies: Modernization, Interdependence, and Externalization." *World Politics* 22(April): 371–392.

———. 1976. *Modernization and the Transformation of International Relations.* New York: Free Press.

Niou, E. M. S., and P. C. Ordeshook. 1994. "Less Filling, Tastes Great: The Realist-Neoliberal Debate." *World Politics* 46:209–234.

Norman, E. H. 1975. "Feudal Background of Japanese Politics." In *Origins of the Modern Japanese State: Selected Writings of E. H. Norman,* edited by J. W. Dower. New York: Random.

Northedge, F. 1976. "Transnationalism: The American Illusion." *Millennium* 5:21–28.

Nye, J. S. Jr. 1987. "Nuclear Learning and U.S.-Soviet Security Regimes." *International Organization* 41: 371–402.

Oatley, T., and R. Nabors. 1998. "Market Failure, Wealth Transfers, and the Basle Accord." *International Organization* 52(Winter): 35–54.

Odell, J. S. 1982. *U.S. International Monetary Policy: Markets, Power, and Ideas as Sources of Change.* Princeton, New Jersey: Princeton University Press.

Onuf, N. G. 1989. *World of Our Making: Rules and Rule in Social Theory and International Relations.* Columbia: University of South Carolina Press.

Oye, K. A., ed. 1986. *Cooperation Under Anarchy.* Princeton, New Jersey: Princeton University Press.

Parks, W. J. 1968. *United States Administration of its International Economic Affairs.* New York: Greenwood.

Pauly, L. W., and S. Reich. 1997. "National Structures and Multinational Corporate Behavior: Enduring Differences in the Age of Globalization." *International Organization* 51(Winter): 1–30.

Peterson, V. S. 1996. "The Gender of Rhetoric, Reason, and Realism." In *Post-Realism: The Rhetorical Turn in International Relations,* edited by F. A. Beer and R. Hariman. East Lansing: Michigan State University Press.

Powell, R. 1994. "Anarchy in International Relations Theory: The Neorealist-Neoliberal Debate." *International Organization* 48: 313–344.

Puchala, D. J., and R. F. Hopkins. 1983. "International Regimes: Lessons From Inductive Analysis," in *International Regimes,* edited by S. D. Krasner. Ithaca, New York: Cornell University Press.

Putnam, R. D. 1988. "Diplomacy and Domestic Politics: The Logic of Two-Level Games." *International Organization* 42:427–460.

Putnam, R. D., and N. Bayne. 1987. *Hanging Together: Cooperation and Conflict in the Seven-Power Summits.* Revised edition. Cambridge: Harvard University Press.

Quandt, W. B. 1988. "The Electoral Cycle and the Conduct of American Foreign Policy." In *The Domestic Sources of American Foreign Policy: Insights and Evidence,* edited by C. W. Kegley Jr., and E. R. Wittkopf. New York: St. Martin's.

Rappard, W. E. 1927. "The Evolution of the League of Nations." *American Political Science Review* 21:792–826.

Rasler, K. A., and W. R. Thompson. 1989. *War and State Making: The Shaping of the Global Powers.* Boston: Unwin Hyman.

———. 1994. *The Great Powers and Global Struggle: 1490–1990.* Lexington: University Press of Kentucky.

Ray, J. L. 1989. "The Abolition of Slavery and the End of International War." *International Organization* 43(Summer): 406–439.

Raymond, G. A. 1997. "Problems and Prospects in the Study of International Norms." *Mershon International Studies Review* 41(November): 205–246.

Reinsch, P. S. 1911. *Public International Unions: Their Work and Organization: A Study in International Administrative Law.* Boston: Ginn and Company.

Resende-Santos, J. 1996. "Anarchy and the Emulation of Military Systems: Military Organization and Technology in South America, 1870–1914." In *Realism: Restatements and Renewals,* edited by B. Frankel. London: Frank Cass.

Reus-Smit, C. 1999. *The Moral Purpose of the State: Culture, Social Identity, and Institutional Rationality in International Relations*. Princeton, New Jersey: Princeton University Press.

Rittberger, V., ed. 1993. *Regime Theory and International Relations*. Oxford: Oxford University Press.

Rochester, J. M. 1986. "The Rise and Fall of International Organization as a Field of Study." *International Organization* 40(Autumn): 777–813.

Rose, G. 1998. "Neoclassical Realism and Theories of Foreign Policy." *World Politics* 51(October): 144–172.

Rosecrance, R. 1986. *The Rise of the Trading State: Commerce and Conquest in the Modern World*. New York: Basic.

———. 1996. "The Rise of the Virtual State." *Foreign Affairs* 75(July/August): 45–61.

Rosecrance, R., and A. A. Stein, eds. 1993. *The Domestic Bases of Grand Strategy*. Ithaca, New York: Cornell University Press.

Rosenau, J. N. 1966. "Pretheories and Theories of Foreign Policy." In *Approaches to Comparative and International Politics*, edited by R. B. Farrell. Evanston, Illinois: Northwestern University Press.

———. 1967. *Domestic Sources of Foreign Policy*. New York: Free Press.

———. 1969. *Linkage Politics*. New York: Free Press.

———. 1976. "Capabilities and Control in an Interdependent World." *International Security* (Fall): 32–49.

———. 1980. *The Study of Global Interdependence: Essays on the Transnationalization of World Affairs*. London: Frances Pinter.

———. 1988. "The State in an Era of Cascading Politics: Wavering Concept, Widening Competence, Withering Colossus, or Weathering Change?" *Comparative Political Studies* 21(April): 13–44.

Rosenau, J. N., and E. Czempiel, eds. 1992. *Governance Without Government: Order and Change in World Politics*. Cambridge, England: Cambridge University Press.

Rosenau, P. 1990. "Once Again Into the Fray: International Relations Confronts the Humanities." *Millennium* 19:83–110.

Rosenbluth, F. 1989. *Financial Politics in Contemporary Japan*. Ithaca, New York: Cornell University Press.

Rowen, H. 1989. "The Dollar Confounding Experts, Central Banks, Continues to Rise." *Washington Post*, 23 May, A1.

Ruggie, J. G. 1983a. "Continuity and Transformation in the World Polity: Toward a Neorealist Synthesis." *World Politics* 35(January): 261–285.

———. 1983b. "International Regimes, Transactions, and Change: Embedded Liberalism in the Postwar Economic Order." In *International Regimes*, edited by S. D. Krasner. Ithaca, New York: Cornell University Press.

———. 1998. *Constructing the World Polity: Essays on International Institutionalization*. New York: Routledge.

Russett, B. 1995. "Review Articles: Processes of Dyadic Choice for War and Peace." *World Politics* 47(January): 268–282.

Schelling, T. 1978. *Micromotives and Macrobehavior*. New York: Norton.

Schlesinger, P. 1994. "Europeanness: A New Cultural Battlefield?" In *Nationalism*, edited by J. Hutchinson and A. D. Smith. New York: Oxford University Press.

Schweller, R. L. 1998. "The Progressive Nature of Neoclassical Realism." Paper prepared for the Conference on "Progress in International Relations Theory." Arizona State University, 14–17 January.

Schweller, R. L., and D. Priess. 1997. "A Tale of Two Realisms: Expanding the Institutions Debate." *Mershon International Studies Review* 41(May): 1–32.

Scott, A. M. 1982. *The Dynamics of Interdependence*. Chapel Hill: University of North Carolina Press.

Sewell, J. P. 1966. *Functionalism and World Politics: A Study Based on United Nations Programs Financing Economic Development*. Princeton, New Jersey: Princeton University Press.

Shimko, K. L. 1992. "Realism, Neorealism, and American Liberalism." *Review of Politics* (Spring): 281–301.

Smith, A. D. 1991. *National Identity*. Reno: University of Nevada Press.

Smith, D. 1996. "Reconciling Identities in Conflict." In *Europe's New Nationalism: States and Minorities in Conflict*, edited by R. Caplan and J. Feffer. New York: Oxford University Press.

Smith, S. 1984. "Foreign Policy Analysis and Interdependence." In *Interdependence on Trial: Studies in the Theory and Reality of Contemporary Interdependence*, edited by R. J. B. Jones and P. Willetts. New York: St. Martin's.

———. 1996. "Positivism and Beyond." In *International Theory: Positivism and Beyond*, edited by S. Smith, K. Booth, and M. Zalewski. Cambridge, England: Cambridge University Press.

Snidal, D. 1985. "Coordination Versus Prisoners' Dilemma: Implications for International Cooperation and Regimes." *American Political Science Review* 79(December): 923–942.

———. 1991a. "International Cooperation Among Relative Gains Maximizers." *International Studies Quarterly* 35(December): 387–402.

———. 1991b. "Relative Gains and the Pattern of International Cooperation." *American Political Science Review* 85(September): 701–726.

Snyder, J. 1990. "Averting Anarchy in the New Europe." *International Security* 14(Spring): 5–41.

———. 1991. *Myths of Empire: Domestic Politics and International Ambition*. Ithaca, New York: Cornell University Press.

Solomon, R. 1982. *The International Monetary System, 1945–1981*. Revised edition. New York: Harper.

Somit, A., and S. A. Peterson. 1999. "Rational Choice and Biopolitics: A (Darwinian) Tale of Two Theories." *PS: Political Science and Politics* 32(March): 39–44.

Southard, F. A. Jr. 1979. *The Evolution of the International Monetary Fund*. Essays in International Finance, no. 135, December. Princeton, New Jersey: International Finance Section, Department of Economics, Princeton University.

Spero, J. E., and J. A. Hart. 1997. *The Politics of International Economic Relations*. 5th ed. New York: St. Martin's.

Spinelli, A. 1966. *The Eurocrats*. Baltimore: John Hopkins University Press.

Spirtas, M. 1996. "A House Divided: Tragedy and Evil in Realist Theory." In *Realism: Restatements and Renewals*, edited by B. Frankel. London: Frank Cass.

Spruyt, H. 1994. *The Sovereign State and Its Competitors: An Analysis of Systems Change*. Princeton, New Jersey: Princeton University Press.

Stein, A. A. 1983. "Coordination and Collaboration: Regimes in an Anarchic World." In *International Regimes,* edited by S. D. Krasner. Ithaca, New York: Cornell University Press.

———. 1991. *Why Nations Cooperate: Circumstance and Choice in International Relation.* Ithaca, New York: Cornell University Press.

———. 1993. "Governments, Economic Interdependence, and International Cooperation." In *Behavior, Society and International Conflict,* vol. 3, edited by P. Tetlock et al. New York: Oxford University Press.

Sterling-Folker, J. 1997. "Realist Environment, Liberal Process, and Domestic Level Variables." *International Studies Quarterly* 41(March): 1–26.

———. 1998. "Between a Rock and a Hard Place: Assertive Multilateralism and Post-Cold War U.S. Foreign Policymaking." In *After the End: Making U.S. Foreign Policy in the Post-Cold War World,* edited by J. M. Scott. Durham, North Carolina: Duke University Press.

———. 2000. "Competing Paradigms or Birds of a Feather? Constructivism and Neoliberal Institutionalism Compared" *International Studies Quarterly* 44(March): 97–119.

———. 2001. "Evolutionary Tendencies in Realist and Liberal IR Theory." In *Evolutionary Interpretations of World Politics,* edited by W. R. Thompson. New York: Routledge.

———. 2002. "Realism and the Constructivist Challenge: Rejecting, Reconstructing, or Rereading." *International Studies Review* 1(Spring).

Strange, S. 1976. *International Monetary Relations.* London: Oxford University Press.

———. 1983. "*Cave! hic dragones*: A Critique of Regime Analysis." In *International Regimes,* edited by S. D. Krasner. Ithaca, New York: Cornell University Press.

Tajfel, H., and J. C. Turner. 1986. "The Social Identity Theory of Intergroup Behavior." In *Psychology of Intergroup Relations,* edited by S. Worchel and W. G. Austin. Chicago: Nelson-Hall.

Thomson, J. E. 1992. "Explaining the Regulation of Transnational Practices: A State-Building Approach." In *Governance Without Government: Order and Change in World Politics,* edited by J. N. Rosenau and E. Czempiel. Cambridge, England: Cambridge University Press.

———. 1995. "State Sovereignty in International Relations: Bridging the Gap Between Theory and Empirical Research." *International Studies Quarterly* 39(June): 213–233.

Thomson, J. E., and S. D. Krasner. 1992. "Global Transactions and the Consolidation of Sovereignty." In *International Politics,* edited by R. J. Art and R. Jervis, eds. 3rd ed. New York: HarperCollins.

Tilly, C. 1975. "Reflections on the History of European State Making." In *The Formation of National States in Western Europe,* edited by C. Tilly. Princeton, New Jersey: Princeton University Press.

Tranholm-Mikkelsen, J. 1991. "Neofunctionalism: Obstinate or Obsolete? A Reappraisal in the Light of the New Dynamism of the EC." *Millennium: Journal of International Studies* 20:1–22.

Urwin, D. 1995. *The Community of Europe: A History of European Integration Since 1945.* 2nd ed. London: Longman Group.

Vasquez, J. A. 1997. "The Realist Paradigm and Degenerative Versus Progressive Research Programs: An Appraisal of Neotraditional Research on Waltz's Balancing Proposition." *American Political Science Review* 91:899–912.

Volcker, P., and T. Gyohten. 1992. *Changing Fortunes: The World's Money and the Threat to American Leadership.* New York: Random.

Wade, R. 1992. "Review Article: East Asia's Economic Success, Conflicting Perspectives, Partial Insights, Shaky Evidence." *World Politics* 44(January): 270–320.

———. 1996. "Japan, the World Bank, and the Art of Paradigm Maintenance: The East Asian Miracle in Political Perspective." *New Left Review* 217:3–37.

Waever, O. 1998. "The Sociology of a Not So International Discipline: American and European Developments in International Relations." *International Organization* 52:687–728.

Walt, S. M. 1987. *The Origins of Alliances.* Ithaca, New York: Cornell University Press.

———. 1998. "International Relations: One World, Many Theories." *Foreign Policy* (Spring): 29–47.

Waltz, K. N. 1970. "The Myth of National Interdependence." Iin *The International Corporation,* edited by C. Kindleberger. Cambridge: Massachusetts Institute of Technology Press.

———. 1979. *Theory of International Politics.* New York: McGraw-Hill.

———. 1993. "The Emerging Structure of International Politics." *International Security* 18(Fall): 44–79.

———. 1996. "International Politics Is Not Foreign Policy." *Security Studies* 6(Autumn): 54–57.

Weatherford, M. S., and H. Fukui. 1989. "Domestic Adjustment to International Shocks in Japan and the United States." *International Organization* 43(Autumn): 585–624.

Webb, C. 1983. "Theoretical Perspectives and Problems." In *Policymaking in the European Community,* edited by H. Wallace, W. Wallace, and C. Webb. New York: Wiley.

Weber, S. 1994. "The European Bank for Reconstruction and Development." *International Organization* 48(Winter): 1–38.

———. 1997. "Institutions and Change." In *New Thinking in International Relations Theory,* edited by M. W. Doyle and G. J. Ikenberry. Boulder, Colorado: Westview Press.

Weinstein, M. M. 1998. "Twisting Controls on Currency and Capital." *New York Times,* 10 September, C1+.

Wendt, A. 1987. "The Agent-Structure Problem in International Relations Theory." *International Organization* 41(Summer): 335–370.

———. 1992. "Anarchy Is What States Make of It: The Social Construction of Power Politics." *International Organization* 46(Spring): 391–425.

———. 1994. "Collective Identity Formation and the International State." *American Political Science Review* 99(June): 384–396.

Wendt, A., and R. Duvall. 1989. "Institutions and International Order." In *Global Changes and Theoretical Challenges: Approaches to the World Politics for the 1990s,* edited by E. O. Czempiel and J. N. Rosenau. Lexington, Massachusetts: Lexington Books.

Williamson, J. 1985. *The Exchange Rate System: Policy Analyses in International Economics.* Rev. ed. Washington, DC: Institute for International Economics.

Williamson, J., and M. H. Miller. 1987. *Targets and Indicators: A Blueprint for the International Coordination of Economic Policy.* Policy Analyses in International Economics 22. Washington, DC: Institute for International Economics.

Wilmer, F. 1996. "Indigenous Peoples, Marginal Sites, and the Changing Context of World Politics." In *Post-Realism: The Rhetorical Turn in International Relations,* edited by F. A. Beer and R. Hariman. East Lansing: Michigan State University Press.

Wohlforth, W. C. 1994/95. "Realism and the End of the Cold War." *International Security* 19(Winter): 91–129.

———. 1998. "Reality Check: Revisiting Theories of International Politics in Response to the End of the Cold War." *World Politics* 50(July): 650–680.

Woods, N. 1995. "Economic Ideas and International Relations: Beyond Rational Neglect." *International Studies Quarterly* 39(June): 161–180.

Yarbrough, B. V., and R. M. Yarbrough. 1987. "Cooperation in the Liberalization of International Trade: After Hegemony, What?" *International Organization* 41(Winter): 13–26.

Young, O. 1969. "Interdependencies in World Politics." *International Journal* 24(Autumn): 726–750.

———. 1986. "Review Articles: International Regimes: Toward a New Theory of Institutions." *World Politics* (October): 104–122.

———. 1989a. *International Cooperation: Building Resources for Natural Resources and the Environment.* Ithaca, New York: Cornell University Press.

———. 1989b. "The Politics of International Regime Formation." *International Organization* 43: 349–376.

Zacher, M. W. 1992. "The Decaying Pillars of the Westphalian Temple: Implications for International Order and Governance." In *Governance Without Government: Order and Change in World Politics,* edited by J. N. Rosenau and E. Czempiel. Cambridge, England: Cambridge University Press.

Zacher, M. W., and R. A. Matthew. 1995. "Liberal International Theory: Common Threads, Divergent Strands." In *Controversies in International Relations Theory: Realism and the Neoliberal Challenge,* edited by C. W. Kegley Jr. New York: St. Martin's.

Zacher, M. W., with B. A. Sutton. 1996. *Governing Global Networks: International Regimes for Transportation and Communication.* Cambridge, England: Cambridge University Press.

Zakaria, F. 1998. *From Wealth to Power: The Unusual Origins of America's World Role.* Princeton, New Jersey: Princeton University Press.

———. 1992. "Realism and Domestic Politics: A Review Essay." *International Security* 17:177–198.

———. 1992/93. "Is Realism Finished?" *The National Interest.* 21–32.